Foreword

The Reverend John Thomas Wilson was bc ... ia's reign and he died at the end of Edward VII's re ... ere tremendous advances in technology; oil lamps ... to electricity; travel advanced with the coming o ... the "horseless carriage"; communication progressed with transatlantic cables and telegraphy and the telephone, whilst improved printing presses saw the start of the local daily and weekly newspapers; working conditions improved the lot of the people, and franchise aroused an interest in politics and trade unionism; educational opportunities increased and there were great advances in medicine; above all, at home at least, peace prevailed.

The "penny post" had been in existence since 1840, but in 1870 a printed halfpenny postcard made communication even cheaper, and these were particularly useful to people living at a distance from post offices. The "picture postcard" as such did not come into being until towards the end of the nineteenth century, but thanks to his skill as an artist, and his talent for small but nonetheless distinct handwriting, the reverend gentleman made excellent use of the space available. His communications to his friend John Worsley over the seven years from 1876 to 1883 were carefully preserved in albums and have survived for over a century.

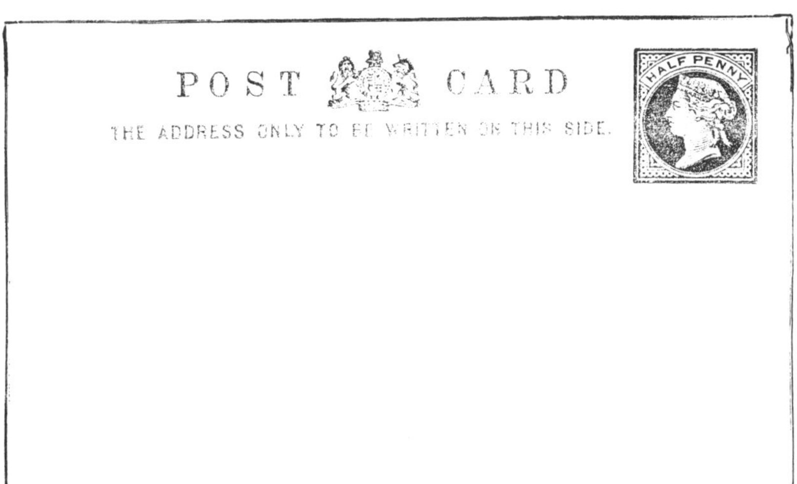

CERTIFIED COPY OF AN ENTRY OF MARRIAGE

GIVEN AT THE GENERAL REGISTER OFFICE, LONDON

Application Number 8174B

18 74. Marriage solemnized at St James' Church in the Parish of Eccleston in the County of Lancaster

No.	When Married.	Name and Surname.	Age.	Condition.	Rank or Profession.	Residence at the time of Marriage.	Father's Name and Surname.	Rank or Profession of Father.
8	April 28th 1874	John Thomas Wilson	Full age	Bachelor	Clerk in Holy Orders	Heskin	Nobl[illegible] Wilson	Clerk in Holy Orders
		Mary Margaret Morris Marsden	Full age	Spinster	—	Heskin	Laurence Marsden	Gentleman

Married in the Church of St James according to the Rites and Ceremonies of the Established Church, by Licence ~~or after~~ by me,

Thomas Evans
Curate in Charge of Wrightington Colliery Church

This Marriage was solemnized between us, { John Thomas Wilson, Mary Margaret Morris Marsden }

in the Presence of us, { Rowland Howe, Margaret E Morris Marsden, Mary Ann Marsden }

CERTIFIED to be a true copy of an entry in the certified copy of a register of Marriages in the Registration District of Wigan

Given at the GENERAL REGISTER OFFICE, LONDON, under the Seal of the said Office, the 4th day of March 1982

This certificate is issued in pursuance of section 65 of the Marriage Act 1949. Sub-section 3 of that section provides that any certified copy of an entry purporting to be sealed or stamped with the seal of the General Register Office shall be received as evidence of the marriage to which it relates without any further or other proof of the entry, and no certified copy purporting to have been given in the said Office shall be of any force or effect unless it is sealed or stamped as aforesaid.

MX 715553

CAUTION:—Any person who (1) falsifies any of the particulars on this certificate, or (2) uses a falsified certificate as true, knowing it to be false, is liable to prosecution.

GENERAL REGISTER OFFICE ★ ENGLAND ★

Form A513MX Dd 8264217 60M 1/81 Mcr(2017)

Biographical Notes

John Thomas Wilson was the son, and possibly the only child, of Noble and Sarah Wilson. He was born on 31st March 1837, in Rakefoot, Westmoreland, where his father, a curate, was a contemporary and friend of the poet William Wordsworth.

John Thomas studied at Bishop Hatfield's Hall, Durham University, obtaining his B.A degree in 1861, his studies having been interrupted for a year by the death of his father and his mother's poor health. He applied for holy orders in 1862, was ordained as a deacon that year, and became curate at the church of St John the Divine at Pemberton, Lancs. Significantly, one of the referees supporting his application was William Worsley, vicar of Norbury, Cheshire, perhaps the father of his friend, John Worsley. John Thomas was ordained as a priest by the Bishop of Chester in 1863.

In 1868 he was appointed vicar to the church of St James the Great at Wrightington, living first in a house called Pyebrook, but moving in about 1871 to the vicarage at Heskin. On 28th April 1874 he married Mary Margaret Morris Marsden, at St James Church, Eccleston. She was the same age as he; they had no children but appear to have lived happily together until her death in July 1910. By then his own health was failing and he resigned his living at Wrightington, but his successor, Revd W.J.F. Baker, had him remain at the vicarage, where he died on 23rd November of that year. Amongst other bequests he left £300 to his successor for the provision of a Sunday School.

Notes

It would appear that John Worsley did not start to put the postcards into an album until he had several, and the earliest dated, which were not entered chronologically, tend to be at longer intervals than later correspondence. There are frequent references to his having disappointed John Wilson over unfulfilled promised visits, and perhaps saving the postcards was a sop to his conscience.

April 25th 1876 — P.O.O - a Postal (Office) order; a service which was of considerable use to folk living in rural areas.

June 15th 1876 — Mr Wilson took pleasure in using styles of writing and phrases arising from his conversations or readings of the day.

Sept 18th 1876 — John Worsley, to whom the correspondence was directed, was a 'surgeon dentist' living in Fishergate, Preston. Born in 1845 he is described as single in the 1871 census, but was a widower by the next one in 1881, when his household included his sister Mary (Miss Worsley, 8 years his senior); his son Jack (John, born 1874); Henry, a stepson, born 1870; and two domestics.Henry's mother, presumably a widow at the time of her re-marriage, may have died giving birth to Freddy - a sickly infant who can be assumed to be the 'poor Fred' whose death is commented upon briefly in January 1881. From illustrations there would appear to have been a girl in the family too (Sissy) - perhaps she was away from home on Census Day in 1881.

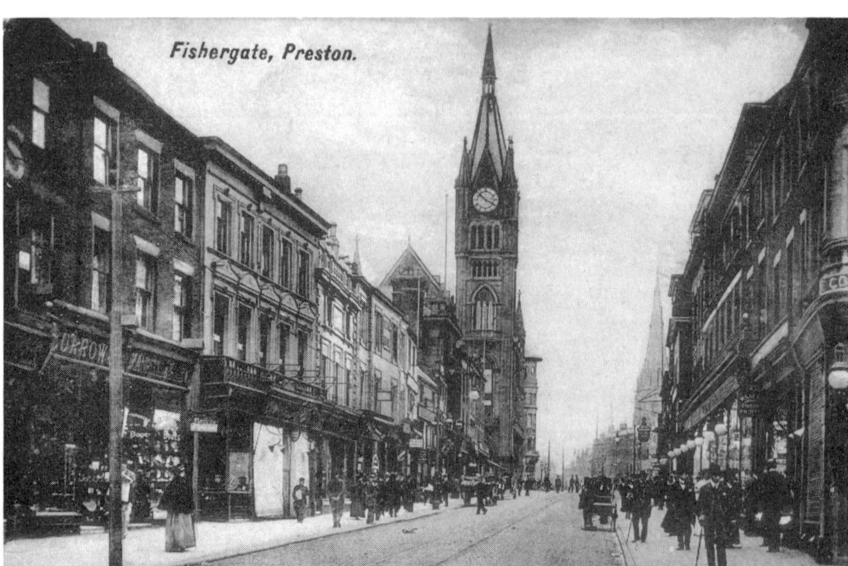

April 25th 1876... If the weather be favourable next week and no rain prevailing I shall be in Preston one day but which I cannot now specify but will not forget the contents of letter just now to hand - Many thanks for the same - as also for despatch of P.O.O.* Mrs W. who I rejoice to say seems to be recruiting her strength joins me in best wishes ...

June 15th 1876*... My master, Sir, Yessir - he come 'ome last night sir quite safely - I see him my oan self hentering the door of 'is dwelling at the c'rect 'our at which he were jew - He bid me Sir, my Master did, to introjuice to your notice this morning the 'appy fact of 'is 'aving attained jewly the shelter of 'is oan wigwam - where 'e 'opes to see you also on Mundy nex all being well and weather favourable to dance with 'im and friends merrily round 'is scalp pole and 'ave a palaver afterwards round the Council Fire where every hatchet shall be buried - and firewater and the peaceful calumet be esteemed instead ...

June 25th 1876 ... We were disappointed at your non arrival on Monday week (School Treat) and also sorry you could not be with us since then. We hope however that you will hurry over very shortly and have a look at us. I don't think I shall be in Preston again for a week or two...

July 15th 1876... By express command of my Master I have waited upon you to say that he won't be - so far as he at present knows - in Preston this month. He hopes you are quite well and begs to remain...

Sept 18th 1876... You see I am greatly improved in health and am at home again - I arrived on Friday evening last. I have a good many engagements this week but if you could come over on Friday afternoon or evening and stay all night I should be rejoiced to see you - If Friday be inconvenient to you any day during the week following will do but send me word in any case - a weekday visit would be to myself personally preferable to a Sunday one as it affords me an opportunity of uninterrupted converse free from the divers mental engrossments which the Sunday duty entails - Hoping shortly to be favoured with a sight of you either on a Sunday or weekday my wife & I combine in all kind sentiments to Miss Worsley* & yourself as also Freddy, & I remain most truly...

Jan 4th 1877... Boo-oo-oo why didn't you come and join us? My dear Sir? Truly the night was very stormy and fearfully wet as well as intensely cold. I was nigh starved or chilled to the point of dissolution in the transit from Preston hither - I am conscious of having acquired a little cold but if it gets no worse than it is at present I shall have little ground for complaining. We hope you will take an early opportunity of paying us a visit in lieu of the one you missed yesterday...

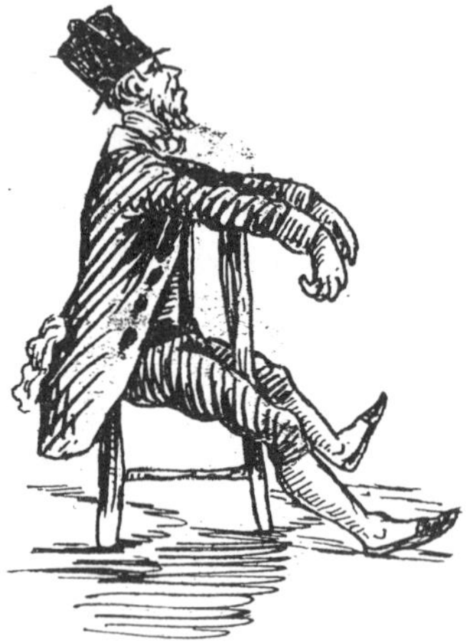

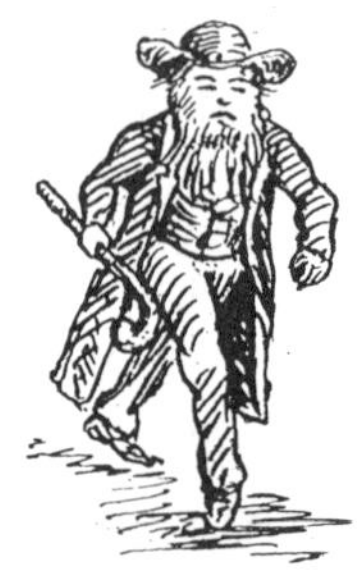

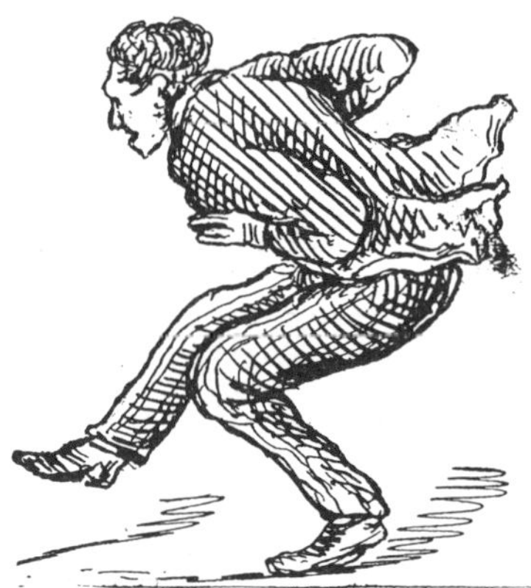

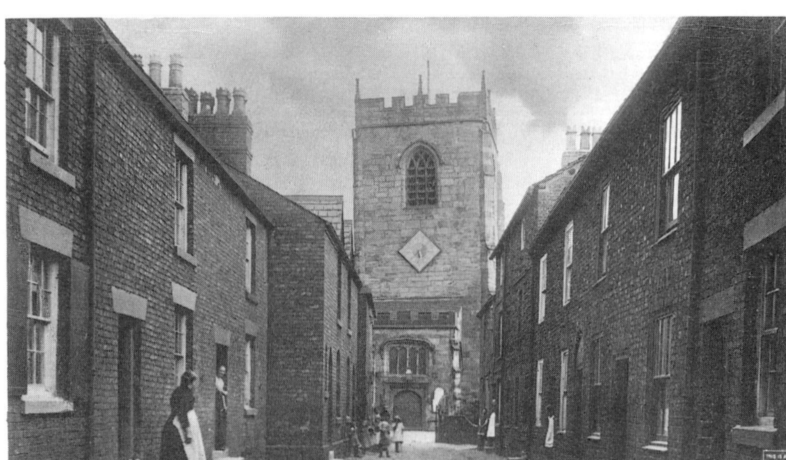
The Parish Church, Croston.
THIS IS A REAL PHOTO

Jan 16th 1877... Ah! my Master Sir, yessir, he sends sir, my Master does, his compliments, sir, and is very sorry to hear sir, as you've got a bad cold sir - He grieves to say, sir, that the partner of his bosom - my Missis sir, has been very poorly and a close prisoner to bed for a week. Doctor, sir, pronounces the complaint to be Bronchitis, sir, and Inflammation of the Lungs - she got up to her bedroom fireside yesterday, sir, for the first time and master, sir, as well as myself sir, is most happy to say she is improving nicely sir - They both, sir, desire to be holden in friendly remembrance by Miss Worsley and yourself sir and my master remains...

Feb 21st 1877... I come with many excuses and an ardent craving that you will kindly pardon my prolix reticence - My partner since I wrote last has had a return of the illness which caused us much alarm - as soon as the Doctor told us the journey might be safely undertaken she removed to Southport where we sojourned for a brief period - We returned on Saturday last - we have now with us Mrs Jackson and family - Her little boy has fallen victim to Scarlet Fever and Diphtheria - and has herself been so ill as to come into Hospital - I will write again as soon as we get the House empty - when we hope that you will favour us with your long promised visit - with combined good wishes to Miss Worsley, yourself and family sincerely trusting you are all well ...

April 5th 1877... We have been greatly pleasured to hear of - and learn from your letter - the felicity which attended you on your return home last Friday - It is a nice walk, that to Croston, and I felt sure you would find delight therein somewhere -We are quite well and shall be glad to hear from you again next week according to promise - You cannot say I am not a punctual correspondent... Jack A. Napes...

Whit Monday... I hope you have got safely back from your Lakeland Tour - and that the weather has been favourable to your enjoyment of it. Here, the times are rather stirring ones - weather is plentiful and we have a power of news knocking about our locality just now ...

June 26th 1877... oh! but my dear Sir - Do come! Don't be unkind - besides I doubt very much whether you have got a pipe or tobacco with you. Mr Parkes has departed today and we are all very sorry to hear of the grievous trouble which hath fallen upon your unfortunate inferior digit - We cherish the hope that vigour & freedom from suffering will be speedily reestablished. And with every good wish mentionable we combine in muchness...

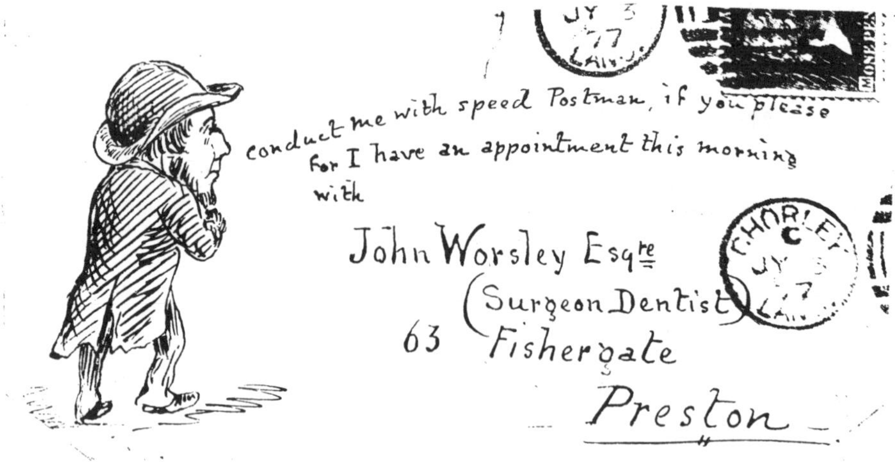

Notes

<u>July 5th 1877</u>

Miss Low (shown as Lowe in the 1881 Census) lived at 15 Adelaide Street, Southport, and may have been an aunt of Mrs Wilson. She was born in 1802 and is described as having an interest in house property.

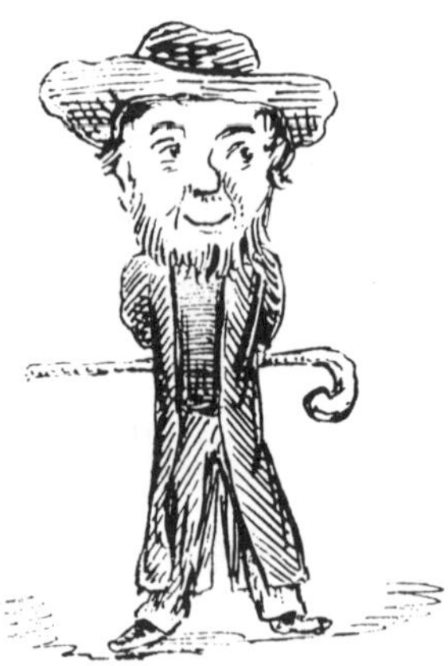

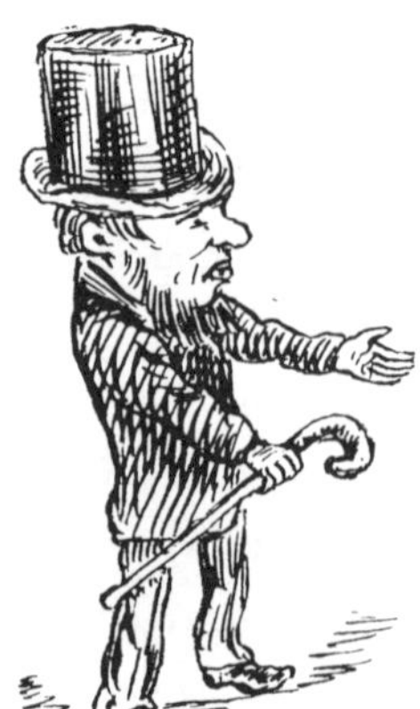

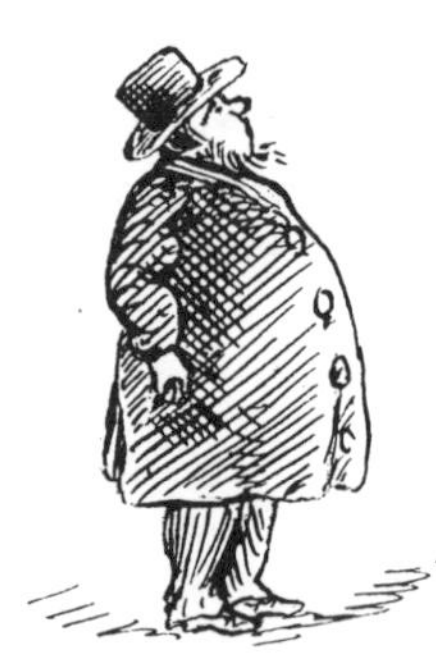

July 3rd 1877... I have just come hastily over to tell you that your sister and the papooses as the East Indians would term them or the piccaninnies as the West Indians would have it came safely to hand last evening., and I need hardly mention that the arrival of a carriage and pair availed to disturb considerably the monotonous flow of our everyday simple Arcadian life...

July 5th 1877... Look here My dear Sir, whenever you come over you will oblige me greatly by bringing if not inconvenient to you a few of those Effervescing Lozenges for my parched Throat - Papooses all thriving so much that a famine is spoken of as probable - By post Miss L * sends a parcel with broken spring - Weather just now most beautiful - Hearty good wishes from everybody...

July 6th 1877... I trust you will kindly pardon me troubling you so soon again with my presence but I have this time the honour to inform you that Miss L leaves us on Monday next and desires the favour of the frames by that day if possible or convenient - May we hope to see you on Saturday? All are well - we hope the little invalid at home has recovered so far as to be transferable - mine partner's gone to Wigan. All unite in muchness...

July 10th 1877... My master sends his compliments Sir and begs to say Sir his Missis been unwell Sir. Happy to say she is improving and 'opes to get up today - all besides, well and 'appy - weather rather cold and muchly wet - please bring when you come over - a parcel - i.e. 1 Dozen packets of Envelopes - moderate quality and also arf a nounce of snurff because my master Sir, he got the snuffles which it's his nose is stopped and wants snurff. Hoping you are quite well as this leaves us at present and that you won't forget the snurff...Please remember snurff S.P scented...

July 14th 1877...tsch scats - this snuff is fresh and brisk and fairly lifts me off my feet - For the snuff just to hand I'm thankful I'm sure My headache and throat it is certain to cure - My household are well - blooming beautifully as the flowers in May and joyously sportive as butterflies in June. With a unanimous compilation of heartiest good wishes ...

Notes

July 19th 1877

The local papers printed weather forecasts of this sort. Published once or twice weekly, they reached Mr Wilson by post, sent by Mr Worsley, and he seems to have enjoyed making reference to some item or other, perhaps by way of showing that they had been read.

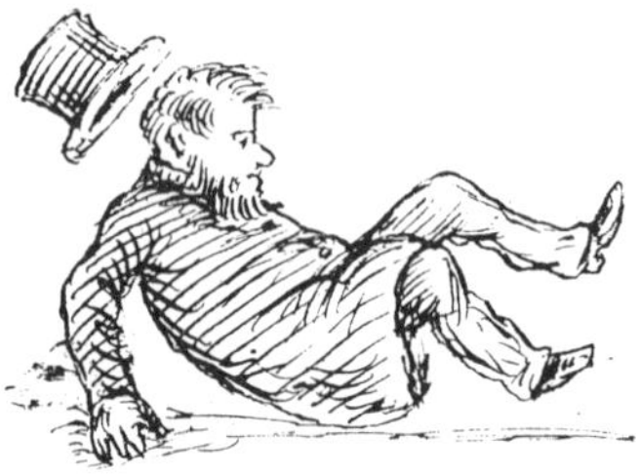

July 24th 1877

Russia declared war on Turkey in April 1877, and Britain sent a squadron through the Dardenelles the following February, which anchored off Constantinople. The San Stefano peace treaty between Russia and Turkey the following month created 'Big Bulgaria' but Britain and Austria were unhappy with the terms of the agreement. Bismarck offered to act as mediator, leading to the Congress of Berlin in June 1878.

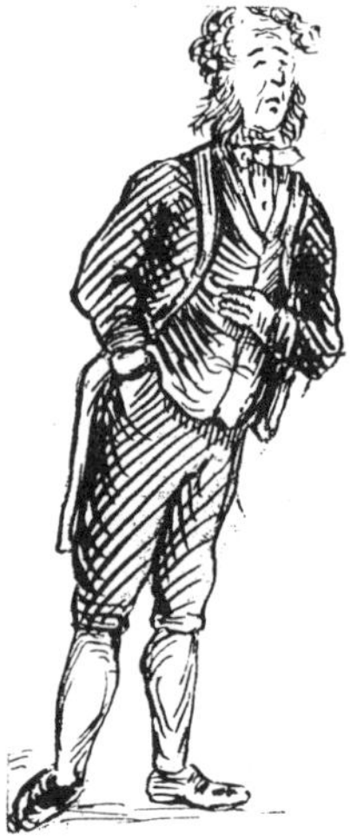

July 19th 1877... Jack is preparing a <u>knockdown</u> for you when he returns to Preston - He talks of asserting a claim to have a long-tailed coat like mine - He considers it probable that my other half may obtain him as her own by stumping down the sum of sixpence as purchase money - Henry spends the shining hours most happily in the society of a wheel barrow which seems to have unfailing charms for him - They are all getting a hue of countenance not very dissimilar to the tints of a hazel nut when full ripe and food begins to <u>dis</u>-appear plentifully where they appear - and really if present portents are to be realised the recent notification of the Weather Forecast and Storm Warning Association* to the effect that an abundant Harvest may be expected is not without a sort of Happy Interest - Thanks for the papers which reach me regularly through your kindness - All join in affectionate sentiments...

... I put no date here on inasmuch as it is merely intended to be a card allegorical of a busy age wherein men run to and fro on divers purposes intent - The moral therefore must be found in the application...

July 24th 1877... I your humble servant am daily receiving tokens of your kind thoughtfulness in the shape Evening News or Evening Mail - But for sich how, my dear Sir, could I know any think about the war* - The childring is quite well and 'appy as the days is long which it's very they are this time of year. We abound in rain with occasional gleams of sunshine but so long as we're 'appy what signifieth, - someone sitting near me picking currants says "tell him I quite expected a letter from him today" - We have acquired quite a large addition to our stock of Ghost lore this morning - there has just been a visitation to one haunt - I cannot give you the particulars in this post card but reserve them as a sensation when you come over. All combine in hoping you are in good health and with earnest good wishes ...

Aug 7th 1877... What the ferrups is up? And there we wuz waiting for you and you never came - and I went to meet you without effect. Till nine o'clock we lingered in doubt - But when it got to that hour our expectance gave out. We wuz waiting and your slippers wuz waiting and you never came - Hope you will be here this evening and not disappoint us no more...

August 14th 1877... just put yourself in my position and see how you would feel for alas! alas!!! Disappointment is my lot - Sunday night and even Monday I lived in hope, yea too on Tuesday but vain was my expectancy - hoping for better luck erstwhiles and trusting that ye all are blessed with complete salubrity..P.S. Note received - snuff plentiful - my store needs no resuscitation at present - thanks ...

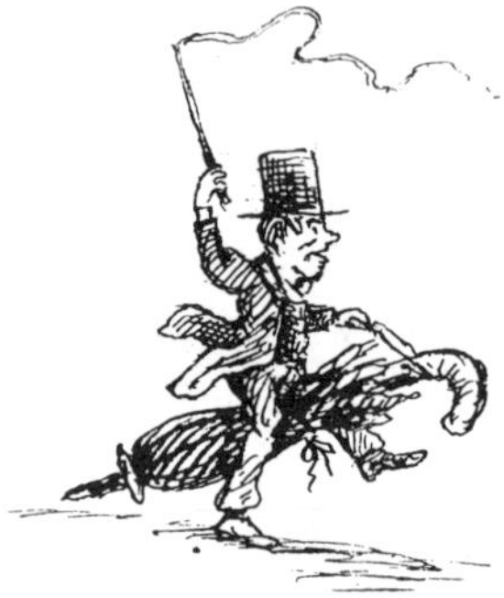

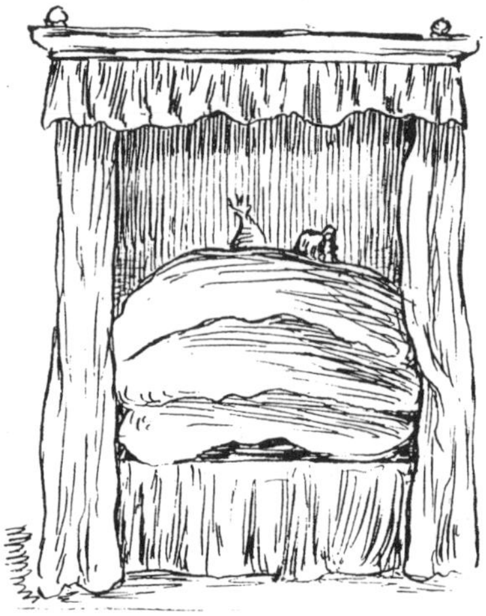

Notes

Sep 5th 1877

As will be seen, Mr Wilson had a copy of Barclay's Dictionary and took some delight in its contents. The 'huge unwieldy proboscian pachydermatous mammifer' is, of course, an elephant.

August 20th 1877... Wet or fair I think you really might either walk or ride over and in either case an umbrella could be useful - Hoping you and all yours are well we cordially cooperate in assurances of sincere esteem.

Aug 27th 1877... My glass has swept the horizon, but to no avail wherever I turn it I signally fail to see you approaching this Heskin direction and so I give up, for I'm tired of watching but let me here say that I'm not without hope that sometime this evening you p'raps may turn up...

...I have just got home and grieved indeed I am to find I shall not have the pleasure of seeing you this evening. Thanks for your letter & pardon I crave for so long delay. Pray do come as soon as you can and present my very kindest remembrances to all...Missis's love to everybody...

Sep 3rd 1877... I trust you quite understand we are merely calling at your hospitable Bungalow for a little refreshment en route and not with the purpose of staying all night - so that night caps need not be provided for us - a pouring rain again, alas! this morning. With warmest regards to all...

Sep 4th 1877... I have just looked in to tell you that we have arrived safely about ten minutes since at our destination - but alas!!! what pens!! Never surely since the day that Troy was built was such a villainous pen as the one I have been wielding been put into the hands of any man - Henceforth my dear Sir save me from an author's pen...

Arctic Regions Sep 5th 1877... I am this morning quite upset - but as soon as I have paid a brief visit to that 'strapping' fellow the 'shaver' round the corner I am purposing to start forthwith upon my travels and pedestrianate with the substantial purposity of the huge unwieldy proboscian pachydermatous mammifer* of which I spoke to you on Sunday last...

Sep 6th 1877... I have climbed the dark brow of stern looking Elleray, Rocks, woods & waters beneath me gleamed misty & wild. The ocean lay sleeping in its Cot far away, Like to some tired and slumbering child, I was near Poet Close's Bookstall yesterday and to this circumstance I must ascribe the rhythmic flatus which has found expression in the above effort - Beyond what I have stated in the verse above written I have nothing to advance - Windermere does not appear to me nor affect me as it used to - I shan't stay at it - I am bent on moving yet further North...

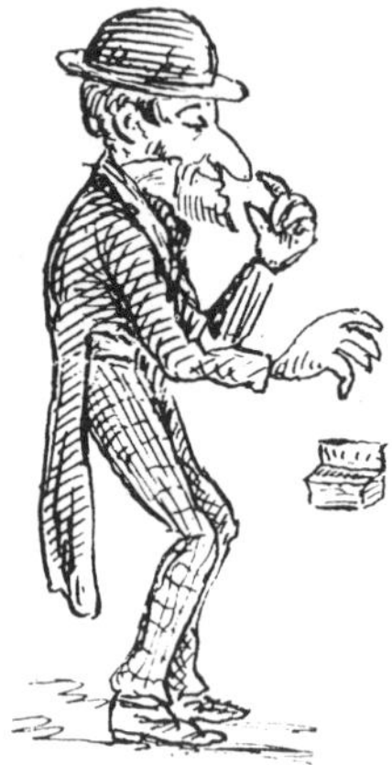

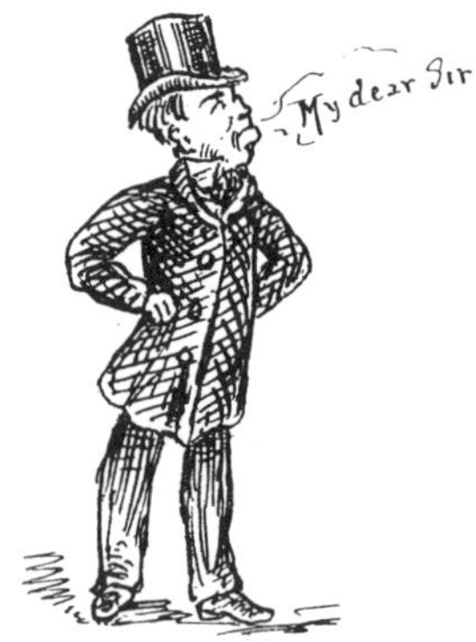

Notes

Sep 10th 1877 Piel Island, near Barrow.

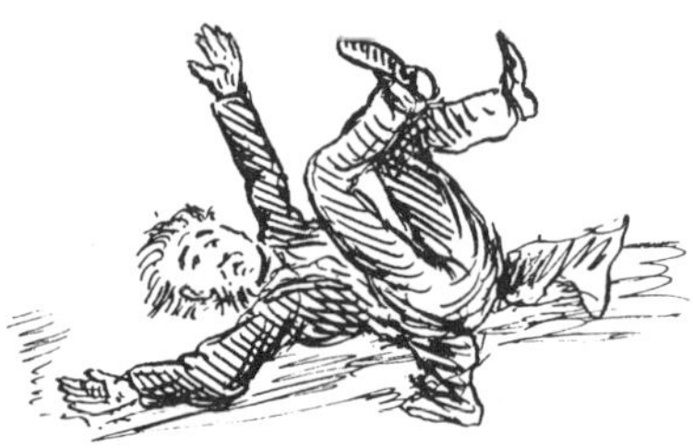

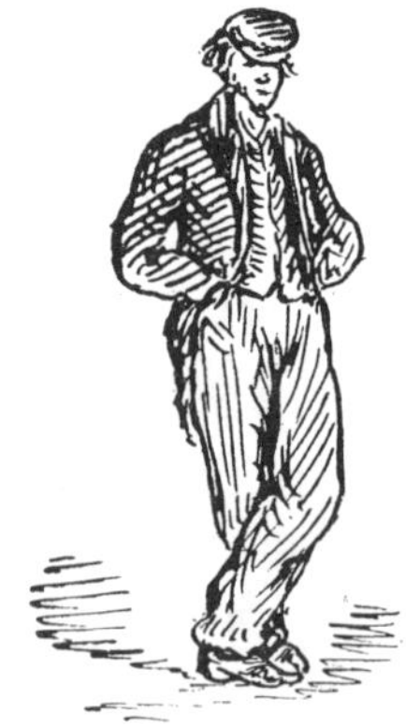

Sep 7th 1877... I am leaving Windermere for Ulverston and neighbourhood today so I expect my next advice will be received by you thence - I was out in a pouring rain - we I should say - but I have caught therefrom a severe cold - Throat raw and sore - Snuff has had to be resorted to copiously but I regret to say causes such irritation of the nose that I have decided temporarily to drop the box. This morning is beautifully bright and mine other half joyous as to the springtime - Yesterday she was complaining a little but the clouds have all vanished and a resplendent halo of Peace and contentment again encircles her - and us...

Bankhurst Villas Ulverston ... Sep 10th 1877 ... Pedestrianation and a severe cold which I caught at Windermere have rendered me quite prostate in a certain sense - But we are about to try the effect of a visit to Furness Abbey, Barrow & Piel* today. My better half is cheerful and well this morning - & unites with me in most friendly sentiments to all...

Bankhurst Villas Sep 11th 1877 ... You will be glad I am sure, to learn that I have brightened up a little and that Richard is himself again, as the sayin' is. My cold which on Sunday was bad indeed is now almost banished and the cocks shrill clarion awoke me easily from my lowly bed this morn and the matin songs of birds beneath the eaves ministered greatly to my delight - I feel again youthful, healthful perk and vigorous - We are making tracks for Cartmel to inspect the Priory of Abbey Church at that place and assert an Englishman's right to grumble with or without occasion just as occasion may serve. So no more at present from yours most truly - With muchness to everybody...

Thursday ... This humid weather - the fatigue I've gone through and the 'coolth' I've had - have completely knock'd me on my back even as you have the unhappiness to see me here - we sigh for home and rest - 'Domum Domum dulce Domum' - we have fixed upon Saturday next to 'Shee wheels go wound' on railway and shall heave in sight at Preston on the early side of 12 o'clock in the forenoon of that day - we yesterday visited the top of the Tower of Cartmel Church - much gratified - Hope you are all in robust health and with much temerity I conclude; subscribing mineself - mine valued Friend with distinguished esteem thine humble and devoted slave...

Heskin ... You will please be back in good time for Sunday's snuff has to be procured tonight... This is not a letter but a memorandum...

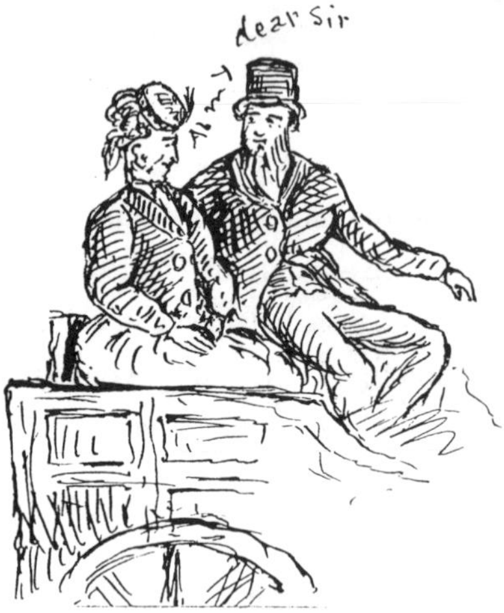

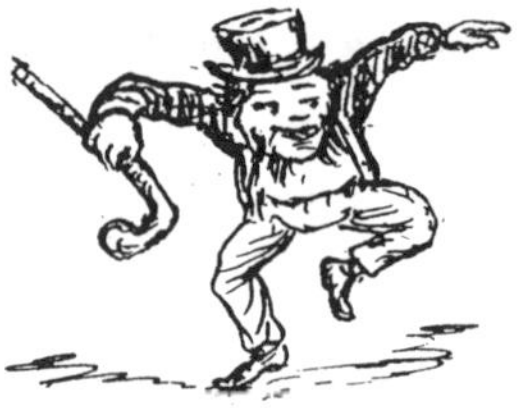

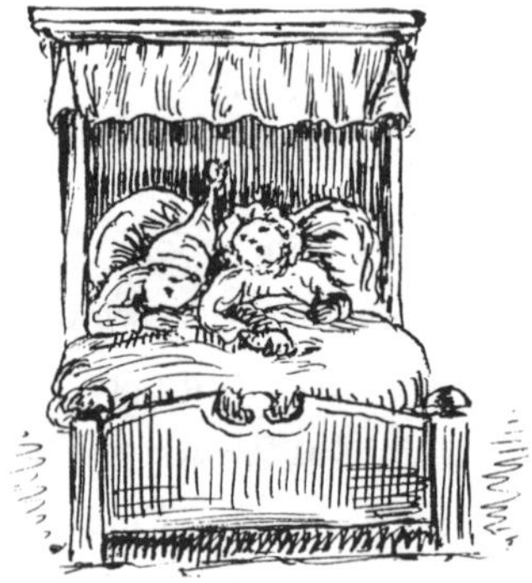

Notes

Oct 1st 1877 Matadore = murderer; Mazard = jaw.

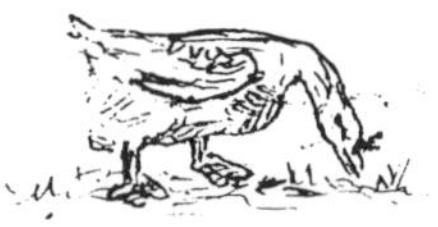

Monday ... We got home quite safely per old Nicholas's conveyance albeit at Croston the water was up to the horse's girths - Mr Parkes purposes to leave either tomorrow night or Wednesday morning early - Wednesday it will be - We hope to be favoured with a visit - pardon haste...

Sep 19th 1877 ... I received your letter duly on returning home from Southport last night - we were greatly disappointed and grieved at being deprived of the pleasure of seeing you - But we cheer ourselves with the hope of an early favour and shall be glad to see you at any time - Mr P took his departure this morning in a - in a - in a what do you call it (I have not my copy of the trusty Barclay just at hand for consultation but chariot or shandry perhaps may answer) in a chariot. I forward by this post a sport paper. The rainy season seems to be setting in again in this neighbourhood although yesterday was quite fine - There's sign, there's sign of grievous rain, beginning in this part again. This poetry comes of seeing I. Close poet when at Windermere.. P.S.. just going out to see for your Goose ...

Sep 22nd 1877 ... Hooray!!!! I'm better again - My headache's all gone and I'm happy again - My eyes however are so inflamed I can hardly see the strokes of my pen - Please look in your Manchester Courier beginning with yesterday's under the heading of Local Gleanings - Lancashire & Cheshire - for something about Heskin School and when you see it you will, by sending it hither place under a deep obligation your humble servant at command - When you feel used up with work come over ...

Sep 26th 1877 ... Honerd Sir .. We are enjoying a good rest after our Northern travels - and are rapidly recovering from the wear and tear of mountaineering. Yet memory bears us back to Windermere's fair scenes, and the picturesque relics that abound in the Northern portion of this County Palatine - and we even now begin to wish ourselves again among them - sailing on the Queen of Lakes, climbing the steep sides of Black comb, moving unceasingly hither and thither and gazing evermore on fresh scenes of beauty - When will ye visit us? Miss L will be here on Saturday ...

Oct 1st 1877 ... In re the Aquatic Fowl mentioned in your favour of Friday last - There's a fine stubble goose in this locality awaiting matadore* (strange word, consult Barclay) tomorrow, and we are negotiating arrangements whereby it may reach you on Wednesday. Trusting it will not too severely tax the mazard* (hie ye again to Barclay) I beg to subscribe myself dutifully and truly.. P.S. I discover that the Goose will come on Thursday per carrier to Preston ...

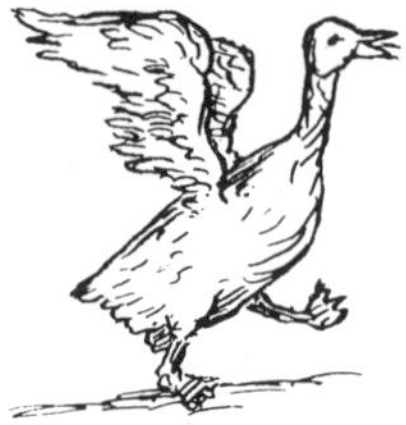

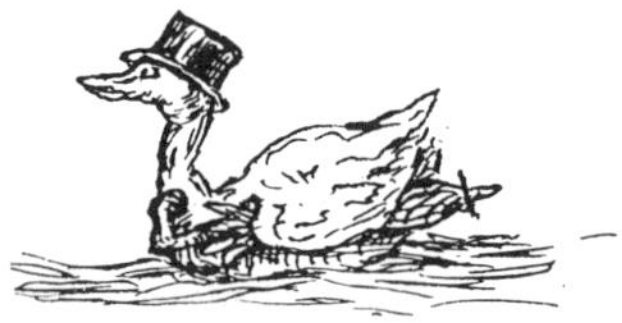

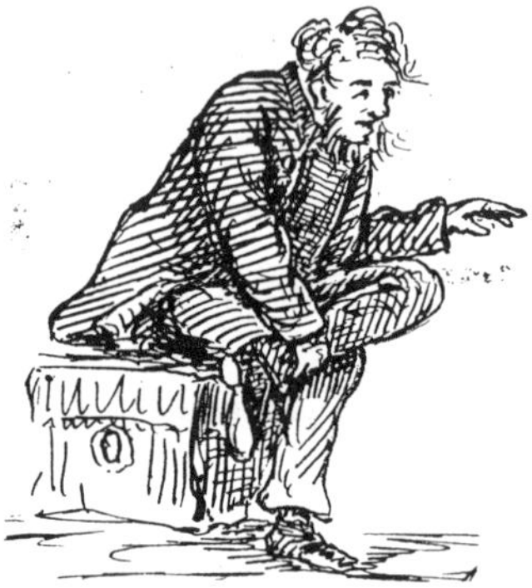

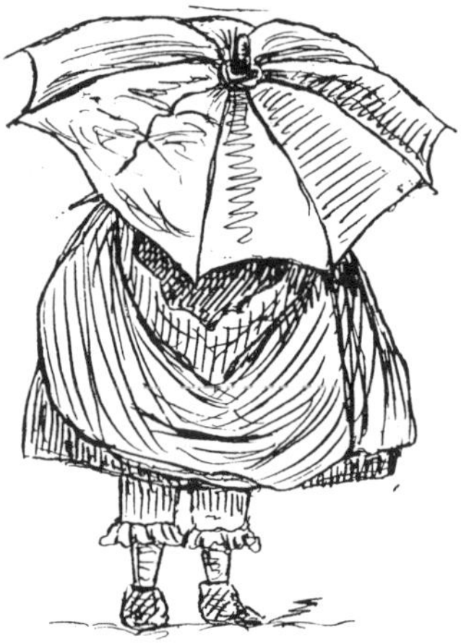

<u>Notes</u>

<u>Oct 23rd 1877</u>

William Henry Marsden was Vicar of St Luke's Church, Southport. Mrs Wilson's maiden name was Marsden, but 'Brother' may be a Masonic reference.

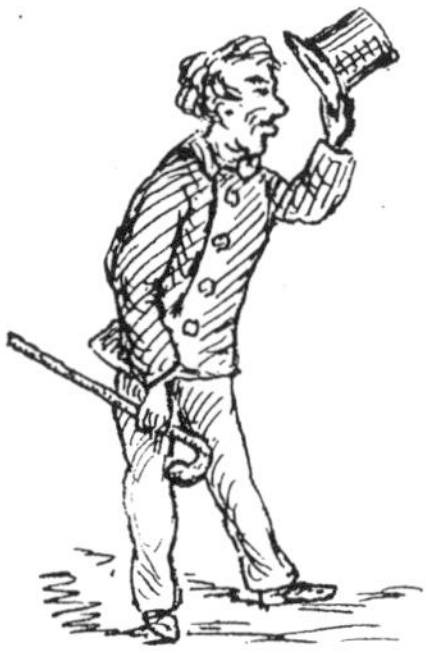

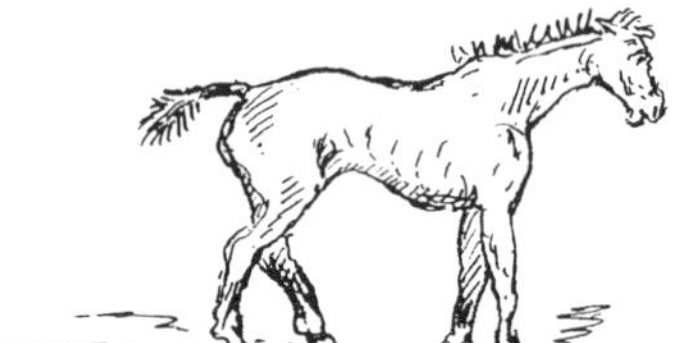

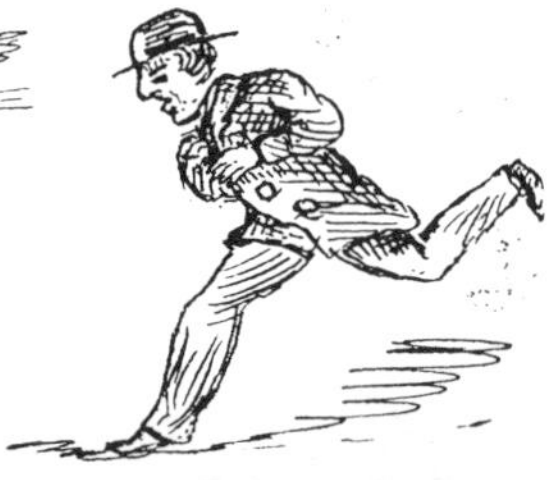

Oct 3rd 1877 (Wednesday).. The Goose is starting on its travels today. It will proceed to the Carriers this evening and will be due in Fishergate tomorrow forenoon - Hoping you will receive the consignment safe and sound and trusting that the goose will prove in every respect satisfactory...

Oct 9th 1877... I am dismally looking forth and expecting the beatification of your presence here - The weather is glorious today & I am sure you would enjoy an out just now - we hope the goose notwithstanding its colour got on swimmingly and gave you all satisfaction. They had killed it other than I instructed them to do owing to some bungle arising from lack of intelligence on their part ...

Oct 12th 1877... We quite expected you on Tuesday afternoon. If you can come over early next week please to send word on what day for be it known we have in our possession at this present time a large fat duck of which we entertain a desire that ye should partake - Hoping you all are well even as we are ...

Oct 15th 1877... I just sit down to tell you that we are going to the great metrolopis (sic) of the Coal District yclept Wigan tomorrow and as it may be late before we return - I write to ask you to come and help us with the duck on any other day <u>but tomorrow</u>. We are undergoing equinoctial outbursts just now but trust tomorrow will prove calmer than today - Our sentiments towards the dwellers at 63 Fishergate, Preston retain their hearty cordiality ...

Oct 19th 1877... as misself & the old Lady proceeded with lagging steps, dejected minds and outspread umbrellas down the Smithy Brow the rain ceased to fall and we felt distraught that we had not further borne you company, albeit it assuaged our grief a little to reflect that the abstention of the threatened downpour would render your walk less unpleasant. We do hope another time you will be able to favour us with longer abidance when you come - Don't let the pleasure be long witholden from us - We trust you found Mrs G better than the message led you to expect ...

Oct 23rd 1877... Pardon me, my dear Sir, venturing a suggestion that you refrain from carrying out your proposal to '<u>trot</u>' over hither this weekend - <u>Come at a run</u> you'll do it quicker so - P.S. Have had a letter from Brother Marsden in Italy.. P.S.2nd.. This is not my week for S'port. I made a mistake in the week - I am at home and shall be <u>till next week</u>..P.S 3rd....Hope to see you on Saturday...

Notes

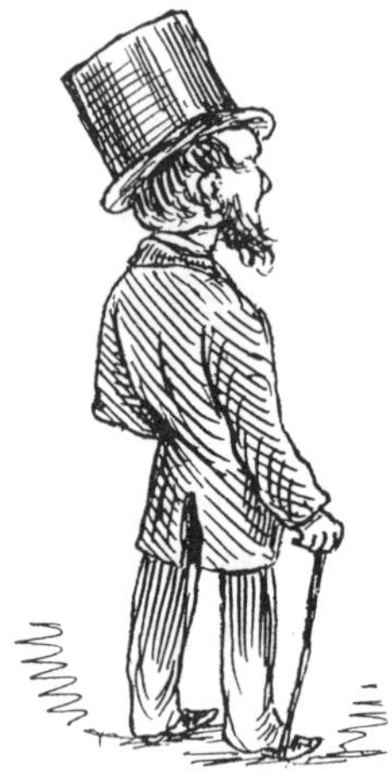

Oct 31st 1877 Rivage = sandy coast.

Nov 8th 1877 Guy Fawkes' night.

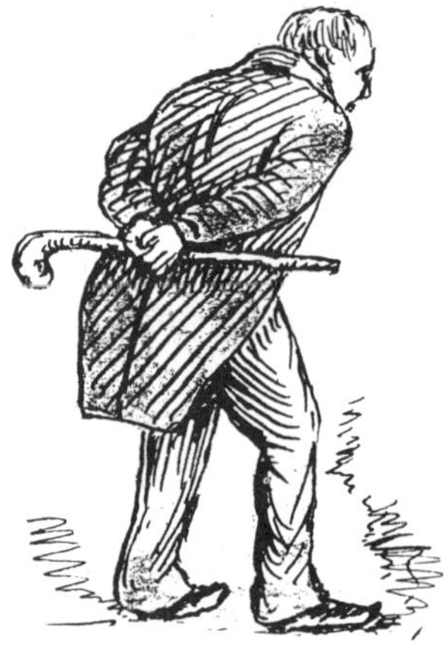

Nov 18th 1877 Cephalalgia = headache.

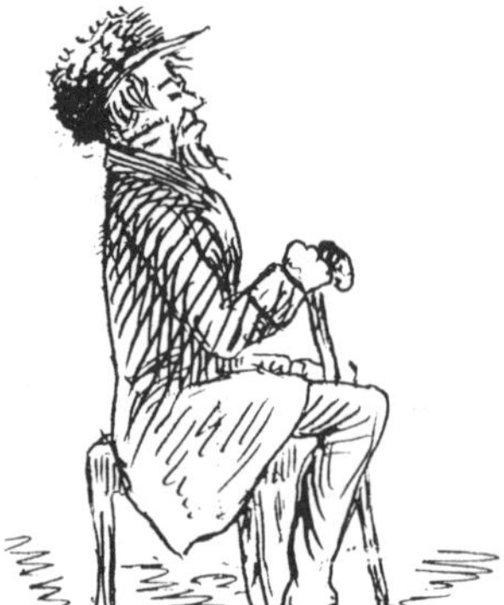

Adelaide Street Oct 31st 1877... Here we are from home afar Genteely treading the Southport shore Where wave lets ripple or billows roar:- Where children prattle and dig the sand And Beauty parades on every hand But stolid now - old fashioned we Practise a grave philosophy - We once were young but years increase:- We pause - we sigh - Our rhyme we cease! On the arenose rivage* I plod my way:- (If my meaning's not clear my dear sir, pray Consult your good friend, the trusty Barclay) But try if you cannot your weary way wend Coppull and Heskin wards this weekend. We beg to conclude with service and duty myself still remaining the humble Deputy...

November 8th 1877... No letter, no paper, no nothink today - I feel in consequence quite trembling and timorous lest you have falled a victim to the perils of the 5th.* I am nearly lost to view amidst figures & Interest Tables &c just now - Hope all are well.. Nov 9th 1877 Two papers to hand today, many many thanks...

Nov 18th 1877... It is a remarkable fact (but nevertheless one which I state with confidence) that I am becoming older daily - The weighty duties of the present time take hold upon me - I have today a bursting headache which necessitates my walking about in the air as here depicted - Thanks for the abstract from Barclay - it goes to prove what a wonderful treasury of information that book is - I have laid the memorandum up in case it should ever be of service - I am grateful for the Papers - My partner is well but I am suffering from the cephalalgia* above mentioned - we hope you are all in a satisfactory condition of salubrity when this reaches you & may long so continue...

Nov 19th 1877... Ah me! my dear Sir this work, work, work is rapidly exhausting me - changing my limber gait and lightsome step into a locomotion sluggish and tardy - I've got the rheumatic in my right shoulder and wrist so if you see anyone in Preston within the next fortnight afflicted in this wise you may with tolerable safety conclude that it is me. I have paused at this particular juncture to refresh myself with a stimulating pinch and now feel sufficiently reinvigorated thereby to commend myself and the partner of my joys and sorrows to the kind remembrance of you all - with every good wish and friendly compliment...

Nov 21st 1877... If there be one thing in this locality of which we have more than another - it is weather - We are never without it - Today it blows hard and rains harder - The atmosphere looks thick & though the time is scarcely half past 2 P.M it is so dark I can hardly see to write. Yesterday being the 20th was a wearisome day of business - I felt very tired yesterday at night fall so am resting & recruiting myself today. In the ardent hope you are all well...

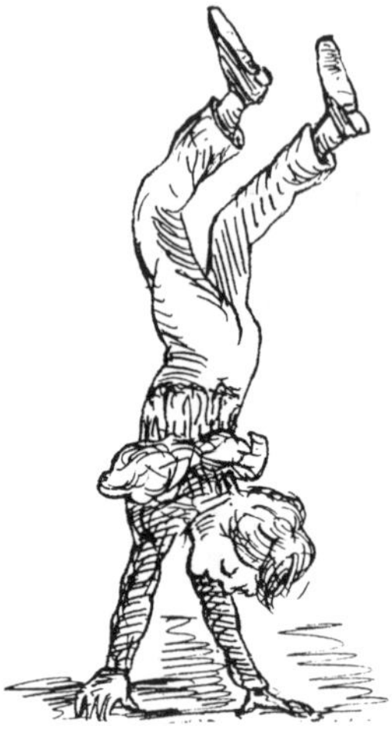

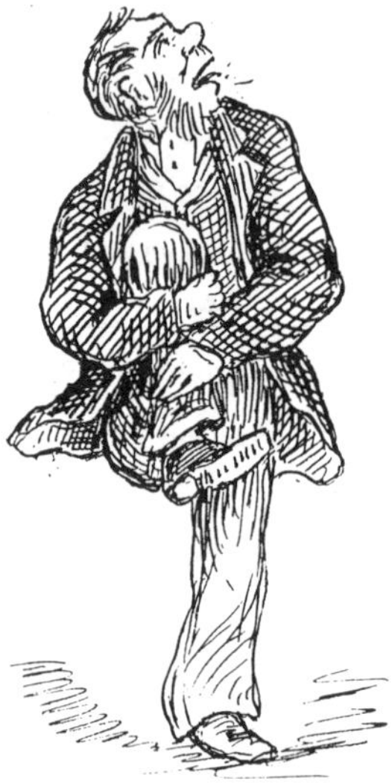

Notes

Dec 7th 1877 — In 1875, to raise money, the Khedive of Egypt sold his shares in the Suez Canal to Britain, and an Anglo-French condominium was set up in 1876 to manage the Egyptian finances.

Dec 12th 1877 — Glike = scoff; arride = deride; alogy = absurdity; cowish = timorous; surbate = footsore; succussation = the trotting of a horse; mansuete = good-natured; comity = civility; edulcorate = sweeten; swap = at once; swink = drudgery; thirling = piercing; dilation = enriching; epulation = feast.

Dec 20th 1877 — Vagous = wandering.

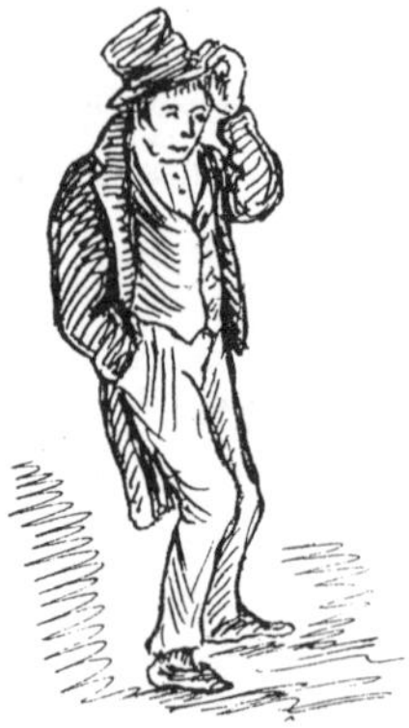

Nov 24th 1877... Many thanks for the papers and letter - with illness, business and divers matters I have been of late so much upset that I have very nearly gone about the wrong end up but upside down or downside up Believe me very truly yours.. In great haste...

Nov 28th 1877... oh, my dear Sir, These corns! These farinaceous excrescences on the minor digits of my inferior extremities! Alas! we are this morning in the number of footsore, travel stained and weary pilgrims. Mine head grew worse and worse while homeward walking and I was brought nigh unto distraction. My fair companions are well but appreciate a rest keenly. They write in desiring, with me, commendation to the friendly regard of yourself and household...

Dec 7th 1877... I have hoped for some time to be able to drop my umbrella or lay it aside at least for a while but alas! me the weather forbids it. I drove out as far as Leyland yesterday and rain poured in just such profusion as if the Suez canal* had been put through a riddle. I, as also my charioteer, the trusty Nicholas - vanquisher of men - got drenched through & through. I have therefore today dropped my umbrella and am keeping myself within doors - Thanks for your continual kindness in supplying me with news. My partner is well and hopeth with myself to be retained in friendly remembrance by you and yours - We combine in distinguished regards...

Dec 12th 1877... I rede ye that ye glike* not at me - nor arride* the alogy* of my cowish * figure as I appear before you surbate* with succussation*, but of your mansuete* comity* be not erk to edulcorate* - swap* - my mental swink* - viz: the remorse I feel at having delayed a day or two longer than I purposed the writing of this communication to you thanking you - not with subditious acknowledgements but with a thirling* dilation* of gratitude - Mine other half and I are promised forth to an epulation* for which - if rain witholds we eftsoon start - We embrace you all in our affection and I abide your unworthy slave...

Dec 20th 1877... Onerd Sir.. Do write me a long letter. I've got 'ome and am glad to report that I found my invalid greatly improved but this morning some of the symptoms had returned but I think there is this afternoon improvement perceptible, I have been out all day and feel both 'umble and mannerly - accept my dear sir my best respex and thanks for the kind hospitality where with you sustained my weary flesh when suffering the exhaustion consequent on a lengthy vagous* circumambulation. The benison of a pilgrim I bestow on yourself and family and mine invalid aforesaid joins me in wishing you all the happiness which the approaching festive season is capable of imparting and trusting further that your store of felicity and blessing may receive large additions the New Year...

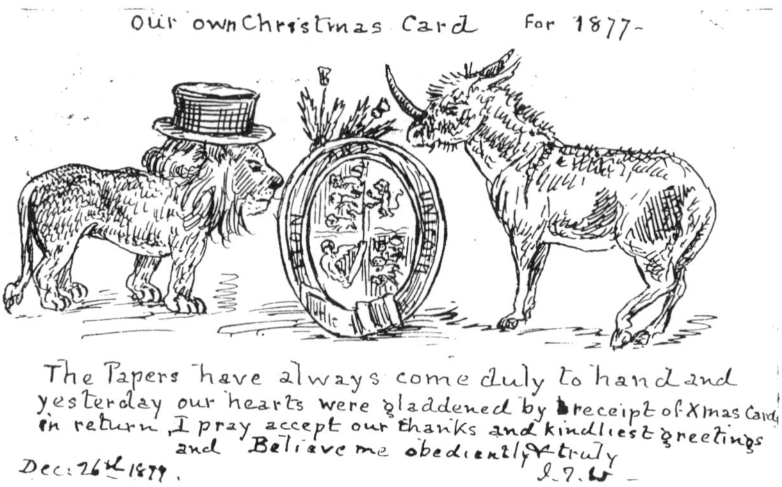

Notes

Jan 8th 1878 Bosky = woody; scaturiginous = abounding in springs.

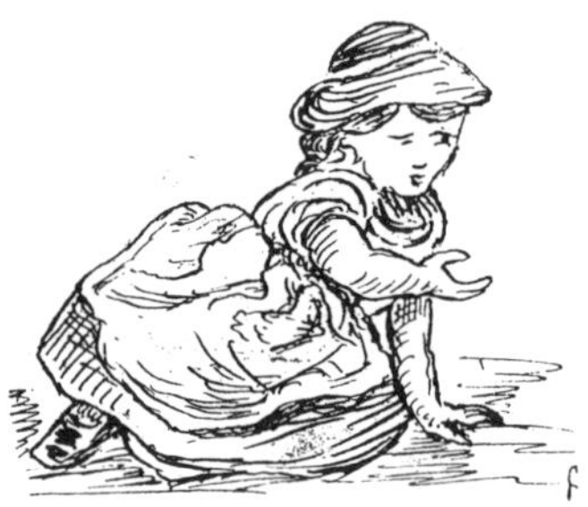

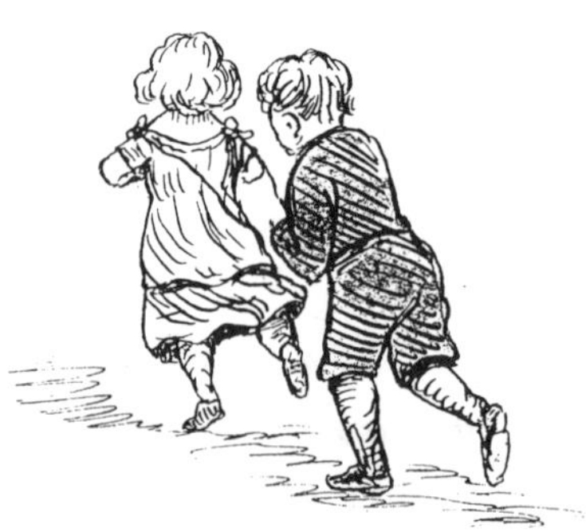

Jan 21st 1878 Peggy was an early form of rounders played with a stick and a 'peg' of wood.

Our own Christmas Card for 1877... The Papers have always come duly to hand and yesterday our hearts were gladdened by receipt of Xmas card, in return I pray accept our thanks and kindliest greetings and Believe me obediently & truly.. Dec 26th 1877

Merry Christmas and a New Year Rich in Blessings...

Jan 1st 1878... Towards the end of my journey yesterday I could scarcely bear the wind was keen as a razor blade and I felt the cold 'steel' over me (should this word be steel or steal?). It was 5 of the clock when old Nicholas having deposited us - his interesting cargo - and meetly refreshed himself drove his wagon home - exposure to the cold occasions a painful enlargement of the parotid, maxillary and submaxillary glands so that I felt as if I was going to have either Tic-gathered face or toothache - but this morning we are better - unite ye in our rejoicing and accept we pray ye our assurance of unchanged esteem...

Jan 8th 1878... Our present moon will attain its first Quarter on the 11th so that if you attain this bosky* hummock with its earsh and scaturiginous firels on the 12th you will I trow have a little light for your transit from Coppull Station hither - we shall be alone and rejoiced to see you - I opine you have by this time got the little folks home again - I am grateful for the papers which through your kindness daily reach me...

Jan 15th 1878... My experience has established the conviction that in this sublunary state we purpose many things and are often disappointed - I yesterday intended to have written to you but a hard fortune prevented me - just as I was searching for a Postcard a friend came in from what in Colonial phraseology I may call a 'clearing' 10 miles distant and engrossed my notice ' from early morn to dewy eve' and at eventide there came old Nicholas's chariot to spirit me away to a place some miles beyond Standish - my whole day was occupied - hence no post card - we have, at home, arrived safe again and venture to hope you were equally fortunate when hence you departed - what a fortunate circumstance you returned when you did, for you escaped the rain & tempest prevalent this morning - mine other self combines with me in sincere regards for all ...

Jan 21st 1878... I thank you over and over again for your long and interesting letter and will you please let Jack come over on Thursday or Friday next to play with me - You need not fear our getting into any mischief or misbehaving ourselves for we shall only take long walks and play at Peggy - should we unfortunately break a window or put a citizen's eye out we won't play at Peggy any more but select another game - Trusting to see Jack on one of the days above named I remain ...

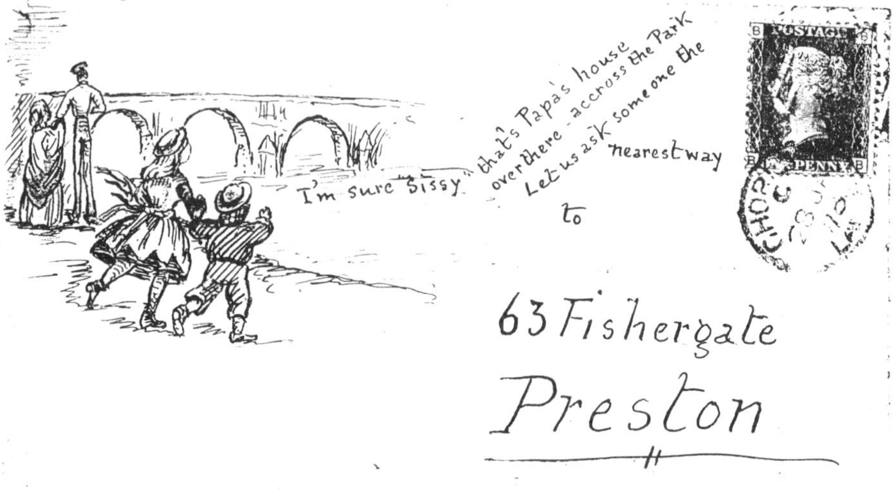
I'm sure "Sissy" that's Papa's house overthere - accross the Park
Let us ask some one the nearest way
to
63 Fishergate
Preston

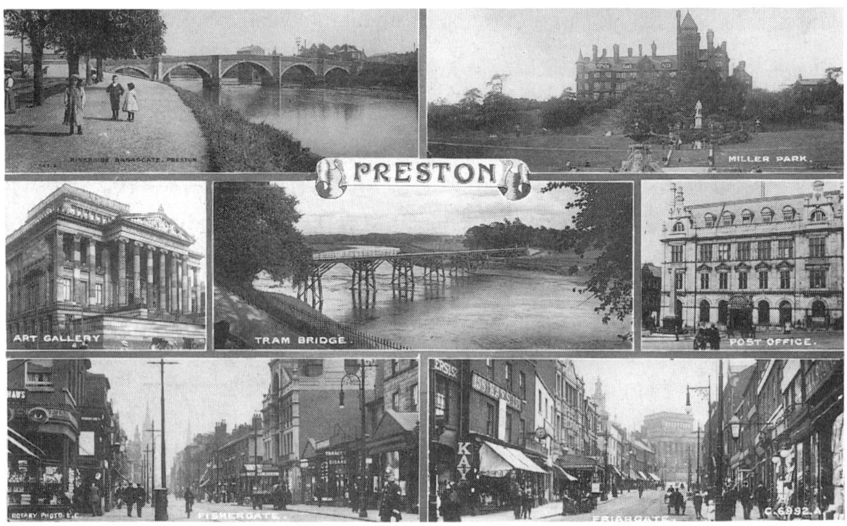
PRESTON
MILLER PARK.
ART GALLERY
TRAM BRIDGE.
POST OFFICE.
FISHERGATE.
FRIARGATE.
C.6392.A
ROTARY PHOTO E.C.

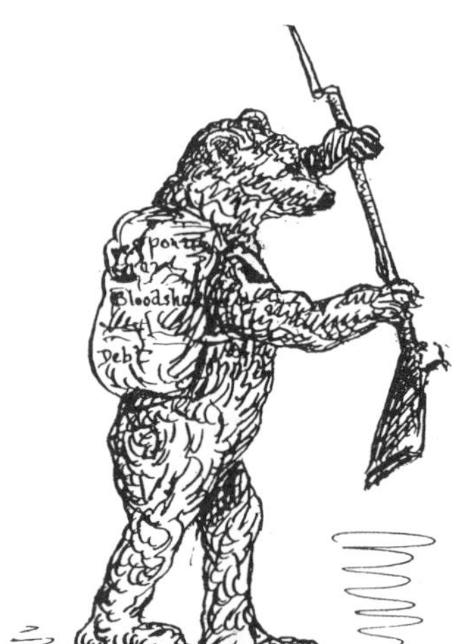
Debt

Jan 23rd 1878... We are setting off to Southport about the middle of next week for two reasons (1) The approach of another first Monday in the month makes it needful for me to go thither & (2) The continued wet stormy and generally unsettled condition of the weather militates against enjoyment of the country - we have therefore decided to take Southport next week and get all our engagements there fulfilled so that we may have the following week entirely at disposal to attend to the comfort of friends when (trusting that the weather will surely be calmer, warmer and drier) we hope to realize the pleasure which we have been anticipating for some time past - viz a visit from Miss Worsley and Jack - Please fix any day in the week commencing on February 3rd except the Monday - the temperature just now is cold enough to starve a Toad - I can scarcely hold or guide my pen ...

... Just one card to tell you the important fact that we have got to Southport and are stopping here for a night or two - The precise day of our return I cannot fix but I dare say Friday will be selected for our departure hence - we have not got much sleep of late because of the storms that have howled around our dwelling in the night time and bid fair to blow it down - We heartily combine in muchness... P.S. I had almost forgotten to mention that I am almost helpless with acute lumbago...

Feb 1st 1878... I am at home again and wish you and yours a very good health - I am myself greatly crippled with Lumbago but hope to be able to lay myself up for a day or two and get well - you don't say in your communication anything about our visitors next week - How will Tuesday suit? - send word what hour and we will one or both try to meet the train at Croston - I suppose by that time the Russians will have taken or have got to Constantopoli and Gallipople - They surely won't want a poor Lumbago victim for a soldier - Hoping to hear from you again...

Feb 5th 1878... So far as I am able to judge of the present phase of the Eastward position I conclude that there is a great possibility that the Russian Bear what's his <u>name</u> will be sent packing as he <u>came</u> - but never mind we hope for the best and are glad to say that the wanderers have come to hand safely - we all got here from Croston at about 1-30 - Jack proved himself to be in good marching fettle - all are refreshed and well - we combine in muchness of kind remembrance & I remain...

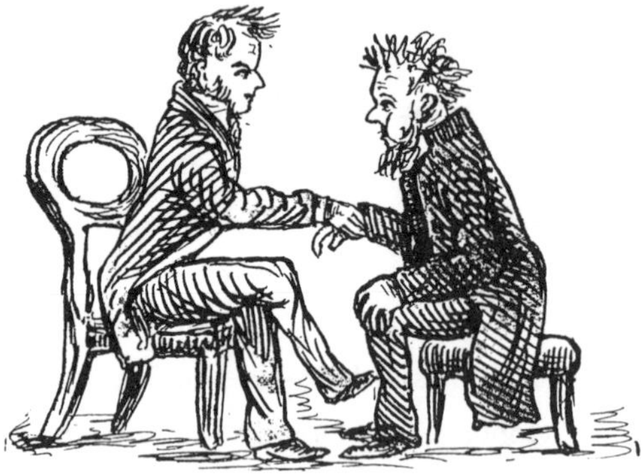

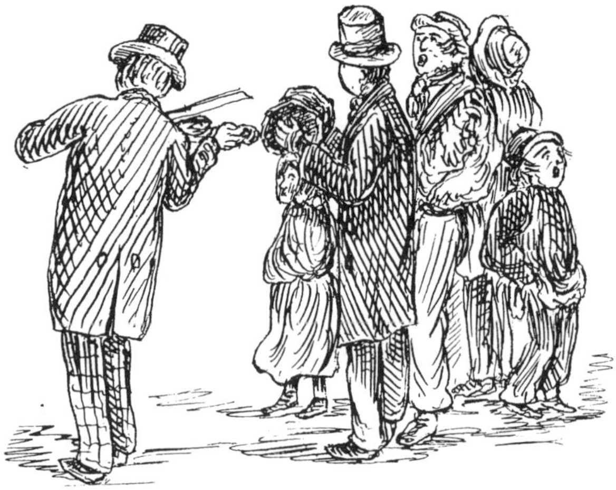

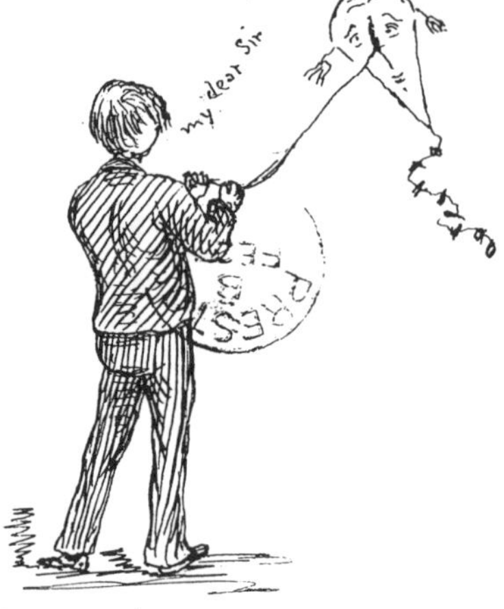
my dear Sir

Feb 7th 1878... I have suffered much from acute Lumbago since this day fortnight and when in Southport had to seek medical counsel - I am rather better today but feel amply able to sympathise with you when you announce yourself ill - ill - most ill - Today is so fine - we have - Lumbago notwithstanding - had a long walk. We have become possessors of a Ham by purchase. Public opinion inclines to maintain in consequence - the expediency of your bringing a trap when the time for return of Household and the above named provision to Preston has arrived - Don't let it be before Monday and if you can spare them longer don't hurry to fetch them - the weather is so lovely just now. Jack has got two pop guns - Bow and Arrow - and of course a rush whip - we all combine in loving sentiments and I remain ...

Feb 13th 1878... just a line to certify you of our joy at learning that the wanderers got home in safety. Jack left behind a parcel of whips and warlike appliances Bows, Arrows, Pop guns - I hope to have the means of sending them shortly. Ginger Ale can be obtained from Robert Kellett in Preston at Fifteen pence per Doz. Our sentiments continue in Concert of Harmony mine whole household combines in friendliness and I remain...

Feb 19th 1878... I'm flying my kite in Southport just at present - from which circumstance you will doubtless draw the inference that my Lumbago is in abeyance - such is indeed the case and I rejoice furthermore to announce that my recent attack of Bronchitis is likewise become almost a thing of the past - My excellent Partner like a true wife as she is has shared my sickness i.e., she has been ill also - and on Saturday night last developed a symptom which occasioned us very great alarm. I felt truly thankful when the crisis was past - We hope and trust your own indisposition is at an end. I thank you with all the warmth of gratitude of which I am capable for the papers which reach me daily - They are at the present political juncture possessed of surpassing interest - Accept a large consignment of our united friendliness and regard.. P.S. Return on Friday...

Feb 25th 1878... I awoke up this morning to a consciousness of being at home once more - I returned from Southport on Saturday much better in health than when I went thither - your letter reached me duly for which many thanks - I am going again to Southport tomorrow - we shall be pleased to see you here this week end - Do come if you can!!!! The hunters were all round us on Saturday and hare hunting was going vigorously forward. Receive our benison...

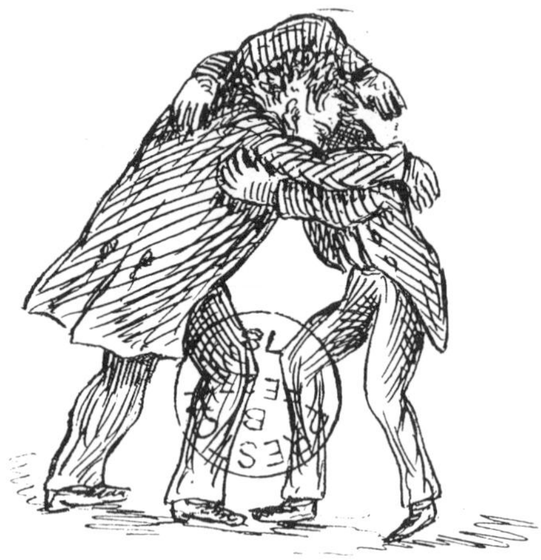

Notes

7th March 1878

This first reference to Mrs Wilson by what is to become a pet name for her may have been occasioned by the weapon, but the Oxford English Dictionary also defines 'torpedo' as 'one who, or that which, has a benumbing influence'.

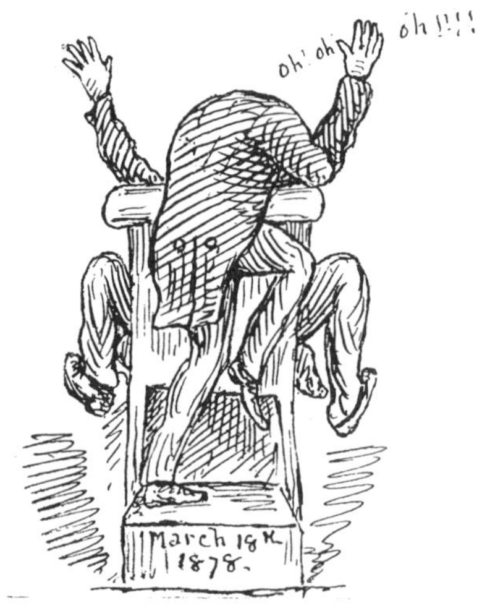

Evidently copied from a George Cruikshank illustration to 'The Toothache, imagined by Horace Mayhew.'

Feb 26th 1878... We embrace and greet ye heartily and well -- we are off to Southport again in a few minutes from now if the rain will cease - a slight sprinkle is just moistening the face of the earth as if with tear drops of silent unaffected sorrow at my departure - I caught cold on Sunday and my cough in consequence has returned upon me - we are expecting to see you this weekend. I return I expect on Friday - Mr Parkes is in Lancashire but not here - whether he will call en route homewards I cannot tell. With large hearted sympathies believe me...

March 1st 1878... I should have jump'd and leap'd and leap'd and jump'd with an ecstatic and bounding saltation had your letter to hand last evening announced that you were going to pleasure us with your presence this weekend - What hinders that ye may not come on the 9th instead of the 16th - make it 9th and I shall be reconciled a little. I learn with grief that your cold and its belongings are still so powerfully upon you - my earnest hope is that you may very soon be as free from cold as I am this minute - with most friendly solicitude towards all.. in haste...

March 7th 1878... I am touching myself up a little - quite in the expectation of seeing you over here this week end - last weekend my dear domestic torpedo* provisioned largely in expectation of your arrival & exploded with disappointment. I hope you by this time feel well enough and that the weather will be sufficiently propitious to admit of your coming - In compliments we cordially coalesce & I remain...

Card Number 2. March 7th 1878... Your letter to hand just this minute has floored me - I am quite prostrate by means of this reiterated disappointment. But so be it !!!! The weather truly is tempestuous and the rain terrific - I cannot get out and about - I am a prisoner - my only companion being a cold - Draughts are holding wild orgies about my chamber and honour with special attentions my head - the hair of which feels as if perpetually on the wave - On the 16th we look for you - by the way we have a concert on that day - if possible come early - <u>so mote it be</u> - affectionate regards to all..P.S. You will probably meet your old friend Mr Howe here on the 16th...

March 18th 1878...oh! oh! Oh!!!! My dear Sir does this represent the process of <u>extraction</u> whereby an aching tooth may be dispensed with? What must be done with the aching heart which throbs beneath or within the waistcoat of the undersigned by reason of your departure? - In loneliness I sigh and wonder how ye gat ye home again last evening - How ye bore the weariness of walking - or how withstood the damp and cold - The old man whom I visited yesterday departed about two o'clock this morning - A fierce wind is prevalent - we hope you found all well on your return - we bear ye in most kind remembrance and I beg to remain...

Notes

30th March 1878

An appeal was in process for the restoration of St James's Church, and the local paper advertised lists of items donated by local worthies.

Henry, here, refers to the local postman, Henry Hitch, who, of course collected post as well as delivering it, and was usually prepared to wait whilst a reply was written, if necessary.

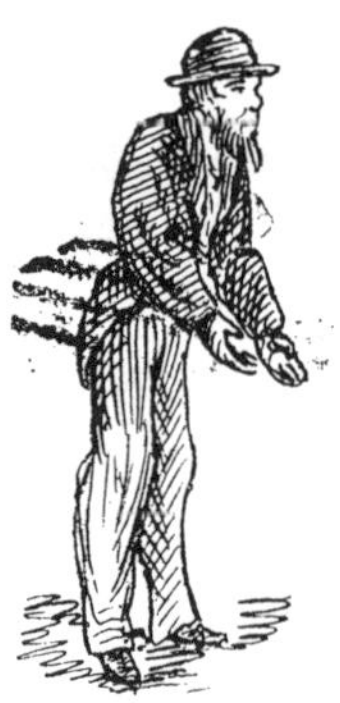

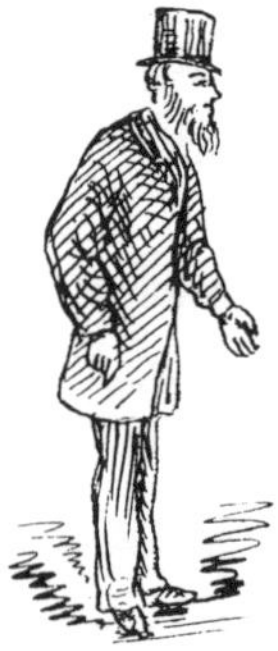

March 26th 1878... I have studied the Eastern Question deeply from the Standard Newspapers with which you so kindly supply me daily and I conclude that War resembles closely a dreaded Dental operation which most persons have at some period to undergo inasmuch as it commences with an amount of subtle negotiation and sometimes finishes with a general upset. I am in haste...

Saturday night. March 30th 1878... I received your favour enclosing receipt for Insurance for which I thank you very much indeed - it is very kind of you to take so much trouble on my account and I should have acknowledged its safe arrival and returned my thanks much more promptly had I not been so fully engrossed with visitation of the sick of whom I have many now and further with an endeavour to accumulate the sum of £150 for an important object* - This last most pressing matter has rendered me oblivious to much of my private correspondence inasmuch as my time for its accumulation is very limited - A stamp affixed inside a Standard which I received today called to mind the fact that I had omitted to respond to your last welcome Communication - It was then too late to rectify the oversight for Henry* had departed - We sent the potatoes off from here last evening and live in the hope that they have reached their destination safely today - We are both better again in health - Trusting that salubrity smiles upon you and all yours in like manner.. My other half amalgamates in sentiments of esteem...

The Bank. England April 1st 1878... I write this at the receipt of usury - A wind more searching than a Custom House officer roars without and nobody comes to visit me within - I have not met the Post this morning or I should have had something to pass my time with - Newspapers letters or something - One door opens - one way of Pastime appears - I have a Post Card and I proceed to utilize it - That Ghost I hear has been at its antics again - **** I was just about to enter upon this terrible hair erecting topic when a client appeared - others have followed and I have for a little space been very busy - my Labours are now over but before I depart I just address myself to the completion of my Post Card - with every friendly compliment to all ...

Southport April 2nd 1878... I am here again but only for today, or till tomorrow morning at the longest - so please don't alter the direction of Standard - The Potatoes which I hope have duly reached you are 5/9 the measure - My 'Sternerhalf' says if you will send word when they are done she shall be happy to get you more if such you wish - with cordial sentiments...

Notes

April 11th 1878

Feriation = holiday from work
Whirligig = a windmill
Adolphe Thiers (1797 - 1877) - a statesman and President of the French Republic. The local papers carried these snippets of information.

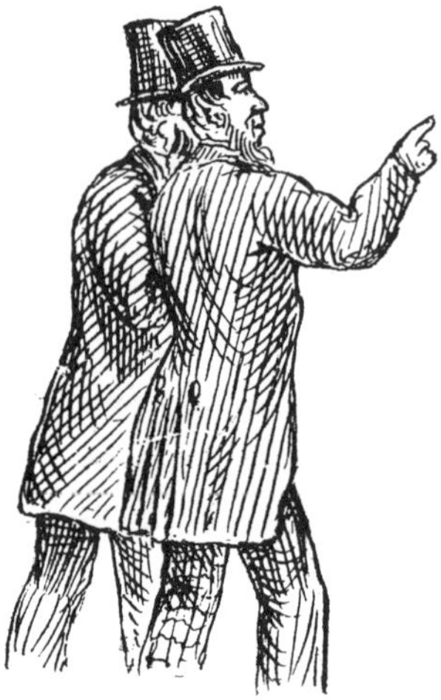

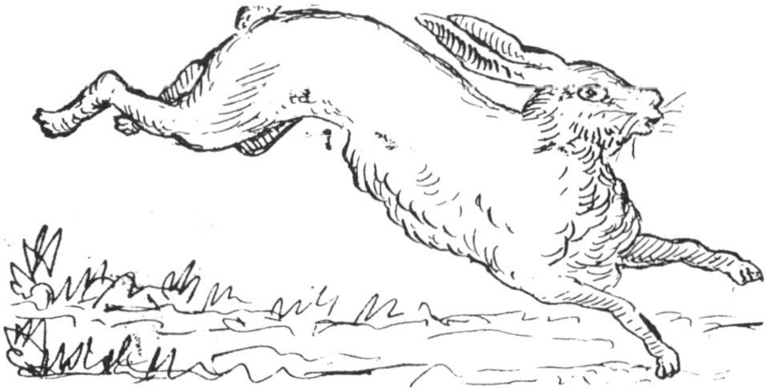

April 30th 1878

Mr George Parkes of Billington House, near Stafford was another friend receiving Mr Wilson's illustrated postcards.

April 11th 1878...after a long period of arduous and anxious labour I am today assuming to myself the delights of a temporary feriation* and am well nigh minded to betake myself to the relaxation of a Country walk through this vigourous Eastern breeze - We have Baby Pie once more with us and have been officiating as 'Nus' girl in so far as Perambulatory duties are concerned. I have furthermore made the terrible but interesting infant a whirligig* at the end of a stick - with which instrument of infantile delight the wind has been actively engaged - The little lady has been with us since Friday last - she is, and has been aforetimes greatly benefitted by the Country air albeit the prevalent East winds have given her a cold - Mine Better Half has also a cold and seems muchly indisposed with it - That perfect salubrity is the portion of you and yours is our earnest united hope...

...Let me point out to you the important fact that notwithstanding the rain now freely falling this 16th day of April - the Tuesday in fact, before Easter 1878 will be about 13 hours and 48 minutes in length and though there is no wind prevailing the Tide at this very minute viz: two minutes past 10 o'clock A.M. will be 19 feet six inches on the Southport rivage - It is furthermore worthy of being remembered that on this day of April 81 years ago L.A. Thiers* was born and just five years ago a great Fire broke out at Santiago in Chile occasioning damage to the extent of Twenty four thousand pounds - We have Baby Pie and a little American lady (Age 4 years) a smart child, abiding with us. That the day finds you all in health is our ardent hope ...

April 23rd 1878... we reached this place an hour agone having accomplished our journey with a bounding speed like unto that wherewith the gentle timorous hare is wont to elude the pursuing hounds - We effected our transit pleasantly - By the way are you going to the Rocky Mountains to see the total solar eclipse? I see that in consequence of special charges observers can go there and back again for about £34.. P.S. I omitted 6d out of the money yesterday - will write again tomorrow...

April 30th 1878... I am in Southport again but only for a day, or two at most - I have informed our Reverend friend of the Templars meeting in May - and have added largely to Mr Parkes' album* recently - A voluminous sequel to the Horse Pages detailing his dental experiences consequent upon severe cold occasioned by his unwonted struggles in achievement of supremacy over his rebellious Nag - Betsy is married and Jane Hann also. The air is still thick with matrimonial rumours - A delightful rain today is falling. In the matter of salubrity we twain are satisfactory. Hoping ye are all abundantly blessed...

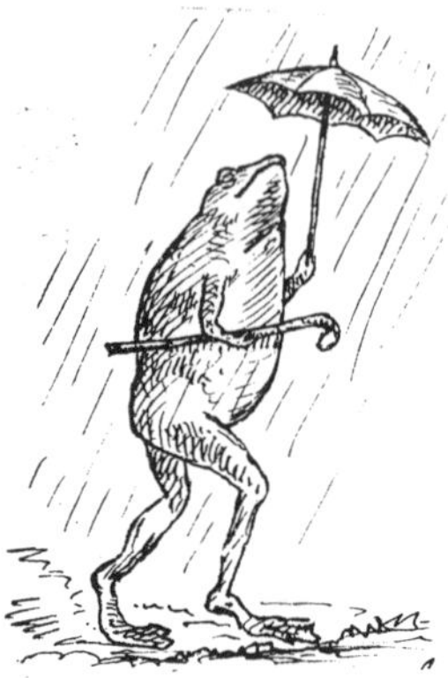

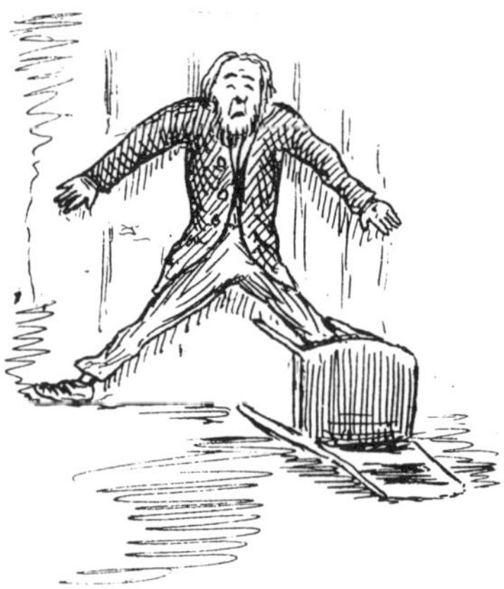

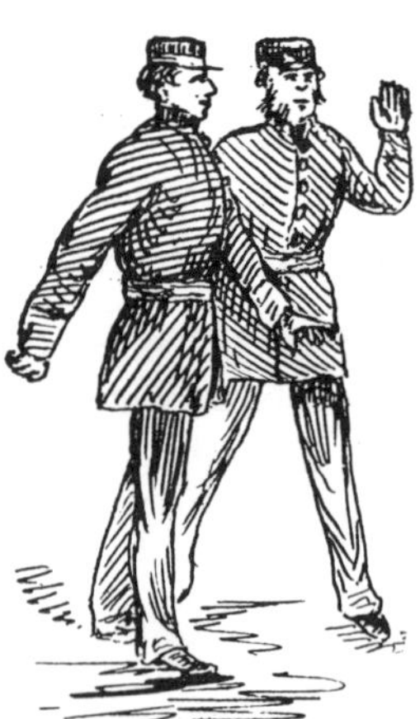

May 3rd 1878... There is a beautiful, productive rain just now falling which makes the gardens, trees and hedgerows look delightful but it renders it rather damp for us inhabitants of the fields and whether wet or fair I suppose we shall have to effect a general migration (Southport was abandoned yesterday - even there we had rain). My observation about a general migration has reference to the 3rd day of June which we trust you will bear in mind - out of one field at least we shall have to hie us on that day - War still lifts its gaunt form in the not distant future but its approach is tardy - Pray accept this notification of our return and Believe me...

May 16th 1878... Condole with me for I am greatly out of fettle today - Partly in consequence of the prevalence of thunder and partly from the operation of cold - My limbs are heavy - weariness pervades my frame and I experience a slightly painful enlargement of the left cheek - My partner shares my indisposition - but we hope when the thunder is over we may feel better - our cordial greetings to you all...

May 22nd 1878... The swelling and painfulness of my face proved to be nothing very serious after all - If I had come to Preston during recent & perhaps present excitement I might perchance have had not one cheek only but both something in this like condition - Thanks for your note - Don't, we pray you, be unmindful of the 3rd of June - Neighbourhood lovely and fresh but the wind a little cold - Kindness & esteem towards all...

May 31st 1878... oh, my dear Mr Worsley.. I am quite intirely done this morning - we got back from Preston yesterday about 4 o'clock and afterwards proceeded direct to Up-Holland whence we did not return till nearly midnight - Exposure to the Night air I feared would leave a token behind it in the form of cold, or cough, or Gout, or Rheumatics or Something but happy, three and four times happy we - no cold results, nor cough nor gout are present and yet we feel as depicted <u>done, quite intirely done</u>. We are all deep in speculation as to the weather prospects with particular reference to Monday - we are hopeful - with love to all...

June 13th 1878...<u>We</u> had nothing whatsoever to do with the Report - It was all Rowland that did it - with wonderful diversity of arrangement in the various papers - Day was lovely - the Party a complete success - We are delighted to hear of your safe return from the sister Isle - can you ascertain from or by reference to your Album the date of the day of our visit to Windermere last year and also the date of our return from Ulverston - when convenient and you feel minded to pleasure me with a line please mention - The Papers have regularly reached me - my Gratitude is heartily yours, with sincere regards...

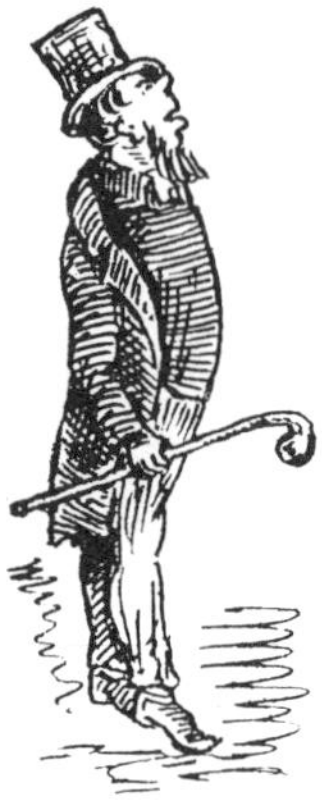

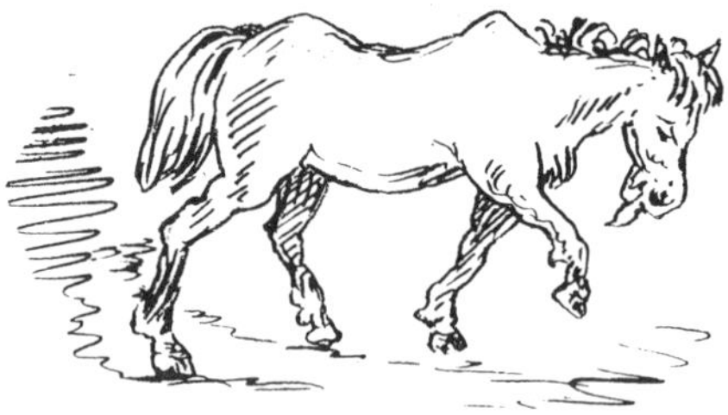

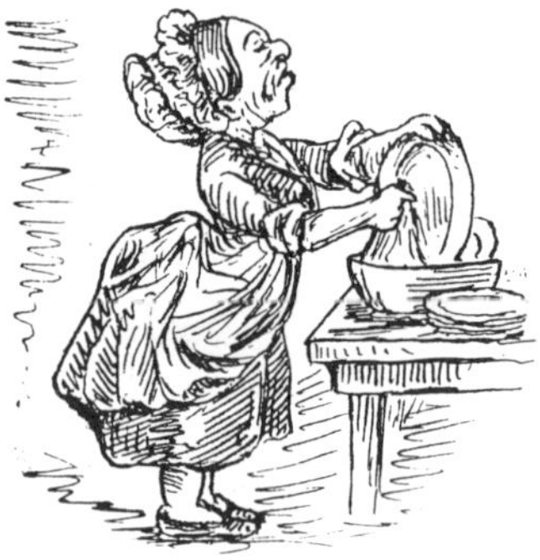

Notes

June 29th 1878

The Berlin Congress limited Russian naval expansion, and obtained Turkish recognition of the Balkan states. It was attended by Lord Beaconsfield.

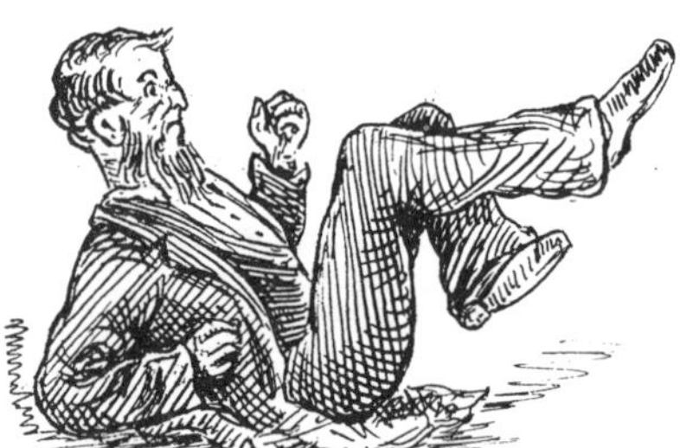

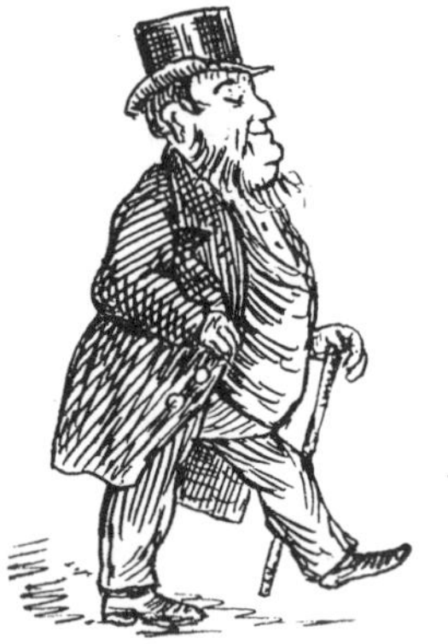

Heskin June 15th 1878... I thank you very much for the information which your note by post today brings me - I hope you have quite recovered from your visit to Hibernian. You haven't been to Epsom or to see the Derby - did you - I write in haste...

June 20th 1878... You may be very well sure, my dear Sir, that there has been a great deal of washing up since the Tea Party but the rectification and straightening up process having been brought to a state of completion we went up yesterday morning early to the top of Harrock to catch the early breezes and revel in the bright & warm sunshine. The scenery there is at its best just now - It was glorious and we returned entranced with the beauteous spectacle - We are still entranced. The effect has been of a lasting character - Commend us to all your family...

June 27th 1878... I have just returned from a very long walk and finding a newspaper awaiting for which I am indebted to your kindness I proceed -(while the thunder bursts and the lightnings flash around) to convey to you a hurried expression of my thanks - Roses abound in our hedgerows just now. Miss L left us yesterday - The Tea Party therefore lasted till yesterday...

June 29th 1878... Your letter is this minute to hand. I am rejoiced to be able to announce in reply that now the Tea Party is quite over I am beginning to get up my flesh again notwithstanding the prevalent temperature which is somewhere between a 'Bake oven' and a 'Blast furnace'. Every one feels it and it is a topic more general here than the Berlin Congress* - whenever I and my neighbours hold a congress, conference, or what not in house, road, or hayfield we always give the heat priority - It is more oppressive than the sirocco from the plains of Libya or the Harmattan which dries up the verdure of Africa and blisters even Ethiopian skins...

July 5th 1878... I am tired this morning - weariness and exhaustion pervades my whole frame & fatigue percolates through every limb - I beheld Harrock yesterday at its best - In addition to the natural beauties of the place the scenic effect was heightened by such artificial adjuncts as Champagne, Salmon, Fowls, tongues &c &c - as well as that beauty of more exceeding charm, to wit, feminine - The occasion was a great one - a Gigantic Picnic was being holden whereat we participated and partook of pleasure abundantly - This morning we're fatigued, yet in our overpoweredness we warmly think Upon ye - Bear us in kindly remembrance and commend us to yours..P.S. Have not been able to send for a Wigan paper today...

Notes

<u>July 20th 1878</u> From 'The Chorley Guardian' of 27th July 1878...

SCHOOL FETE AT MAWDESLEY

On Saturday a double event was expected to take place at Mawdesley, viz., the laying of the foundation stone of a new chancel in connection with the church, and the holding of the annual school festival. Unfortunately, through some hitch in the arrangements, the ceremony alluded to above was postponed, but the school feast nevertheless was held and proved a brilliant success. The heat was intense about noon and very few cared to stir abroad. About 12 o'clock however, the children began to assemble in the environs of the school and shortly afterwards a procession was formed and after a rather uncomfortable perambulation of 4 miles of country under a scorching noonday sun, the processionists adjourned to a field which had been kindly lent for the purpose of the festivities by Mr H. Southworth. At the end of the meadow nearest the rectory a large tent had been erected in which tea tables had been fixed, and in this cool retreat a substantial repast was partaken of by relays of people who in the aggregate numbered about 600. After tea rustic sports were indulged in and, the band being present, the opportunity of dancing was availed of to a large extent. Several races for small prizes took place, and as the evening wore on and the air became somewhat cooler, the number of participants in the sports increased and the scene was lively and enjoyable.

<u>July 29th 1878</u> Mr Wilson lived in the house called Pyebrook in 1872 before moving into Heskin Vicarage.

<u>Aug 1st 1878</u> The annual Southport Horticultural Show.

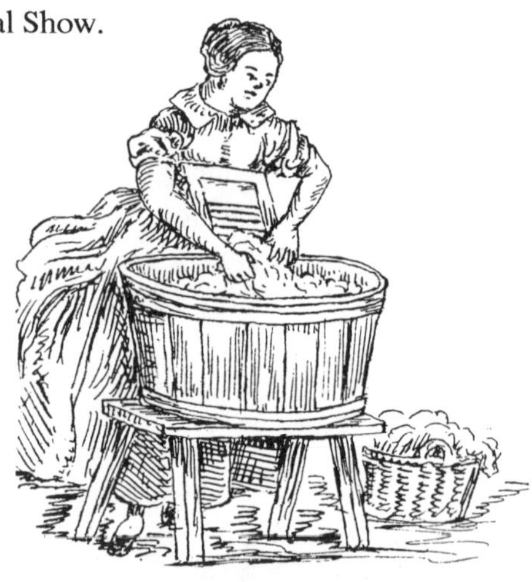

July 15th 1878... I am still the recipient of your favour and kindness in the matter of a diurnal paper. My gratitude for your thoughtfulness is sincere and deep and I beg you to accept my thanks in greater measure than I am able, on a Post Card, to express - I venture to offer also my respectful duty and remain...

July 20th 1878... I am myself upset with this fierce unbearable heat but nevertheless grieved to hear of your indisposition, but earnestly trust you are by this time recovered - We are in a chronic state of sunstroke - but yet by Fern leaves &c in our hat we preserve our brain from utter disarrangement - The Picnic referred to in my previous holograph was not an enterprise of my promoting - I had merely the honour of a guest's position at it - & in such capacity perpetrated large consumption of delectable viands and partook freely of the pleasures of the occasion - It is Mawdesley Tea Party* today but we are not going - when will you slip over and spend a week end with us? Devote attention to this subject in your next...

July 22nd 1878... I have had my attention fixed upon the chapter & verse you name for some weeks past - It is certainly interesting and I am grateful for your most kind letter - I am sure you would find it warm at Southport - Accept my congratulations on your victory - We regard with intense satisfaction the probability of a visit from you this week end & trust nothing will occur to prevent it & deprive us of the pleasure of yourself & household...

July 29th 1878... It is washing day at our house today and if you could only see the soapsuds in flakes of froth flying about the wash house you would think there was a snow storm prevailing - We last evening, after leaving you, waddled round by the School and old Pyebrook* at each of which places we paused awhile - but notwithstanding - reached this domicile about 8-15 - at 8-20 we were indulging in conjectures as to how far you had got on your homeward way - It is now 8-22 A.M. and Mr Jackson has just gone...

Aug 1st 1878... We were in Southport yesterday and found the place a scene of bustle, dust and heat - It was in fact the eve of the Culture Show* - the heat, the bustle, and the dust were overpowering - It really seemed as if to step out of one's skin and sit for a while in one's bones - in a free and airy fashion would be - to say the least of it - a change - Southport we rejoice to record is well supplied with advantages in the shape of seats for a heat smitten Public to sit upon as well as Lamp Posts for the aforesaid H.S.P. to rest against. We delight in the cool and quiet of the Country today and feel exuberant - we even envy not the dwellers in Preston..P.S Thanks for Graphic and Mercury...

Notes

Aug 6th 1878

Having consideration to the poor state of the country roads, which were of course unlit, accidents to carriages and pony traps were frequent occurrences, and as will be seen, Mr Wilson suffered in this way on more than one occasion.

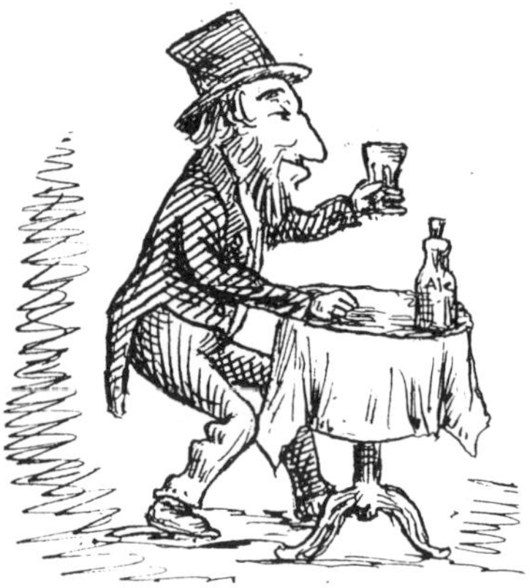

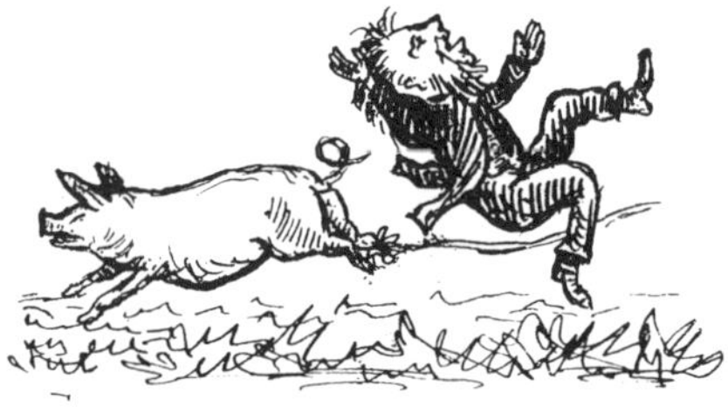

Aug 28th 1878

Monition = instruction.

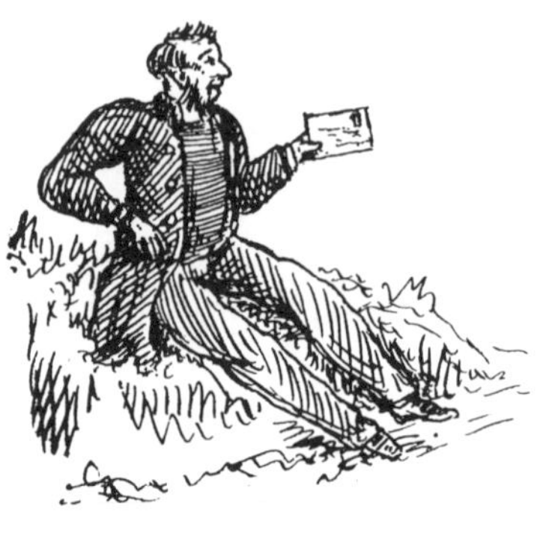

Aug 6th 1878... Receive an old man's blessing and permit him furthermore to inform you that the 'Eating up' Party will be holden here on Friday evening next. Mr P will be here and probably Miss L - shall we have the additional pleasure of your presence on the occasion? We anticipate that more than 30 persons will take part in the eating up process and their labour will be considerable. We had an accident* in the road near here yesterday - a carriage drawn by a pair of horses upset - no one was injured (fortunately) but the carriage is invalided & wheelless at Grundy's...

Aug 12th 1878... I was truly sorry to hear of your indisposition which unfortunately deprived us of the pleasure of seeing you here at the 'Eating up' Party on Friday - but with your permission I will - just to show that a kindly feeling still animates my bosom drink your health hoping you are by this time quite restored to vigorous salubrity. Mr Parkes is with us - Mr Cummings presence is looked for in a day or two - Party passed off well - at about two o'clock A.M...

Aug 16th 1878... I have been much upset by a Pig - twenty eight shillings worth - that was brought us some few days ago - but am sufficiently recovered to assume my pen to admonish you that the time is at hand for your promised visit to Billington near Stafford - Mr Parkes is arranging it for the second week in Sept. Mr Howe, Mr Marsden &c promised also to go and will be communicated with as soon as Mr Parkes has heard from you - please write by return and say if 2nd week in September will meet your convenience - Address G. Parkes Esqr at this place - where he yet abides but which he threatens to leave daily - Hoping all yours are well and with kindest compliments from Mr P and self - (sister Mary, Margt absent)...

Aug 19th 1878... Your letter is to hand and for the sake of an additional card and pen & ink figure being contributed to your album Mr Parkes insists on me being scribe on the occasion - You mistake - it is not a 'day' visit which Mr Parkes reckons on - He expects you to stop with him a year or at least a very sensible proportion of twelve months - I look forward to a week's sojourn amid the lovely scenery which encircles our friend's residence - Banish from your mind the thought of 'a one day's visit'...

Aug 28th 1878... Your most valued letter has just come to hand this minute - so far as I know the arrangements to which you refer it is expected that on Sept 9th - the Anniversary of the Battle of Flodden in 1513 - or on Tuesday 10th at latest ye and we and brother Marsden will turn up at Billington House in the County of Stafford - I doubt not our Stafford friend will administer to you further monition* touching the matter and to ourself also he may transmit additional despatches - anyway - on Sept 9th my especial notice is at present fixed. Hoping we shall meet under our friend's roof tree - as above...

Notes

<u>Aug 31st 1878</u> Harrogate

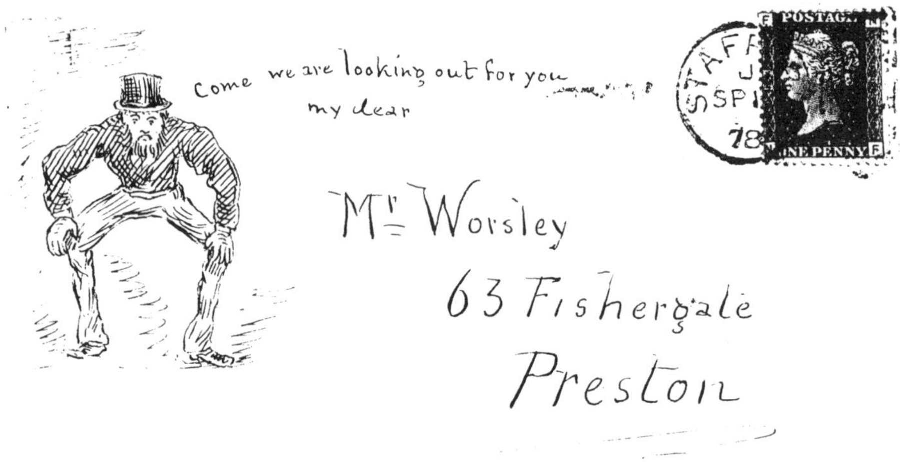

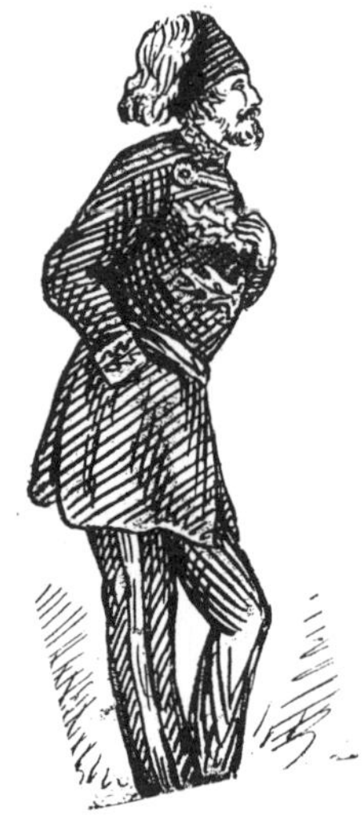

<u>Oct 9th 1878</u> A few more years were to pass before the causes of these diseases were identified.

Aug 31st... We are setting off on Tuesday next to a place called Harrowroot* - situated far up among the Highlands of Yorkshire - we shall return at the weekend (both Missis & us) in order to journey to the far off Stafford...

To Arrogate (verb Active) This 3rd Day of September 1878... I am to enjoy my first sleep at this place tonight - Harrowgate contains a collection of Houses - each of which is covered with what is termed in the vernacular of the locality 'a roof' - The chimneys too are so arranged that they each point directly to the zenith - There is also a Well...

Sep 5th 1878... I'm running back again on Saturday - we have had fine weather and much enjoyment - There are, I find, several wells - but the water is not well suited for tea making - in haste..P.S. we go south from Wigan (DV) on Monday early - Mr P I believe is expecting us on that day...

Sep 16th 1878... I am back again - we returned home on Saturday last - by train to Wigan and from Wigan in cab - Mr Parkes had provided two conveyances for the use of his guests - and often and often we regretted your absence as day after day we drove leisurely about through most lovely scenery. It was just the sort of out you would have been delighted with. We are nearly tired out with repeated jauntings and are glad once again to partake of home rest. I hope you are all well...

Sep 26th 1878... Don't think that the Eastern Question is setlled yet - complications will follow on complications to result I fear within a very few years in a general war - I regret to have to inform you that Fever (spotted) has agin visited us - It is strange that with so healthy a neighbourhood this scourge should once and again find its way in among us - Careless exposure to wet and inattention to Diet I apprehend are the causes in the present instance - I was visiting at nearly midnight - This morning I feel achy and chill - I have got cold - Torpedo well - Baby Pie also - Hope you are all salubrious...

Oct 9th 1878... Those Diplomatists are up to nothing - and there will be no Peace in the East I am convinced till these Diplomatic people step aside and let us go in - You would then see what a rough five months or so would do towards the settlement of matters - I am not well but yet have no desire to exchange places with either the Caimakhan of Svornick or the Akhoud of Swat - I seek not their dignities - weather woeful, Spotted fever and Typhoid* prevalent - rain pouring heavily - yet amid it all our heart is warm and we hold ye each and every one in affectionate esteem...

Notes

Oct 15th 1878 Report from 'The Chorley Guardian' of 26th October 1878:-

LAYING THE FOUNDATION STONE OF A NEW CHURCH AT SOUTHPORT

The foundation stone of St Luke's was laid on Friday week with full masonic honours by Brother the Right Honourable Lord Skelmersdale, Deputy Grand Master of England and Right Worshipful Provincial Grand Master of West Lancashire, whose zeal in the direction of church expansion, as well as in connection with Masonry not only in his own province but throughout the United Kingdom is so well known and appreciated. The popularity of his lordship in the Masonic world was again clearly shown by the very large and brilliant attendance of brethren from nearly every part of the extensive Masonic division of Lancashire, the bulk of the brethren hailing from lodges in Liverpool. There were altogether about 400 present.

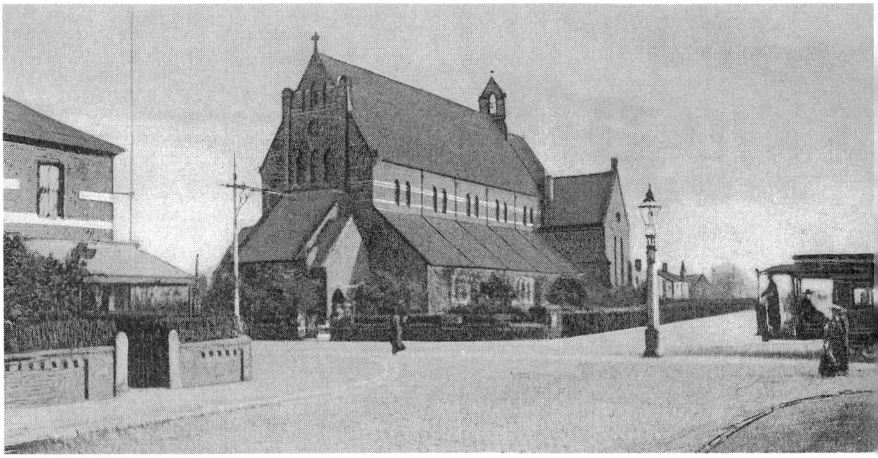

St. Luke's Church, SOUTHPORT. 202

Many professional men belonged to the Freemasons and did good work in raising money for churches. Although Freemasonry started from the establishment of guilds and lodges set up whenever masons were assembled for a large building project from as early as the 14th century, by the 17th century non-operatives were being admitted as patrons in certain lodges and the movement swung more to benevolent and social activities.

Nov 25th 1878 The traditional goose at Christmas was to be ousted in popularity in due course by the turkey, still a novelty in 1878.

Oct 15th 1878... Believe me, I am looking forward to the pleasure of meeting you at the laying of the Foundation Stone of St Luke's Church*, Southport on Friday next, October 18th. We twain are going thither and many Masons* - It is in fact, to be a matter of 'so mote it be' - Commend us to your sister and household and of our sincere esteem be assured...

Oct 29th 1878... Brother Mason Marsden is going to preach in our church on Sunday next - Mr Parkes is with us - We hope ye will be minded to journey hitherward also - on Saturday evening, and abide with us until Aurora ushers in next Monday - Our Partner like ourself and friend ardently desireth your presence - Pray send us word whether the desired pleasure may be with sureness anticipated, every kind compliment to all and sundry...

Nov 7th 1878... Now look here, my dear Sir - we were greatly disappointed that neither yourself nor our Masonic Brother favoured us with presence - The latter was prostrated by an attack of Bronchitis - Mr Parkes is still with us but returns home tomorrow - If convenient to you on Saturday next and agreeable we shall be gratified to see you over here...

Nov 12th 1878... I cannot stand this weather - it is so cold and the snowy roads are very slippery - I am due in Southport one day this week but except the weather change I hardly know how to get there. My visit will only be for an hour or so - I am promised forth to the consecration of St James's Church, Chorley on the 18th at ll a.m. I hope you are all well even as we are. We hold ye in loving remembrance...

Nov 21st 1878... A little while ago I looked forward with a degree of confidence to the approach of skating weather but this nasty fog I did not anticipate - we hope your cold is better and your household all well. We ourselves rejoice in a fair measure of salubrity - we spent last Monday in Chorley at the consecration of St James's Church - we combine in cordial compliments...

Nov 25th 1878... I cannot account for it but I feel completely wrong end up this morning - I am very cold, and shockingly out of fettle - We have got an Eastern Question now to look after. Miss Low has given us a Turkey* - Have you got any likenesses - My 'explosive' says she is bothered to death about them - Fog gone - weather now beautiful - so look me up and bide a wee - I shall probably be in Preston next week, but don't put the ringers under instructions or organise a Reception until you hear from me ...

Notes

Nov 27th 1878

Afghanistan was the scene of a long struggle as Britain attempted to prevent Russian infiltration. Mr Wilson was evidently much taken with the newspaper references to the terrain out there.

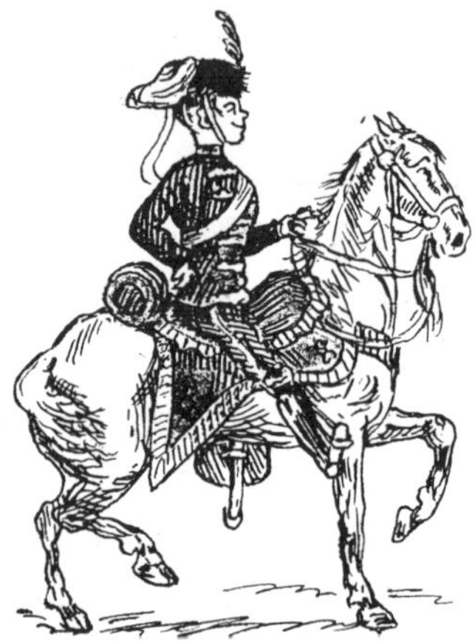

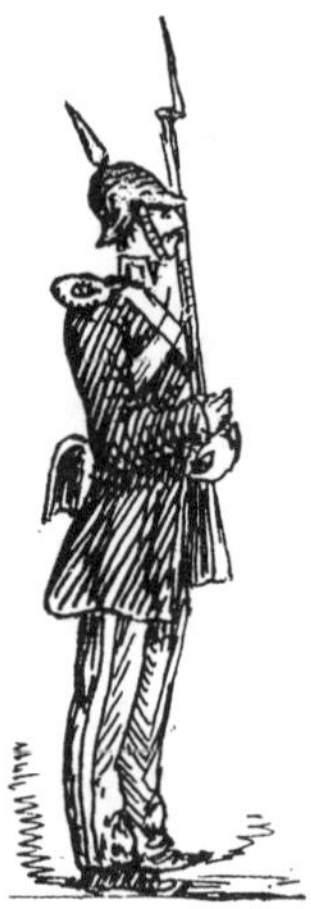

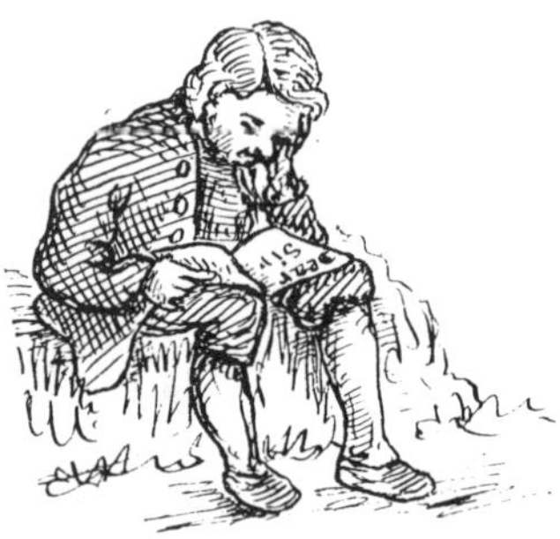

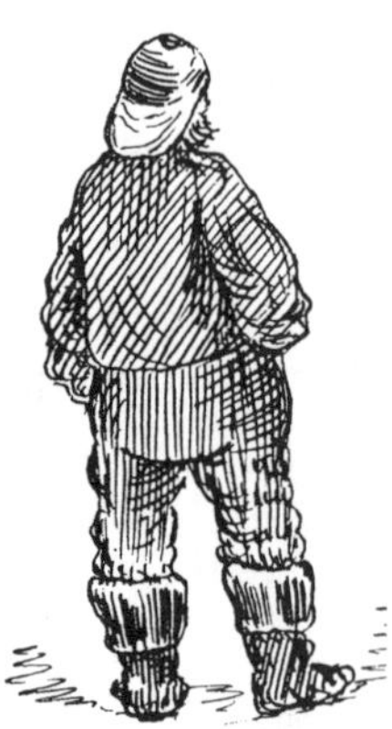

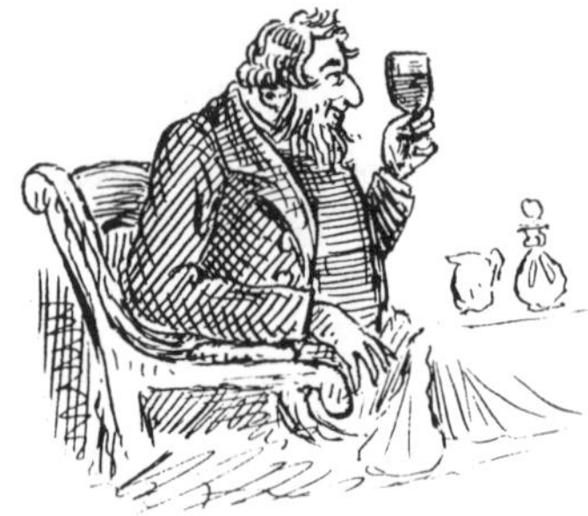

Nov 27th 1878... I read the Afghan* News with avidity in the Journal with which you are kind enough each day to favour me - The Infantry & Artillery have already had their innings and when the operations are extended to the open country the Cavalry will doubtless make their appearance - We have again this morning enjoyed a dense and raw fog but this afternoon the air is much clearer - I, however, venture out of doors very little in consequence of the fog's effect upon my weak chest - I feel much better today than I have done for a week or so. My other moiety is not I regret to say quite well yet - with friendly greetings...

Dec 4th 1878... I am agin off furlough and on guard at home - our retreat from Preston last evening was most keen and trying - The breeze swept over the hoary fields as bleakly as in the days of Moscow. Fast ran the horse and faster yet the driver's nose - we crossed the Howbrook nullah about 10 minutes to five o'clock - and rapidly ascending the southern slope from the Brookhouse Pass we promptly effected a junction with the friendly Tribe occupying the Vicarage Kho - The Kotas was quickly surmounted and our Passage Train brought to a halt by five o'clock - Our force was early astir this morning and we have surveyed all the paths and Passes over the Harrock Kho - The clergyman who represented Brother Marsden was Mr Hatfield. Receive our friendly salutations...

Dec 11th 1878... I am by the fireside - afflicted with a severe and feverish cold - sore throat - raw chest and soreness all over - I am better today than yesterday but still much room for improvement. Hope to be all right by Saturday next - Weather beautiful. Shall be glad to see you - Trust your cold is better and all the household well...

Dec 16th 1878... Permit me, my dear Sir to hope that you successfully surmounted the difficulties of your journey homeward yester even - and that your own dwelling was attained in ample comfort without misadventure of any kind - I have got no additional cold and hope all at 63 are well - very truly thine...

Dec 17th 1878... I rejoice to hear of your safe & pleasant return. I thought to have been at Southport today fishing for health - but snow too deep for travelling. My cold is no worse - I have been out a little this morning the snow notwithstanding. Robert in high fever this morning but quite sensible at times - To all commend us...

Dec 23rd 1878... Here's wishing all of you at 63 Fishergate Preston a very enjoyable Christmas and a most happy New Year and begging to remain as ever I subscribe myself as heretofore...

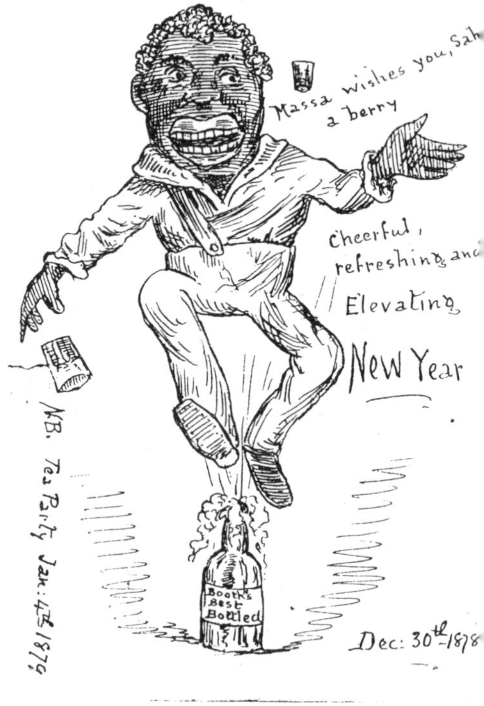

Notes

Jan 21st 1879 Mr Howe

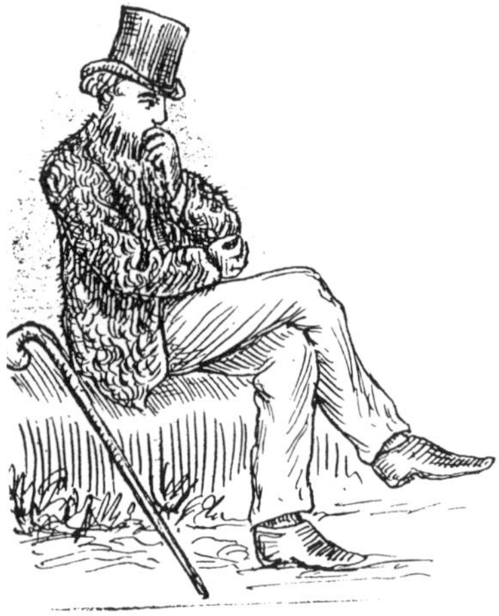

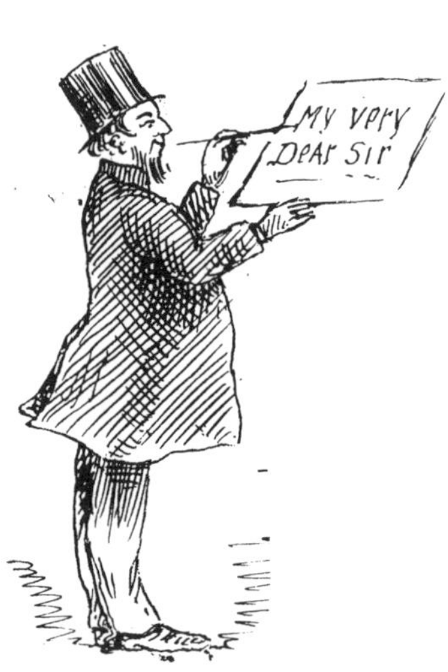

Dec 30th 1878... Massa wishes you, Sah a berry cheerful, refreshing and elevating New Year..N.B Tea Party Jan 4th 1879...

Jan 10th 1879... It is cold, cold, very cold if I mistake not - The winds are Easterly and piercing - our Party nevertheless was a great success - Mr Parkes & Mr Howe were both present. They have waddled forth this morning to Appley Bridge Station en route for their respective homesteads - The great speech of the evening you will doubtless find reported in most of the neighbouring newspapers - Miss L left us on Tuesday last. I go out no more than is needful on account of the effects produced by these bleak winds upon my chest and throat - I have a cold but my Explosive is well and joins me in manifold kind sentiments to you all...

Jan 21st 1879... How have you endured this Christmas season just past? Colds of course you have endured like the rest of us but what I would ask more particularly is - How is your heart? Has the Festive season and the opportunities it affords left it <u>all your own</u> or is the ownership of it 'in fee simple' now claimed by another? I am a prisoner to the house - <u>almost</u> - for though as favoured with health as most people I have to keep vigilant watch and ward this cold weather against my old foe - Bronchitis - Have you had a Glossop paper from the Great Orator*? The ground here is white with hard frozen snow and the roads are so slippery that people have to tread slowly and with great care - My Worthier half is well and joins me in affectionate regards to ye all...

Jan 27th 1879... I have been sitting and thinking deeply about this cold weather and the probable duration of it - people hereabout speak of the probability of it lasting until the middle of April but if so what is to become of us all - It is fortunate that we have little sickness or the look out would be terrible - During service yesterday afternoon a swarm of mice invaded the Sanctuary - driven by the cold from outside and attracted by the warmth within - They promenaded the aisles and careered about the seats - occasioning a degree of apprehension in some feminine minds - causing feet to be transferred from floor to seats & more close arrangement of skirts - In the hope that you are all well we abide as heretofore...

Feb 7th 1879... No newspapers came to hand yesterday. A thaw has come at last and pouring rain has taken the place of snow & frost - My esteemed old neighbour Grundy is no more - about 5 o'clock in the evening of the 27th he expired - I was present at his departure - he died as he had lived - quietly - My Partner is undergoing a bilious assault today but combines with me in the hope that you are all well...

Notes

Feast of St Valentine

The Zulu War arose from disputes between Zulus and Boers over land on the Transvaal border. Cetewayo, the Zulu chieftain had expected British support, but instead received an ultimatum to disband his army. A surprise attack by Zulu warriors led to the massacre of 1600 men.

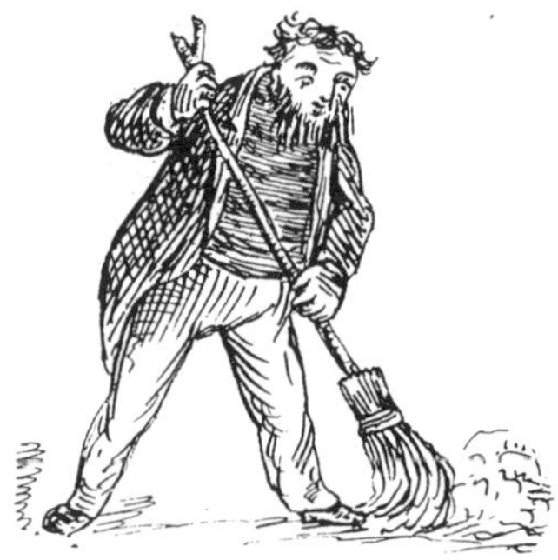

March 4th 1879

Prince Louis Napoleon, only son of Napoleon III, was serving with the British army under the command of Lord Chelmsford. Owing to a blunder he was sent out on a patrol in the course of which he was killed by the Zulus.

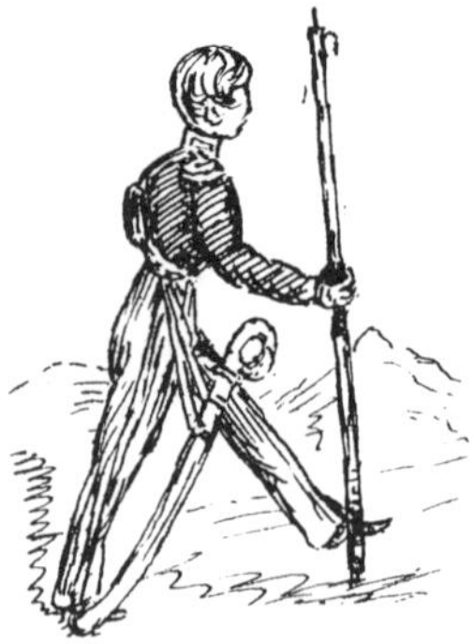

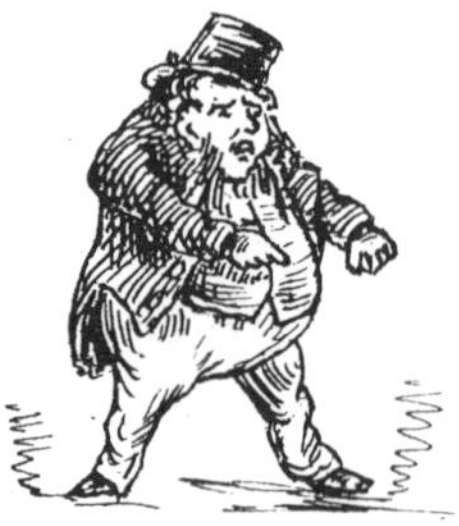

Feast of St Valentine 1879...The anxieties occasioned by the recent severe weather are much allayed by the reappearance of brighter skies & milder temperature but our minds are now harassed and distraught by the unhappy occurrence on the Ingela river* on the 22nd ult. It has produced a profound sensation all the world over but nowhere more than here where we may be said to be patriotism itself - Have you been largely favoured with tender missives this Feast? It is quite a treat to be able to get out of doors again - Accept an assurance of our affection and believe me ...

Feb 21st 1879...I have again given all diligence to keep my own doorstep clean - winter has returned upon us - the snow lays thickly, so that the services of a besom have been rendered needful in order to make this dwelling accessible. However is the weather just now in and about Preston? The air is so thick with haze that we cannot see further than a few fields breadth - Preston is quite beyond our range of vision - I really should rejoice if the snow would depart not that it proves, so far, very detrimental to myself but as many are thrown out of work by it. We are all well and join in the hope that this will find you & yours in like happy case..P.S. Your letter just to hand...

March 4th 1879...Louis* I see has gone off to Africa on the Staff - does it mean anything like here depicted i.e. a walking tour through that interesting portion of the dark continent - not of course a Promenade to Berlin - I cannot go - I am prostrate with Bronchitis and Influenza - and the draughts occasioned by these high winds make my cough dreadful at times - I was obliged to get up at 2.30 this morning - and not a bed has borne the weight of my prostrate corpus since - I will send you another card when I feel a little better - our friendliness to all...

March 7th 1879...Now look here, My dear Sir - I may be rotund and an ungainsome - unwinsome - un-wee-thing yet I must assert, and experience proves, that I am not constitutionally strong. It has been as much as I could achieve this time to keep body and soul together. I have managed to preserve the union and feel much better today - The crisis, I think, is past - I am on the road to recovery but the sharer of my vicissitudes is prostrate - her little world extends no further than the linear circum measurement of her bed - Further advice in a day or two...

Notes

March 12th 1879 — Dr Hilton was the local Medical Officer of Health.

Pollie, a vicarage maid, is not to be confused with the horse acquired later, and called by this name!

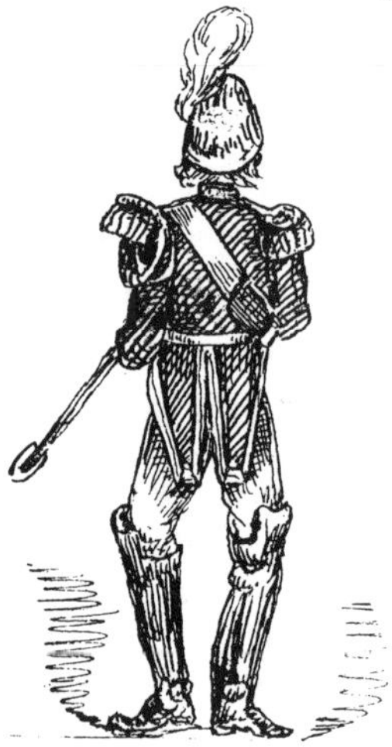

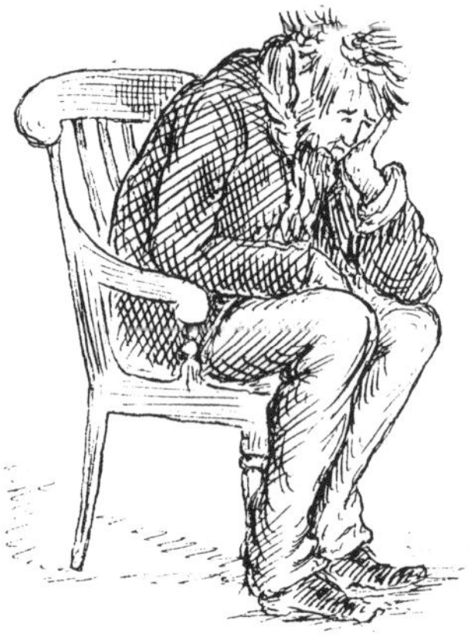

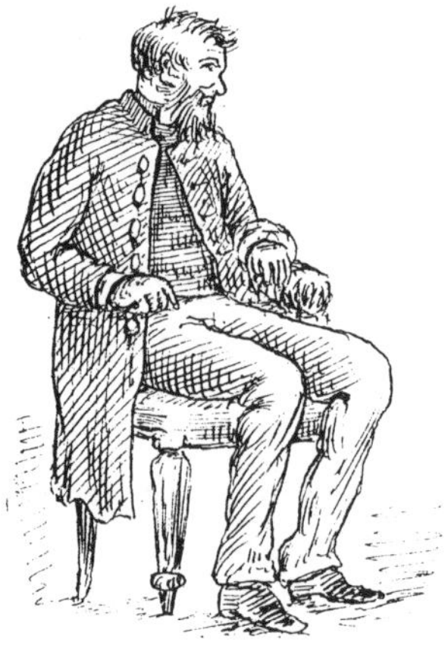

March 12th 1879... In reply to your welcome letter which, by the way, did not reach me until eight o'clock last night, I beg to say that we are still carrying on the campaign actively against the attack made upon us by Bronchitis - my comrade has been a prisoner of war for just one week but is to be let out of bed on parole for a few minutes today through the intervention of our esteemed Regimental Surgeon 'Hilton'* - under whose able and kindly care she has been since Saturday - as for myself - though wounded in the engagement - I am regaining slowly my strength under the skilful and patient treatment of the before named estimable medical gentleman - albeit I, like my comrade - am in the condition of a prisoner of war - my bedroom being utilized as a 'guard room' - for the present. We have Pollie* established here as sick nurse - she makes an indefatigable one - thoughtful, willing and prompt - affectionately remembering ye all in our improvement we combine in craving your kind reminiscences...

March 22nd 1879... I have been 'quite intirely' this way - antiquated and feeble - but with the return of spring time and more genial weather I am putting forth fresh growth and strength - My cough is much improved as also that of mine 'Helpmeet' - In fact I may say our coughs are almost gone - but yet so great tenderness of chest and throat remains as to make us still prisoners of the house - If we can get well enough by Monday or Tuesday next & the weather permit we may probably venture out for an airing...

March 25th 1879... I am just, as we may say, improving - decidedly better than when I wrote to you last - but still I feel languid and inert and possibly may continue to feel so as long as these piercing and most bitter Easterly winds are prevalent. My more tender moiety is likewise advancing in strength but the aforesaid orient gale irketh her full sore - We contemplate a migration to a slightly milder clime so soon as ever the wind's keen edge is blunted - I think our friend Parkes's little Eden will be the 'ultime thule' the goal in fact of our pilgrim steps - He has bidden the pair of us to come thither for nursement - shortly therefore we shall we trust thitherwind be tending swathed as to our heads with wrappers - shawls &c till a beholder would find it difficult to determine perhaps whether we were human beings or a pair of guinea pigs - meanwhile in the hope ye are all well...

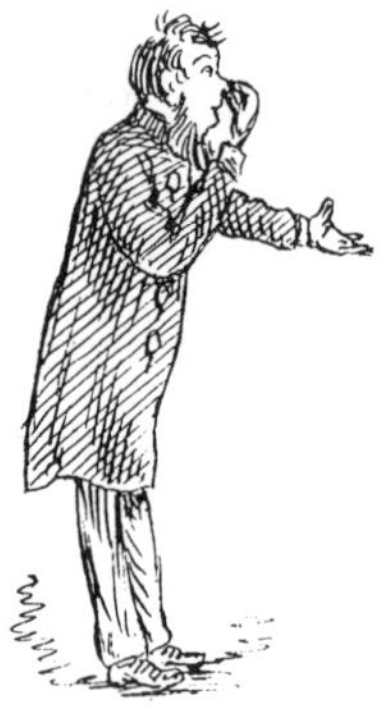

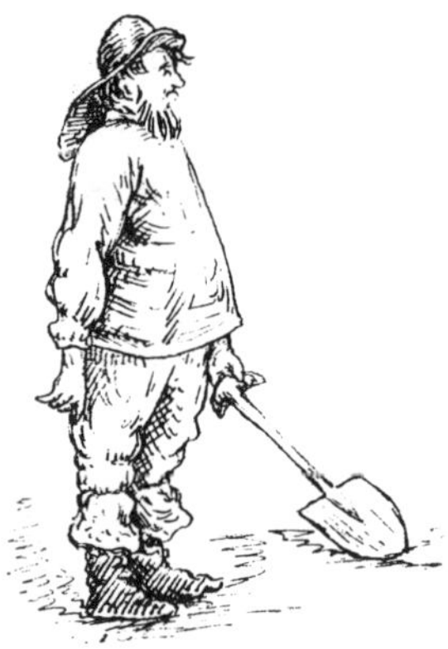

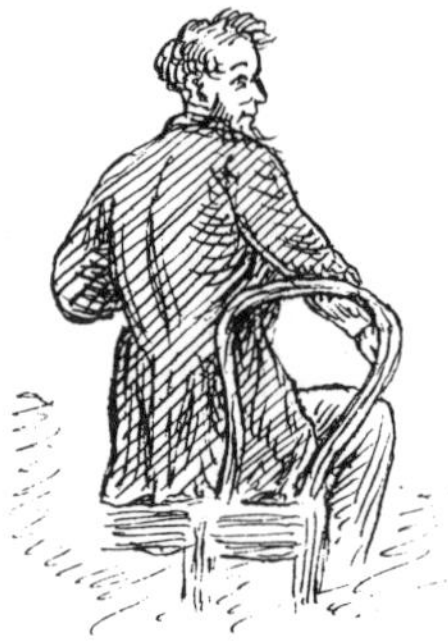

March 29th 1879... You should just have felt my nose the last few days and I am sure you would have felt sympathy for me - my poor facial prominence has been swollen and sore as to be scarcely touchable with any degree of comfort - You will perceive that we are now in Staffordshire whence we purpose returning to Lancashire about the middle of the week- Thanks for the papers which together with all letters have been forwarded to me per favour of Rev. W.G. Lule B.A. As we were coming here - while en route for the station - old Nicholas's trap (the new & elegant one) broke down with us - The axle tree smashed asunder in consequence of a jolt on a very bad piece of road (it was a patent axle) and I am induced to exclaim with Hudibras or some other man - Ah me, what dangers do environ, The man that meddles with cold iron ..Billington - Stafford.

April 2nd 1879... As I begin to feel once more fitted for doing a fair day's work for a fair day's wage I have arranged for our return to Lancashire and hope to be again beneath the roof tree of my own little upland retreat tomorrow (Thursday) evening. We on Monday visited Boscabel House & the Royal Oak famed as the scene and means of King Charles' escape from the hostile pursuers of British Royalty - the Monarch of the Forest interposing his sturdy arrow to shield from death the Sovereign of the Realm - of course I could not leave the spot without creeping into the King's Hole where I had well nigh perforce remained - my Form being so bulky as to render egress difficult and the possibility of it even doubtful without the paring of a half inch from my circumference all over - Tomorrow morning at 8 or thereabout we start from Stafford - with our Benison we remain...

Wigan April 3rd 1879...10.47 A.M.. Ah! how are you all, my Lancastrian friends just now - you see I am once more among you or at least in your county - I have about ten minutes ago arrived in this town of Wigan - am now off to Southport purposing to return hither this afternoon and pass on by hired fly to my journey's end. With profound esteem...

Notes

<u>April 10th 1879</u> Miss Lowe and Mrs Marsden.

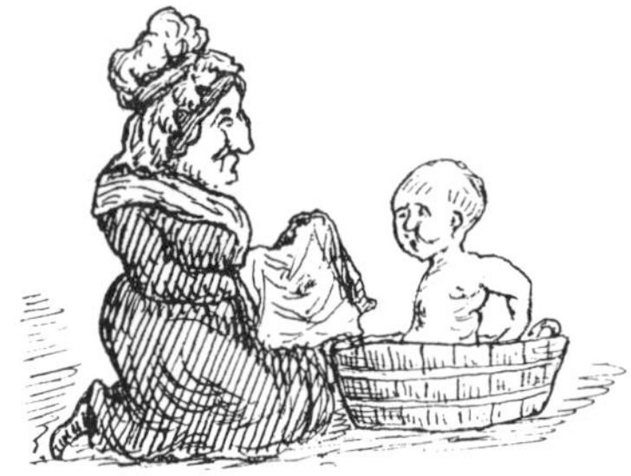

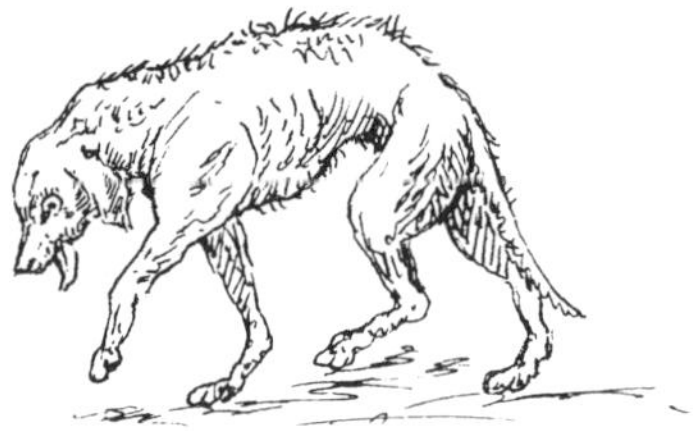

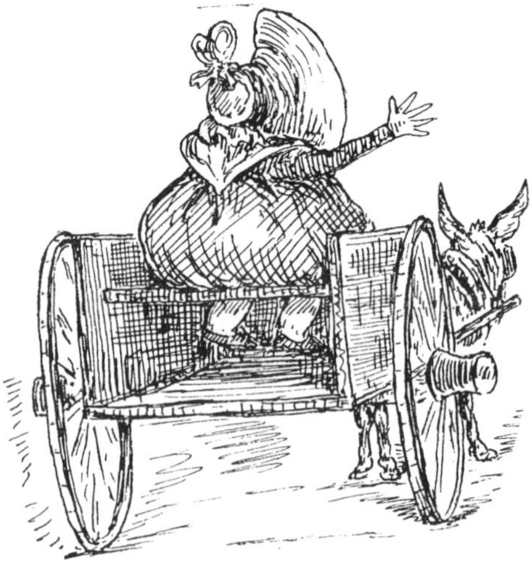

April 10th 1879... Just a line to announce to you the happy fact that we continue to progress towards completely reinstated salubrity and now feel refreshed and blithesome as a child which under experienced maternal supervision hath been 'Well tubbed' - great care is still requisite because the temperature is so changeable and return of cough and soreness of throat is often threatened. Mrs Parkes is with us - not the wife but the mother of our Mutual friend - On Monday and Tuesday last we had all headaches hereabout - Gardening has begun and great part of our seeds are in the ground - On Monday or Tuesday next we expect Miss L. and Mrs L.M* from Southport over here - the rabid ruthless East wind is recklessly running its rural race round our rustic rath in capital form this morning - There are rumours of a rabid dog having been about the neighbourhood - the poor creature has been shot - to you and yours a poor and obscure hedge priest's benison in which his partner joins ...

Wigan April 18th 1879... I am once again in this great coalopolis of Lancashire - I have come hither unaccompanied having no business in the Town but induced to visit it solely for exercise and change - I left all well in my own domicile - Mrs Parkes is still with us but our Southport friends have witholden hitherto their projected visit - I think I told you in a previous communication that we had a rabid dog on the march through our neighbourhood committing great havock. We are only just now settling down to a quietude again. With profoundest homage to all in your home I beg to remain ...

April 26th 1879... ah, my dear Sir, I have just come over (or been conveyed over) to thank you for your note and the continued favour of Daily News per Standard. We shall be glad to see you any time that you can make it convenient to pay us a visit - our 'gee up' is not in good Form or we would meet you at the station - will you look us up next Saturday if the weather be fine? - come either on that or any other day that suits you best - Some people think they see signs now of the winter drawing to a close - all sigh for springtime & we cordially unite in all friendly compliments to you all ...

May 8th 1879... now look here, my dear Mr Worsley - I have received duly your letter and found with much regret that you could not visit us last week end. I detected with unfeigned concern too that you made no mention as to when we might look for the happiness of your visit - Now this is to certify you that you had better hurry up and come as <u>a fortnight from tomorrow</u> a mutual friend from a neighbouring sea side resort is purposing to be here - you will probably prefer coming before her visit takes place - You need not send word when you will be here but come when the weather and your convenience will permit - We hope you are all well - air still rather cold but those experienced in weatherology are of the opinion that it will be more than a month or two now till we have spring upon us ...

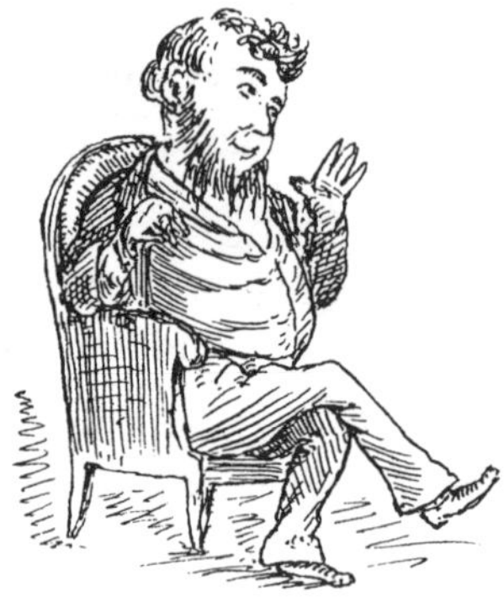

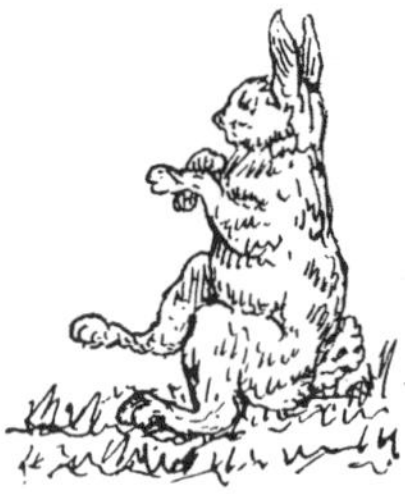

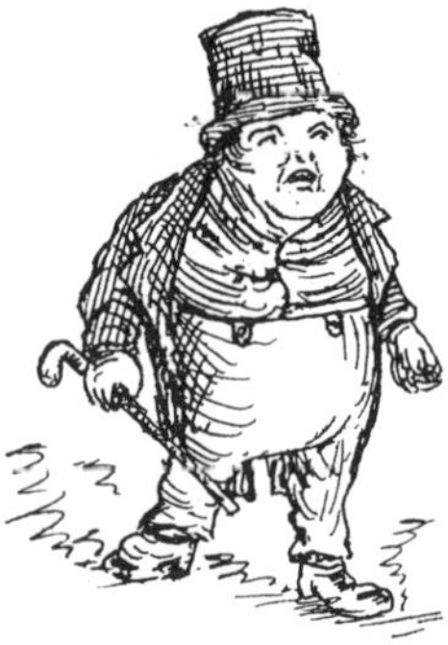

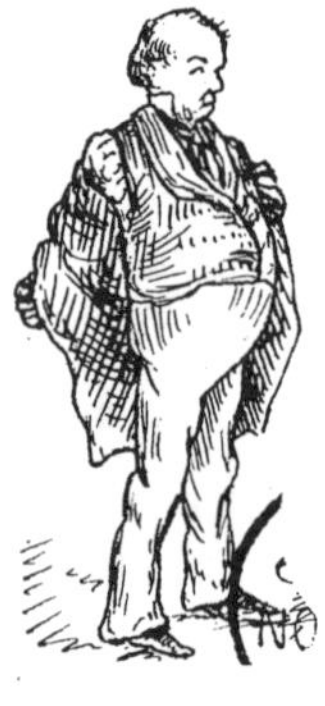

May 14th 1879...We expected you last weekend, wherefore came ye not? May we anticipate your presence here on next Saturday? Mrs P leaves us on Friday so that we shall be alone. The gentle rain this morning has made the fields look fresh and green and beautiful - we have got a colony of rabbits established in our neighbourhood. They sport in the garden and leisurely take their enjoyment each evening & morning immediately in front of my windows - we are all well and wishing you all heartily the like blessing...

May 23rd 1879...I am just this minute in great anticipation - I am to be honoured with a visit from a Lady - a friend whom you know from Southport - I am sitting awaiting her arrival which is now momentarily expected - country lovely - suppose we shall not have the pleasure of seeing you now till the guest chamber is once more at liberty...

May 27th 1879...Here, I say, my dear fellow, I'll tell you what it is - my pleasure's spoilt - How can I go to Scotland or anywhere else, do you think in such an outfit as this? I consider my figure naturally is very passable but just look at what a sight those confounded tailors and outfitters have made of me - the coat doesn't fit me; and as for the waistcoat it causes me quite a bad pain in the chest which I think is either a sore throat or a stomach ache - I really think you will have to excuse me going to Scotland with you this fitting unless I travel in my every day things for don't you know I don't want the scotch folk to take me for a Guy Fawkes. I am yours in grief...

June 9th 1879...well, thank goodness we're back in England again, and look here, my dear Sir, if ever you catch me any more going to Scotland in the capacity of a Tailor's locomotive 'Lay Figure' to set off his bad work to advantage just tell me of it - will you? And what's more I'm blest if I'll ever put on again this horrible abortive Antediluvian specimen of a Gentleman's best coat - I'll just pack it up carefully and send it off to the British Museum where it will be a lasting memorial of myself, and a proof to after ages of the misery inflicted upon humanity by the Tailors in our own day - I am glad to know that you are safely back again and hope the very natural weariness will rapidly wear away - Our Annual Summer Tea Party will be on June 23rd but Miss L has made arrangements which will preclude her being present with us on that occasion - cannot you drive over and join us on that day and bring with you Miss Worsley and your family - It would add muchly to our pleasure to be favoured with the presence of ye all...

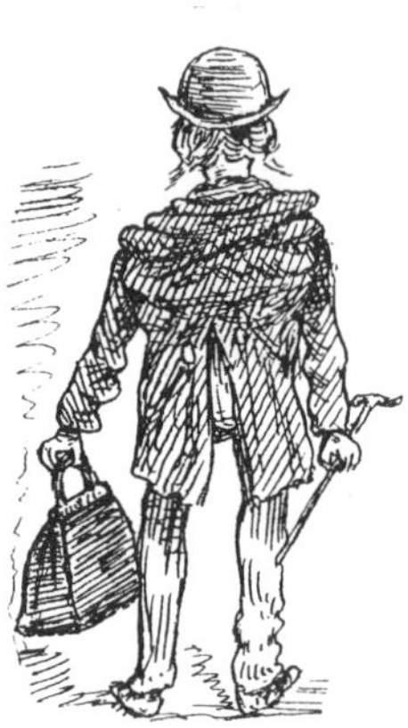

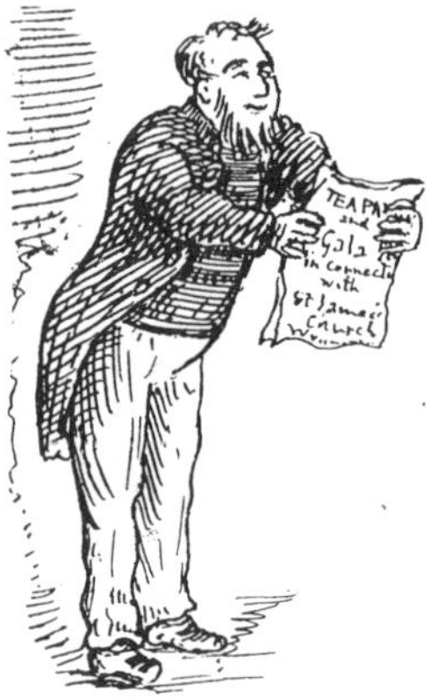
TEA PA
and
Gala
in connecti
with
St James's
Church

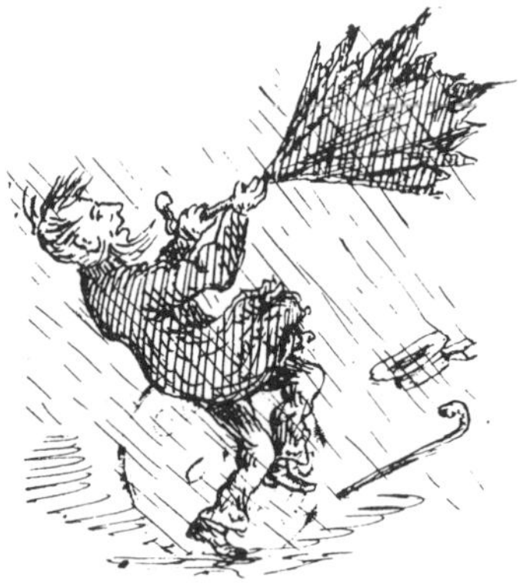

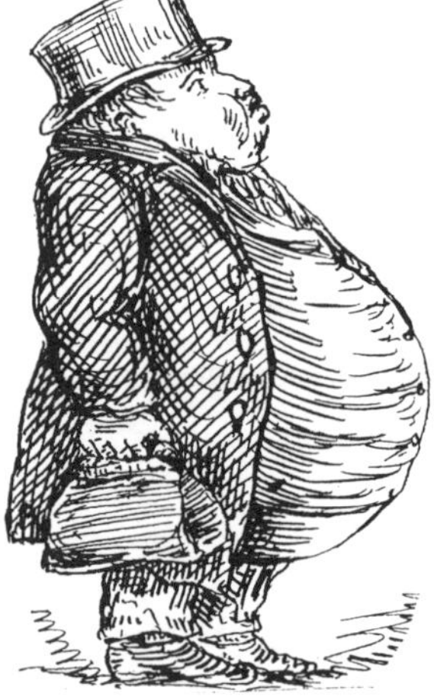

June 11th 1879...I forgot to ask you whether before the coat was taken off and laid aside you observed particularly how that odious garment looked from behind - of course a little awkwardness in the fit is not at all times a serious defect yet in some instances may, besides detracting from the elegance of a manly figure, considerably incommode the wearer if in 'Tour'ing he has luggage to carry, and requires the free use of his arms when climbing the steep sides of mountains or moving with a swinging gait across rough moorlands. Trusting you will kindly pardon my perhaps unnatural curiosity on this matter...

June 28th 1879...I have been so busy that I could not write to you earlier this week - You see it has been our Tea Party and with house full - field full and mind full I have positively until now been completely unable to attend to anything in the way of correspondence - We were disappointed at your absence and that together with the prevalent pluviality detracted considerably from the plenitude of our happiness - The lady whom I informed you would be absent subsequently decided to be present, but still several of the friends of former years were unavoidably absent - The Prebendary was in Normandy at the time - on the whole the day was a pleasant one and a pecuniary success...

July 4th 1879...Did you ever know such a summer? Did you ever experience such weather before in the month of July? The winds are just now as potent as in March or September - caterpillars abound in consequence of the great destruction of Birds during last winter and the fewness of them this summer - I fed the birds during the winter & protected them so that my garden has become a favourite resort and I have not seen in it one caterpillar - while round about me, among my neighbours, whose superior wisdom led them to lay poison during the hard weather in order to exterminate the 'bird pest' and secure good fruit crops this season - the outcry is great for their berry trees are almost leafless - We should have been in Southport today but for the rain & wind..P.S. Thanks for the invitation...

July 9th 1879...You would I feel sure have been pleased to learn that our 'Mutual friend' from Glossop was present at the Party this year - I give here as good a presentiment of his commanding figure and general aspect as a Post Card will admit - You see him here as he appeared when (black travelling bag in hand) he set forth again for Glossop. Upon his open brow time writes no wrinkle but there is a slight increase of expansiveness in the region of the waistcoat - That is the only visible change...

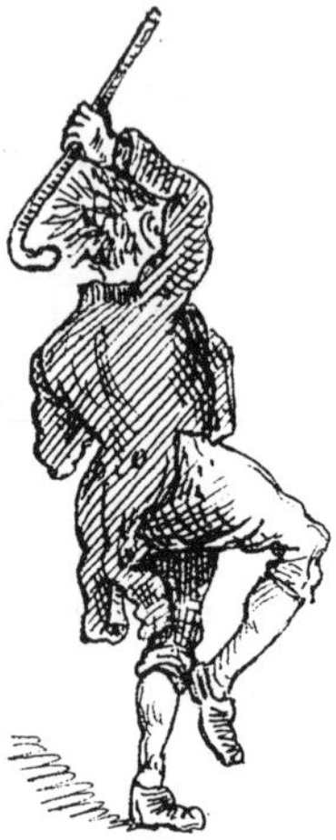

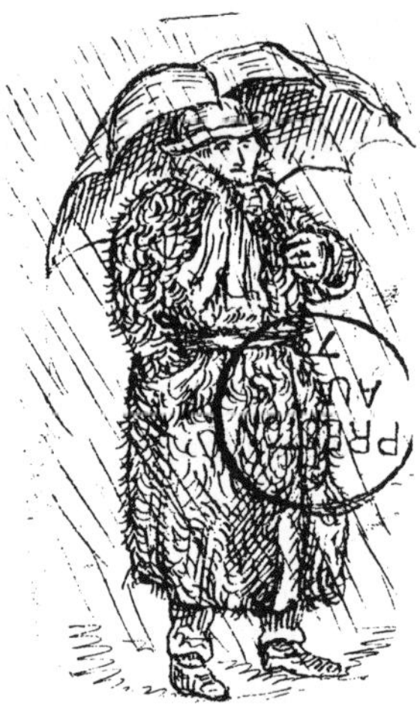

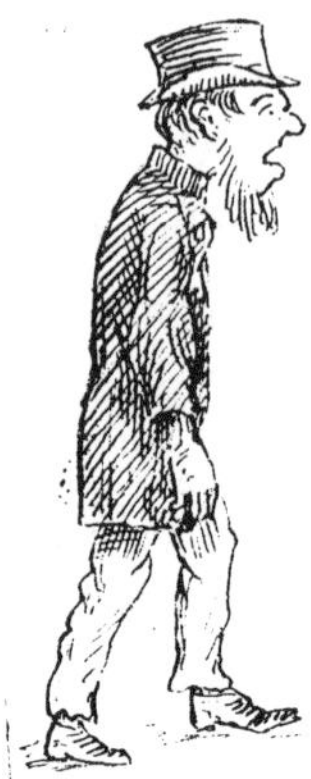

July 14th 1879...What can you expect? I am very grateful for your kindness but truly in such weather as we are at present enjoying it is quite out of the question for a semi-invalid & hot-house plant like myself to make arrangements which will take me far from home on any given day and stated hour - since February last I believe I have only been to Southport once - my worthy other self on all occasions having most affectionately acted as my Deputy in travelling - I saw recently in a Newspaper that a number of lambs had been frozen to death at Edale in Derbyshire on the night of July 1st in this remarkable year of Grace one thousand eight hundred and seventynine - when returning from Southport on Wednesday I was caught in a thunder shower and a severe cold has since been my portion so that I feel sure, if I were to avail myself of your most cordial invitation and essay to get to Preston in this drenching weather, there would by the time of my arrival at 63, Fishergate be little left of me to dine - with every friendly sentiment...

July 25th 1879...Arrah now, me honey!! Sure it isn't meself that would be after putting up wid that toe at all, at all - Why don't yez ask somebody to lind ye a stout shtick and give the crater a good bating wid the curled ind iv it - wouldn't it make it plain to ye in what part the pain was? I remember you had a bad toe once but don't recollect the nature of the soreness - If from tight boots or too much walking a few doses of aconitum & then arnica might relieve - If gout be the evil & the part red a few doses of aconitum followed by sulphur would give you relief - If the soreness is the result of a mechanical injury & the skin has been scratched or rubbed off procure one ounce of vaseline ointment and apply freely it will soon rid you of the plague - I shall be glad to hear from you again in a few days - I received the portrait of 'what is it?' duly - If I had time now I would copy it upon another card & send you the pen & ink reproduction...

Aug 5th 1879...If I had not the good fortune to possess a substantial top coat or two, a spacious umbrella and an ample muffler I could scarcely weather this peculiarly bleak and humid summer of 1879 - Yesterday morning early the pluviality was second only to a water spout and today we are enjoying a persistently pouring plenitude of pattering plashing rain while the thick atmosphere and low temperature remind one mightily of November - as to health these meteorological conditions notwithstanding we twain are tolerable and combine in heartily hoping that Miss W & yourself and juveniles are blessed equally with ourselves. We have had about us of late much diphtheria but have fortunately been unaffected by it - craving to be retained in kindly remembrance...

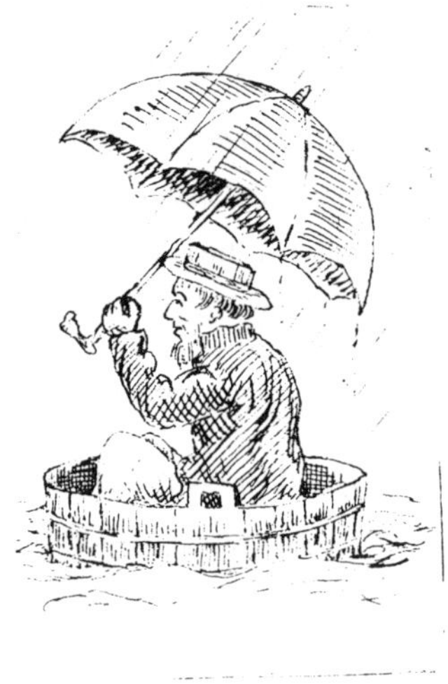

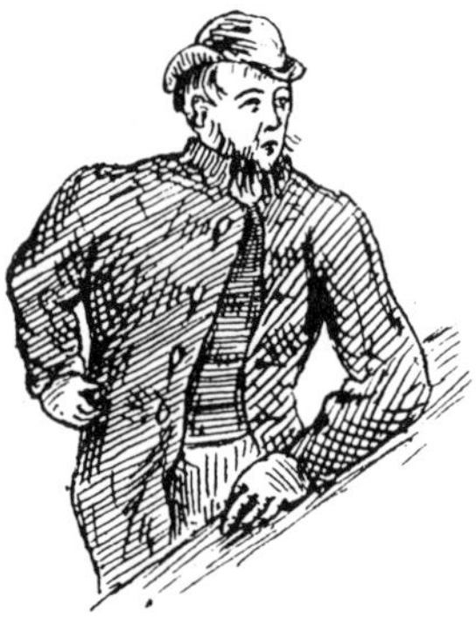

Notes

Aug 13th 1879 — This holiday house of the Worsley family, possibly at Harrock, is referred to later as 'the smoke room'.

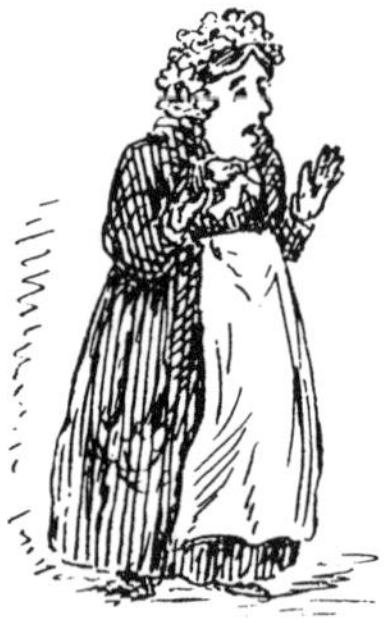

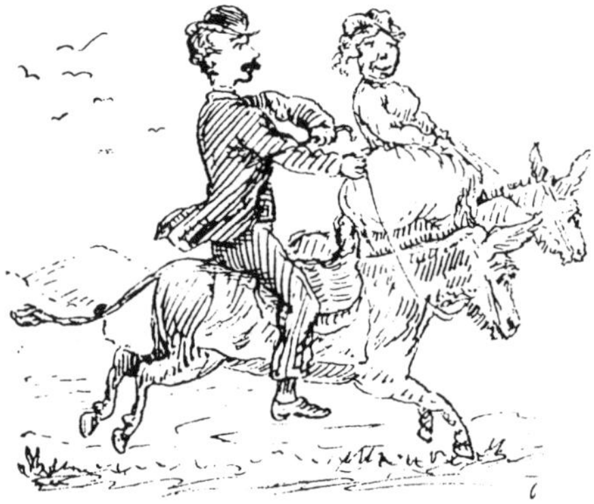

Aug 9th 1879... I am greatly grieved to learn that the card which I provided with an umbrella for its protection suffered severely from the rain - I hope this one will have better fortune. The weather is at present a little more favourable and I trust the improvement may continue - You will be pleased to learn that during the recent showers and floods I have got on swimmingly...

Aug 13th 1879... Just a hurried line to say that the Standard is to hand and my eye has alighted upon the notice of decease which you had marked - cause of death is not specified but I suppose it would be old age and natural decay - My priceless Partner bids me to ask if you are ever going to let us look at you again in Heskin & when? Sunday, Monday & yesterday were fine. Today thunder is passing over us but we trust the disturbance is only temporary - Will you look us up this weekend - I have once or twice recently visited your summer house* on the Hill - Hoping for the pleasure of your presence with us shortly and with our combined sentiments of tenderness to ye all...

Aug 21st 1879... what? catching a train again - He surely lives on the railway for he seems to be always there - I'll see if I cannot get him a Post as Engine Driver when I go over - exclaimed my excellent Partner as with uplifted hands she hearkened to the reading of your last favour; and partly probably with a view to afford herself this opportunity and partly more probably with other motives she announces her intention to visit Preston (if the weather &c permit) next week and bring me with her - on what day she does not know - so you must not expect us - we shall just look in and take pot luck - gloomy damp weather still prevailing and withal unhealthful - we have been bidden to an excursion around Conistone and also to a nutting enterprise near Windermere in September - with sincere regards to all...

Aug 27th 1879... I regret to think that there is not much chance of this sort of thing being done this week for the weather is even worse and worse - I am sure you can neither go to Blackpool, Lytham nor Southport - Today (unto the present time) I don't think it has for one minute ceased raining. I am a close prisoner in my dwelling, labouring under the twofold disadvantage of dark, depressing weather and an execrable pen. I hope next week to look you up - meanwhile accept a simple Hedge Priest's blessing and believe me full truly...

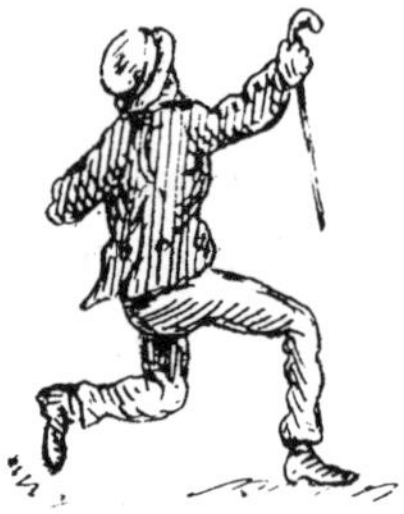

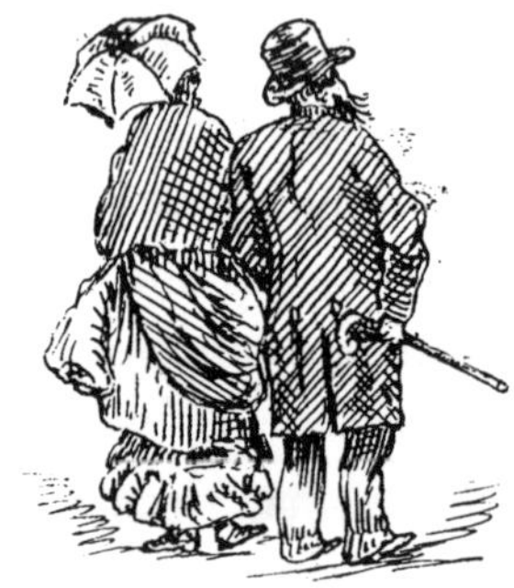

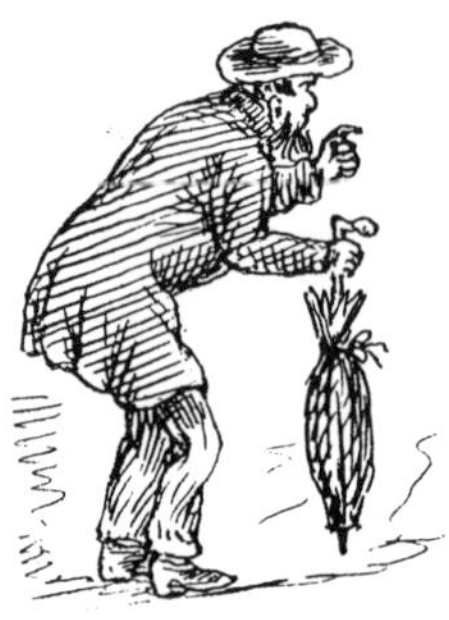

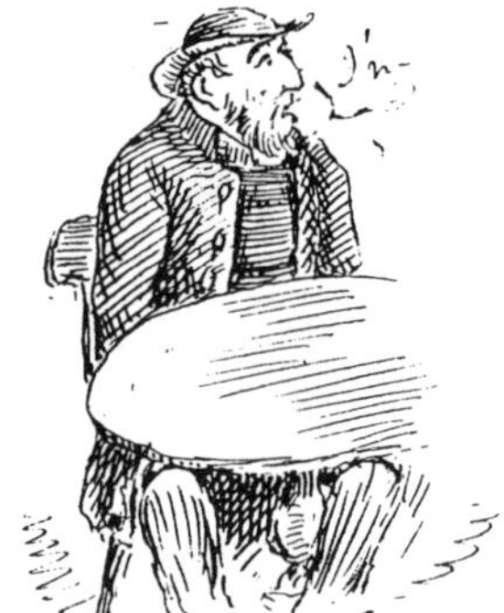

Aug 30th 1879... I am fully bent on 'running over to see you' some day shortly but am now not quite sure whether it will be during the coming week as I and my other moiety are planning a run northward even nigh unto Scotia's borders and we will en route drop in at 63, Fishergate - This Northward Excursion will scarcely eventuate before next Monday but one - we may then look you up. Thanks for your long letter - we are neither of us superabundant in robustness and feel the necessity of a change. Permit us both to wish your youngest scion many happy - most happy - returns of his Natal day - and with fervid compliments to Miss Worsley & yourself..P.S. Truly a season to be remembered...

Wednesday Sep 3rd 1879... My beloved Duplicate and my highly estimated self intend to invade 63 Fishergate Preston either before or after Breakfast on Monday next Sep. 8th - we shall tarry but a little space being, in fact, on a migration Northward - to the city of Durham, thence passing on to Newcastle and back home via Carlisle - i.e. if weather favours us. Today is fine and we are full of hope - albeit the beloved Duplicate, aforesaid, has had to seek medical aid this morning - we trust rectification may be effected before Monday morning...

Sep 5th 1879... Look here, Sir - I have just received your note and while thanking you very earnestly for it I am desirous to make it very clear that our purpose is for Monday the 8th Inst - We hope to be in Preston about 8 o'clock a.m and crave the indulgence of 'Breaking our Fast' beneath your thrice hospitable roof tree - somewhere after 10 o'clock (say half past) the Flying column under command of the undersigned will operate in a Northern direction towards the Grampians - advancing against Barnard Castle - Durham Castle and Newcastle. We shall have about two hours for rest and gossip which may suffice to render us both easy until we meet again (or effect a junction) in proximity to Harrocks leafy height at the weekend. With distinguished devotion...

Carlisle Sep 8th 1879... I'm waiting for my dinner, my dear Sir, why do they call 'em Refreshment Rooms when they don't have refreshment ready for the hungry viator - The hour is 21 minutes past 2 and the rain has for the first time in our journey begun to fall - we are trying to persuade ourselves that it will only be a shower - alas!! appearances are against it. Hungry but fondly we remain...

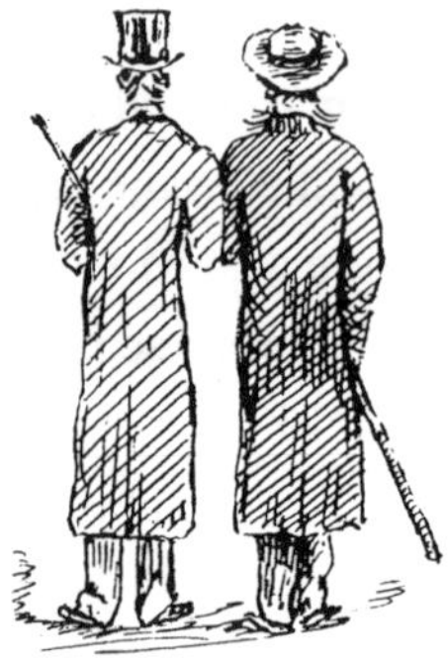

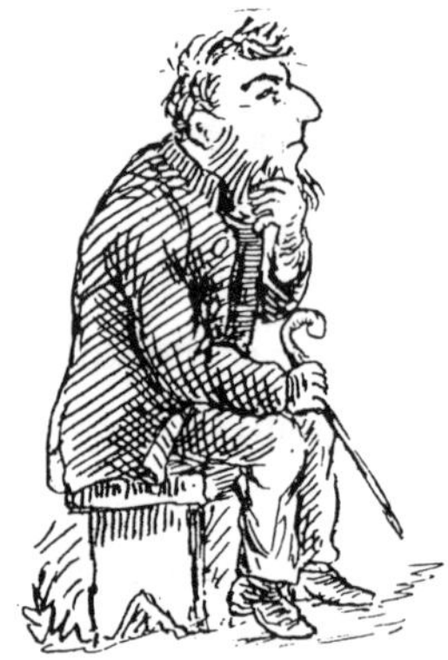

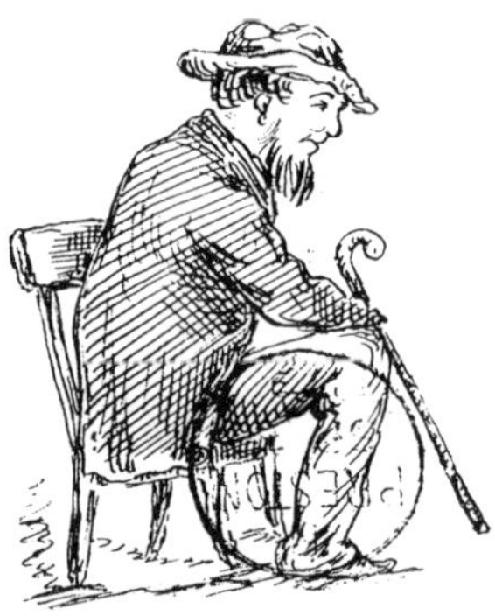

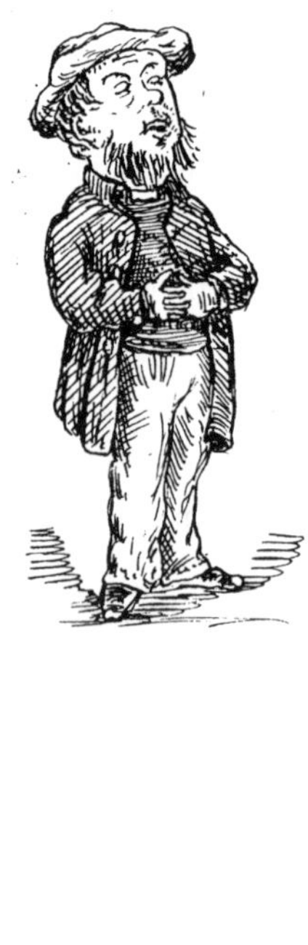

Sep 9th 1879... I have at length arrived at Daum - which is the villainous pronunciation of the word Durham and patronized by no body but the natives who ought to know better. I wish your professional duties and inclination pemitted you to join me that we might walk together and view the stately towers and gems of scenery which adorn this ancient spot. The scenery would have been enhanced by two figures like the above - My Partner joins me in devotion...

Wigan Sep 24th 1879... When I come to think of it I cannot see that you can do better than carry out your proposal for Saturday afternoon next (the 27th Inst) - By the early train I shall look out for your arrival; and much I trust the weather will be favourable as today - My energetic charioteer when I was riding with him on Monday evening last unfortunately ran over a man - there was very little light and the man seemed to shoot across from the roadside and seize the horse's head - I think he was under alcoholic influence. I leaped from the vehicle to look at him & beyond a poke in the ribs from the carriage shaft he seemed to be little the worse...

Southport Sep 30th 1879... ah, who can count the ploughing waves That break upon the sand-strewn shore - so, my dear Sir I muse while by the waters sitting. From this you will perceive that in accordance with our purpose we are here - Having arrived yesterday at 2o'clock p.m. I know not yet how long we may abide but will write you further - Standard is to hand this morning & your letter also - For both I thank you - & rejoicing to learn of your safe advent to 63 Fishergate we combine in all cordiality my self remaining as ever ...

Oct 1st 1879... I am still here and happy. The autumn winds are sighing - The leaves all around are dying - But to be happy we are trying and bent on care defying. I send you a hurried line to resuscitate old acquaintanceship - remind you that ye are not absent from my thoughts, and inform you that we shall be at home again on Friday next - we venture to hope that your waistcoat hangs out more loosely than when you left our dwelling last - We rejoice to report ourselves in good health - and beseeching a place in your affectionate memory still I remain...

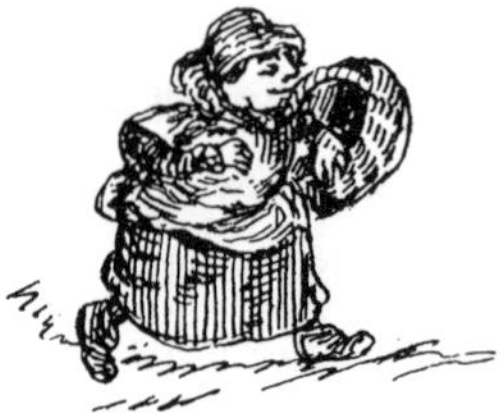

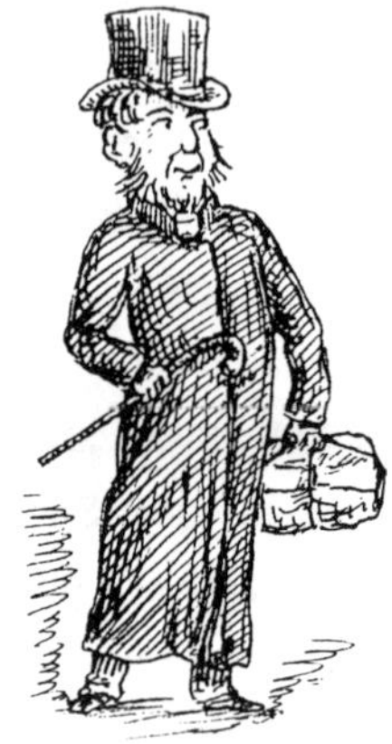

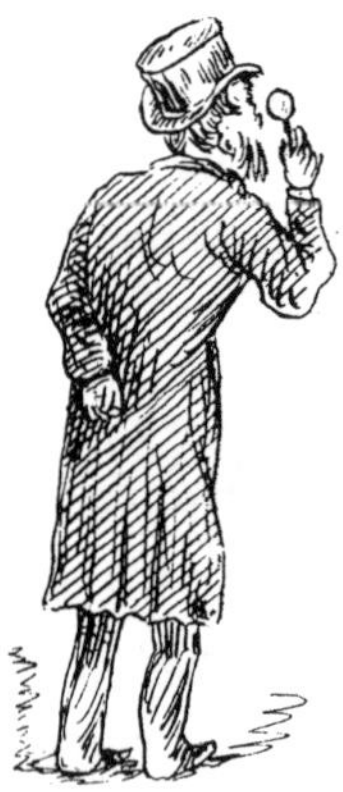

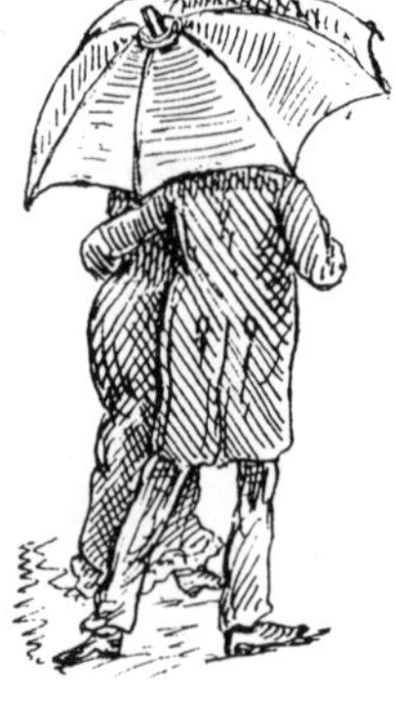

Oct 8th 1879... I ain't got no time for nothink scase (sic) my venerated friend Mr Parkes is with me, my engrossments are manifold - and my mind is harassed with preparations for St Luke's Bazaar - I have had visitors every day and found it necessary to run about for Provender. How strangely hazy is the atmosphere and damp withal - I can scarcely see fifty yards from the house. Is it October or November at which we have arrived - November here & perhaps October in Preston. The seasons are so incomprehensible nowadays - Mr P. came through direct from Blackburn to Croston. With our united cordial esteem...

Oct 10th 1879... I wish I could just pack up a few necessaries in a paper parcel and join you for a few days in the great 'Metrolopis' of the Empire - Mr Parkes has left me this morning en route for Blackburn Accrington and Ramsbottom from which last named hamlet he proceeds tomorrow morning direct to Stafford. The weather has brightened slightly so that on Monday we shall, all being well, make tracks for Southport - where if we cannot sell anything else we will try to sell the unwary in the Fine Art Museum. Mr Parkes a little while ago in cutting a low branch from a laurel bush cut himself severely & nearly bled to death. If he does it again with fatal results this will be his epitaph:- From laurel bushes lopp'd he many a limb But now alas! grim Death hath lopp'd off him...

Oct 14th 1879... You really ought to bring your magnifier and come over to inspect the varied and interesting specimens in the 'Art Museum' of St Luke's Bazaar - There may be many good 'shows' in England at the present time but of this feel assured that if prizes were offered for excellence this one would at least be found to possess a <u>second</u>. A Ward, showman...

Oct 15th 1879... I record herein my conviction, which is the result of close & attentive observation, that Bazaars - whatever else they may do - minister large (may I say <u>ample</u>) facilities for flirtation - not content with the interior of the building, young people in whom tenderness is a prominent quality, erect their umbrellas when <u>only the dews of night are falling</u> and <u>so</u> in some cases proceed homeward - I - nay - '<u>We</u>' shall be home again on Friday - Being very busy I shall probably be unable to send you further advices till I reach my own domicile & the quietude of my usual haunts. With all friendly consideration, remember me...

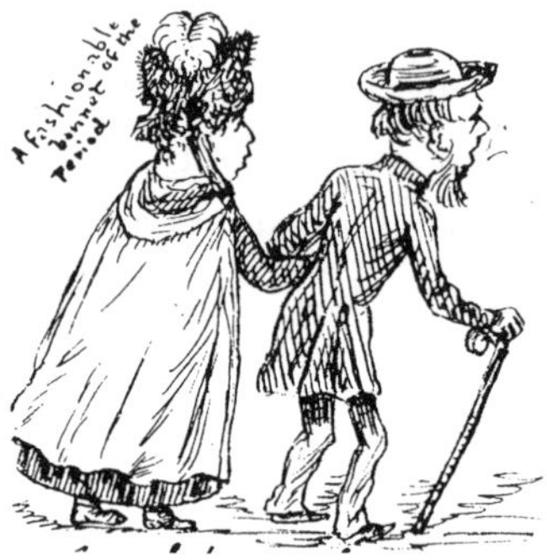

Notes

Oct 24th 1879 Fane= temple.

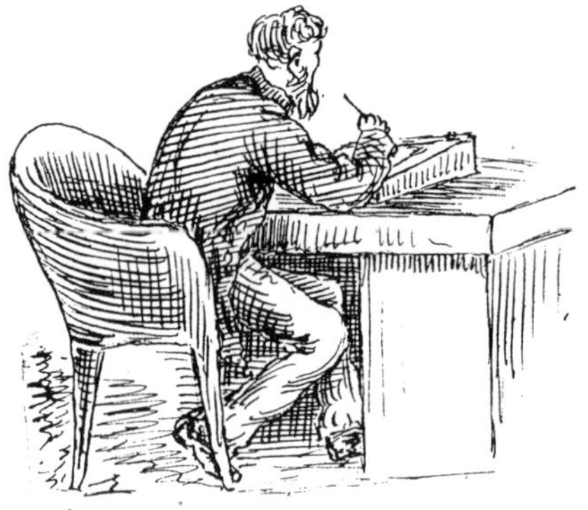

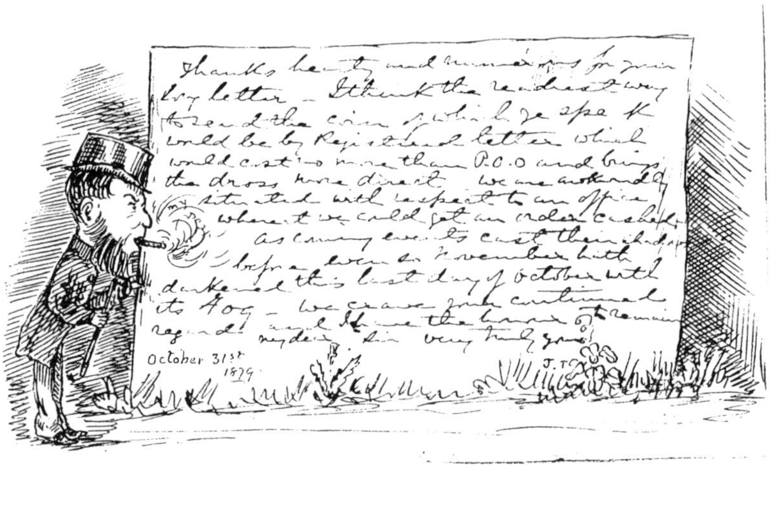

Oct 21st 1879... Mr Worsley! Mr Worsley! my dear Sir, Heigh!! We're back again don't you see - weary, and, as to Bazaars, thoroughly satisfied - I believe the enterprise was a great success but falling ill on the Friday and leaving early on the Saturday I saw very little of it after Thursday on the night of which last named I left it hurriedly to look at a fire which had broken out in the Town but which was soon extinguished. I caught cold at the fire and hence my illness on the Friday - we return home to find storms and tempests here abundant - We both feel better again - on Thursday next a Southport friend purposes to join us and abide here for a little space - We combine in cordiality...

Oct 24th 1879... Let me see - I usually begin 'My dear Sir' - I will begin so now - My dear Sir - our Southport friend has arrived & on Saturday a clerical brother from Wigan is due to abide with us till Sunday evening & one from Southport I am told has declared his intention of nestling with us for a week. The decoration work has commenced in the Modest 'fane'* of this upland Parish so that it is now needful that friends who have collecting cards be kind enough to send in the coin which their eloquent advocacy has been instrumental in evoking from the generous and well-disposed - aid is largely needed and craved with earnestness. We are well & with all good wishes I remain...

Oct 31st 1879... Thanks hearty and numerous for your long letter - I think the readiest way to send the coin of which ye speak would be by Registered letter which would cost no more than P.O.O and bring the dross more direct. We are awkwardly situated with respect to an office whereat we could get an order cashed. As coming events cast their shadows before even so November hath darkened this last day of October with its fog - we crave your continued regard and have the honour to remain...

Nov 6th 1879... Hooray! Hooray! my Friend behold In one hand's your note - in the other one gold - Pardon I beseech you my tardiness in acknowledgement - I have been from home much, and largely occupied - We are having a Christmas tree in aid of Restoration Fund which I find will have to be largely augmented in order to achieve all that is required. The roof or ceiling of which I spake e'erwhiles is proving much more costly than I anticipated - Postman here - must close abruptly & with many thanks...

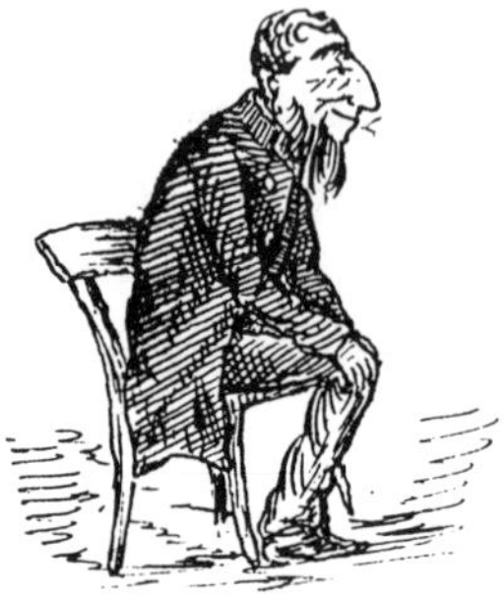

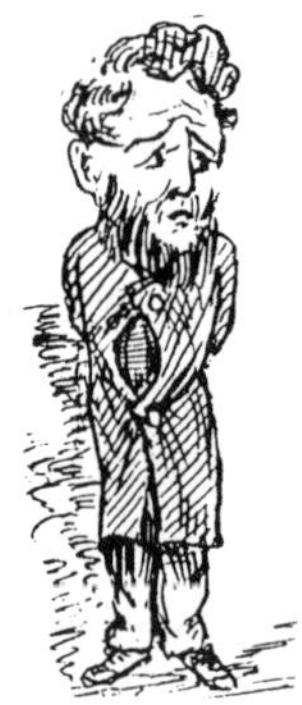

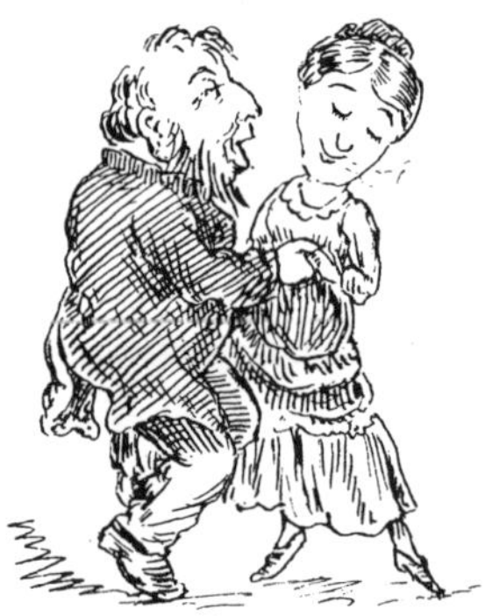

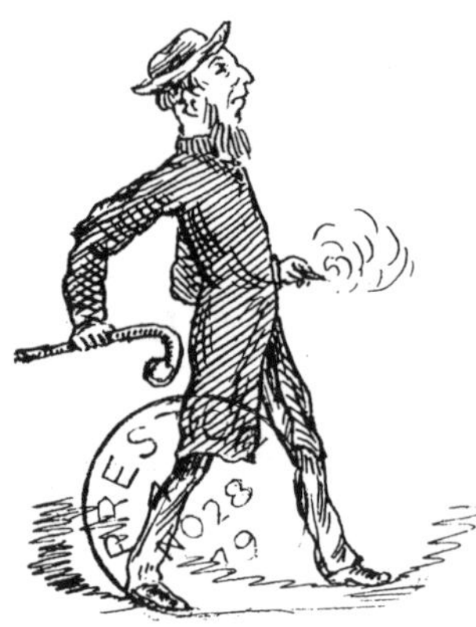

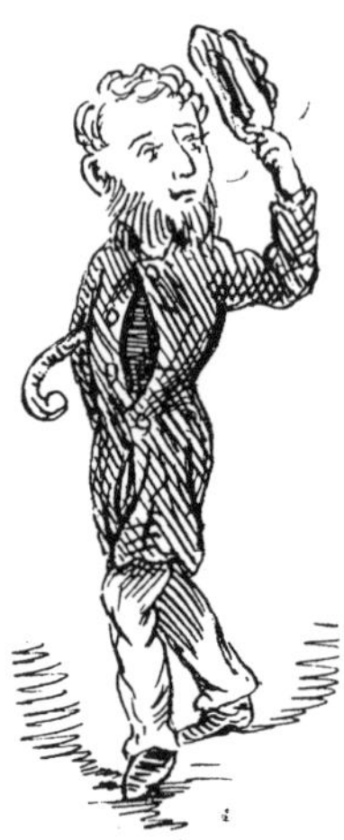

Nov 13th 1879... It is of course no use grieving about it now but still it troubles me a little to think that I was in Wigan on the day and about the hour at which you passed through it - yet being ignorant of your presence, I went not to the station to greet you - My unfortunate ignorance and consequent abstention weighs upon my mind greatly - What tempests!!!! On Tuesday night the storms of wind and hurricanes of rain coupled with whirlwinds of Hail and attended by rattling of sashes - banging of doors - moaning & howling in chimneys as well as other divers discord kept us awake through no small portion of the time of darkness. We hope you are all well and have found travel beneficial...

Nov 18th 1879... November has come at last - we have a dark morning with dense suffocating Fog - oh for Electric light or otherwise for the bright sunshine once again. Our house is full of coughs, colds, catarrh &c and yet great and diligent are the preparations being made for a Christmas Tree, Bran Pie Concert & Stall for sale of work on Saturday December 20th 1879. This is with a view to raise further coin for our Repair Fund - at Rufford also there will be an ingathering on Advent Sunday - Mr Howe has written to me - requesting me to do my best endeavour to find him a situation as 'son in law' in a wealthy family - From this I conclude he is still single - with combined muchness to all ...

Nov 24th 1879... Your promise last night set us dancing with delight and our hearts were merry and free we caper'd and flung - we laughed and we sung - and passed the time merrilee. We trust you got safely home and escaped cold - cough, asthma and what not - a lovely morning - sun bright - fields white - I think I may say it's quite a Christmas sight - we commend ourselves to you and yours and I remain ...

Nov 27th 1879... What do you think of this 27th day of November 1879 - ground white with hoar frost - sky clear and a bright sun just peeping over the horizon in the south, south east - Just the sort of morning for pedestrianating - were I a votary of 'the weed' I should delight to go forth for a rapid spin accompanied by my stick & cigar. We rejoice to hear of your pleasant and safe return - I wonder if we shall have the star shower tonight - Remember me to all and sundry ...

Dec 3rd 1879... Good morrow, How do you do? I hope well - such weather as this really makes walking pleasant - I am myself taking ample advantage of it. In a few minutes I am starting forth to Appley en route to Wigan. Hoping to see you on Saturday I remain ...

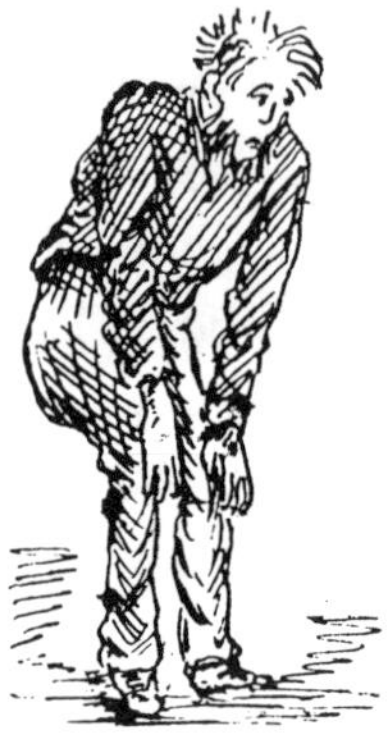

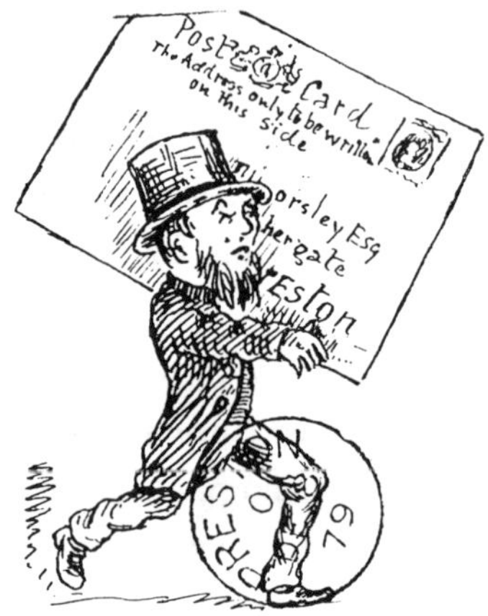

Card
on this side
79

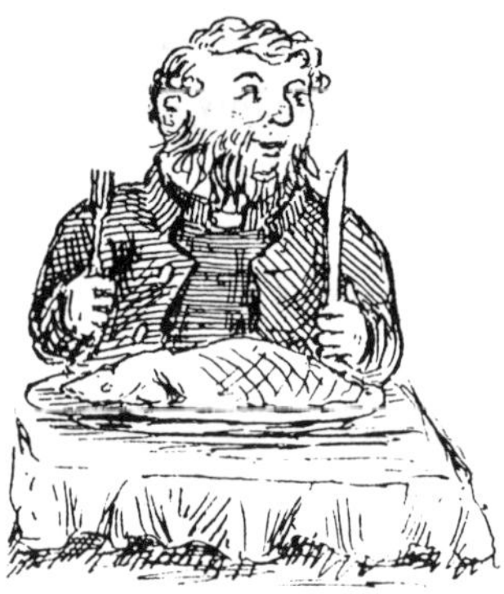

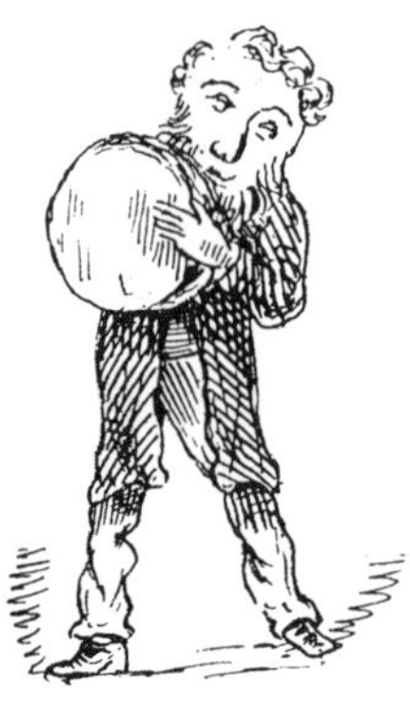

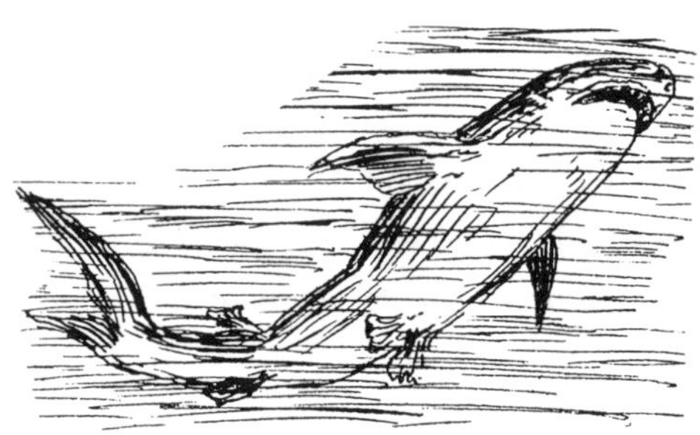

Dec 5th 1879... 'come now sure yer Hanner's only got to give a bit iv a slorr this weather an' yer here in a minnit'. The snow is falling freely and we believe the cold has been greater the last day or two than any time during last winter. What never occurred then has taken place now - viz. one of our taps is frozen - The pipe connected with runs down the inside of an interior wall and the tap is in the middle of the house & yet it is frozen - The weather though cold has been beautifully fine - we hope (and shall be pleased) to see you on Saturday - i.e. tomorrow ...

Dec 8th 1879... Though numb with cold and my fingers stiff withal I hasten at your desire with a Post Card - I suspect you are at this moment passing by the Bar or in close proximity thereto - The sun is beaming more brightly than he has done for many a day - so that your walk I feel sure will be a pleasant one - With ardent friendly reminiscence ...

Dec 9th 1879... I regret to inform you that I yesterday loitered below 'par' nor acquired my wonted vigour until after I had brandished a knife and fork over the delicious 'sole' you brought us - and transferred a fair portion of the delectable fish from the platter to my internal organism - Then and not till then, warmth returned and I regained my wonted vivacity and force - as a happy conclusion to my card I thankfully report that I am myself again - The soreness & stiffness have fled from my muscles so that I can pedestrianate with ease as erst.. (grateful for sole many thanks)...

Dec 9th 1879... We were greatly grieved when at Tea yester even to discover that in the distraction consequent on your departure I had omitted to fetch out the cheese you were good enough to approve - My dear Partner though at the time so poorly as to render the necessity of Medical aid probable indulged in an address which - to express oneself as mildly as possible - had about it a flavour of censure - I am bidden to assure you that we shall yet have an opportunity of attacking that cheese ...

Dec 16th 1879... Mister - You'd better have your Meter froze than be druv out of the house by it in this way - You'd better have candles and frost than gaslight and explosion - I should prefer a frozen Meter to a bursten pipe pouring through ceiling and passage a flood of water up which came swimming plasterers, white limers, painters and charwomen like so many sharks to worry one - Go along with you Mister and don't grumble no more with this rebuke and counsel - so no more at present from your very truly..P.S. Our taps are all right again ...

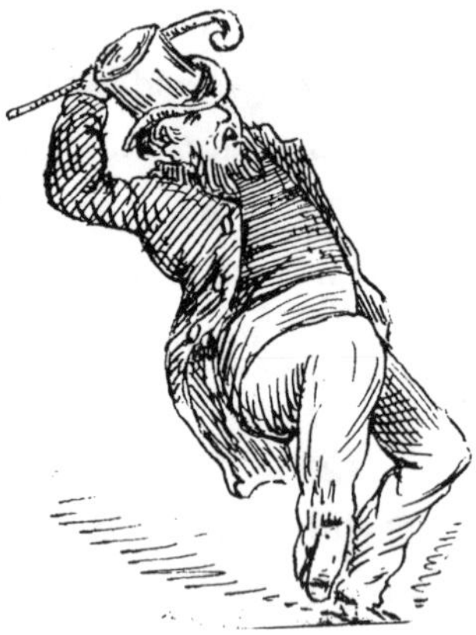

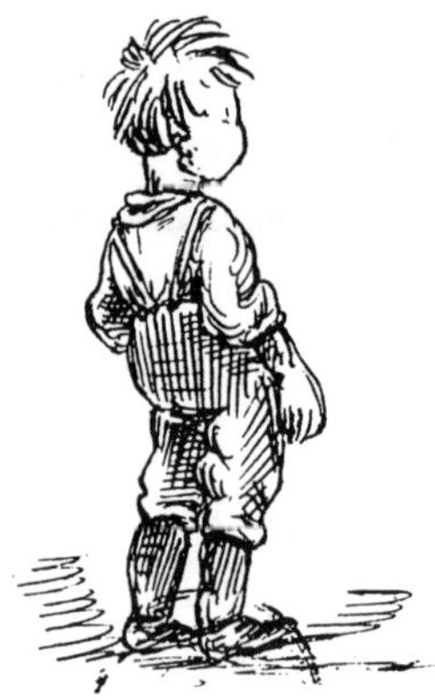

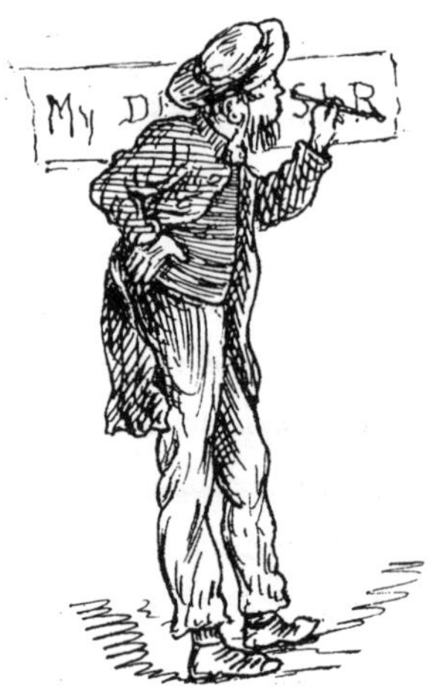
My D
SIR

Dec 16th 1879... I rejoice with you that the thaw has come for the roads during last week were not fit to walk up - It was difficult for even an experienced and agile pedestrian like me to keep his feet - I have been compelled to assume all manner of contorted attitudes to preserve my balance - On Sunday coming down 'Smithy Brow' I got such a slip that I verily believe if I had not learned dancing in my youth or boyhood I should have fallen full upon my back and in that supine posture have attained the bottom of the brow - by a nimble bound of this kind I regained my feet and averted catastrophe - Sorry to hear you will not be with us on Saturday (20th) ...

Dec 22nd 1879... This is December 22nd - on Saturday last Dec 20th we had according to arrangement our Christmas tree - Day fine, all jolly - good success - Have not yet heard the total of gains but am told that when all expenses have been paid we shall have at least a clear gain of £15 - I am done up - am full of cold - can scarcely walk and have an attack of Bronchitis - I am almost speechlessly hoarse and am doing my best endeavour to prevent it becoming serious. Mr Parkes is with us ...

Dec 27th 1879... The writer's down on his back with an attack of Bronchitis - never got out of doors on Christmas Day - even writing is a labour to him - He can't taste - can't smell and can scarcely guide a pen - pen goes skating like - its point flying from under it - All good wishes .

Dec 31st 1879... I'm vastly out of fettle still - I don't feel half the man I was - the high & boisterous winds accompanied by storms of sleet are very trying - I encounter draughts everywhere, and renewed chest irritation is the result. I continue to move about the house but have to wear my hat or otherwise protect my cranium with shawls, antimacassars &c - and I neither look nor have a sprightly feel - I combine with my Hobididdles in wishing you each and all a very Happy New Year - Yours feebly but most truly ...

Jan 2nd 1880... Just a line to inform you that I feel much better this morning - My Breathing occasionally short and panting still but my cough is nearly gone and I am moving about indoors once more without needing to be enveloped in shawls &c - The sun has broken out at last but the high wind continues and this last night bid fair to blow us over - Hoping you are all well - I reiterate our combined good wishes for the New Year on which we have now entered & I remain...

Notes

Jan 5th 1880 — On December 28th 1879 excessively high winds tore down part of the Tay Bridge and a train crossing the bridge at the time fell into the river with the loss of many lives.

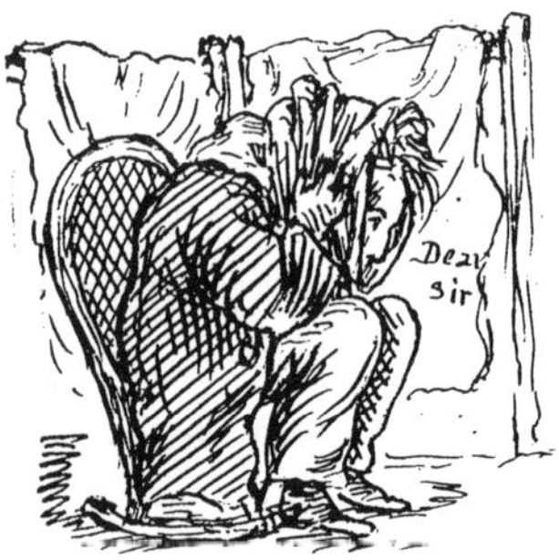

Jan 17th 1880 — Miss Lowe

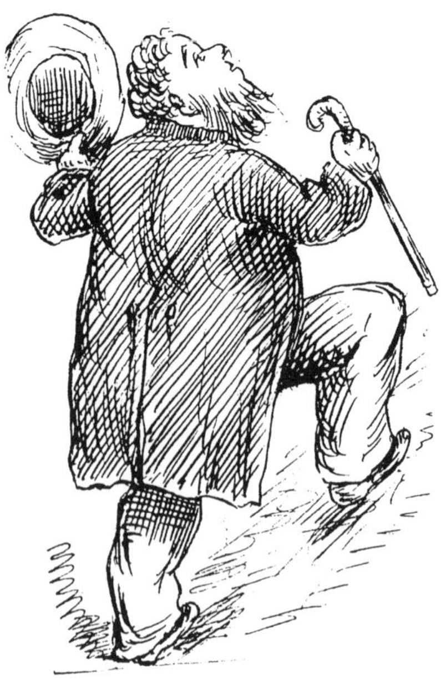

Jan 5th 1880... I should have been well some days ago, but for the terrible currents of air which the recent high winds have sent whisking about my dwelling - The odious plague has notwithstanding all precautions on my part threatened my life and made it needful for me to put up a screen near the fireside and with my shawl over my head crouch the livelong day behind my extemporised and anything but effective shelter - You have a heart, I know, that can feel for another's woe and if you had been here during the past ten day that heart would have felt a great deal. The Tay Bridge Calamity* has been truly shocking - I have still strength left to entertain good wishes - Accept a liberal measure of them for yourself and family...

Jan 15th 1880... Although my chest was no doubt primarily affected I suspect from my feelings that my liver too has been considerably involved - You generally make a point of refusing to have anything unless I join you at it - now why don't you join <u>me</u>-? I don't feel any pleasure in the sole enjoyment of this illness: perhaps partnership in the matter might render it more agreeable - I am much better than I was but am far from feeling yet thoroughly reestablished - My possessions are on the increase - besides a Bronchitis and Liver derangement I have now two pigs - As I write this the sounds of revelry are ringing through my dwelling as we have today a children's party and they are just now in the height of their enjoyment - To the friendly regard of all we commend ourselves ...

Saturday night Jan 17th 1880... My experience during the present week has been that of very uphill work - I have been nursing or superintending the nursing of a good friend* in Southport whom you know - My Vigil has lasted through night and day - my patient has been very nearly dead and is still, though better, in a most critical condition - watching and waiting I have felt little inclination, or rather, <u>fitness</u>, for letterwriting. I have just got home. It is late and I have to return to my duties tomorrow night. Accept my good wishes and believe me ...

Jan 21st 1880... Now who's made that little snip in the edge of the card - it is really a pity that it could not be left in its pristine condition of entirety - I am you will perceive in Southport once again - Our patient is for the present improving but still incoherent and critical - what may be the ultimate issue we cannot yet determine - I am kept very closely occupied with my duties of Nurse - I may not be able to write again this week but will send you a line from home - Hope you are all well ...

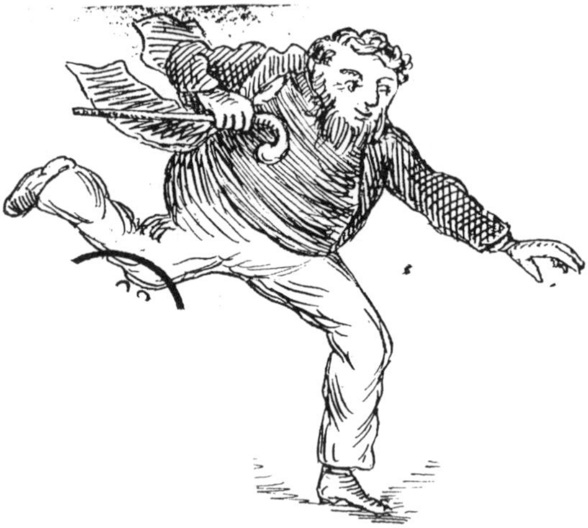

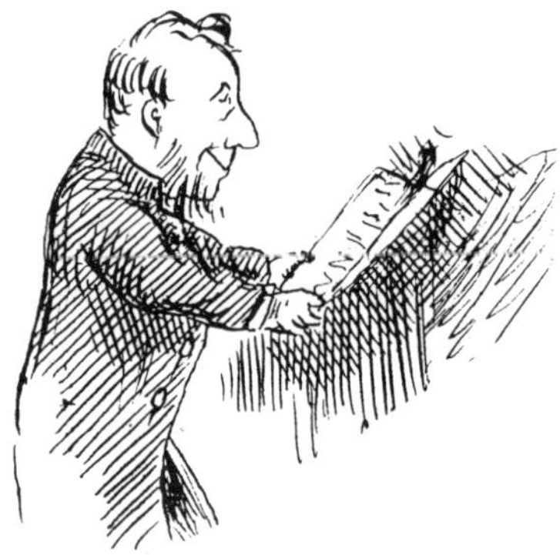

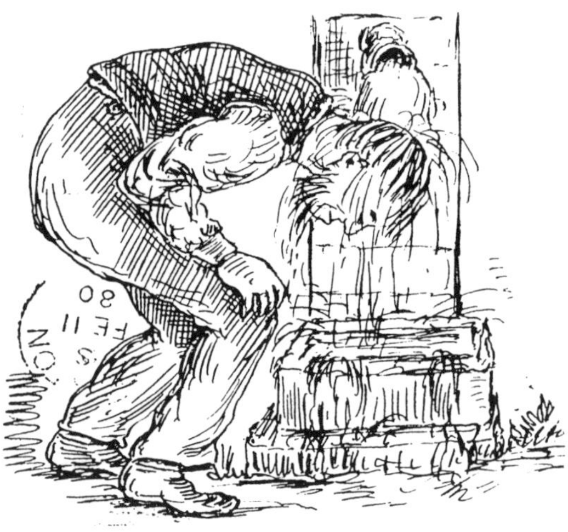

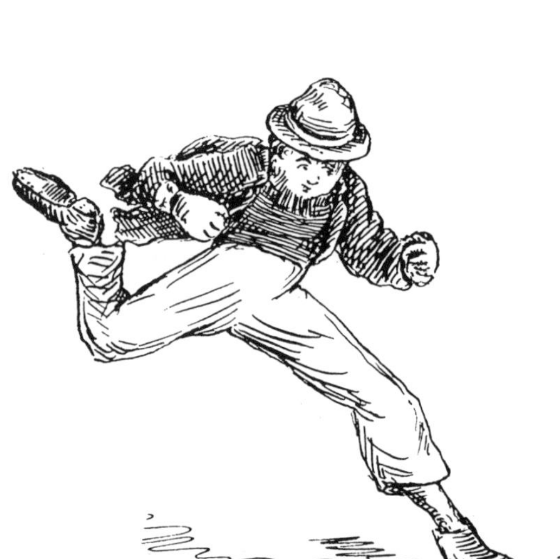

Feb 2nd 1880... I am hurrying back to Southport either today or tomorrow - Please send papers to me thither - our Patient we left on Saturday sitting up in an easy chair eating, but the Friday week before she had been given up - The issue of her illness is still doubtful - Her condition most critical. Hope you are all well - my 'Elevator' is quite knocked up with nursing & loss of rest...

Feb 4th 1880... Thanks, many thanks for the newspaper just now in hand - Your kindness is very large and great too is my obligation. I arrived here yester even and rejoice to report our patient much better - on our arrival she managed (of course with considerable assistance) to walk from her bedroom in to the one in which I am now writing to have Tea with us - mental quietude & composure is not yet complete but decided improvement is 'perceptible' - My beloved 'elevator' 'Dynamite' Torpedo or what not is muchly indisposed - I am 'wenting' forth to Wigan at noon but return this evening & I suppose will remain till the weekend - To all and sundry our felicitations...

Feb 4th 1880 Evening... I have decided this evening to return home tomorrow and so take the opportunity of adding another communication requesting you to forward the Standard until further arrangements are made to my country domicile. I find Southport so relaxing that it feels like shortening my days - East winds & sudden change from intense cold to damp thick enervating weather makes me languid and miserable - I am writing almost in darkness...

Shrovetide 1880... I have taken to the use of cold water of late pretty largely - Though comfortable and refreshing I fancy I get cold from the manner of using it - I shall have to adopt some other plan - My cough is rather bad but my invaluable partner seems to have quite regained her health - How are ye all - I hope well and enjoying your pancakes this Shrovetide. Believe me...

Feast of St Valentine 1880... You will I am sure excuse haste. I am hurrying home again - I got here on Thursday night and am returning with all despatch this morning - I don't think I shall be here at all next week - Patient is recovering admirably - far beyond our most sanguine expectation - a visiter by this post - you will perceive that I write from Southport - Believe me...

Feb 16th 1880...I am here it is true but I am off again - health and weather permitting - on Tuesday between which date and Friday my address will be as usual contiguous to the Ocean's brink - I am due on or after Feb 26th at Bradley to preside - or at all events to take part in - a concert - not as a singer - but yet as a vocalist in some fashion...

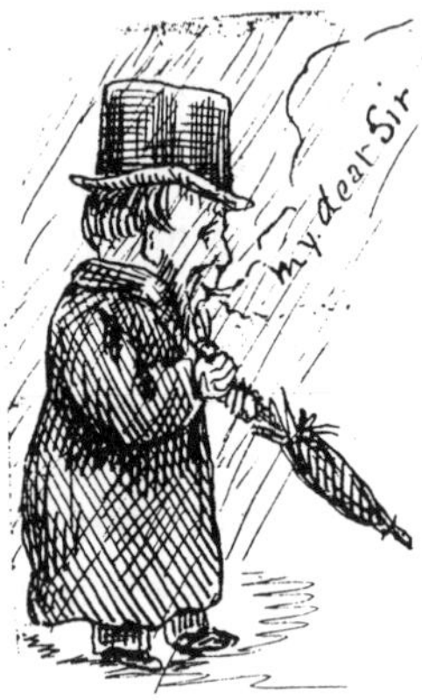

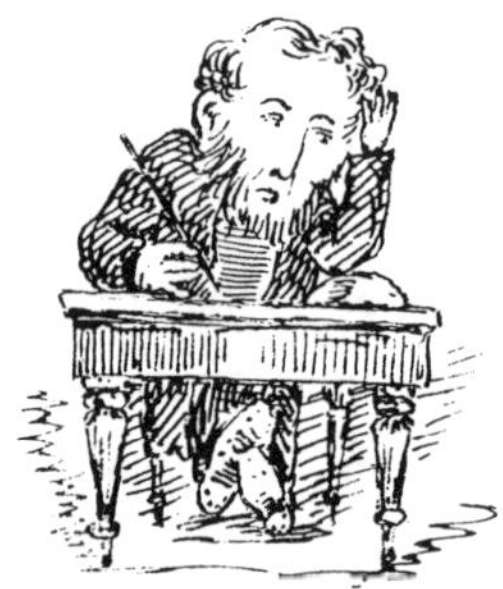

Notes

March 2nd 1880 Mr Howe

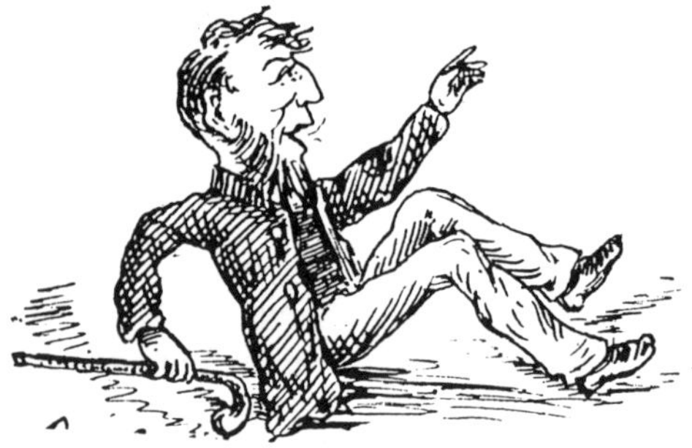

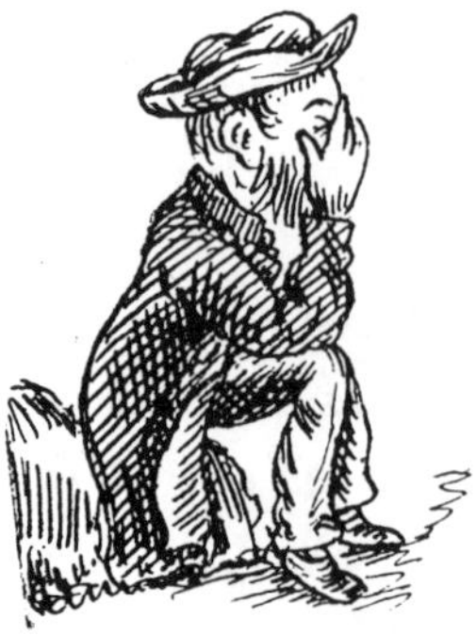

Feb 23rd 1880... I am just setting off to Staffordshire where I am promised to preside at a concert - The weather though mild is not very inviting in some respects but yet under the guidance of my Elevator and accompanied by my trusty umbrella I hope the journey may be accomplished in safety & perhaps conduce to my benefit - for I need a change muchly - Methinks I hear you say ' surely you have had enough of changes recently' well, yes, I <u>have</u> of a certain kind but I want rest now and quiet. Believe me...

Staffordshire Feb 25th 1880... I said I was coming, now didn't I? Well, I've come and feel woebegone at times and poorly but on the whole I flatter myself that I can detect a little improvement from the change of air and hope to be able to sport myself decidedly better when I return to Lancashire which I expect will be probably on Friday next - Torpedo is with me - also Baby Pie - Mr P is well but very busy as also is Baby Pie only in a slightly different way - we all combine in amicability and I remain as heretofore...

Staffordshire Feb 26th 1880... This is the date of today and tomorrow we propose returning to Lancashire where it is our intention to abide awhile beneath the shadow of our own wigwam - The Morbid whom we have been nursing during the past seven weeks is there already having arrived before we left - I am glad to report that we both feel benefitted by the change - but I am not a Samson yet - The muchest of muchness to all and believe me...

March 2nd 1880... I am '<u>settled down</u>' once more in my simple 'ome - The toil and bustle of travel are over and I hope for a space of quietude and rest - our invalid is still with us and I rejoice to think improving - I heard on Saturday evening with great regret that my esteemed brother* in Pemberton has suffered the loss of his excellent partner who departed this life in Rome. We have winter upon us once again freely - snow laying deep but I don't expect it will remain long - accept a measure of our fraternal affection & Believe me.. P.S. No Standard this morning...

March 10th 1880... I am ashamed and grieved at not writing sooner. I have got quite muddled with regard to the flight of time and it seems to me that it is at least a fortnight since I wrote last. Miss L. and Miss L.M. are still with us - the former improving very fast in body - there is also perceptible improvement in memory - we have now a dark dull atmosphere - harbingers, I opine, of coming storm - My Mezereums are out in full bloom - I have two white ones - with amplitude of affectation...

<u>Notes</u>

<u>March 11th 1880</u> The dissolution of Parliament following the resignation of Disraeli.

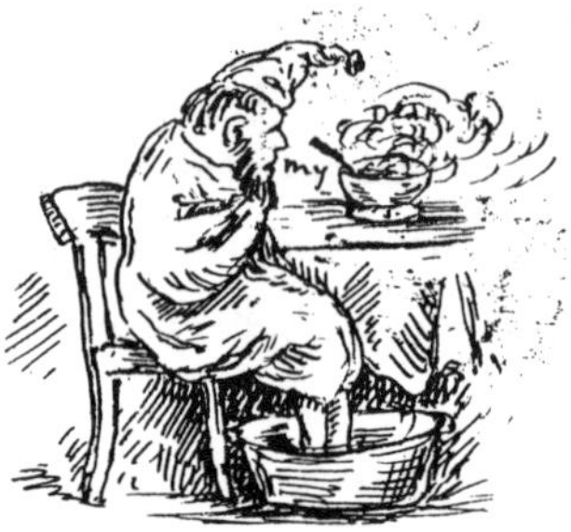

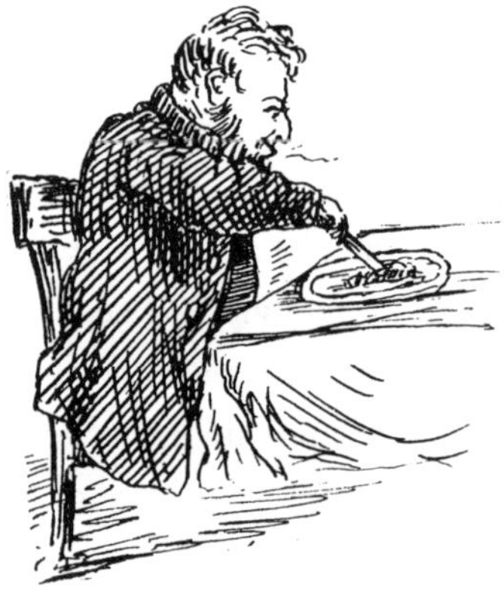

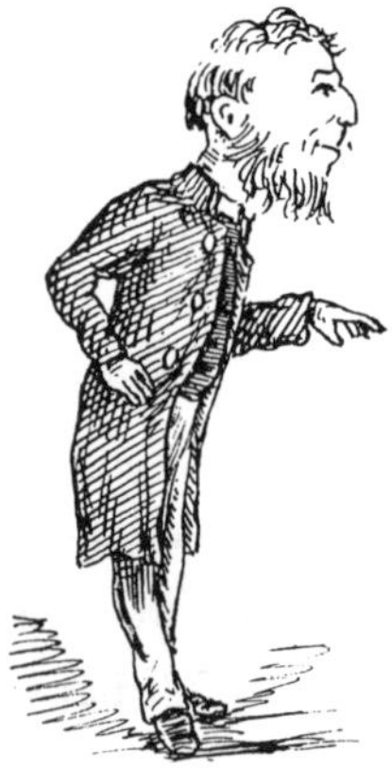

March 11th 1880... I have to write to you in snatches just as I can get the opportunity - for with children among my guests nothing seems to be in its place and no place seems to be where it should be - We have got into gloomy wet weather again and enjoy the additional infelicity of smoky chimneys - We are in a state of excitement about the Dissolution* and shall await the issue with much interest - We have had our pigs rung so I don't fear their going rooting in election matters - with fervid affectation...

March 15th 1880... I had despatched my other card before I read your letter to hand by today's post - The Standard to whose non-arrival I made reference e'erwhiles next day came to me accompanied by a letter but I have been so diversely disconcerted & exercised that it is quite possible that I may have omitted to mention them - You see I have promptly taken my pen in hand again & trust this attempt at rectification will secure your approval...

March 22nd 1880... With the exception of a slight catarrh I think I may describe myself as being in excellent electioneering Form - our Invalid is still with us and I rejoice to say receiving benefit from our pure air - On Friday last she went to Wigan and bore great fatigue - The weather here is splendid but the wind is at times distressingly East - I have commenced gardening and have achieved some really first class work - not great in quantity but of quality unimpeachable ' as fine as meighl' welly - such my quondam gardener would pronounce it - In the hope that you are all well with a hearty shake of the hand I salute you...

March 24th 1880... My catarrh is nearly gone and my appetite for food is such as an elephant or a Hippopotamus might envy. I can scarcely see or hear of a dish without harbouring a craving for it - in fact for deglutition and assimilation I am always ready - This is considered by self and sundry a good sign - We have lovely weather still and a delightfully nipping East wind - our Invalid and my Torpedo were at Southport yesterday - They describe their 'out' as having been exceedingly pleasant but cold - Permit me to hope that health is abundant in your household. Thanks for the newspapers which are especially of interest at this time - Receive the salutations of me this 24th day of March 1880.. P.S Have just got your letter - why not come here for an 'out' -? We shall rejoice to see you ...

March 27th 1880... Your letter reached my hand in due course yesterday (Good Friday). My last card was sent off in the hope you might be minded to look us up this Eastertide - but that unfortunate cold of yours it seems is to stop the way - Its presence is greatly to be regretted as it is such beautiful weather - The air quite glistens with sunshine - the American Telegrams predicting cyclonic depressions notwithstanding - accept a poor Hedge Priest's Easter benison and Believe him to remain ...

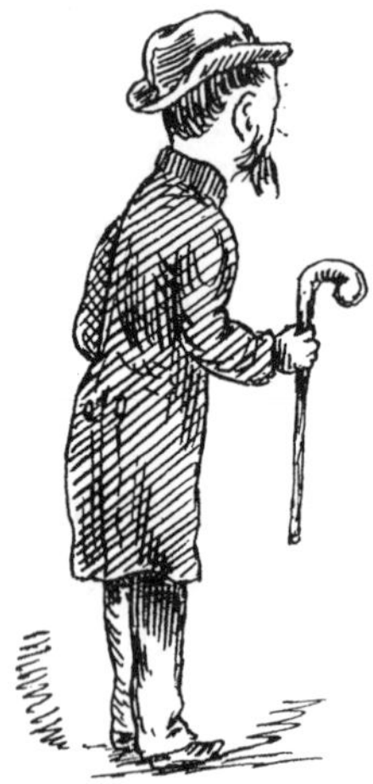

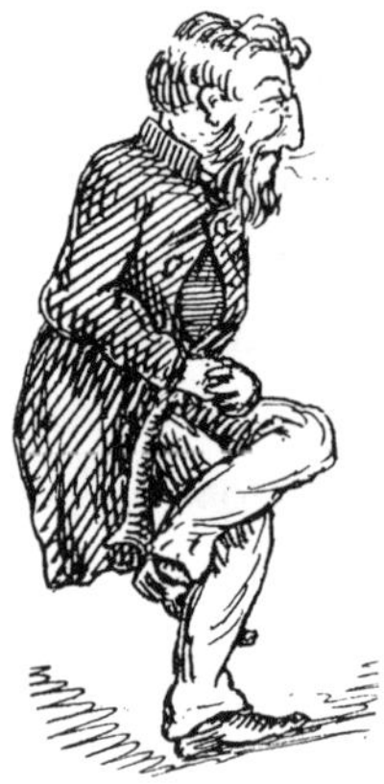

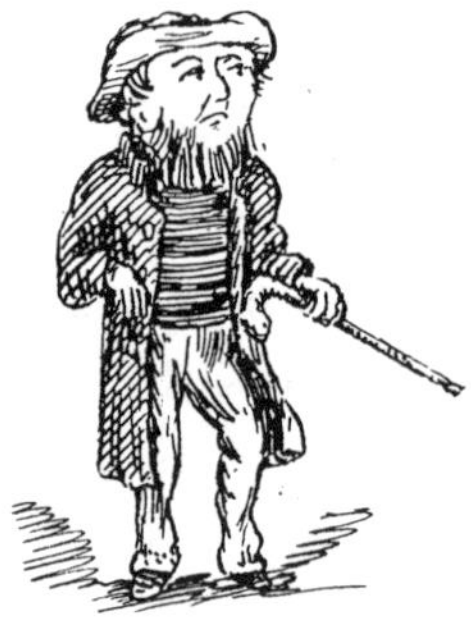

April 3rd 1880... I am in readiness awaiting Duty's call to go to the 'Poll' - 'Poll' is derived from Dutch Bol which in Low German becomes Polle, and signifies a 'bulb' - a 'head' hence a register of 'heads'or 'bulbs' - Has your 'bulb' been registered yet? - I suppose it has - I am taking my Bol or bulb for registration on the 10th - when, I trust many thousands of bulbs entertaining political sentiments of harmony with my own may also be registered - With affectionate tenderness ...

April 7th 1880... ah, my dear Sir, say nothing about it for I, like <u>you</u>, am doing my best, but really it gives me quite a stomach ache. We have today had a vehicle upset near here - horse - conveyance - and passengers precipitated into a wide and deep ditch - I think nobody much hurt, horse dug out alive - harness broken - vehicle moderate in condition when rescued. Don't see immediate prospect of getting to Preston - will send a bit of <u>the</u> cheese but Torpedo thinks you don't deserve any if you won't fetch it - Hope all yours are well - to each commend us .. P.S make it known that we expect Mr Parkes in a few days ...

April 13th 1880... you've done well, and <u>I've</u> done well so I am sure my dear Sir nobody can blame us - Our success is gratifying and we can look with pleasure alike upon the Icy North - Your own abiding place and the region of the Winter Sun Setting to wit, the South West - but the exertions and anxieties of the past fourteen days have left me, as you see, a little thin and shaky - We have been daily expecting a storm which up to this present has not come albeit the skies have looked very dark - My Dynamite accompanied Miss L. to Southport yesterday for a few hours and got nearly petrified with cold. I duly affected the registration of mine own bulb on Saturday last - I did it at Standish and I did it early - I went thence to Croston just to look at how matters were proceeding in that quarter and felt like an embryo member myself - I was back in the retirement of home by one o'clock. Mr Parkes is here - He arrove last evening and combines in cordiality...

<u>Notes</u>

<u>April 17th 1880</u> Mr Storey was the defeated Liberal candidate for North Lancashire.

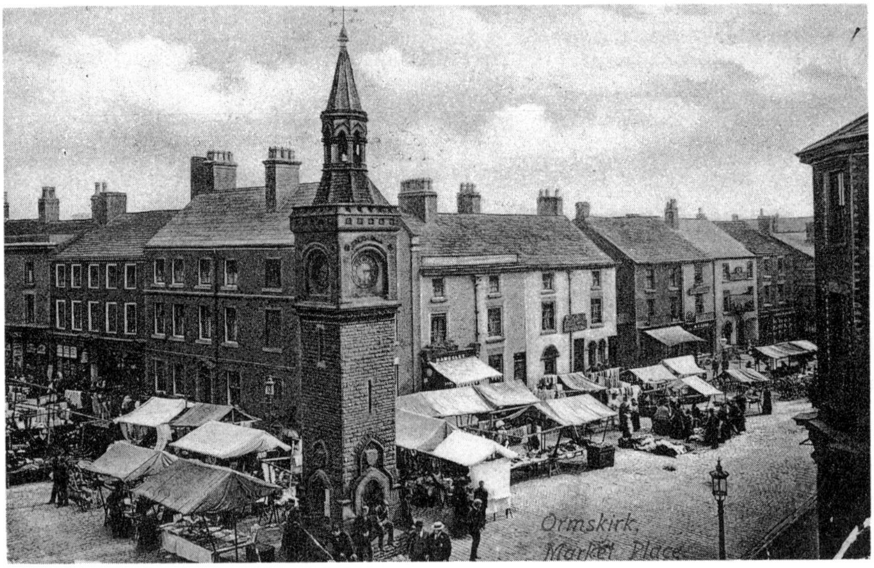

Ormskirk and the Bell Tower.

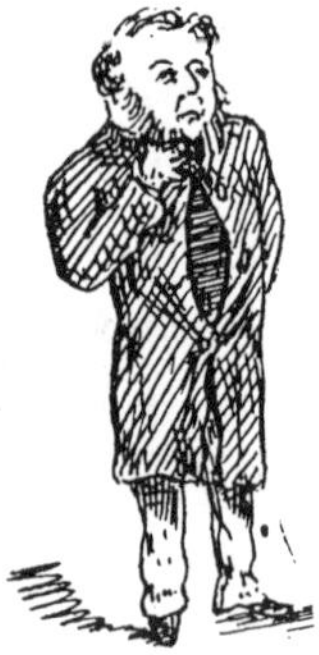

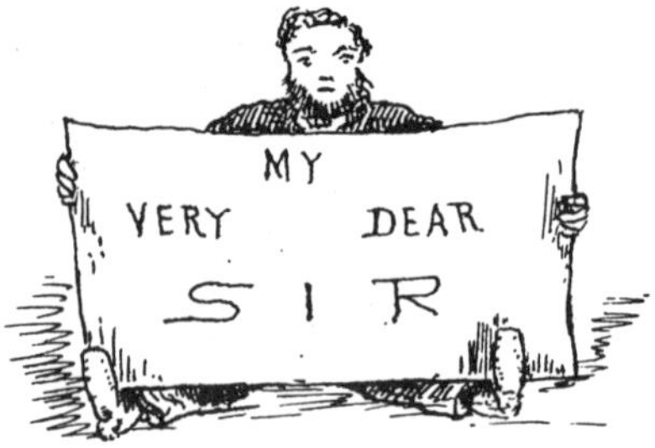

April 17th 1880... Hooray for North Lancashire. Hooray! for Preston - I should come to Preston but engagements Bahr my way - when will this exciting time be over? Our own Division like many another has told its Storey* of defeat and our neighbours in the South West have been Very Cross - Mr Parkes and I visited Ormskirk on Thursday last to inspect the bell tower* in its Market Place - It is a meagre gingerbread structure which would look all the more noble for a little more stone and dimension - The design is pretty enough but the good folks when they were erecting it should have got leave to approach a little nearer the clouds with the top of it - The Town stands greatly in need of a covered market - We conclude that the Election excitement has now quite subsided for having journeyed hence thither in an East wind and open vehicle we were blue with cold when we passed through its streets yet no one assaulted us for displaying that Party Colour - Our old Bachelor friend proposes to seek again the great emporium of leather on Monday next. He appends himself to me in the bonds of fervent amicable regards towards your household & self and I remain...

April 20th 1880... I have given up all interest in political matters for the present and don't care how the remainder of the Elections go - It is pleasing to know that the era of prosperity has already set in - I am told that eggs even now are both bigger and more for the shilling than they were before the elections. We are glad to learn that the cheese reached its destination duly and gave satisfaction. I write in great haste ...

April 26th 1880... The Tornado in America seems to have been very terrible and we have looked forward apprehensively to the storm announced from New York as probably qualified to cause disturbance here - with a few lively gales and a little rain it has passed over - of thunder & lightning we have had none - Damson blossom is making the gardens white and the whole aspect of the country is fresher since the more genial breezes and little rain - We are pretty well. Take us on the average - Miss L is still with us - My Reverend Brother from Pemberton has returned from Italy - To you & yours greetings - health and every blessing ...

Tuesday May 4th 1880...I write just a line to let you know we are all in excellent health and trust ye are in the possession of a like beatification. Heard the cuckoo first on Sunday evening ...

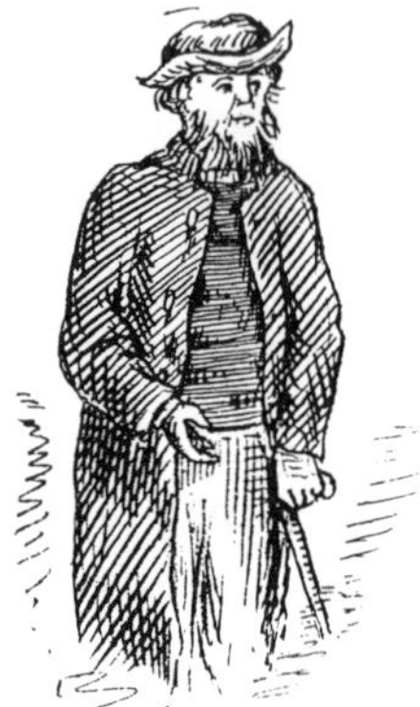

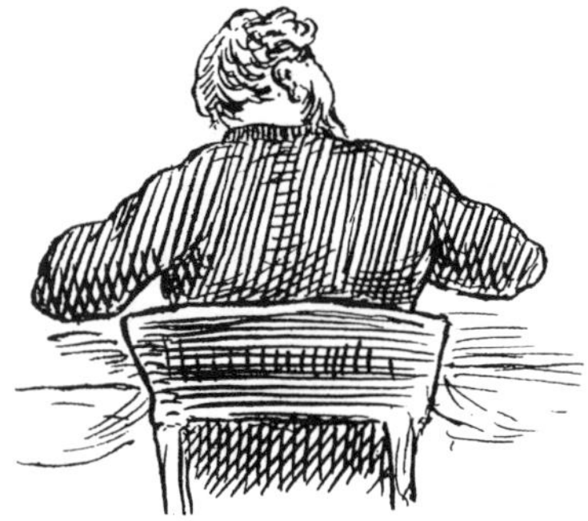

Notes

May 17th 1880 Gladstone's second ministry.

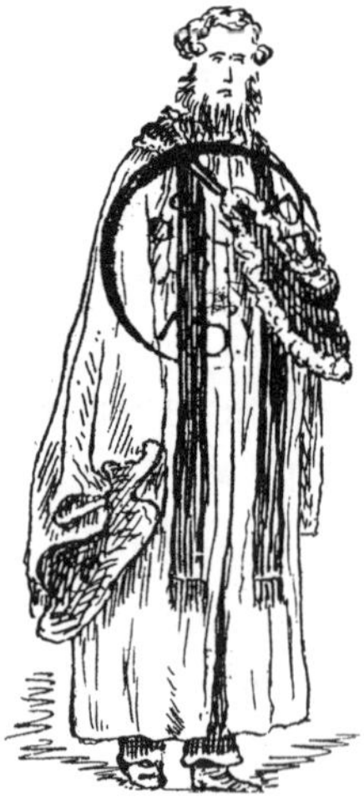

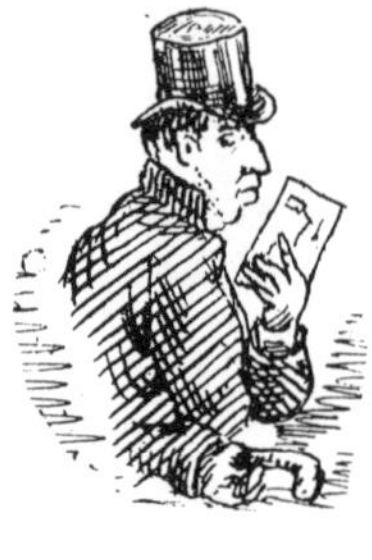

May 10th 1880... for a fortnight nearly we, who were last year altogether complaining of wet, have been sighing for rain - Glasses have generally stood high and sea weeds have persistently remained crisp and dry but when we had all abandoned hope of showers falling - rain has unexpectedly arrived - a gentle, spring like rain which is making the buds unfold and all nature look fresh and lively - We can almost see the mustard & cress and grass grow. I intended to be up early this morning and spread upon my walks several cart loads of gravel but the rain has effectually checked my plans & stayed my purpose...

May 17th 1880... I am staying at home replenishing my corporeal organism by enjoying my food regularly instead of wearing the flesh off my bones by jaunting off as many do at Whitsunday-tide - Besides, be it known, I have many duties to retain me here even if disposed to take an airing and a holiday - Folks here generally are sighing for rain - Frosts are becoming hurtful and the growth of grass is tardy - yet we don't despair - We have a new government and have been promised prosperity - The present Cabinet* of course will make it all right. Don't cry therefore but do your best to endeavour to be cheerful. Accept my salutations...

May 22nd 1880... On the 27th Inst St Luke's Church Southport is to be opened - The corner stone was laid as you will remember with Masonic honours. Will the Brotherhood be taking part in the opening? We are bidden to grace the ceremonial with our presence so that if you attend and chance to see in the procession a cleric of imposing stature and wearing withal a kindly aspect; and attired muchly as we have here depicted that processional cynosure will most probably be us, ourself. Need we add how largely your esteemed presence would add to our pleasures on the occasion. For a week we have been awaiting rain - leaden skies and a lower temperature have given grounds for expectancy - but as yet expectation has been vain - dust is flying in clouds and riotous gales are in the ascendant. To all we send our salutations...

May 25th 1880... with very great concern we learned the cause of your silence - Though the weather has been fine of late I think the East winds have proved rather detrimental to health - Glandular swellings and inflammatory irritation in the eyes as also pains in the ear and face have been prevalent - Mr Howe is expected to be at our Gala on the 14th of next month - as usual 'he holds his letter in abeyance and hesitates to send it' but he will turn up for all that - Either come and abide under one thatch on that occasion or drive over and bring your household for a gambol in the country - with a cordial conjunction in all amicable sentiments...

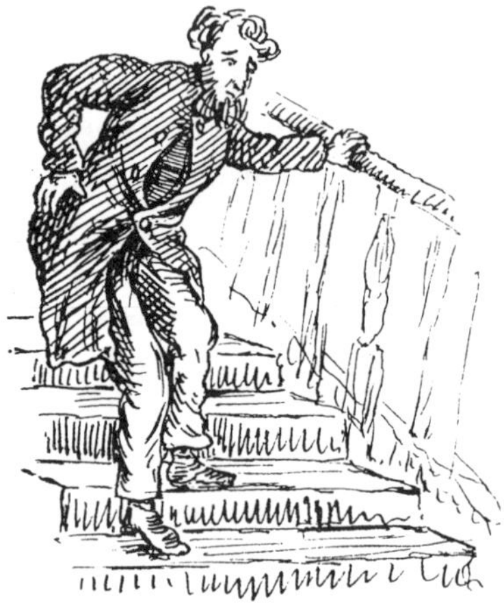

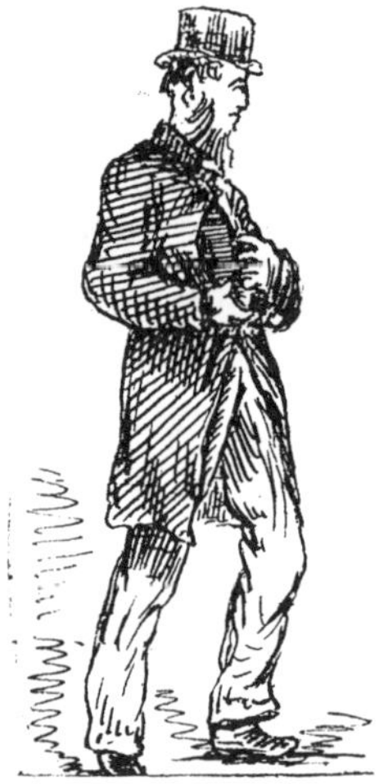

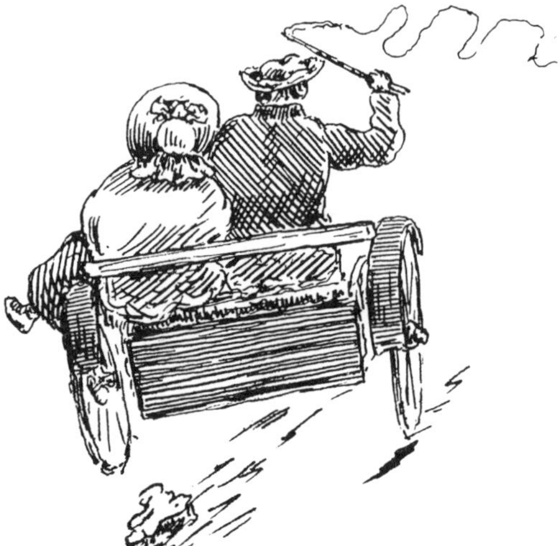

May 31st 1880... I had the responsibility of a distant predication laid upon me yesterday or rather yester-even - at Newburgh, to wit - and exposure to the rain pouring heavily as I rode home has given me cold in the lumbar muscles so that I can scarcely get up and down stairs without a degree of caution and some feeling - I hope the ophthalmic irritation has subsided or so much so that you now suffer no discomfort. The rain has continued with little intermission today - Receive a certificate of our distinguished esteem...

June 5th 1880... I was in Wigan yesterday and partly in consequence of the prolix pedestrian preamble needful to attain the station followed by the patient plodding homeward I am tired - rest is needful so I am taking a day of it - I am alone with the exception of a domestick left to look after me - All are well and hope your optics are regaining their wonted repose and freedom from irritation - Why don't you come over and try our salubrious air - a sight of the country would do you good - The Westmoreland hills as also those of Cumberland have been twice visible this week - a sight for sore eyes - Monday next but one - our Gala - Torpedo, Miss L &c gone to Southport on a marketing excursion...

June 11th 1880... Now come, my dear Sir, won't you join us on the 14th - our dwelling is beginning to fill very nicely. Two guests from Ormskirk already here - one from Stafford due today, one from Glossop either Saturday or Monday - Brother Mason Marsden on Monday &c &c &c. Weather again beautiful but sometimes much more like September than June - We do hope your optical affliction has been banished ...

June 18th 1880... We've got a small conveyance now and might have had a 'turn over' to Preston before this to look at you but we are still in the throes of parochial Festivity. Monday a party for scholars & general public - Wednesday a Party for teachers and tomorrow (Saturday) a Party for scholars only - Hope your eyes are improving ...

June 21st 1880... Our local Festivities have so greatly engrossed my time during the past week that I have found it impossible to correspond with my usual regularity. Your wonted consideration and liberality of sentiment encourages me to indulge in confident anticipations of your forgiveness - We had gatherings on Monday, Wednesday and Saturday - Mr Howe - fickle man - came not - our Billington & Ulverston friends visited Preston on Saturday - but rain in the one case and evil tidings in the other sent both of them unexpectedly off to their respective destinations. Are you better?...

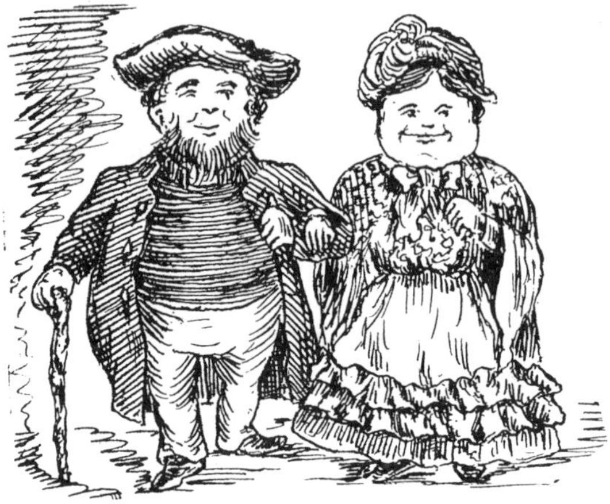

Notes

June 26th 1880 Well-sinking was a common practice.

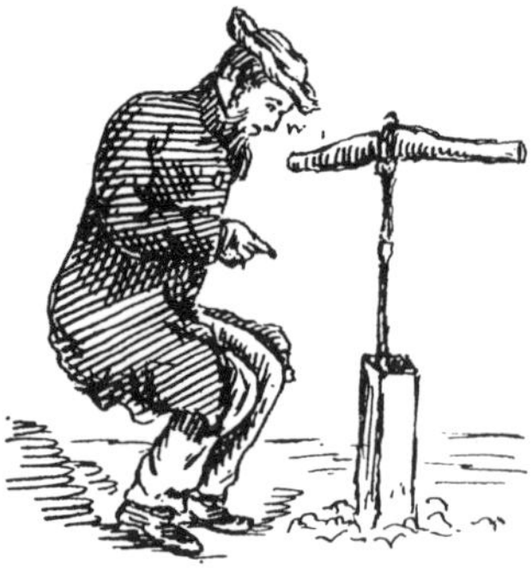

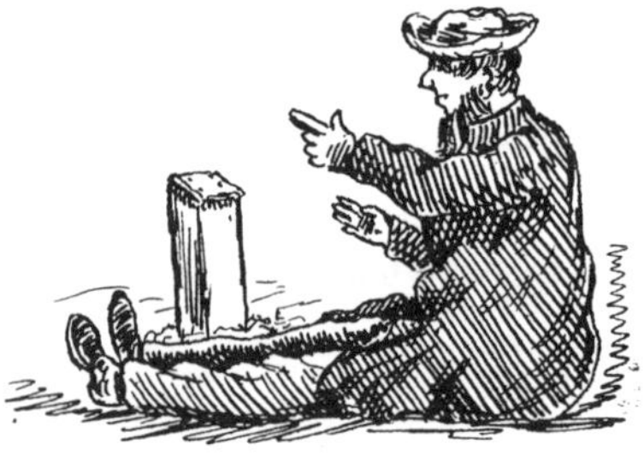

June 24th 1880... Me and the dear partner of my joys and sorrows have decided to have an out for a little fresh air - We intend to go as far as Wigan - The Sulphur in its Atmosphere like the Sulphur in the Harrogate Waters will we hope be highly beneficial to us - Besides a walk to the Station (Railway not Police) may not be without its advantage. Why don't you come over some weekend? the views have of late been grand - Ferns, wild hyacinths; foliage, &c beautifully flourishing. Post just to hand an hour and half before time - I conclude in haste...

June 26th 1880 (evening)... During the past week the Atmosphere has been so clear that I have, between showers, stood and looked around me - Croston, Longton, Bretherton, Leyland, Eccleston, Chorley, Lytham, Fylde Country - Whittle Hills, Pendle, Longridge and Preston have lain spread out before my gaze as on a Map - The view would have filled you with delight and much I marvel that you come not - We are expecting sinkers here on Monday to make a Well* - If they chance to strike '<u>Ile</u>' we shall have a Limited Liability concern very quickly afloat - value of shares not yet determined - Our Pigs are nearly ready for the Butcher so if the sinkers strike 'ile' during their operations we may perhaps preserve the swine in the 'ile' and export them - a great commercial future is opening out. Shall we send a 'prospectus'? Colds are prevalent - The household concatenates with cordiality...

June 29th 1880... My good men there is no water in that deep hole which you are boring - depend upon it - and if as you say you have already arrived at rock my opinion is that you will neither find Water nor strike 'ile. Draw out your boring rods - unscrew the shell - nail a 'bit' wood over the boring box, then close your labours and come sit down and rest - So spake we to the sinkers - The operations yesterday came to nothing - All's well that ends well - but we still have no 'well' ...

June 30th 1880... your suspicions respecting the Advertisement in Standard are well and truly based - perhaps the more correct Masonic formula would be 'well and truly laid' - <u>'so mote it be'</u> - Miss L and mine 'other half' being in Southport today I take advantage of their visit to get this card into the post expeditiously - When are you hasting hither? can you come on Saturday? I beg leave to bow my compliments & remain...

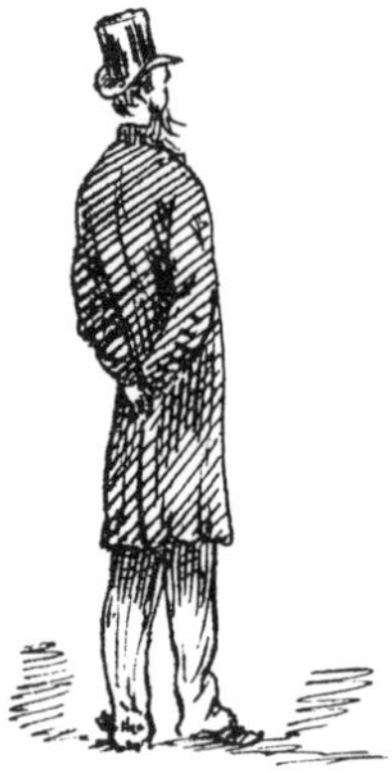

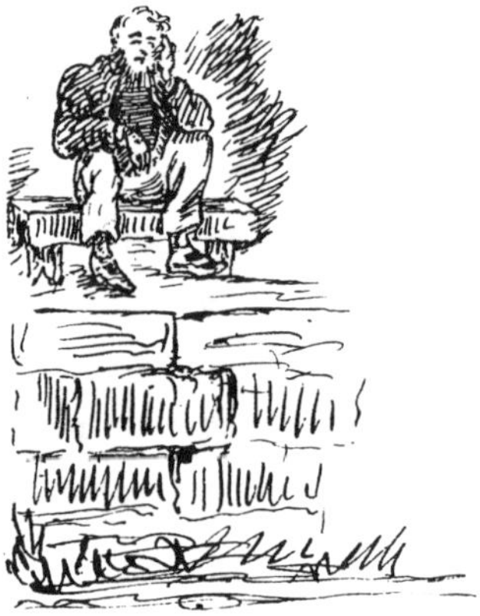

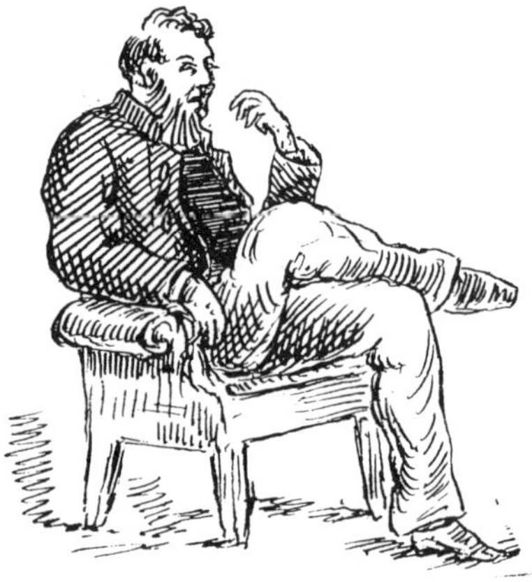

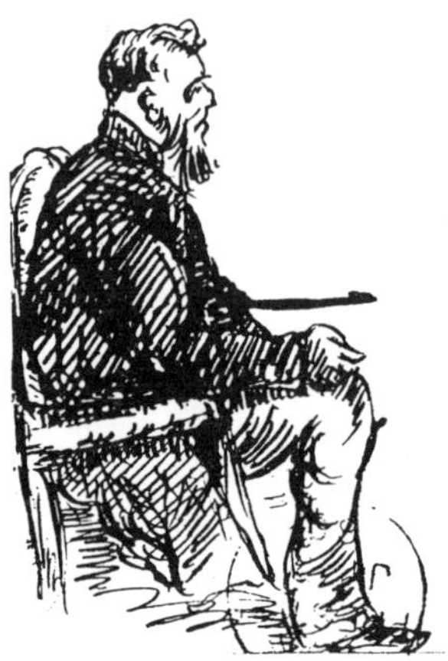

July 9th 1880... Well, how are you all getting on my dear Sir? 'We' are moving about mostly amid rain and divers kinds of storm - Electricity loads the air and Farmers are sighing for fair weather and sunshine. Our visiter of the past few months has left us this morning so that the house contains none but members of the family for the first time since the middle of January last - Most members of the family too are gone to Wigan so that all is very quiet and if I can just spy an opportunity of running between the falling rain drops without touching them I shall be off to Wigan too - not because I like the town, far from it - but because I am gregarious and want company - Receive my salutations - My household all salute you - Greet for us your entire family and indulge credulity at least so far as to Believe me ...

July 13th 1880... The Thundery state of the atmosphere continues - I am languid and inert - I sit in weariness - unable to get to Preston, Southport or anywhere. I am compelled however to make an effort to get out to attend to certain duties today so inviting your indulgent judgement on my brevity I have the pleasure of wishing you a very good morning & Believe me ...

July 20th 1880... I don't know exactly whither I am going but I am bound to be off somewhither. Torpedo is taking me - South or Mid Wales I think it probable we may land in. I have even a design to breathe the air of freedom on Snowdon's top - I have a 'touring' mania on me strong - Don't write to me till you hear further as the address on your letter might not be strictly accurate...

July 22nd 1880... I set forth yester morn at daybreak to revel mid the romantic scenery of the Principality. Our expedition however came a cropper as the saying is at Wigan - Torpedo fell ill - Day wore on and no improvement - I myself joined the sick list with severe headache - We took a cab and came back - I am rather better this morning but I fear Torpedo will have to seek medical counsel - We hope you are all well now. The twain of us combine cordially in muchness ...

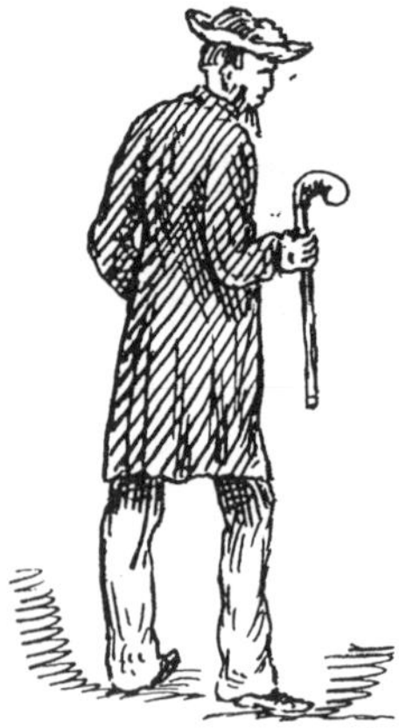

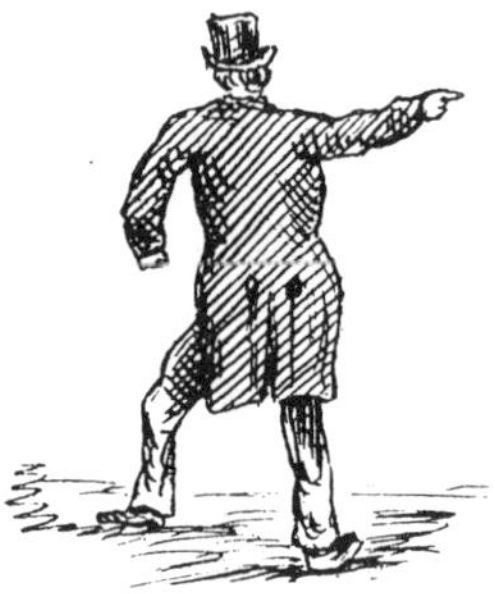

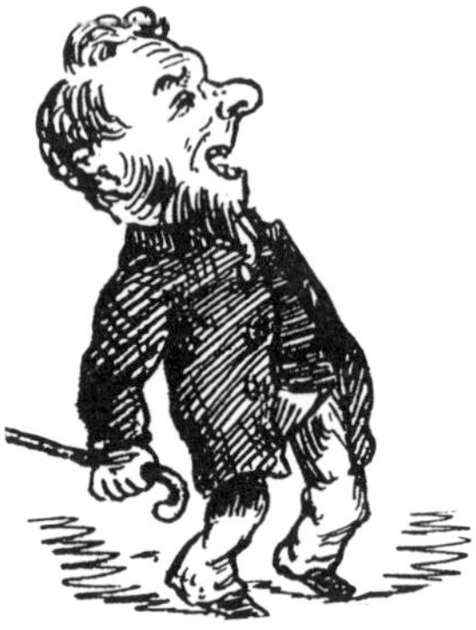

<u>Notes</u>

<u>Aug 6th 1880</u> Apparitions had been reported at Knock and some 500 Roman Catholics took part in a pilgrimage, many of them crippled or otherwise deformed.

July 24th 1880... Permit me, good Sir, to acknowledge the receipt of your (letter) and to thank you for the kind expressions of sympathy which it contained - we have both been very ill. In fact the Doctor's aid has been invoked and I rejoice to say that improvement is apparent - Tonight (Saturday) my Partner seems much better - and I though still much out of sorts am in like hopeful 'finding'. Now in reference to your coming over hither ye can I am sure bear us witness that ye have been bidden often enough to really have no need to interpolate your reference to a visit with the hesitating parenthesis (If I may). We shall be at home all week - no more contemplated escapades Southwards yet awhile - so come over any day - there is a bed as well as knife and fork at your service - I have one eye very much irritated - Poor hay weather for the farmers - receive for yours and you an assurance of our continued esteem ...

July 30th 1880... Come on, my dear Sir, join us this weekend. Your Southport friend will be here again next week - The house will be more clear and free - and withal to your liking this week - come therefore my dear Sir - come. My eyes are, I regret to say, much inflamed but I can still get about. I hope to see you early on Saturday at the latest - Write and specify the hour - esteeming ye as ever ...

Aug 2nd 1880... come Sir, I say, what the ferrups does this mean? Do you wish to provoke me to have recourse to personal violence - eh? Keep my temper! Do you say? Not get excited!! eh? How can I keep my temper? How can I avoid being excited - when I loitered about home awaiting every train on Saturday afternoon which might bring you - and so ardently expectant was I that besides walking beyond the Bar to meet you I witheld presence from the Mawdesley Tea Party until after sundown and then, with a view to being back the more early, took a conveyance - Keep my temper indeed! Not get excited forsooth!!!! I should like to see who could be placable under such disappointment - Ah! my friend! 'tak shem tae yersel' - and receiving the kind wishes of all here...

<u>Wiggin</u> Aug 6th 1880...Ha-ha-ha!!! my dear Mister - my last card I doubt not, would have a slight flavour of asperity - and ever so likely that it should considering that I couldn't coax or beguile you hither - Have ye joined the pilgrimage to 'Knock'* in Ireland? Have ye been travelling under the name of Goschen to the Porte -? Or is your nom de plume Leppel Griffin, and your whereabouts Cabul? On all these points I'm in a cloud of mystery - Write I pray ye and all shall be forgotten - I have thought of utilising the agony column in a leading Journal with a view to finding you. I am yours forgivingly...

<u>Notes</u>

<u>Aug 10th 1880</u> Dr Tanner was an American who fasted for forty days and forty nights. In 1881, however, he went to Amsterdam to repeat the feat for £2000, but before he could start his fast he fell down the stairs of the hotel he was staying at, and died of concussion.

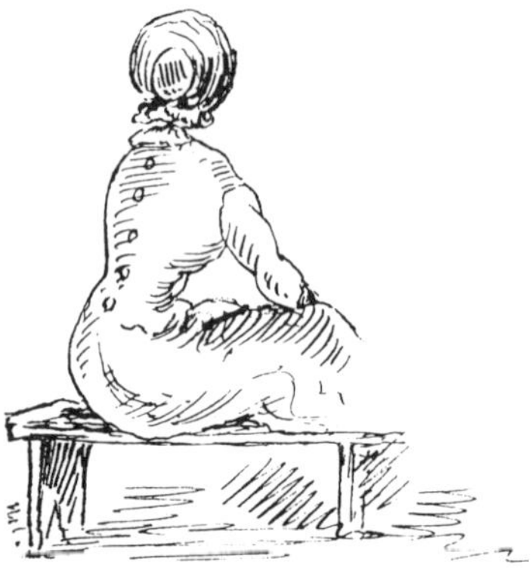

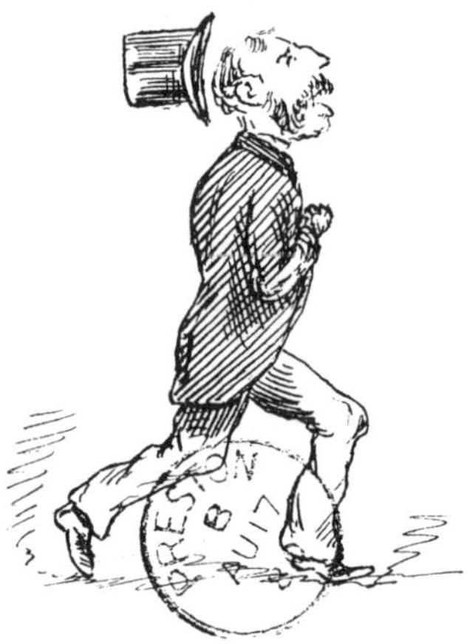

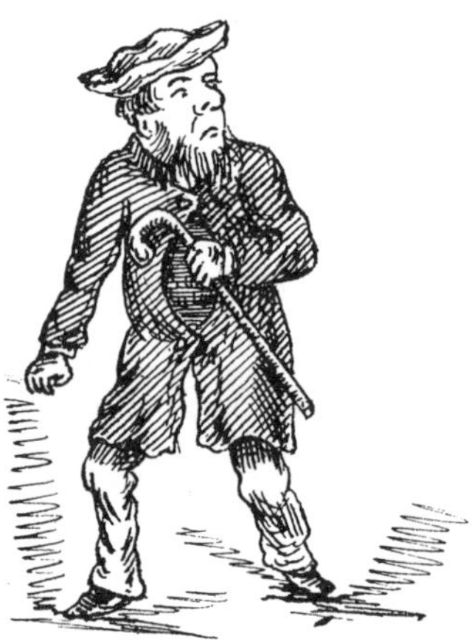

Aug 10th 1880... This weather is really hot - enough to reduce one to the skeleton like proportions of Dr Tanner* - I have walked a good deal lately & from fatigue and perspiration feel vaporising and evanescent - why don't you come over - I last night from the top of the Hill saw Black Comb in Cumberland. The whole range of the North Lancashire, Westmoreland & Yorkshire hills - the mountains of Denbighshire also the Great & little Ormshead. I think I am going from home today but shall not stay longer than Friday night or Saturday morning. I have not been fasting but I do feel 'Tanner' like, Miss L returns home today...

Aug 13th 1880... Dearest - The fact becomes more patent annually that you have the misfortune generally speaking to be in the wrong place at the right time - Here have we been visited by a most beautiful and accomplished young lady - possessing a heart entirely free and unfettered yet instead of heeding my call and pleasuring me with a visit you go, for ought I know, 'Knock'ing about Ireland pilgrim fashion - This augurs badly for an early settling down in matrimonial Bliss. We return homeward tomorrow morning and shall feel joy at seeing you in the evening tide to abide with us till Monday ...

Aug 16th 1880... To see you nipping up the road at the rate of four miles and threequarters in the hour on such a smoking hot morning as this was a stirring sight - a moving spectacle. Ah, how I wish my pen could move with like despatch, but alas, alas, it may not be - As the fingers of my timepiece point to 8.5 AM this minute I venture to picture you to myself as located in a melting mood beneath the grateful shadow of the roof of 63, Fishergate - In the ardent hope that you feel in no way worse for your rural visit I am bold to commend myself to your friendly regard and I remain ...

... I will meet the train which leaves Preston at 6.20 PM tomorrow (Thursday) - The walk will do me good - Now see you come and don't disappoint me - I was not at Wigan on Monday - surely you must have mistaken my method of writing Aug for Wigan - Anyway I sent the card per post from here as usual - remember tomorrow evening. I shall appear as here depicted ambulating to Wittle stocks unless it be <u>very</u> wet at the time named...

Aug 20th 1880... I will meet you of course (all being well) according to our agreement - Will take the Town Lane and Pyebrook route - Hoping the weather may prove fine and trusting that ye all reached Fishergate in safety last evening...

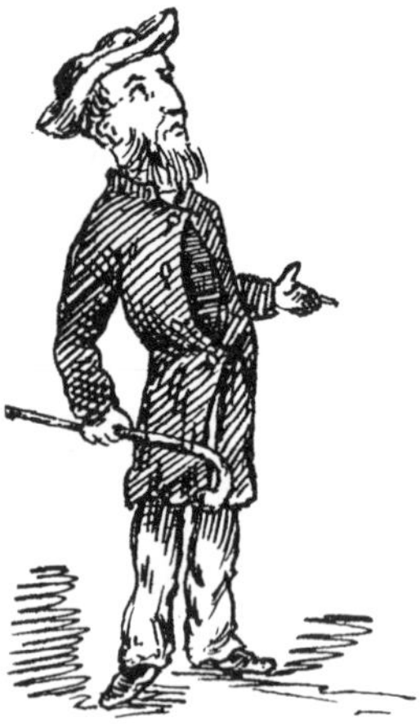

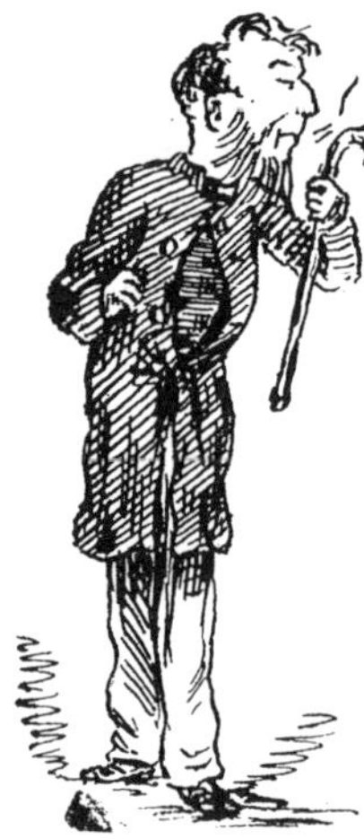

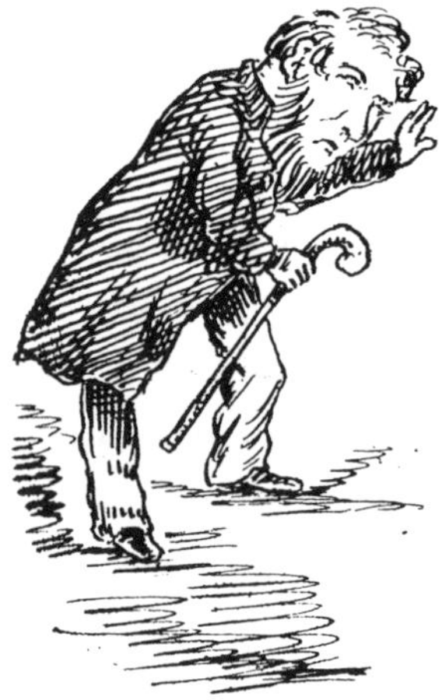

Notes

Aug 30th 1880 Tergiversation = evasion.

Aug - 1880... Now my dear, good Mister, is it fair or just to come and see a friend in a Bilious attack and leave him again in a hurry? You really might have stayed till Monday morning and borne me company for a little longer space - The shades of Eve surround us - The household planet burns brightly on the table around which we are gathered and on which a tender Duck but a brief half hour agone was figuring - we speculate and sigh - and many a wonder is expressed as to whether ye have yet reached the shelter of your Bungalow - We hope to see ye all as per arrangement - don't fail herein - mind that -come which way ye like but 'come' even if a Balloon be the vehicular medium you select. Receive our cordial Good night and Believe me ...

Aug 24th 1880... I stick to my promise like I stick to my stick - I grasp it tenaciously, but whither away good sir, with yours? Ye promised me a note to hand today yet none hath come - I am going to Southport tomorrow (Wednesday) - And hope to see you there on Thursday - Write immediately you receive this and tell me what train you will come by - Address to me as usual in Adelaide Street - I will meet you at the Station alone so that we may have a stroll and spend a few hours together. A change and 'rouse up' will do you good - I am quite surprised not to hear from you by today's Post - I do hope you are not worse - See ye fail not to join me at the briney main and see ye withold not a letter as per above. The cordial greetings of Torpedo and self accept ...

Aug 27th 1880... Come this is too bad - Alas! Alas! here have I been waiting and hoping and apprehending - to find out at last full surely that I may not have your company at the Sea side nor enjoy the felicity your presence in my upland demesne is calculated to import - wherefore thus? My dear Sir - remember Mrs Dombey - make an effort - if you don't feel first class in the matter of health - make an effort - Nobody from here will be with us on Sunday - you need not send word but if you feel you can come - come - there will be something to eat and country air as usual, and we shall be pleased to see you ...

Aug 30th 1880... now, now Sir - not one word I beg - I don't wish to hear you say one word about it either in the way of justification, explanation or tergiversation* - for shame, for shame of you - the day was glorious and the ride out hither would have done you good - yea and your family good also. I thankfully add that we had an amplitude of success. The Organ got duly opened but it required a vast of strength to do it ...

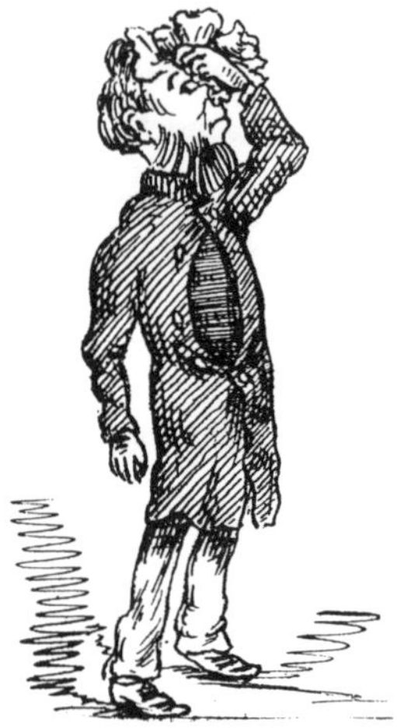

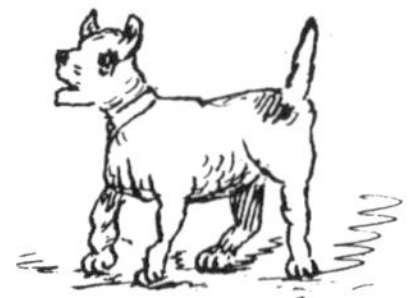

Notes

Sep 4th 1880 — A character from Dickens' "Martin Chuzzlewit" - popular reading of the day.

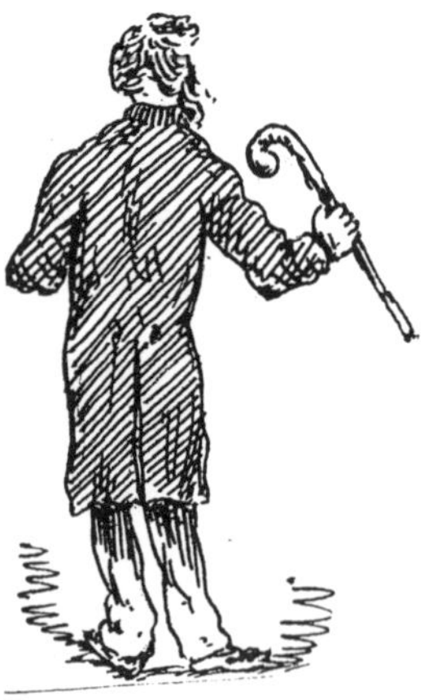

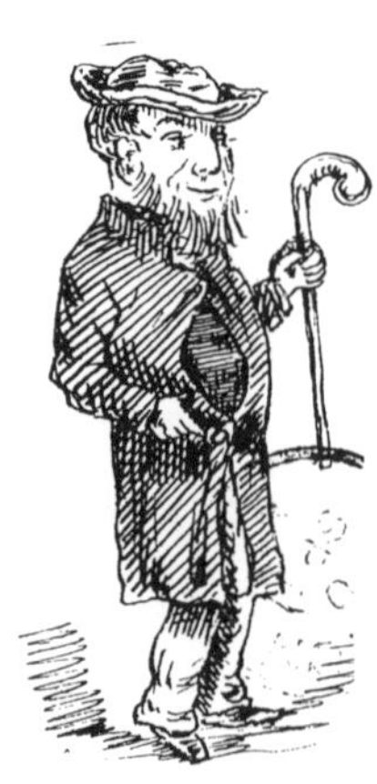

Sep 2nd 1880... Oh! my dear Sir - This weather, this weather - It is fast causing me to vanish into thin air and hoary mist - you may expect to see me if it continues present a sort of half pitchfork - half feathery appearance. Our new canine guardian arrived on Tuesday evening 'Cave Canem'- Its fierceness is not yet such as to occasion alarm but in time it may be - I hope you are better ...

Sep 4th 1880... I think I told you in my last that I had become the possessor of a 'dawg' which though very active and an excellent runner is nevertheless as quiet as quiet; and enjoys a disposition which I am sure may be described as benignity itself. You don't need to fear it for it would be most pleased to see you - I walked fourteen miles yesterday in the summer heat so that weariness and perspiration have reduced me to the unpretending condition here faintly represented. Really what glorious weather we are being favoured with. I found your note waiting me on my return home last evening - change & rest may do great things for you - come when so 'disposed' as Mrs Gamp* might put it ...

Sep 7th 1880... I am sure that if you were really so minded you could come over anytime with as much facility as I can twirl my stick - I have not felt quite so well for a few days past - I think I have become thinner as you will perceive by a close observation of the back view of me as presented to you here - I have had two children bearing me company and two old folks - but all have vanished like morning mist before the rising sun - The carriage that came for them had an accident at Smithy Brow & the coachman was sent hurtling through the air. The horse & he were hurt ...

Sep 11th 1880... The days are cutting shorter and shorter - The glistening haze of Autumn hanging over the harvest fields each morning admonish me of two things viz. If you mean coming hither and enjoying a vesper and a Matin walk you must make a push, not delay longer. Secondly you may be getting your skates ready for in six weeks from this date an occasional Frost may testify to the proximity of Winter. The grass and stubble sparkle with the drops of dew - The smoke room begins to look rather autumn like - Indeed the face of Nature is just now beautiful. I move about a great deal - my shoes and stick are in constant exercise. With unabated regard ...

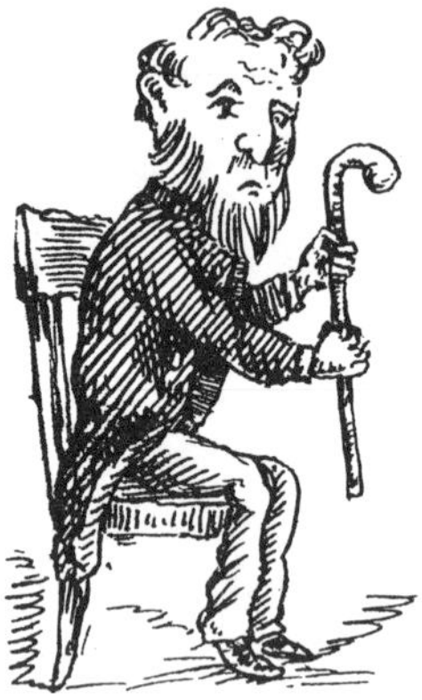

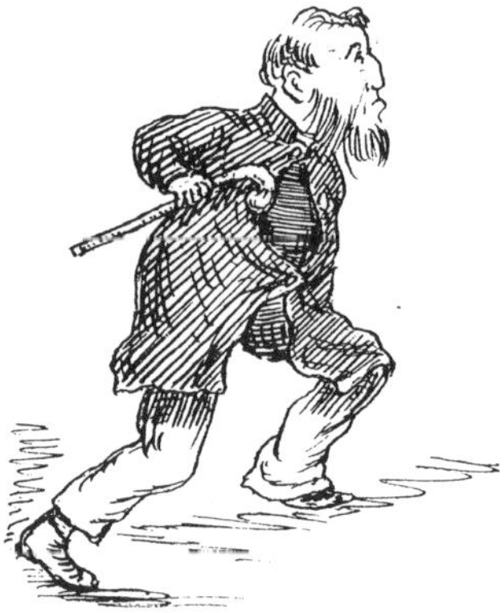

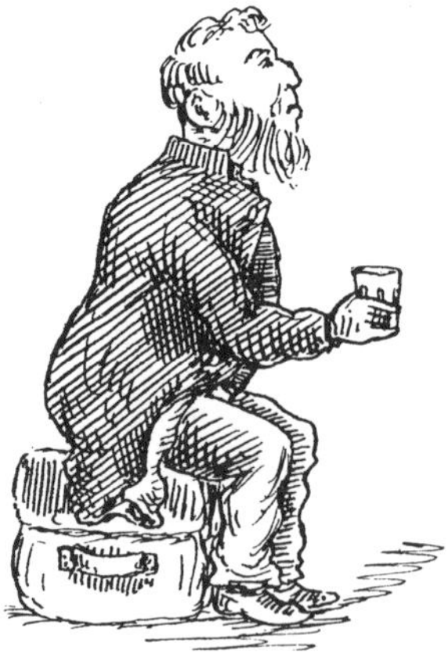

Sep 13th 1880... now, do I look happy My dear Sir? Do I look happy think you, eh? If you don't - then why don't you come over to comfort me - You have dallied and waited till rain has returned and I here all this time ready to go out with you on the breezy hills to sniff the balmy zephyrs - The harvest time has been glorious and much of the corn here has been housed - I am expecting this week our Glossop friend - "Little 'Frill' doth jump about Running sometimes in and sometimes out The rain outside comes down amain Abates at times then pours again" As high class poetry of this description comes in expensive I cannot afford any more on a half penny Post card so with distinguished regards...

Sep 22nd 1880... Let me tell you, My dear Sir, seriously, that you will provoke me to make unpleasant use of my walking stick - if you go running anywhere about the country but to this portion of it - I consider it, Sir, scarcely fair to myself or the many friends who would have been pleased to see you here - You have missed a treat which would have done you a power of good by banishing anything in the shape of Melancholia for many a long week - I will reserve particulars till I see you - Mr Parkes hath failed us - this time - but Mr Howe is here and greeteth you - You see we have rain and tempest once again - The fair summer is past and gone and the Voice of approaching Winter is already heard around us - hoarse and harsh - All conjoin in the desire to be commended to you ...

Sep 27th 1880... I'll come over and fetch you Sir if you delay much longer - so long as twelve miles lay between myself and Fishergate fear appears to have no place in your bosom - but have a care, Sir, shut up Newsham and 'make tracks'. Bright autumn has returned and we have once again right lustrous mornings and full cheerful days. I was at Mawdesley yester even. My Friends there were collecting coin and I 'picked up' a cold. If you hear of anybody having lost one they can have mine by applying promptly ...

Sep 29th 1880... I shall have great pleasure in taking a glass of water with you; and hope for an early opportunity of doing so - I am happy to inform you that we are well - with the exception perhaps of my new dog 'Frill' - he looks pale this morning and keeps his tail constantly on the travel ...

Oct 2nd 1880... You see you have put off your visit till it rains again - The bright sunshine and the balmy breezes are no more with us - but never mind my dear Sir, only come and the past shall be all forgiven - aye! I will even go so far as to lend you an umbrella - If its proportions are 'gamp' like it will be found to be an article of great service - Effective in warding off from you the pluvial distillations of the tearful clouds. I was in Southport yesterday - I am today <u>in</u> weariness ...

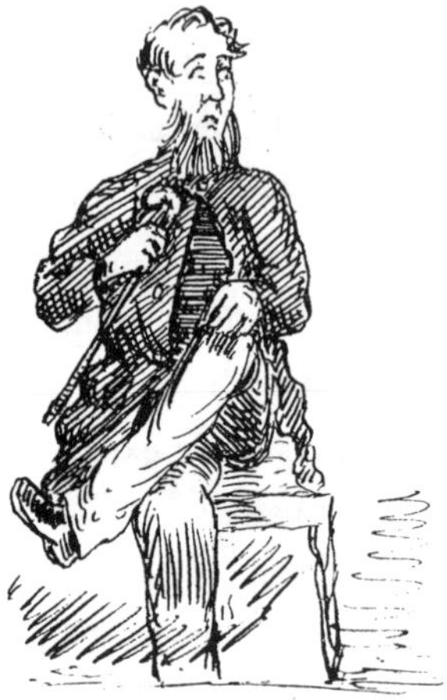

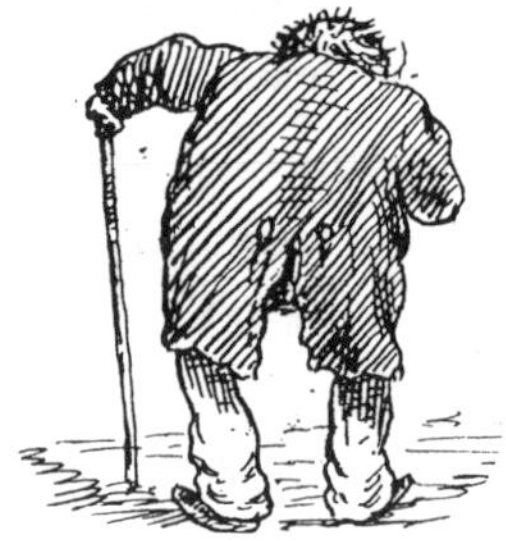

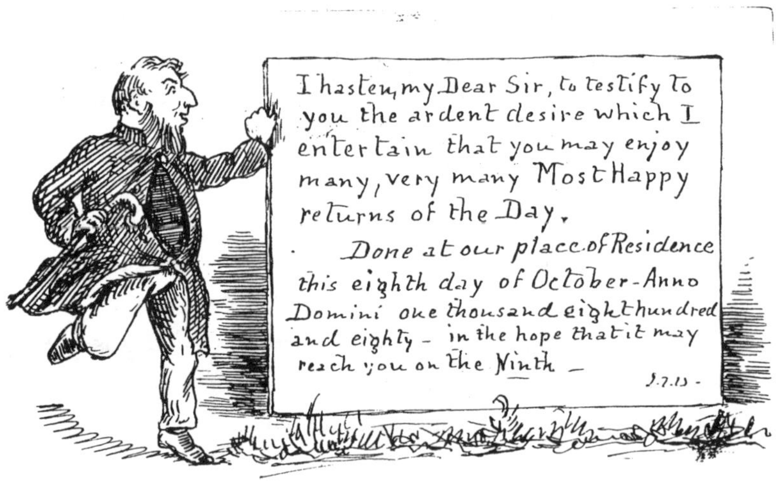
I hasten, my Dear Sir, to testify to you the ardent desire which I entertain that you may enjoy many, very many Most Happy returns of the Day.
Done at our place of Residence this eighth day of October - Anno Domini one thousand eight hundred and eighty - in the hope that it may reach you on the Ninth -

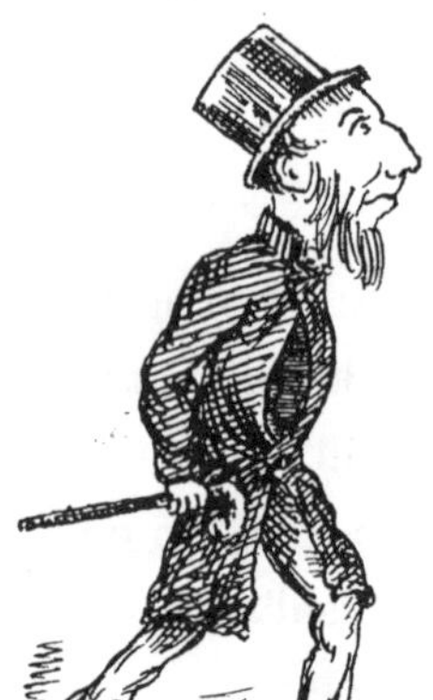

Oct 4th 1880... Here I've been waiting and waiting yet you've never come - ah! If naught but your presence would give us comfort we might go for a long time without it - Now stern winter breathes upon us and I opine that soon you may skate hither - my dear Sir. Yours disappointedly and rather starved ...

Oct 6th 1880 ... Good morning my esteemed Friend and fellow citizen you are surely not growing into an old man like myself; and yet forsooth appearances are insignificant - you neither write or come - I'll just tell you Sir, what it is - this new dog of mine, our 'Frill' - though only a pup is growing rapidly and beginning to enter upon the world of Discovery - He has already found out in a mild sort of way what his teeth are for and to what uses they can be turned - so that if you don't be coming over and make his acquaintance while yet some of the tenderness of canine infancy remains upon him he will perchance further on select a bite as the most suitable salutation when he sees you - Accept these friendly counsels and discard promptly your present condition of reticence and invisibility - The hurricane is over - calm, with leaden skies and hazy atmosphere prevails ...

... I hasten my dear Sir, to testify to you the ardent desire which I entertain that you may enjoy many, very many Most Happy returns of the Day. Done at our place of Residence this eighth day of October - Anno Domini one thousand eight hundred and eighty - in the hope that it may reach you on the Ninth ...

Oct 12th 1880... I have taken to wearing a tall hat of late and, my dear Sir, I rejoice to say that the result is satisfactory - The article is said by friends to import a gracefulness to my figure and in every way to become me exceedingly - Some say it makes me look more spiritful and energetic than I was wont during the wearing of those soft 'felt' constructions. What is your opinion of the effect generally - is it worth the outlay of 10/6 by which it has been brought about? Shall we see you this weekend? In great haste ...

Oct 13th 1880 ... Be it graceful or ungraceful I wear the tall hat under a protest. It sits uneasily and is provocative of bad feelings and it would require but little more discomfort to stimulate me into open revolt against it - I will be beguiled no more by any hatter however famous or however suasive - oh! that I had your gentle ear at hand whereinto I might pour my trouble - but - enough - Time presses & I must hie me to a close...

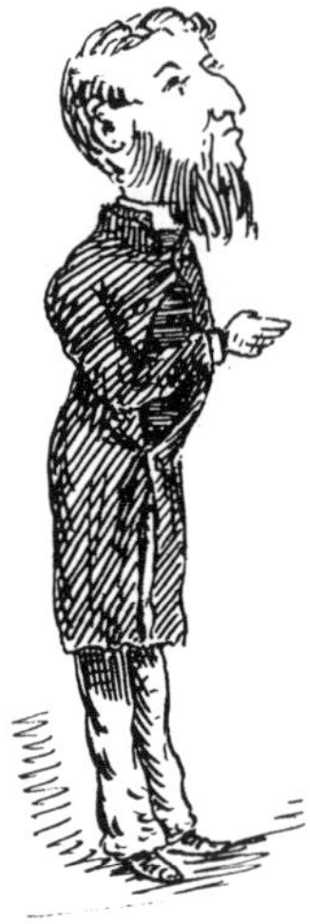

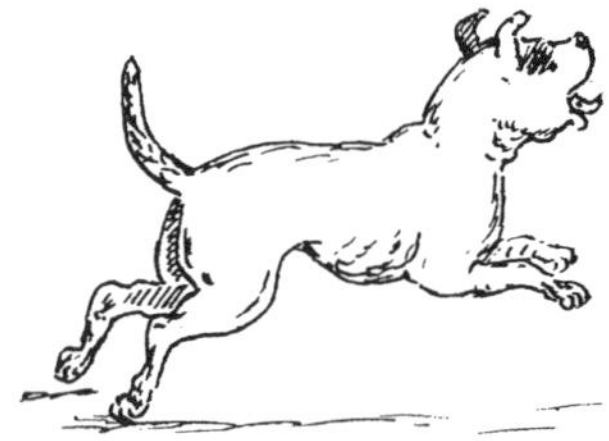

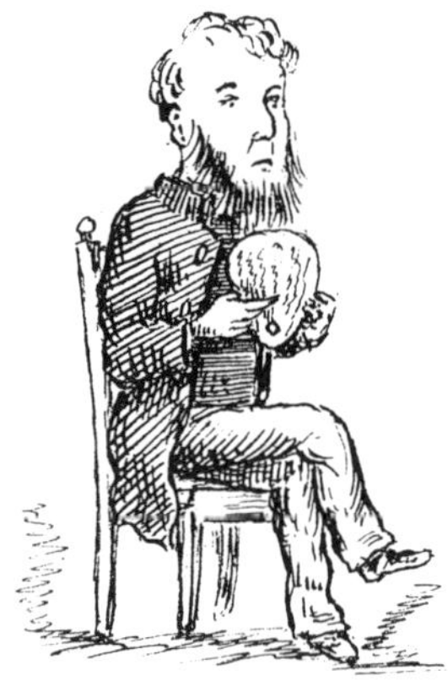

Notes

<u>Oct 22nd 1880</u>

Planchette was, briefly, a popular pastime, and consisted of a small board supported on castors and incorporating a vertical pencil. The participants each placed a finger lightly on the board, which, in reply to questions, might 'move', forming words or sentences on paper placed below the board.

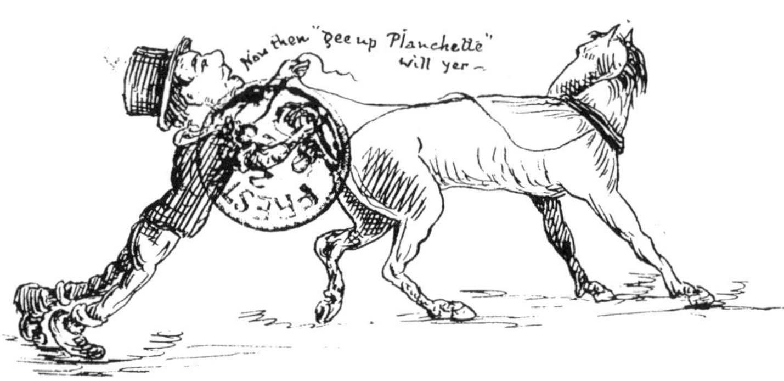

Oct 14th 1880... I am in Wigan - en route to Pemberton where I purpose staying all night - I return home tomorrow (Friday) where I shall be happy to see you on Saturday evening - 'Torpedo' is with me. We have left 'Frill' (our new dog) to keep house in our absence. He is getting very demonstrative but very docile and not dangerous. I will have his throat muzzled on Saturday so that he may not swallow you...

Monday Oct 18th 1880... Now talking about tall hats, my dear Sir, let me tell you that I detest them so much that it is always under protest I wear one - and last night - when after your departure I went forth to spend a quiet hour or so with Mr H. I left that uncomfortable, Pompey's Pillar-like head device on a convenient hat peg in this dwelling and garnished as to my head with a sensible soft felt construction pedestrianated cheerily underneath the quiet stars and blandly beaming moon - By the way have you ascertained who were the twain who had so nearly been your fellow passengers - I hope ye got safely to your destination without coolth - P.S There is rather a powerful odour of tobacco about this room this morning - It has slept here last night and not yet started on its travels ...

Oct 20th 1880... I am here in Southport amongst all the rank and fashion - the beauty and learning from other places - I have come to seek counsel about my chest - I am only here for a portion of the day and shall hie me back again as early as I can - A young lady & gentleman are abiding with us; they came to hand yester even - How long their sojourn will continue I am not informed - I have brought my tall hat because I want to wear it out speedily before the fashions change then to tall hats, farewell ...

Oct 22nd 1880... 296th day of the year ... I cannot make Planchette* do anything - In answer therefore to the enquiry what does Planchette say? my response is nothing to me anyway - I cannot get it to move - so must bring it over for a lesson - I paid down six shillings honest money for it and it seems hard that it should refuse to do something for its keep. Health and weather favourable it is not improbable you may see me and Planchette & Torpedo next week ...

... I should without fail have driven over to see you today if I had had my horse but in any case when we come we must be home again before dark - out of Preston we must be before 4 o'clock - It is as well my purchase of that horse fell through for if I had a horse just now I should have to keep a groom also to harness and unharness and attend to the horse generally...

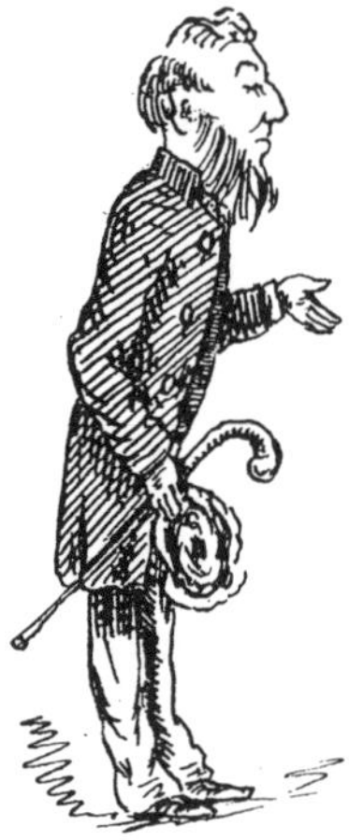

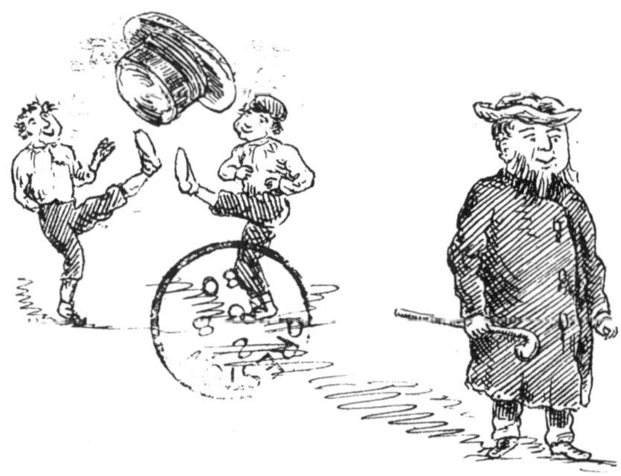

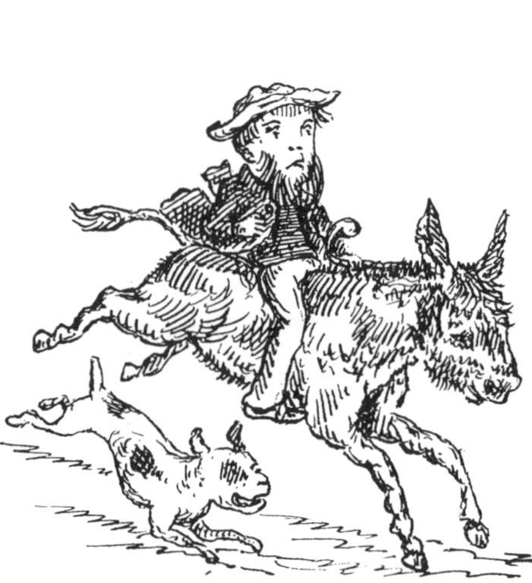

Oct 27th 1880...oo-o-o-o-oooh dither - dither - dither!!! It is cold, cold, cold, very cold - we got home at 5.20 - It is now half past and aren't we cold - It was cold and sleet in Preston but here it is cold and hurricane. I fairly tremble with the cold and fear for it seems only a question of a few minutes whether the house wont be carried away. I am on the western side of it but on the eastern one it is appalling. You see me here shivering with cold - our kindest compts are due to your sister and self for the cordial & hospitable reception of us today ...

Nov 3rd 1880... I need hardly say that I look forward with pleasure to the advent of Saturday next and trust the weather may prove propitious - The season is just now delightful - about enough frost to brace the corporeal organism and enough sunshine to remind us that summer has been and again will be - I am much engaged and must perforce be brief...

Nov 8th 1880... I am resolved that there shall be no more disputes about the qualities of our respective hats. I have abandoned my tall abomination and intend henceforth to wear only my soft and easy fitting Felt. My tall aversion I am giving to the local Football club so you may now bring your old straight up tile without fear of competition. We hope you got home safely and dry-ly ...

Nov 9th 1880... Look here Mister, this I am sure is not the thing - for how can I be expected to turn out respectable when other people wear my clothes. I'll tell you what it is - you have just gone for to put my limp Felt completely out of shape by wearing it on Sunday last and getting it wet in the storm. It hardly looks the same article. It points awkwardly out in front and sits shapeless and uneasy at the back - while the crown of it - oh my!!!! it's undescribable - It has gone more the shape of a church spire than anything else ...

... If Brother Doig will be prevailed upon to lend me his donkey the difficulty of transit will be overcome - so that 'Frill' and I might run over many a time and see you - but until this happy consummation can be attained you must really excuse my sparse visits - 'Colonel' returned safely and is well...

Nov 16th 1880... I was up and astir this morning very early - Daylight had in fact scarce struggled through my window blinds when I had finished my 'matin' shave - In mind I am revolving many projects and have much wherewith to exercise my self - Painting - plumbing, joinery, plastering, Landsurveying, begging - with the numerous etceteras which fall ordinarily to my care - Our 'Fane' will be complete towards the close of next week. I am suffering from a vacuum in my chest - I mean the chest which e'erwhile contained our Restoration Fund. More grist is needed for the Mill and on myself falls the task of seeking for it ...

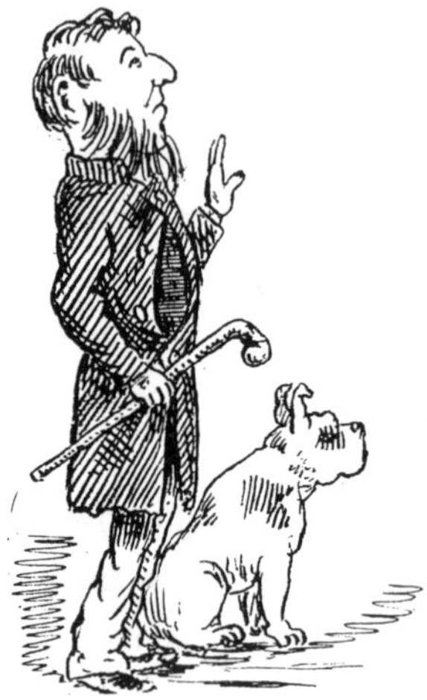

Notes

<u>Nov 23rd 1880</u> Decoration was in progress at Mr Wilson's church, money having been raised by public subscription, and Mr Worsley was a contributor.

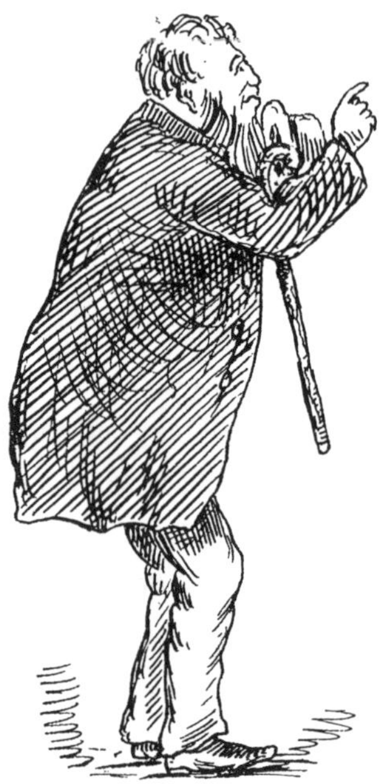

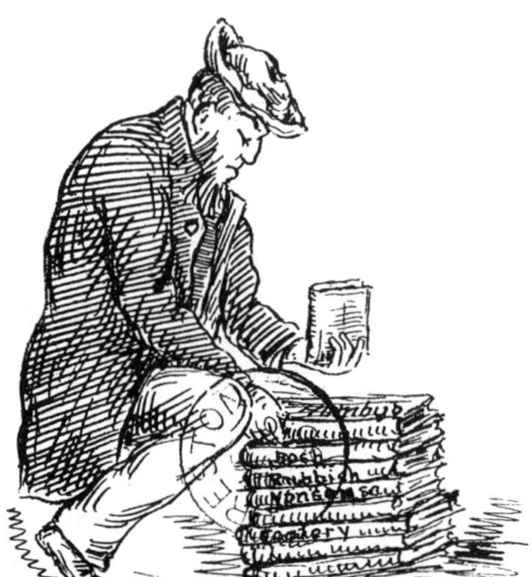

Nov 17th 1880... Now don't expect it, my dear Sir, and don't be offended - don't be offended now I beg if I don't write this next week as regularly as aforetime - for I really haven't leisure - I really haven't - I may be more at liberty by & by, but indeed for the present you must bear with me - you must indeed for I'm ever so busy. Time fails me to say more - except to solicit your kindly remembrance of me which - grant me and believe me ...

Nov 23rd 1880... You will readily understand Sir, that Frill and I are fully occupied - Frill attends to and looks after the rats and I - well what don't I attend to and look after? The dog also very faithfully accompanies me in my outgoings but during the last few days while the ground has been carpeted with white I have been at times much exercised to know which was Frill and which was snow - They seemed to get mixed somehow only poor Frill looked a little colder than the snow - I regret to inform you that my Domestic Bombshell has been & is very unwell - Though happily tokens of improvement are becoming visible - a severe cough and cold - I am myself in tolerably tidy fettle - but busy - my dear Sir, busy... P.S Decoration* still going forward they have begun your portion of the work today ...

Nov 27th 1880...I'm tired my dear Sir, I'm tired and sigh for a little rest - my eyes are much irritated by overwork and exposure over and anon to the bleak winds which have been and are holding wild revel hereaway. My sight is dim and the eyes look dark - I can scarcely read the writing on this card - Perhaps you say that's no wonder - if it was better written it would be easier read - I received a communication from an eminent and learned Government official a few days ago - I cannot tell you his name for I could not read it. It was much after the style of Planchette - the two names are one word and not a letter formed - Planchette is far the better writer ...

N.B Dec 1st 1880 ... Don't you see Sir - as I've told you before - the reason I don't write quite so often just now is I'm busy - very busy but you don't need to tell any body that I said so - you know. Thanks for your compliment per Mr Seddin - Decoration is proceeding when I went up yesterday a man was occupied lettering your portion of the work - I was at Wigan yesterday also, but stayed only two hours - During the darkness of the evening I was trucking about my neighbourhood till a late hour obedient to the calls of duty ...

Dec 6th 1880...eh, Dear Sir, these books, these books - A parcel of them reached me from London on Saturday and what, let me ask, can I do with them - I've no time for reading, for sickness and cetera, cetera, cetera keep me continually busy - On Saturday continued going straight on all day - no time to turn round - today unvaryingly turning round - no time to go straight on - one day is like another only in one thing - on each and all I'm busy - Yours, as far as I have time to be...

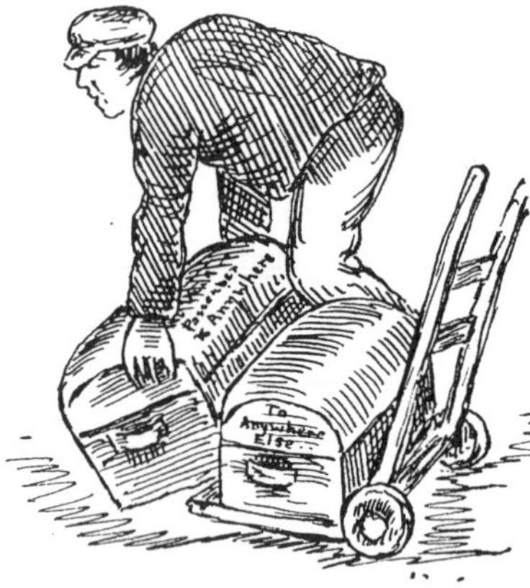

Notes

<u>Dec 14th 1880</u> Violence and terrorism were rife in Ireland as Gladstone tried to get a new Land Act (passed in August 1881) through Parliament.

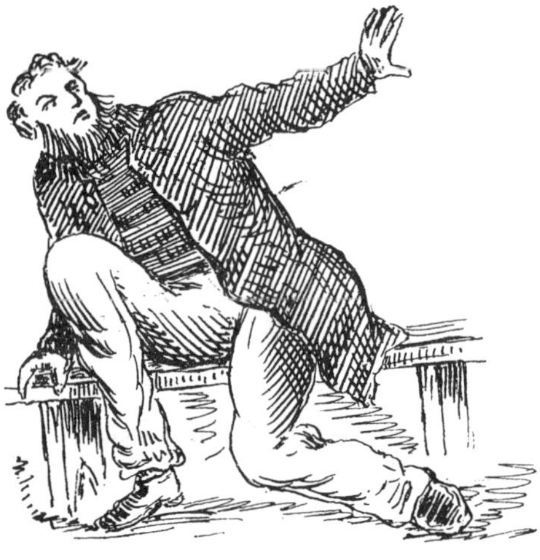

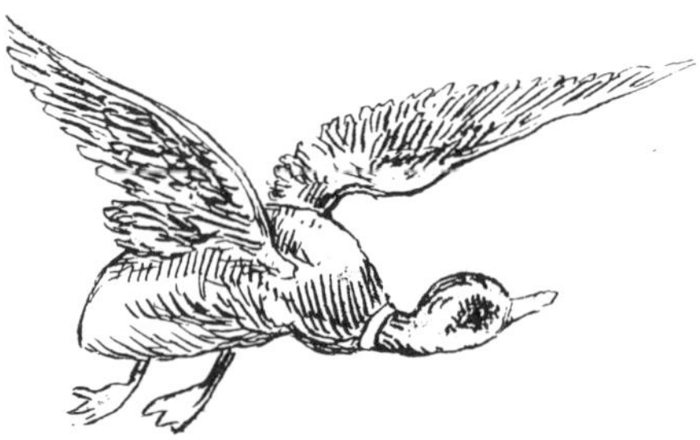

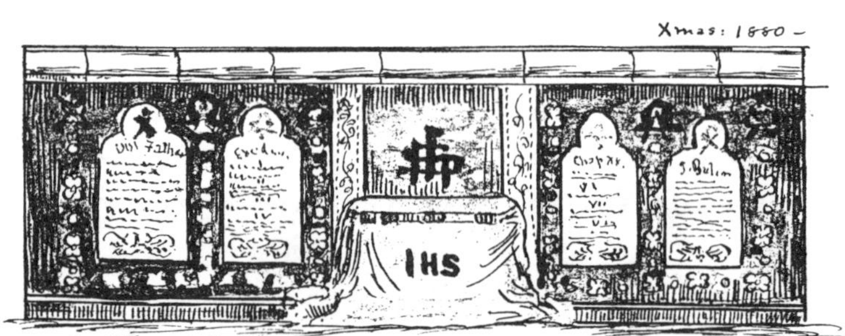

Dear Sir. The Lamp is lighted and my sight feeble at the best is yet more
dim by artificial light - but while conversing with frends who have come in
to see me I have endeavoured with a camels hair brush and such colours
as I have at my disposal to give you a sort of idea of one part of our
decoration in which you have an interest - but from uncertain sight
the strokes are to some extent haphazard and besides of course
the whole is done roughly and offhand from memory. - I got home
safely - but it was very cold by the time we got halfway hither
- The horse was very tired but the pie occupied a place of honour
in the equipage - it has been partaken by all the household today
and much enjoyed - very truly J.W.

Dec 10th 1880...I really think that if I could I would get our luggage to the nearest railway station and send off in search of health and rest - for we are both out of fettle 'Partner' makes no progress - cough worse - congestions frequent - Has not been out of doors for three weeks and without a change for the better not likely to be so for three weeks more - I am myself unfit for active duties - Headache all day yesterday and irritated eyes - If we could get well enough to seize upon a change anywhere I believe it would do us good - I expect Brother Evans on Monday - Torpedo joins me in good wishes to you & yours ...

Dec 14th 1880... I wouldn't really My dear Sir - I wouldn't for a pension live in Ireland at the present time* - If you go there for a tour don't ask me for I shan't go - I regret to say that my house is not much less of a hospital than it was when I wrote last - but hospital or no hospital I won't go to Ireland - Torpedo still laid up - but I am myself better than at the close of last week. Of your household & self we cherish kindly hopes ...

Dec 22nd 1880... Oh! o,o,oh! my dear Sir - I cannot do with this frost at all - Tumble, tumble, tumble - it's not pleasant for a man of my weight and bulk. Besides how can a man be a white man when he is black and blue all over in consequence of falling on the slippery ice. I must say that in these hard times when standing and walking are next to impossible sitting is sometimes scarcely a luxury. Torpedo has been under medical care and still is - though I rejoice to say improving nicely - We ourself are not quite so well as we would wish to be - I have been suffering from much eye irritation and today when I was felicitating myself upon a decided improvement in my left eye, cold struck suddenly into the other one - But for our condition of health we should have been in Walton at this very minute - We hope you and yours are happy and will remain so - We pray ye each and every to receive our cordial regards ...

Xmas 1880... I wish you all the Compliments of this festive Season - (excepting coughs, colds, Tic and Indigestion) and to you and yours may Christmas be amply happy - and the New Year full of Joy ...

Xmas 1880...The Lamp is lighted and my sight feeble at the best is yet more dim by artificial light - but while conversing with friends who have come in to see me I have endeavoured with a camels hair brush and such colours as I have at my disposal to give you a sort of idea of one part of our decoration in which you have an interest - but from uncertain sight the strokes are to some extent haphazard and besides of course the whole is done tonight and offhand from memory - I got home safely - but it was very cold by the time we got half way hither - The horse was very tired but the pie occupied a place of honour in the equipage - it has been partaken by all the household today and much enjoyed ...

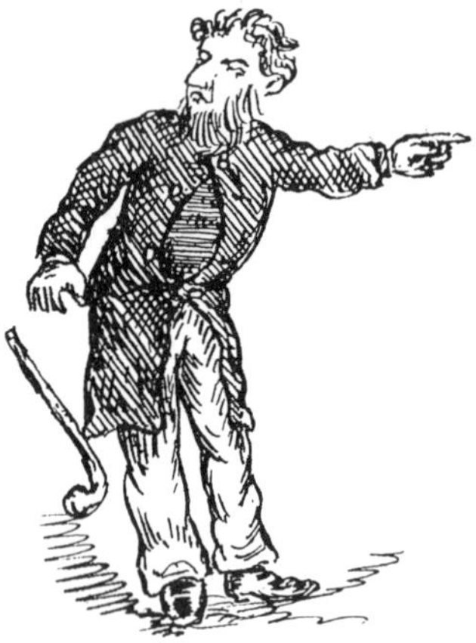

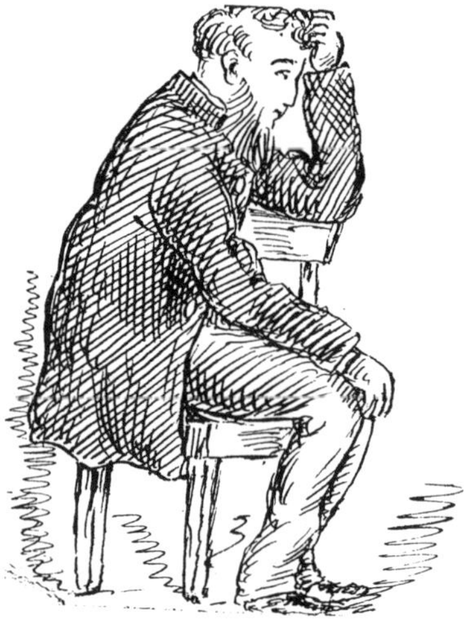

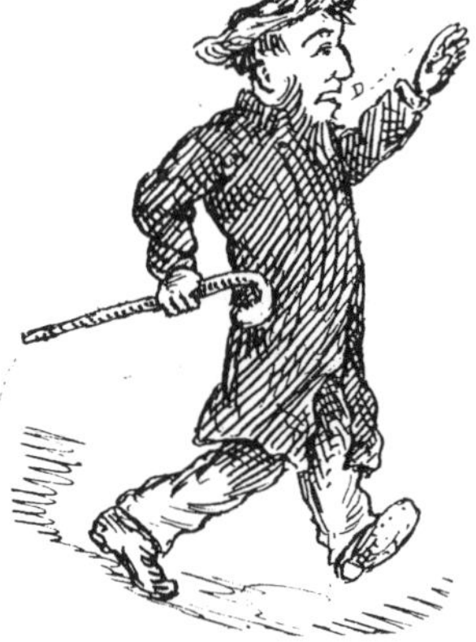

Dec 29th 1880..."Well - 'eres your werry good 'ealth and many on 'em" (as the saying is) and may the New Year be a prosperous and happy one to you and yours - From three o'clock this morning the rain has teemed unceasingly and we incline to the opinion that there has scarcely been such rain since Noah's flood. The undulating fields around us seem filled with reservoirs. I had made arrangements to visit Southport today for an hour or two but if I had been adventurous enough to make the attempt I fear the transit between Burscough and Blowick would have had to be by raft or Canal boat - not by rail - we are most of us a little better but the real Director of the Establishment still unable to face the outer air ...

Jan 3rd 1881... The Old year's knell has sounded - The hoary veteran has been laid to rest - so now I bid ye - go forth to meet the shadowy Future, without fear and with a manly heart - We have had but little sunshine since the New Year came in - The weather in fact has suggested November, rather than January - Our invalid's health is improving, but only slowly - Eyes better - appetite better - cough better - but debility and depression still linger about - I hope your sister of whose illness you spoke is well again - With all seasonable sentiments of cordiality...

Jan 8th 1881... I am sitting here puzzling my head as you see with a view to finding out or determining when I wrote you last - my cogitation proving vain I am under the necessity of going ahead irrespective of the date of my last card - The cold here is so raw and penetrating that I really cannot keep warm even by the fireside - The East wind on Thursday went very nearly to giving me Bronchitis - I know the symptoms well but timely remedies and much care helped me through it - so that I still remain free - Torpedo also much better ...

Jan 12th 1881... The whole country round about us this morning white with snow, which has fallen softly and silently during the night - to the depth of near two inches. This is very unpleasant for a person like myself who is such an easy dupe to bronchitis and have to be out and about so much just now. How fare ye? I hope well. My other self I regret to perceive has got cold again - her cough is rather worse this morning but I trust it may not prove a serious aggravation. I have just been out of doors to spread for the Robins, sparrows and other birds which favour my garden with their presence their breakfast of crumbled bread - On window sill and swept walks they are all busy and from their numbers I should conclude they have generously invited some neighbouring birds to join them. 'Frill' - our 'dorg' has been for some days indisposed. On the day his Licence came he entered for the first time on the active duties of his Station - the barking and work he did that day he has not yet recovered from ...

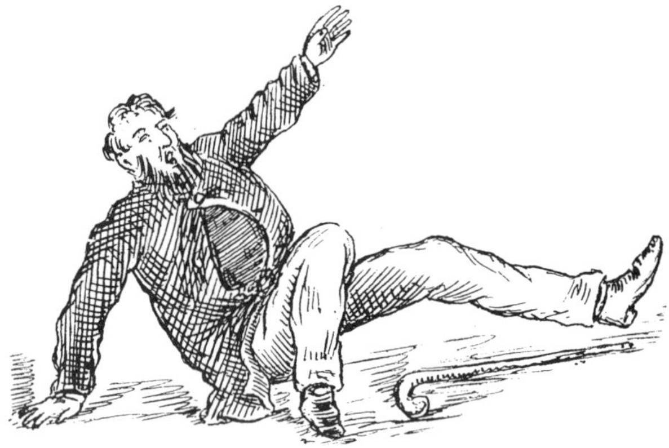

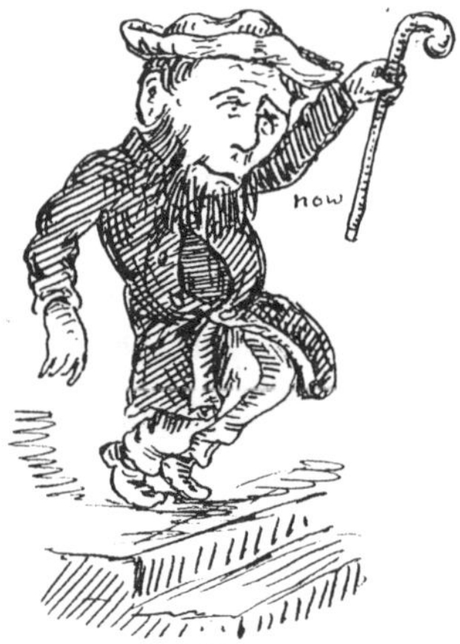

Notes

Jan 24th 1881

A severe strike of miners in Lancashire, where over 40,000 men were idle, came about as a result of disputes between masters and men over the adoption of the Employers' Liability Act. Riots broke out and the infantry was sent to keep order.

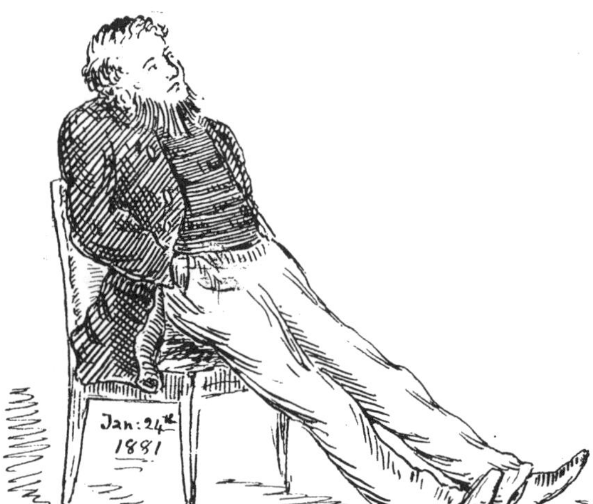

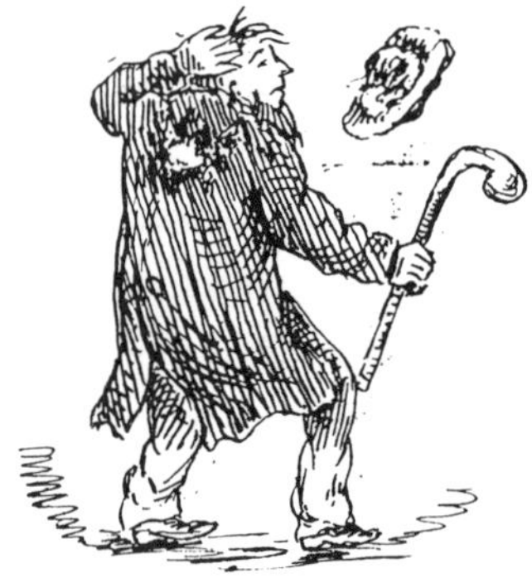

Jan 17th 1881... Have <u>you</u> measured your length yet this season upon the cold, cold ground - Really, with the snow and frost and onerous Duties of Life it is quite a labour for one to keep upright - Yesterday morning was, like last Saturday week, bitingly raw - a frozen mist drifting through the air nearly nipped off a body's ear tips - On Wednesday about noon the snow began - then yesterday about the same hour there was an additional downfall. On Saturday evening the 15th was our Tea Party - in spite of snow and cold there was a full muster. Our taps are frozen - all water has to be fetched from a distance - The snow is from nine to eleven inches in depth and rapidly 'balls' on the soles of one's boots - again I say those who like old fashioned winters are welcome to them for my part I give preference to something milder. Hope you are well ...

Jan 19th 1881... now me darlint It's not for the likes uv me to be afther venturing out into such dape snow at all, at all - a bitter east wind yesterday - more snow falling - meself with a bad cold, and my domestic superior back into Bronchitis coupled with the horrors of ear ache - no sleep last night - Today much exhausted - The cough at times almost suffocating. I want to go out but hesitate to put my feet off the clane door step into the swate cold snow lest the cold of my feet should increase the cold in me head and completely fraze the Tay when I'm afther drinkin it - No Standard reached me yesterday so that I don't know if the Lague - the Land Lague I mean has yet completely swallowed the rint...

Jan 24th 1881... I have heard of your devotion to meteorological studies - until half past 2 a.m Brother Mason Sale tells me ye kept watch and ward anxiously scanning the sky and noting the portents of the weather. What a fortune we might make if we could only dry this snow and sell it for salt. I was in Wigan on Saturday last - The Town seemed to be in much disorder - streets filled with miners and military.* Present to all your family assurance of our sincere regard...P.S Domestic Superior still an invalid ...

Jan 27th 1881 (morning)... I always consider that the most disagreeable part of snow falls is the snowballs - and after the sleet of last night the deep lying snow all about us is in splendid condition for manipulation by those thoughtlessly energetic youths who delight to make travelling unpleasant and perilous to us old folks who have to trudge on foot along Life's pathway - The health of my 'domestic superior' is better in some respects but an invalid prisoner still - The improvement brought about in one day is banished in the next - as for ourself we have we are thankful to say, had singularly good health considering the changeable and sometimes piercing winter. On the whole we have little sickness in our neighbourhood...

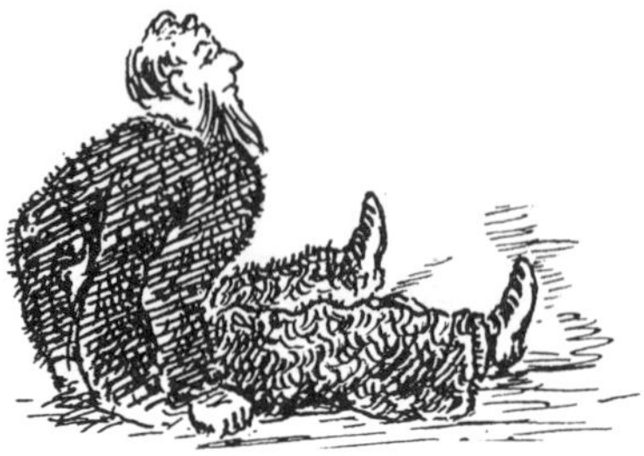

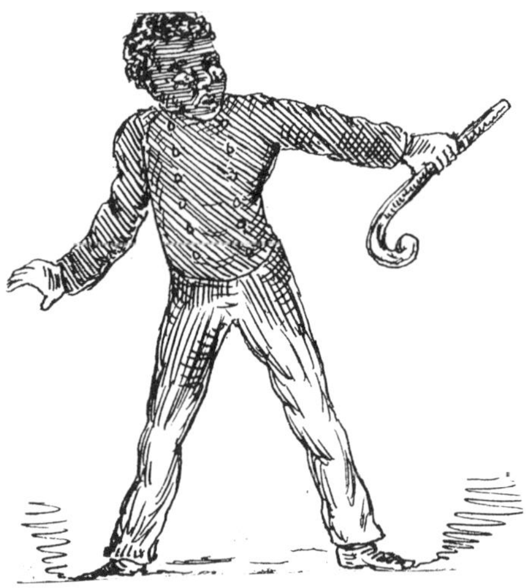

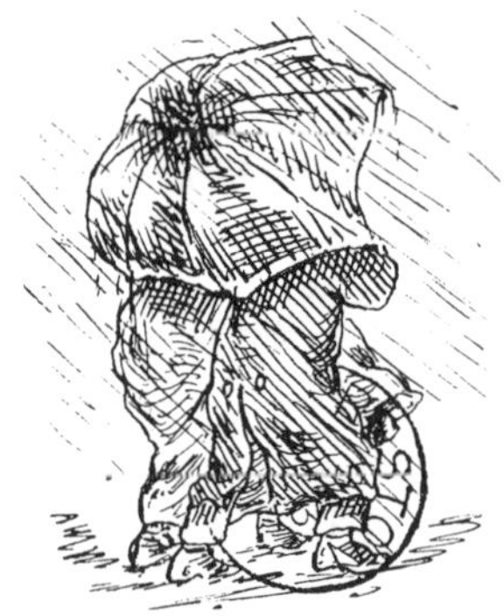

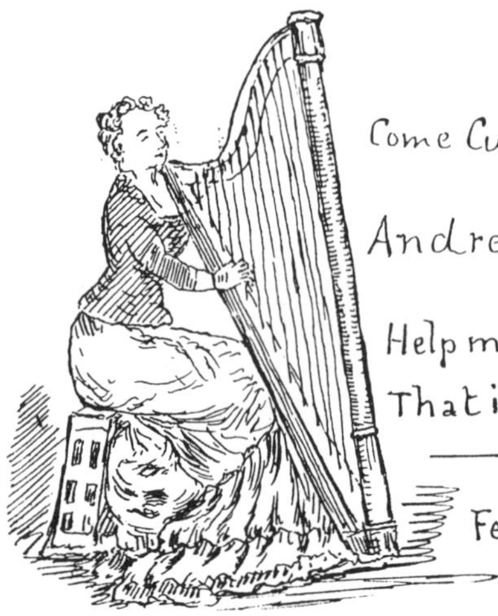

Come Cupid, stay thy flutt'ring
Wing
And rest thee near me while I
Sing:
Help me to tune this Harp of mine,
That it may charm my Valentine.

Feast of the Loving Saint
1881

Jan 31st 1881... I was thoroughly down on that snow and am heartily thankful that it is gone - we have again got frost with us but I hope the snow will keep off. I am sorry to hear of the cause of your visit to Leamington? Poor Fred, his life was brief. How are things in Preston? Here they are flat enough and in Wigan a hundred fold worse - what is the present anarchy going to culminate in -? Looking round the world we surely see now distress of Nations with perplexity - My fairer moiety is I am glad to say improving again - I sincerely hope she may soon be well. When think ye of coming our way?...

Feb 3rd 1881... Just a line to inform you my dear Mister that my better half is greatly improved in health and has during this present week been out several times. The rain yesterday and today have been a sore hindrance to our outdoor exercise - We should have visited Southport today had not the rain come down so heavily this morning and thwarted our purpose. How fare ye in Preston? I assume that ye like ourselves are now freed from snow - there remaining only here and there the remnant of a drift to remind us that there has been winter. The roads are a little quieter there having been for the past two days fewer wanderers in search of alms. Our charioteer 'Nicholas' is very ill - Bronchitis. Are you coming this weekend? We can furnish accommodation and shall rejoice to see you. Frill has just caught a mouse ...

Feb 5th 1881... The outlook hereaway is just now miserable for a rain is pouring heavily but I am told the Dress Circle at the Alexandra Theatre Liverpool on the afternoon of Monday the 24th day of January in this year of grace one thousand eight hundred and eighty one looked beautiful - very beautiful and in some respects rather suggestive of Preston. Many thanks for the evening paper which you were kind enough to send me - It was surpassing in interest - Parliamentary news is just now lively reading - To each and all dear Sir our love ...

Feb 9th 1881... The storms have ceased & the sun shines forth once more - I hope for the felicity of your presence this weekend...

Feb 11th 1881... As our King Coffee Calcalli sends the golden axe so my master sends his stick saying he awaits you this weekend - another disappointment like rejection of axe means war... Your humble servant Sambo...

Feast of the Loving Saint 1881... Come Cupid, stay thy flutt'ring wing And rest thee near me while I sing; Help me to tune this harp of mine That it may charm my Valentine...

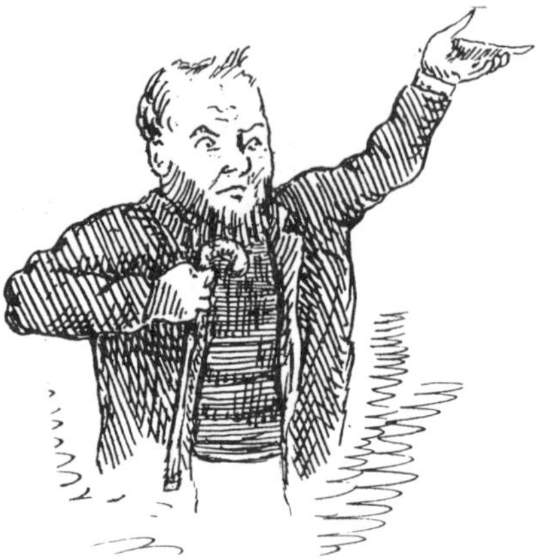

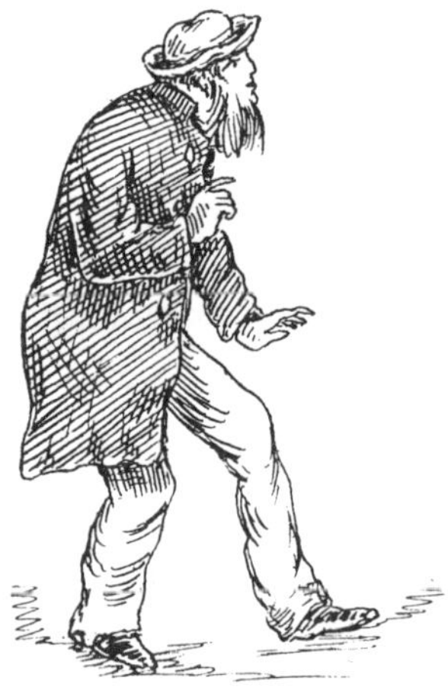

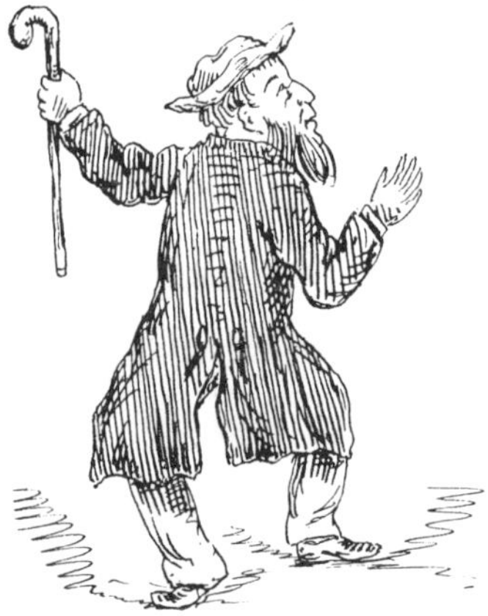

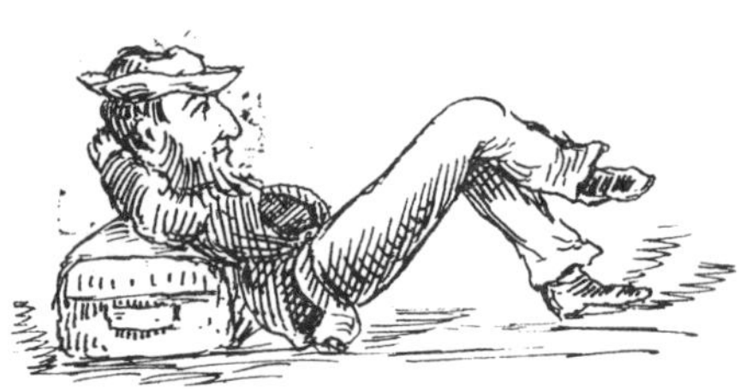

Feb 14th 1881... You did well, Sir, You did well in going home last evening and I cannot too highly applaud your wisdom for it really is not fit to turn a reindeer out this morning - nor know I of a surety whether the persistent and sweeping rainfall would not avail to wet through even the great coat of a Hippopotamus - A seal would hardly endure it for a moment - and even a Rhinoceros methinks would scarcely venture out wishing for the loan of an umbrella - We have decided not to leave home this week in consequence of funerals - therefore if there be a fine day come ye.. come one, come all, come young, come old, come great, come small.. all combine in amity and I am ...

Feb 19th 1881... I approach my task with nervous timidity - Having been so busy all week I had nigh forgotten to communicate to you the fact that we intend, purpose and design to visit Walton or Kirkdale during the week next ensuing - It is withal likewise within the scope of our intention to glide to and fro through the streets of Wigan on the Monday if so be that the begging obstructionists who therein do congregate will permit us - A Masonic Brother of yours from Southport hath abiden here this week and went hence no later than yester 'even'...

Feb 21st 1881... I have not had a minute to spare for I am right off this moment to Wigan - Torpedo has already started. In fact she is walking leisurely on before with the understanding that I shall overtake her. A nasty keen east wind blowing - a forbidding sort of morning - Tomorrow we are due in Liverpool or some other foreign part not much wide of it - We purpose spending a few days thereaway - We are going thither for change of air and scene. Receive our best wishes ...

Feb 23rd 1881... ah, my dear Sir, I'm a great traveller I've got as far as Liverpool, nay I have penetrated even to Kirkdale - and now I'm resting awhile in my wandering - 'Pedo is with me - We may hasten homeward any time - our stay in these foreign regions depending greatly upon how the air agrees with us - It is of course a great change from our fields and dells where conies sport at will, and Fairies saltate. Though distant ever truly yours ...

Feb 24th 1881... You must know my good Sir that it is not our intention to remain here for ever. We have visited the river - been aboard ship - Inspected the public buildings and permitted the corporation to retain them - Partner & self are both well and have enjoyed ourselves muchly - a nice sharp frost this morning makes us feel quite at home - and it is our purpose to return thither tomorrow - getting ready now in fact - with love to everybody I remain... P.S. atmosphere thick & raw but still we're hopeful...

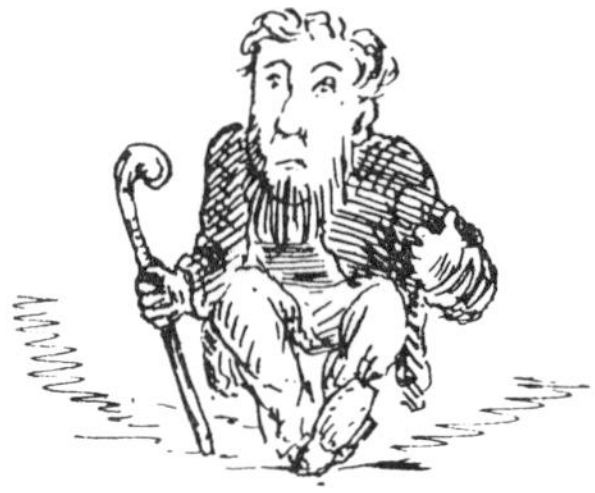

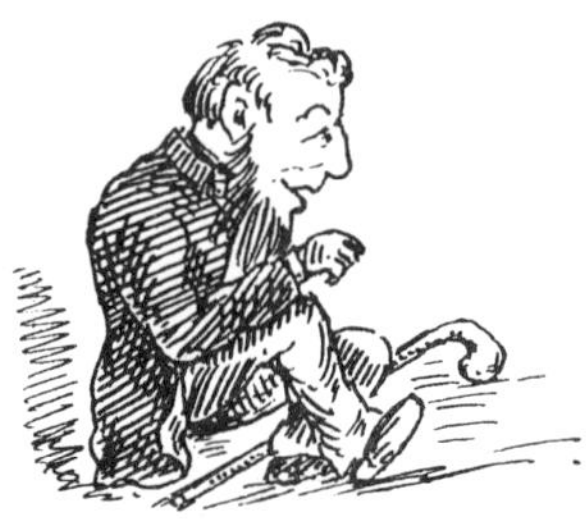

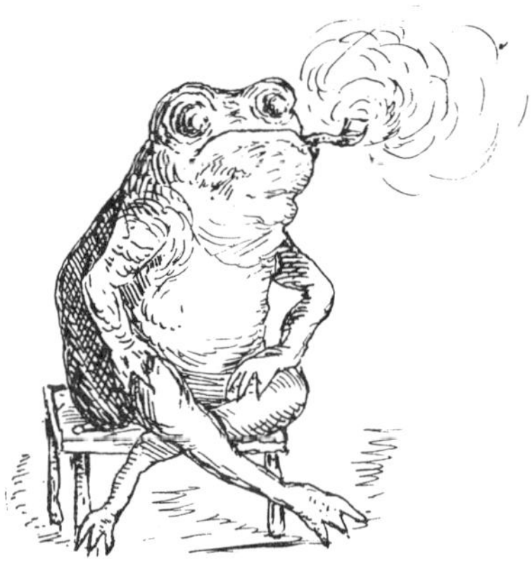

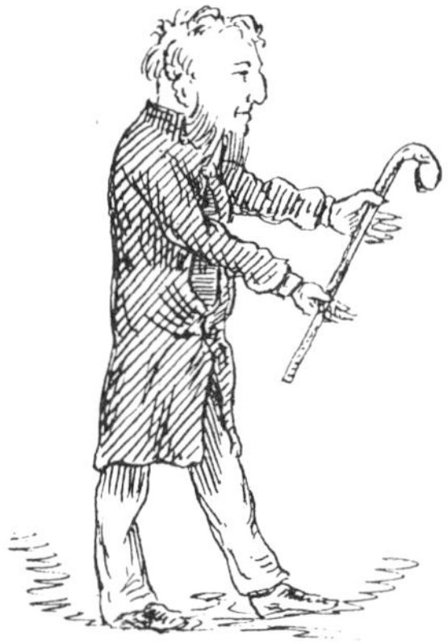

Feb 26th 1881... I am back again, my dear Sir, from that 'ere what d'ye call 'em - we've both had much enjoyment - but are tired, very tired and stand now in much need of rest and tranquillity - This we intend trying for at home before setting off somewhither again - We got hither last night. Have had no time to read a news paper while I have been away and so when I have written a few cards it is my intention to devote the morning to reading through the Standards which have accumulated during my absence - We shall be at home all this next week so you may drive over with pretty safe expectation of finding us - we have no one with us - House empty - snow on house tops and yet more falling - Hail stones at 11.30 last night ...

Feb 28th 1881... If, as you say, I'm smirking - it is a smirk of satisfaction for don't you see I'm having a rest and getting over my fatigue nicely - What shall you be doing on Wednesday? Could ye not all come hither and look at us - The ground is slightly white but as the sun is shining brightly the whiteness may have all vanished by Wednesday - Tomorrow, Tuesday, I am thinking of going to Wigan to take my niece a pancake - leastways to eat, or toss and eat one with her - 'cum on Wensdy' as aforesaid - With love from all of us ...

March 3rd 1881... I'll tell you what, Mister, this weather isn't suitable for the likes uv me - where is the dewy grass? - under the snow, where the rippling Brooks? - Icebound all of 'em. Where the ponds & pits for bathing, sport and fishing -? Frozen, aye frozen, each and all - Tis enough to make one sit and Fume - Tis thus we dwellers in the country feel keen winter muchly - and ere ye come not to our rescue - our solitude ye break not in upon - well be it so - we await with patience Saturday the Twelfth, the moon and ye - Meanwhile believe me shiveringly yet warmly...

March 9th 1881... This stick and I have travelled many a mile since the 'Day Orb' arose on Monday - ah me - 'twas one o'clock this morning when I stepped inside my domicile and sought repose - but as I sank into slumber the elements awakened and howling gales from the west suggested the existence of an atmospheric coercion Bill operating over Ireland and occasioning a rush hither. The snow is all gone, in fact it disappeared on Saturday - we are all well and look for your appearance & that of others also on Saturday 'so mite it be'...

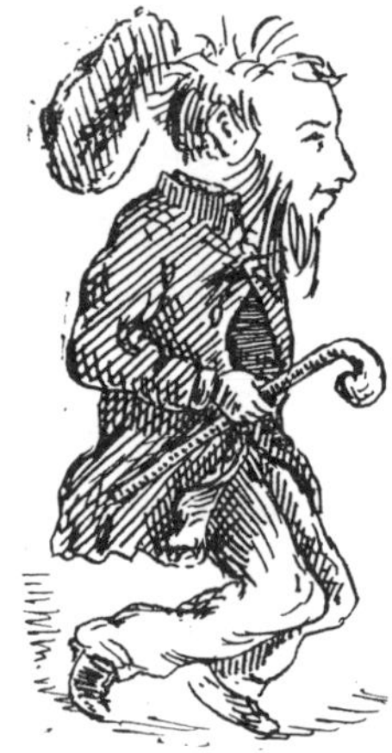

<u>Notes</u>

<u>March 9th 1881</u> Pinguid = fat.

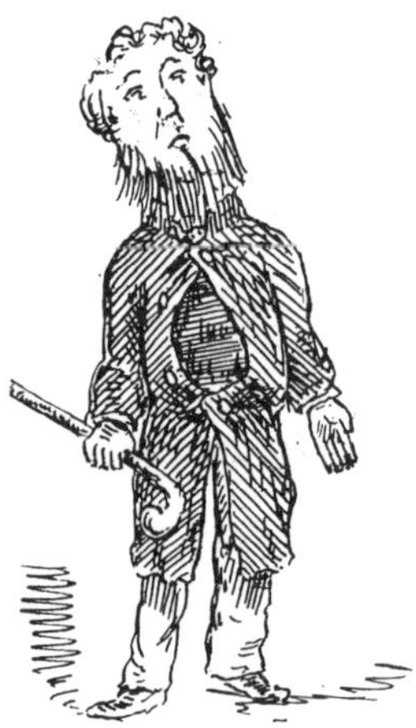

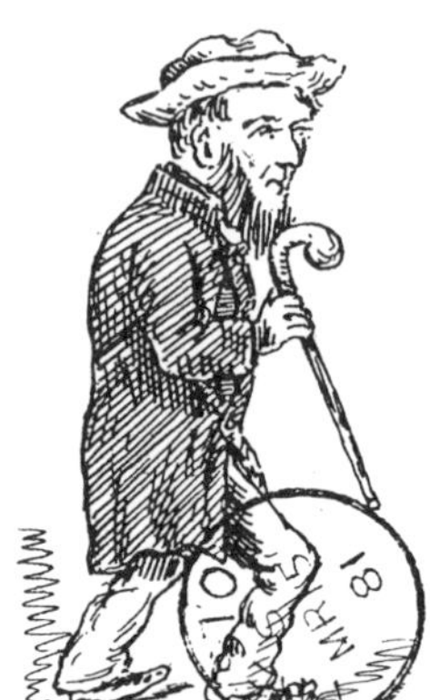

March 9th 1881... I'll tell you what my dear Sir the storm that has been afoot all this day and is raging with yet greater uproar and riot this evening is enough to blow one into the middle of next week - outside it is really difficult to stand - I am reminded very forcibly by it of the tempest which a little past seven o'clock on the evening of 28th December 1879 blew the Tay Bridge to pieces - My shutters are closed and the curtains drawn but through it all I hear distinctly the howling hurricane and pattering rain - and the curtains wave about in quite a spirited fashion - I thought to have been in Southport for an hour or two today but, ah no, I knew better - Frill is getting quite fat. He is now a pinguid* or obese quadruped and becoming useful - He will actually bark at last if a tramp accidentally treads on his toes.. P.S letter just come alright...

March 10th 1881... of course, you know, we can't help the weather - It is not in your power nor in mine to secure calmness and sunshine - therefore we must reconcile ourselves to things as they are and they are stormy - much as I regret the necessity for postponement of your visit I feel that it is even better thus till ye can hither come with reasonable prospect of suitable meteorological conditions. The days too are lengthening fast so that shortly be there moon or no moon ye may be assured of light enough to subserve the purpose of your return journey. I had time and space only to add a line to the card this morning and that line had reference to the contents of your letter...

March 12th 1881... Permit me in the elegant and refined phraseology of this enlightened nineteenth century to ask you with reference to future arrangement & fixtures as to visit &c 'What's yer little game?' How expressive !!!! How elastic is our 'Mother Tongue'!! How figurative and noble our language in this age of universal education. Really English, as often spoken, must be heard to be appreciated - and though appreciated it cannot be always understanded of the people. My enquiry however is plain enough to be repeated 'What's yer little game?' ...

March 15th 1881... I am setting off through the week with a host of engagements and not feeling in exactly the choicest of fettle for meeting them - yet an ye be so minded I shall be hereaway on Saturday to receive ye should ye elect to come - I am today expecting a visit from the Brother of a Brother Mason of yours from Southport - Today is fine but fogs are usual at Eventide - Torpedo well - wants to set a gardener at work but the ground is too heavy and wet - I did a little pruning yesterday ...

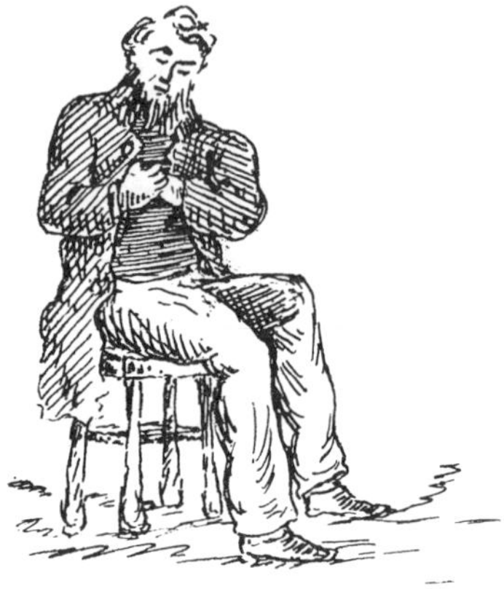

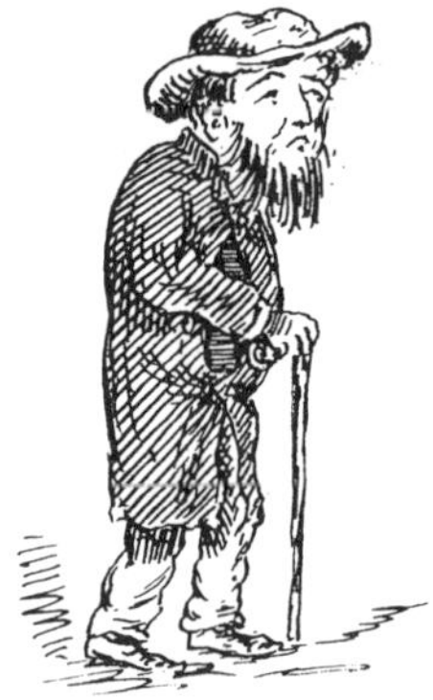

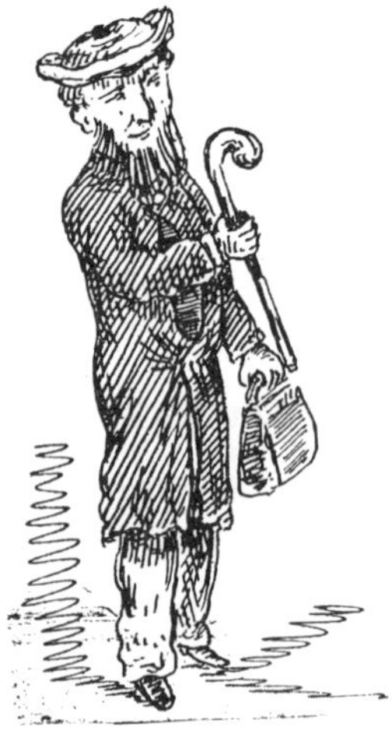

March 19th 1881... eh, dear, I'm done up entirely - I've been abroad since I wrote you last - Anyway I've been to Pemberton - call it what you will. I went forth a hale strong man but have returned a creechy, and complaining hunch back - I've a cold - a cough - a crick in my neck, and complaining rheumatism across the shoulders and upper portion of my back - I got home in good time yester Even - but quickly as I came the cold got up me before I went to bed - We are again in the midst of howling winds - raving tempests, fierce storms - ah, when is the spring time due - Fondly long we for it - ah, me! this rheumatism - Painfully yours ....

March 21st 1881... see, my dear Sir, it is my intention to go abroad again this week - If the weather be fine - health good; and no valid obstacle opposing we are minded to meet his Lordship of Liverpool in Wigan on Wednesday next - we shall afterward abide perchance a day or two in Pemberton - the Torpedo wants a change of air - as the atmosphere here is fine and pure and that in Pemberton is rich in smoke, and impure - the change will be a complete one and that is precisely what is wanted - when we have inhaled a sufficiency of smoke this week we purpose going to Southport next week to adulterate it with ozone - 'Frill' has caught a 'flea' - I don't know where he caught it; but he has been out hunting all morning and has brought it back with him - He is a clever dog is that Frill - agreeable in disposition and pleasant in manners. You should just see him making a bow - I mean of course a 'bow wow'. Receive the tribute of our esteem...

March 23rd 1881... as I threatened you a few days ago I am come to meet his Lordship of Liverpool but oh my! I'm bowed down, drawn in and disquieted by an attack of rheumatism. I caught them on my last visit to Pemberton but they did not set in till the day I got home - However I know very well by the feel of 'em that they are Pemberton rheumaticks - From the base of the skull down the 'back' of my neck and across the shoulders of my 'back' - that's where I feel 'em - and that's where they sit enthroned - and after some days intimate acquaintance with them I with unquestioning confidence pronounce them the Pemberton rheumatics - when they are in good form and active they cause me to look considerably less perk and brisk than usual ...

March 24th 1881... I told you we came over here to meet his Lordship but ah me! what could anyone do with such weather as we came on - why, look you here! My stick was useless - we had to borrow umbrellas instead - and glad to get them - Rain fell and wind blew to such an extent that we frlt compelled to escape to and remain within shelter. This is our second vain attempt to meet his Lordship - on both occasions the rain and storm intervened to thwart our purpose - We are going home now - that's something, so no more at present ...

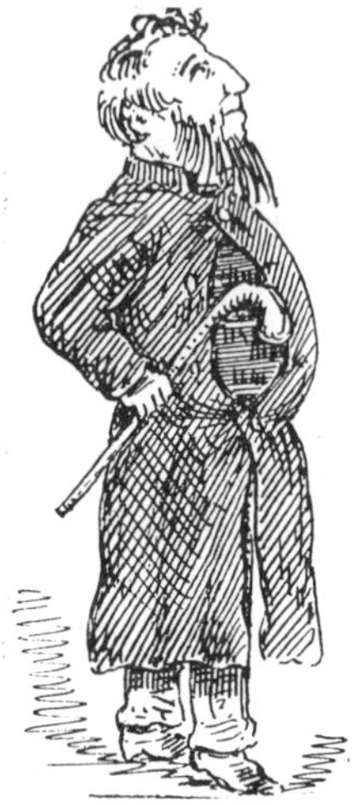

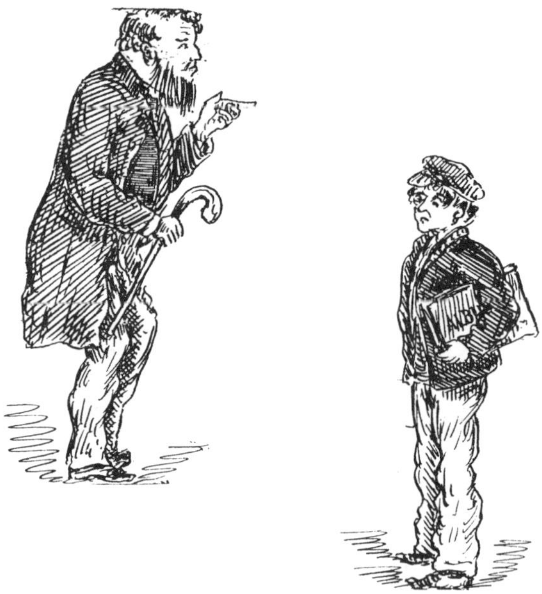

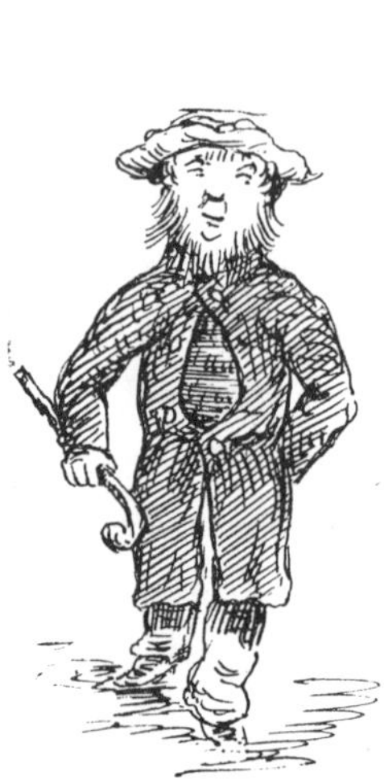

March 29th 1881...Southport.. I am come for the waters at Southport - I'm getting too stout - really too stout - It is quite time I did something so I've come here for I'm not only getting too stout but too stout for anything - in fact I'm almost too stout to go to sleep, especially with the rheumatiz...

April 1st 1881... Look here, Sir, If your master has got that bound and you are taking it home - just tell 'what's his name?' at 63 Fishergate Preston that I am home again - and now the weather is fine we shall be pleased to see him and his tomorrow if he be minded. We expect a house full at Easter - now mind what I say & tell him - I'm in haste...

April 4th 1881... Now just you look here - Sirrah it is precisely 20 minutes past 9 o'clock and though I have, as I told you - walked already a matter of 9 or ten miles, I feel that I could, without discomfort, at this late hour take up my trusty stick and go forth for another 4 or 5 miles pedestrianation - It would in fact merely stimulate the circulation a little and procure me an appetite for sleep - However it is not my intention to go out - The East wind still blows and I am aware that I possess a chest and that I am by reason its most natural protector. You and convoy will by this time doubtless be at home - my earnest hope is that ye have got thither without accident or cold - Receive our very natural affection ...

April 6th 1881... You see this, don't you? You will recognise it doubtless as my stick - That trusty staff which is the unfailing attendant of my walks - The Miser 'Elwes' left his hoarded gains and got him hence - The Great 'Napoleon' after Waterloo left his coach and fled - James II left his throne and betook himself to exile - 'Peace' left his name of infamy and sought the gallows for repose - Your boys yesterday left their sticks behind them - The two long straight rods which I cut for them - on the Hill. Now you would not have caught me leaving my stick for something - No, my trusty stick I stick to - I bear it in remembrance and make it an object of my care. I will treasure their forgotten sticks and let them season - so that they will be more serviceable when next they take them in possession ...

April 11th 1881... come, I don't like this - it's two (sic) bad - how many times now have you promised - and disappointed us -? Ah me! Ah, me that faithless men Should deceive us once and yet again; Should keep us poised on 'expectation's toe' Then never come, ah woe, ah, woe - Saturday was beautiful - sunshine and warm - I felt confident of seeing you early and so put off or set aside all engagements which might prevent me bearing you company in a ramble - our lady guest left us on Tuesday or Wednesday last but returns with Miss L on Thursday or Saturday next - The 'Columnal' Colonel or shall we say General is inspecting his forces in Wigan whither he marched on Friday ...

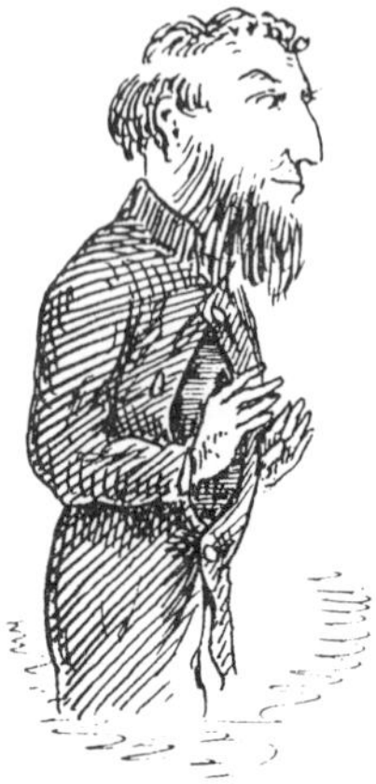

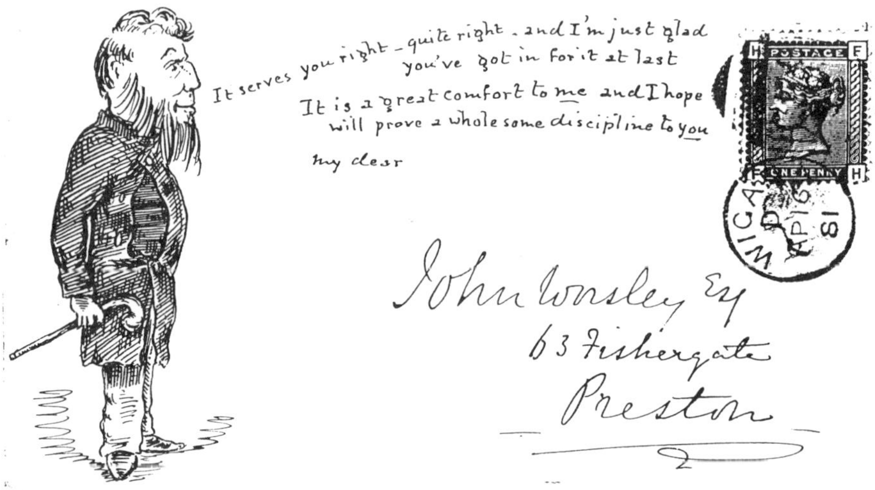

Notes

<u>April 19th 1881</u> A spiritualist called Fletcher and his wife were accused of obtaining property by fraud from a Mrs Hart-Davis. They convinced her that her dead mother was sending messages that she should give them her jewellery.

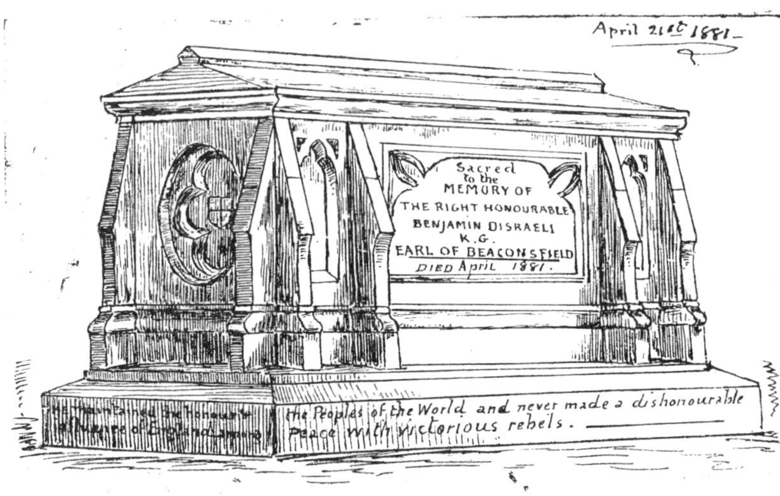

April 12th 1881... I shall be sorry indeed to have the necessity imposed upon me of coming over to Preston and through the instrumentality of a powerful stick instilling into you a regard for our feelings and a tenderness toward our expectations - The importance also of keeping promise and fulfilling covenants - I trow my trusty staff wielded by an arm nerved by a sense of right on the one hand and of wrong on the other would not be long in producing an impression either for better or worse. If I write confusedly rather - I write under strong emotion & with a desire that my stick should suggest more in the way of indignation and retribution than is really conveyed by my hasty indiction - Promptly start forth on the pathway of amendment and 'trek' vigorously - with many a scrunch or scrunch on scrunch. I speak after the manner of spiritualists ...

April 14th 1881... now look here, Mister, will you kindly say how many times, in your opinion, an invitation ought to be repeated in order to be binding - Thunders of denunciation - clouds of wrathfulness - and a pattering rain of fierce invective rang through this dwelling (figuratively) when our hopes were blighted and our fond desires found to be ungratified - I wouldn't be you for something, when next the General commanding in chief hereaway sets eyes on you! The lightning flashes of a direful anger will gleam about you with a terrible brilliance & power which once experienced will not be soon forgotten - However as you have made your bed so you must lie on it - The way of transgressors is more often paved with rough granite sets than made smooth with asphalts or McAdam ...

April 16th 1881... It serves you right - quite right - and I'm just glad you've got in for it at last. It is a great comfort to <u>me</u> and I hope will prove a wholesome discipline to <u>you</u> ...

April 19th 1881... I feel a little tired and no wonder. I have scarce recovered from the fatigues of Eastertide - The nasty East winds too catch us very powerfully and make us almost cough our heads off. The Eastern gales are as unpleasant to us as the Eastern Question is to the powers - The Hart-Davis v. Fletcher (spiritualist) trial* is at last concluded & I suppose the convicted female impostor is now enjoying the 'scrunch' of Justice - The Babes are with me - They are playing with their dolls and whispering in close proximity to my ears - Family cares as discussed by two loquacious maidens in stage whispers are to say the least of it distracting to a scribe. Miss L is here but speaks of returning to her own dwelling on Thursday next - The Post just this minute here - In haste ...

April 21st 1881... Sacred to the memory of the Right Honourable Benjamin Disraeli K.G Earl of Beaconsfield died April 1881.. He maintained the honour & influence of England among the Peoples of the World and never made a dishonourable Peace with victorious rebels ...

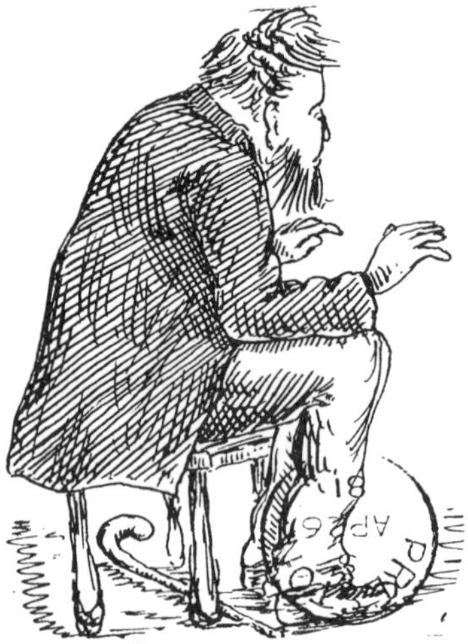

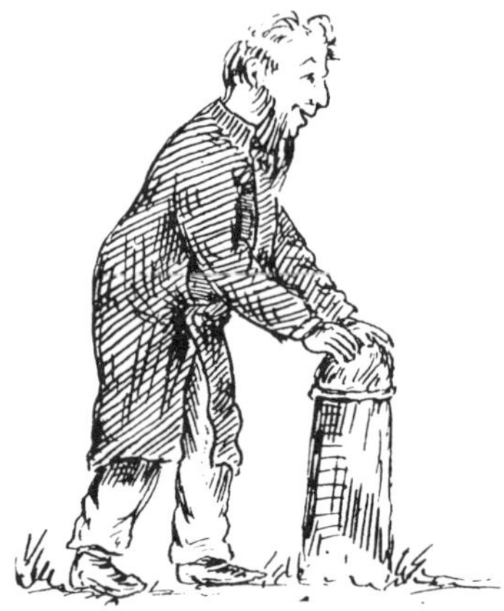

Notes

April 28th 1881 — The election of Francis Powell was disputed on the grounds of bribery by his agents, and a Commission was set up which found the claim to be well founded, with evidence of extensive corrupt practices during the Wigan borough elections.

April 23rd 1881... I sit convicted of folly - I both feel and look simple: for I have walked myself footsore - a thing which a person at my time of life ought not to have done - on returning from Wiggin on Friday - long ere I reached my journey's end I felt a weary pilgrim - when I smiled as I can't help doing (ye know our cheerful disposition) it was like a grimace of pain rather than the effect of pleasure - We have today had the first instalment of our garden seeds inserted in the earth - Before the gardener had quite completed his task it began to rain beautifully - Just the thing to make things grow - I don't remember when we got them in so happily before - we smile a grimace once more ...

April 26th 1881... It has been as much as I could do to keep myself warm during the late East winds - I have crouched over the fire nearly the whole day through endeavouring to obtain therefrom a little warmth - The weather even now is not sultry but the cold is less keen than it was erewhiles - I was in Southport yesterday accompanied by my 'House Marshal commanding in chief' - we both feel knocked up today - we begin to opine that it does not do for old people to walk so much - we indulge full many a grunt at aching bones and weary limbs...

April 28th 1881... It's a grand morning - a glorious morning, my dear Sir - but do you know I begin to think that my days for dancing, jumping and other frivolous pleasures are over for I really this morning could not by placing my hands upon it muster spring enough to take a fly over this low post - I walked to the station at Appley Bridge yesterday but rode back - I also did a little pedestrianism in Wigan town and Park & this morning I feel as stiff as a poor old horse that has had a few days of too hard work - I am writing this at six o'clock A.M! I am the only one astir & have scarcely power to stir ...

April 28th 1881 Number 2 card 8.40 AM... The cuckoo was seen yesterday - we have heard it this morning for the first time this year - The fruit trees are unfolding beautifully into leaf and the hedge rows in places are quite green - This is the anniversary of our marriage and my better half, to wit the 'House Marshal commanding in chief' being minded to signalise the occasion by acts of tenderness and forgiveness, commands us to signify her intention to sink in oblivion the disappointments and covenant-breakings of the past - It is her purpose to banish from her usuage the formulary of invitation - She bids me therefore say that when ye are disposed to come - what you have to do is not wait for an invitation but to come and take your luck of the larder - These are the latest orders from our domestic 'War Office' - The Right Reverend the Lord Bishop of the Diocese holds a confirmation at Standish tomorrow at 11-0AM. We are due there at the hour named. I was informed yesterday that there is to be a Commission of Enquiry into Bribery & Corruption at Wigan* - News is said to have reached the Town yesterday morning...

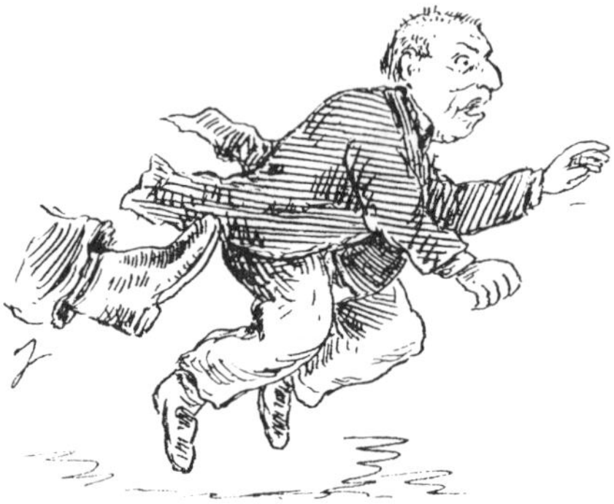

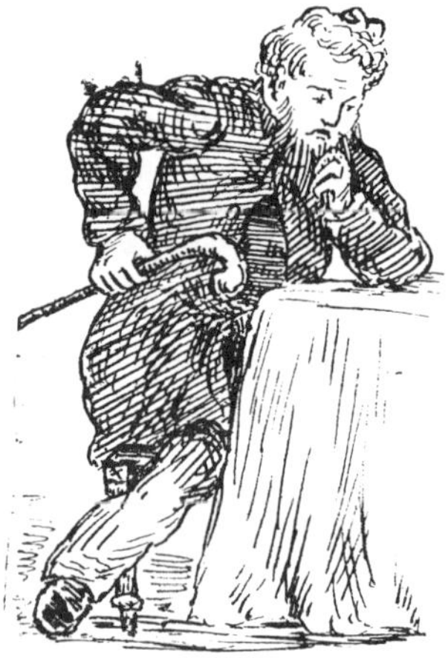

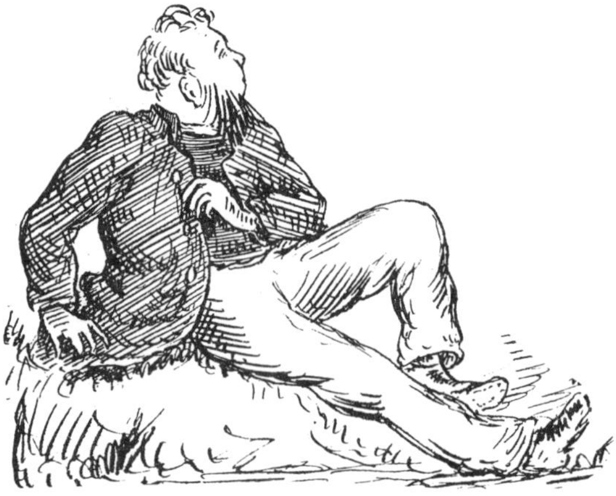

May 2nd 1881... I want you to do me a little favour my dear Sir - You are strong and lithe and nimble and withal given to travel - Will you therefore at your earliest convenience 'trip over' as the saying is and give that Glossop friend of mine a kicking for I cannot get a letter out of him whatever I do - and as I am devoted to peaceful pursuits I am in a measure compelled to employ 'Lay agency' for the application of that stimulation to which only I can look for efficacy since all gentler means have failed - I need hardly suggest the appropriateness of strong shoes - If you undertake the mission - Yours as ever ...

May 5th 1881... Let me see - Saturday to Tuesday was what the letter said and it rather puzzles me - 'Saturday' all right - Sunday also all right for I am at home that day - Monday! Monday! Let me see Monday!! yes Monday all right up to evening certainly up to Tuesday night probably - My dear Mister it is in this wise - We are under a promise to go to Pemberton on Monday evening and stay Tuesday, but this promise is conditional - If our host is at home we are going - if he is away we are not - If business calls him off on Monday he will let us know - If it does not he will expect us - come prepared to stay Tuesday - Saturday Sunday & Monday we hope of a certainty to be here & it is not impossible we may be on Tuesday - any way afford me the three days felicity - Torpedo is wonderfully mollified at present but if ye break faith there will be an explosion & you'll get the most blown up...

Wednesday morning May 11th 1881... venerated and locomotive Sir - I really cannot play your game at my time o'Life. The East wind together with the standing and walking about have done me up entirely. I have taken a spell of about 12 hours sleep and yet the weariness and aching is not out of my limbs and my cough is as bad as ever. A person having heard of our presence in that distant but commanding locality to which you took me on Sunday evening - full of regrets at not having the privelege of seeing me came hither yester even shortly after your departure to ask me to go over today (although the place is far beyond my jurisdiction) to see her mother who is a patriarchal person whose earthly pilgrimage has already extended beyond 90 winters. There is therefore not much chance of a rest for me today - Before eight o'clock yesterday evening a messenger was sent to inform me that the little infant who was brought after me up the hill was dead and its burial fixed for Thursday next. Torpedo laid up with Lumbago and occasional twinges of sciatica ...

Southport News Report - 21st May 1881

St. Luke's Fancy Fair

The Fancy Fair opened in the Cambridge Hall on Tuesday morning, on behalf of St. Luke's Church, has proved the most successful venture of its kind, and indeed, not without cause, for extraordinary efforts have been put forth by those who have had the management of the bazaar. The fair has been organised on a medieval plan, everything connected with it having a tinge of the 'olden time' imparted to it. The result, especially as far as the appearance of the hall is concerned is most gratifying, a very complete illusion being secured, thanks to the clever work of Messrs. Bernasconi & Langford, who fitted up the interior of the place. The interior of the hall has undergone a 'change, into something rich and strange'. The spectator entering the room finds himself at once transported from the present place and the present century back some hundreds of years to such a town as Shakespeare wrote of. All round the room are old-fashioned shops, ramped with the low penthouses beneath, in which the wares are displayed in tempting confusion. These shops are adorned in the 'good old-fashioned' manner with signs such as "Ye Leaguers of Lathom", "Ye House of Hesketh", "Ye Scarisbrick Mart", "Ye Lancashire Witches", "Ye Temple of Mystic Arte", "Ye Moote Hall" and "Ye Banke". At the end of the room is a counterfeit castle, called "The Tower of (Little) London", and above the platform is a manor house girded with trees. The gallery has been utilised, for the windows have been arranged at intervals along the sides, through which the spectators may watch the fair beneath.

Nor was the attraction of appropriate apparel wanting, for stall holders were attired in unwonted dresses, which if not medieval, were at least novel, and in no wise suggestive of the 19th century. Then there were trumpeters dressed in Lincoln green, knights of the shire, the heralds, pages, and all the et ceteras of the 16th century to aid in the illusion, which, as we have said, was very complete.

The fair, which is for the purpose of raising £3000 to free St. Luke's from debt, was opened, not by the Countess of Lathom, as announced, but 'by commission', the Countess of Lathom being prevented from attending in consequence of a recent family bereavement. 'Sir Marmaduke Lyndsay' (otherwise known as Mr Richardson of this town) acted as herald and read the commission which directed the affairs of the fair to begin. At the time the place was crowded to excess. 'Sir Marmaduke Lyndsay' duly attired in the historical costume of the period, and attended by trumpeters dressed in Lincoln green, read the proclamation as follows:-

"O yea! O yea! O yea! Ye ryghte Honourable ye Ladye of Lathome does streightlie charge and commande alle manner of personnes of whatsoever Estate, Degree, or Condition they bee, havynge recourse to this Fayre toe keepen ye peace of our soverygne Ladye ye Queene.
That no manners of personnes schal maken ennis conventicles, Affrayes, or Riotynges, by which ye peace of thys Fayre may ben disturbed, upon pain of Imprisonmente in ye Toure of Lyttel London atte ye discretion of ye Bayliffes.
Also that alle comers hithertoe doe without parley and atte once paye ye prices demanded of them by ye Ladyes atte ye Boothes for alle commodities whatsoever.
Also that alle folk who have filled their pouches with monie before comynge to ye Fayre fail not to empty them before leavynge ye same, so that ye heavie debte of 3000 of pounds maye ben defrayed, and ye newe Churche of Seynte Luke ben made readie for ye consecration.
Also that all good people try theire fortunes, atte ye mennie and divers Rafflynges, that they maken haste in Evenynge to see ye joyfulle and merrie entertaynments, and that whenever they doe feel wearie and hungry, either in ye daie or nyghte, they goe straight waye to ye Refectorie, where Maistresse Conell hath moche meates, confections, fruites, and ye like to refreshen themselves withalle.
And finallie, that when persons soever finden themselves aggrieved, injured or wronged, by ennie mannere of personne in this Fayre, that they comen with their Plaintes before ye Stewardes and Bayliffes in this Fayre assigned to hearen and determine pleas; and they will given to alle parties Justyce, according to ye Lawes and Customes of ye Fayres of thys countrie.
I now therefore declare ye Fayre open God saven ye Queen

When he had finished the trumpeters blew a blast with their trumpets, the Reverend W.H. Marsden then called for three cheers for the Queen and this having been given, the business of the fair commenced.

(Listed amongst stall-holders were Mrs Marsden and Mrs and the Misses Jackson)

Besides the attraction of such a novel show as the antique houses, and dresses, a number of shows were provided and amusements - including a Sedan chair which plied for hire in the hall, tableaux vivants and pantomimic plays being provided in the evening.

The bazaar, on the closing day, had, up to the previous evening, raised £2283. 5s.

May 11th 1881 (evening)...'It's true 'tis a pity and a pity 'tis 'tis true' - In our card this morning we told you of our cold and weariness - we depicted ourself reclining before setting forth to confront the day's fatigues - We have now confronted the day's fatigues and we are supine 'therewith' i.e not the temporary rest, but with the confronting duty - therewith we are supine - what can we say fairer - I'm in fact quite on my back 'intirely'. This remark of course, I use allegorically - I'm tired that's the long and short of it - We are rejoiced to hear that you reached Preston quite safely - and that your country residence had fortified you ...

May 15th 1881... I am placidly looking forward over the intervening wall of days to being in Southport on Tuesday next to witness the opening of St Luke's his 'Fantesie fayre'. Shall ye hie thither I wonder? I feel better - my other half very much indisposed - Lumbago, toothache & Tic - Yours truly...

Southport May 16th 1881... We are here, both of us. We can sit outside a little but the wind is cold and the rain at times moderately copious. Hoarsely roar the distant billows. We hope for a fairer time tomorrow when there will be opened St Luke hys Fantesie Fayre whereat we are minded to be present. Thine Dear Sir muchly...

Maie ye XVII 1881... Ye'll know this stick I suppose eh! man you <u>should</u> have been with us here at 'ye openynge of ye fantesie fayre'* this morning - we are all of us rather in a quaint style - Indeed you would hardly have known most of us. The Countess of Lathom not being present by reason of a family affliction ye fayre was opened with 'moche solemn and imposing ceremonie' by a herald preceded by trumpeters. Rain falling heavily but 'ye fayre' crowded to overflowing notwith standing - too crowded, in fact, for moche pourchasing to be within the range of practical politics - yours, most truly as ever ...

Maie 18th 1881... some friends having regard to my quietude, sapience and good nature would have had me attend the Bazaar in this 'character' but I did not do so - My poor Torpedo has not 'blown up' since she came but has completely 'broken down'. Has had in fact to seek Medical aid - Face ache - sciatica and an acute pain in the left side - cough severe - got to Bazaar for about one hour when I had to get her out into the air to preserve her from fainting - We are returning home on Thursday if possible (i.e if Torpedo is removable). I shall have to go 'whether or not'. If you come to the 'Fayre' come in a character - Free Masonic will do - if not - come in a Sedan chair. Yours truly...

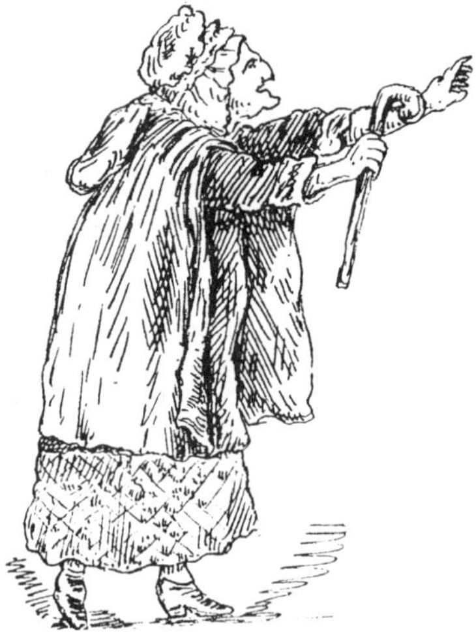

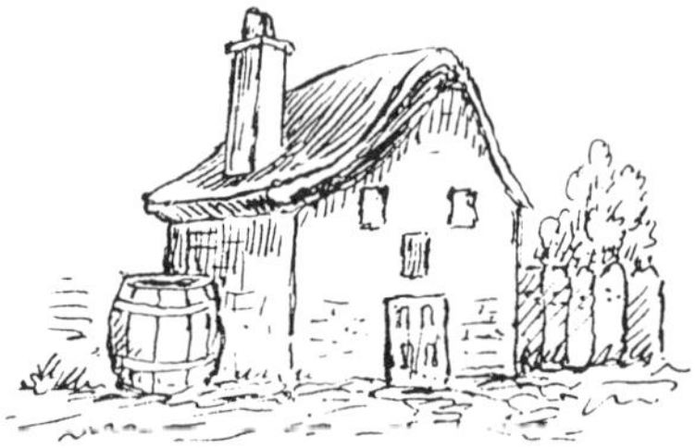

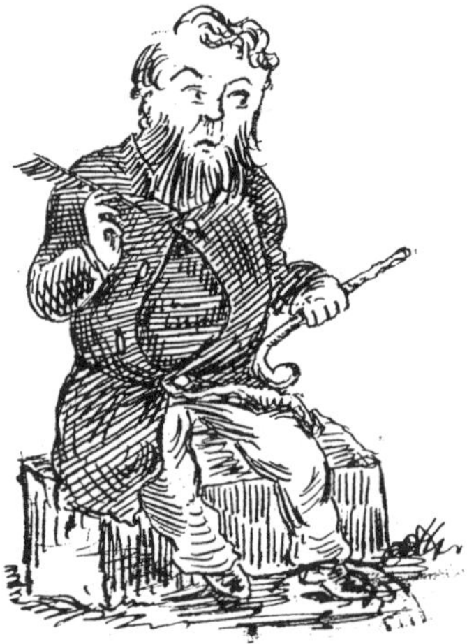

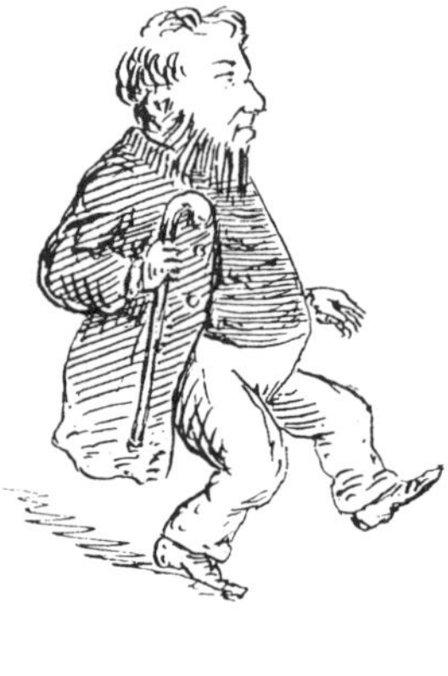

Maie XXIst MDCCCLXXXI... If I had to go much to that Bazaar it would have made me an old man - It was so crowded and the standing about ever tires me - causes a back ache and makes me stoop - Torpedo was under the Doctor's hands all the time - she is now much better - Grand weather we are having - a glorious bright morning 'this' but the wind continues still rather cold - I am picking myself up after the fatigues of the 'fayre' - Believe me ever truly ...

May 25th 1881... Oh, for a little cot, with good outook - pleasant natural features and quietude for Torpedo is recovering from her painful illness and in rambling mood - We are at Southport today and we hie us to Ormskirk tomorrow, to Wigan on Friday and in due course home again - next week if the weather, health and engagements permit we propose to visit Chester to revel awhile among its antiquities - S. Luke hys Fayre hath given us a passion for quaint things & old fashioned places. It closed last night with an auction at which or in which four eminent auctioneers took part. I have not yet heard the total. Yours truly...

May 28th 1881... I don't like this going off so much for it always more or less upsets me and renders me fit for nothing scarcely for a day or two after my return. The change of air worked wonders in Torpedo - but the thundery condition of the atmosphere quite prostrated me - St Luke hys Fayre was a marvel of success £3003 'poundes' being obtained thereatte - ye have said not whether ye vouchsafed presence. Thine most truly ...

May 30th 1881... I reckon nothing of this green ink and I write to warn you not to be beguiled into purchasing it. I had almost set off to Chester this morning - all ready except putting my hat on - but the prospect of great heat and a temporary feeling of all overishness deterred me - The country is truly grand just now - We shall soon be in June & don't you forget the 20th. Believe me truly ...

Wigan June 1st 1881... Well I declare I've been prevailed upon to come skipping hither again. I am afraid I shall begin to fancy by & by that I am a Ratepayer in the Borough. Weather delightful but scarcely cold enough to congeal that mixture of alkanet root, spermacetti and sulphuric other known as the blood of Saint Iannarius. Don't let the 20th day of June (Inst) escape your memory. Yours truly...

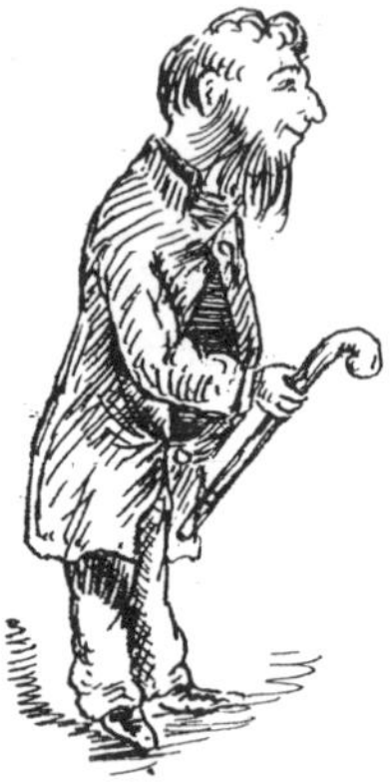

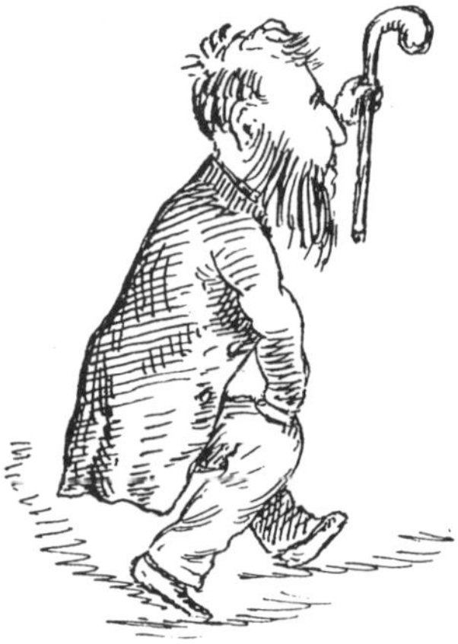

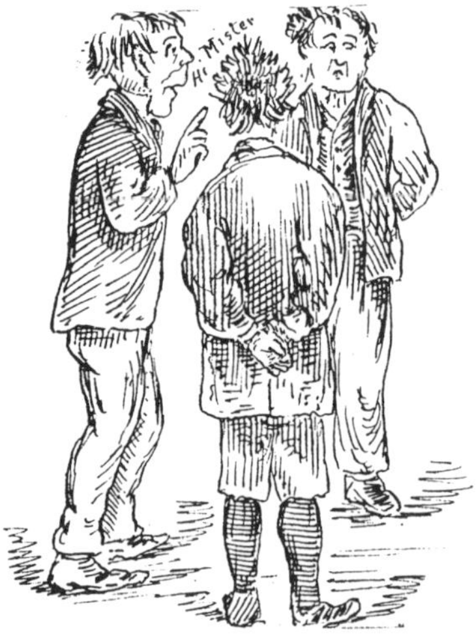
Hi Mister

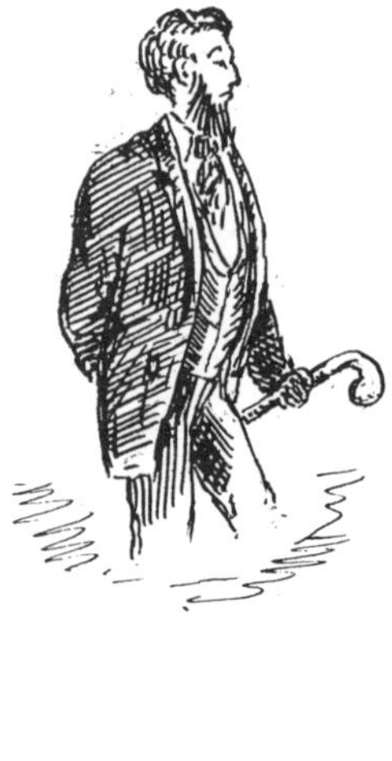

June 4th 1881... I'm back again - I elected not to abide in that obfusc Town on the Douglas - In Herefordshire they call a goose a <u>goose</u> but geese they call goosen the teminal 'en' making it plural, so Wigan is derived from the Saxon word 'wig' meaning a fight and 'en' which makes it plural. Wigan was therefore in good King Arthur's days the place of fights - yea and so it is still - Its 'purring' like that of the cat is famous wherever it is known - King Arthur fought more than one battle in its neighbourhood and I saw one fought in its streets during a recent visit - oh would it were the abode of peace. Yours full truly ...

June 7th 1881... Heigh ! My good Sir, Heigh! You'll excuse me intruding upon or interrupting you, but I wish you just to be good enough not to forget Monday the 20th of this present month - To attempt to describe the country at this time present would be to attempt the impossible. It is simply grand and lovely - We have two ladies sojourning with us for a few days - both leave before the Tea Party - alas! Cattle disease has broken out in Eccleston - Two beasts were shot there last Sunday - We are well and hope you enjoy like happiness - To ye both and all we tender our warmest regards and I remain ...

June 10th 1881... Hi Mister we're a Depitation cumn to tell you as you mun mind, like and not forget that Munday 20th of this here month is to be wer Tay Party - and wer Minister yoa know sir, he do say, good man, like a he wants yoa, like, to be there uncommon. We, this Depitation - me and my two mates like, as has come'd to ax yoa please sir to mind as yoa don't forget wer joyful Party begs likewise, with yer pardon for offence which its not wanting to vex you as we wish - begs as you'll be at it and enjoy a bit of a romp and a dish of Tay - start soon whatever yoa dun, and get in handy. We'st to hev a little of refreshments at 12 o'clock - ave prizes gin us at hauf past and go a walking at one - see as you don't forget the day - Its on the Mundy as we go a walkin - for on the Tuesdy we'st hev no walkin in us cause we'st be fit for nuthink, scase. Yours truly ...

June 14th 1881... Bring over with you a gentleman friend - If you have any estimable Bachelor acquaintance give him a chance. I am going to Aughton next Sunday but hope to be back again here at a little after six o'clock - We are very busy just now getting ready for Monday next when we hope for the pleasure of seeing you and your Bachelor (intimate) friends to help them to a settlement and I know of no prospect of attaining that much to be desired issue better than the one afforded by our Gala on the 20th - Rise to the occasion my dear Sir - Rise to the occasion and Believe me very truly yours ...

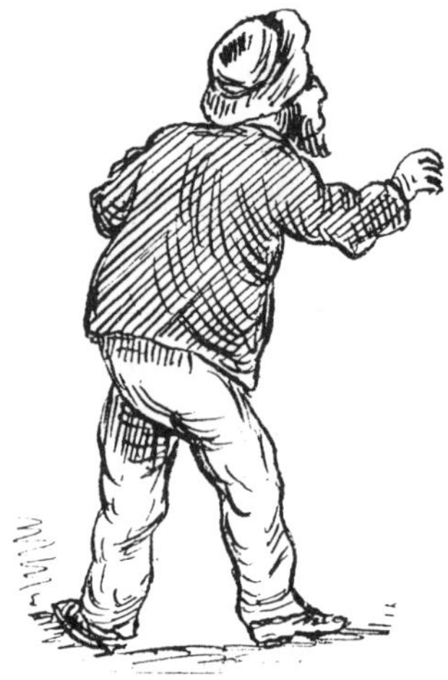

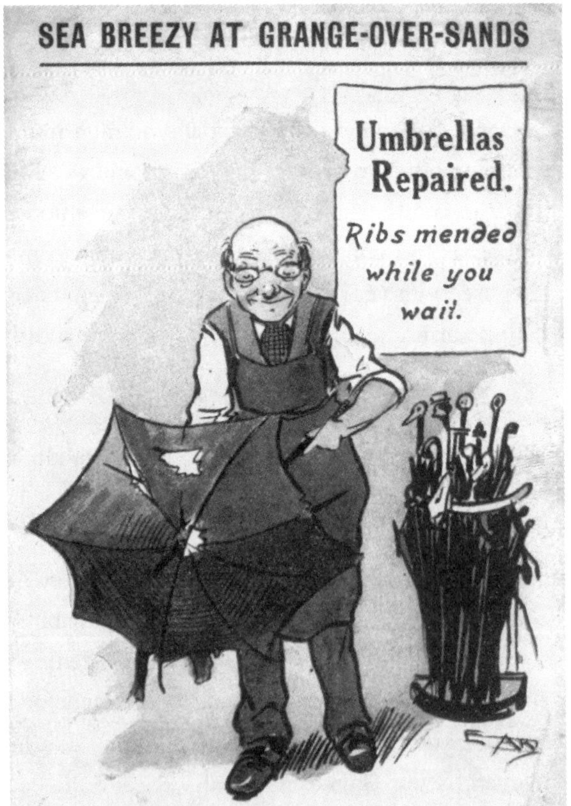

A 1920's postcard very much in the style of Mr Wilson.

June 22nd 1881... Do you know, my dear Sir, do you know? The Party is over alackaday we had not your presence & really under the circumstances we could not expect it. We grieve for your absence and yet more for the lamentable cause. I have been so occupied since the party that I haven't till this evening had time to write to you. We have not yet brought the money & Bills face to face with each other therefore cannot tell the result - but yet our Depitation think that in a manner of speaking - The cop will be enough to fill the Ditch up ...'

June 24th 1881... Heigh, Mr Worsley, Heigh! by all that I can learn - there is a likelihood of some of us getting over to Preston on Monday next - From the shadows cast before I glean that there is probability of a person or persons of the name of Parkes flying through Preston with us - we are in a manner organising a sort of expedition to the Magnetic Pole - I mean 'Grange' where we shall probably abide for a fortnight. I am just starting out to Wigan - as it is Market Day and I have business there. I meanwhile remain ...

June 25th 1881... Let me see, my dear Sir, I am rather puzzled to determine what to do - To come by an early train will upset all our preconcerted plans - I have consulted with 'Torpedo' and she endeavours to help me out of my difficulty by bidding me say that we cannot come before the train leaving Croston at eleven minutes past one and getting to Preston at 1.35 but by that train it is our purpose to come so that a little after half past one we hope to look you up. The weather is unsettled but the sunshine when we have any is bright and beautiful. We all combine in muchness and hoping soon, in health ourselves, to find ye all in health also. I remain ...

Grange over Sands June 27th 1881... I'm here - in fact we're here and I'm completely overcome - It's impossible for us to describe the place but the one word Paradise will convey an idea of the surroundings of - as well as the place itself whereat I'm staying - Position commanding and view extensive - I'm so in raptures that I can say & write but little - We gratefully remember your hospitality as we passed through Preston en route hither and combine in love...

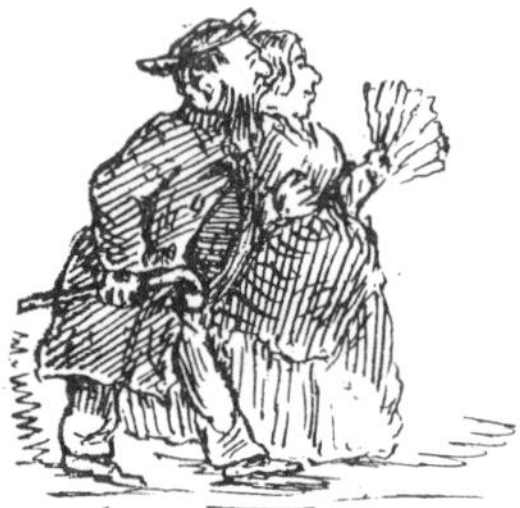
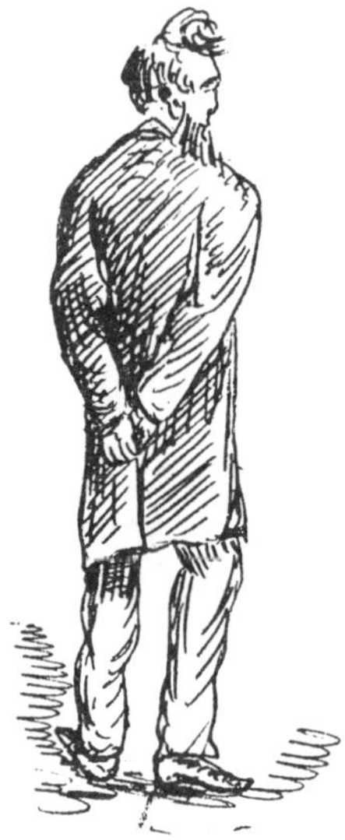
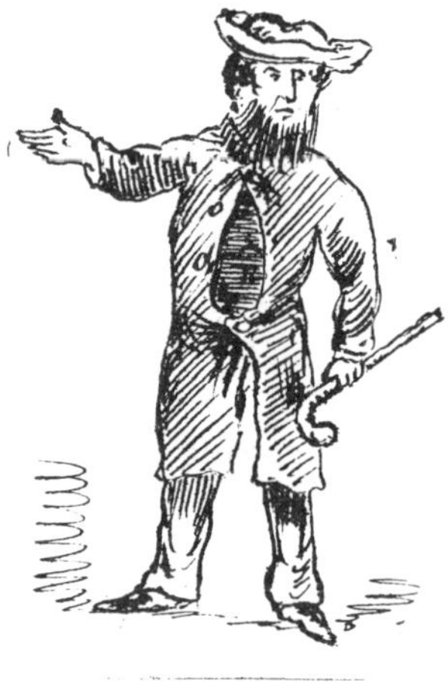
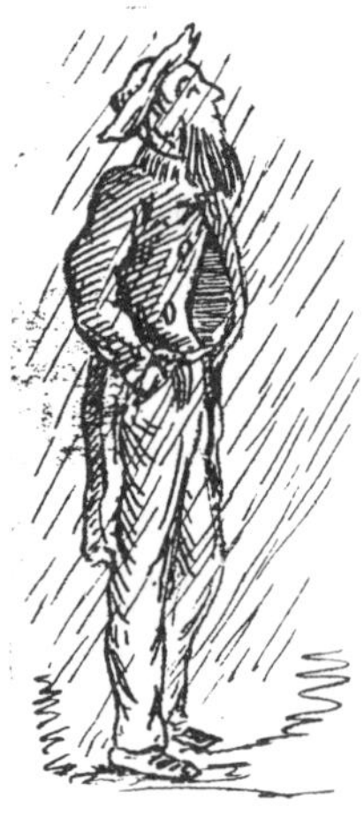

Grange over Sands June 28th 1881... We're promenading here quite happily and comfortable. Grange is a pretty place but required two things to make it perfect one of these was Torpedo's presence - the other was that of self. It has now got both and looks its best - We are promenading freely to the great garnishment of its thoroughfares - The effect is charming, - positively charming - and now, good Sir, make no use of the translation that I gave you - as I am quite doubtful about the mood and tense of one of the words - The print is so small and my eyesight bad - a few days here I hope will work a change and assuage the irritation with which my eyes are affected - When I return I hope to be better every way - am just starting off some miles into the interior - We twain and <u>all</u> are ever truly ...

Grange over Sands June 30th 1881... see here - There is I understand a train from here on Saturday next which is due in Preston before 12 o'clock say 11-17 or thereabout - by that train it is the purpose of myself and other moiety to get to Preston. She I regret greatly to say suffers intensely from Tic - the result of cold. This last night she has scarcely slept a wink and now it is raining potently and in profusion. I want to get out and cannot - ah me, I will come to you for comfort on Saturday ...

July 4th 1881... I don't understand it. What does it mean? We have looked for you but we looked in vain. I'm sure it was a compact - so out on you - I'm not pleased. You would not like it yourself - so say nothing. Full of indignation ...

Grange over Sands July 6th 1881... a grand country, this - a truly splendid country, sir and I am in it once again. But what a thunderstorm awaited me - The first peal I heard at Hest Bank - as we crossed the Bay - rain began and during the evening the thunder was the awfullest - the lightning the appallingest and the rain the copiousest I heard or witnessed - All calm again this morning - Receive our benison ...

July 7th 1881... I know not what to make of this weather I can simply get nowhere except wet. Rain, Rain, seasons written everywhere. I intended to start this morning for Windermere but alas - mists being about the mountain tops, clouds curtain the sky and rain drops are profusely falling. I am informed this morning that Mr P. driven perhaps by despair of anything like reasonable weather here or in Staffordshire has announced his intention to return with us on Saturday - Tuesday's storm surpassed everything of the kind I remember to have ever beheld. My Barometer is not encouraging. With affection yours ...Phosferine has stopped Torpedo's Tic.

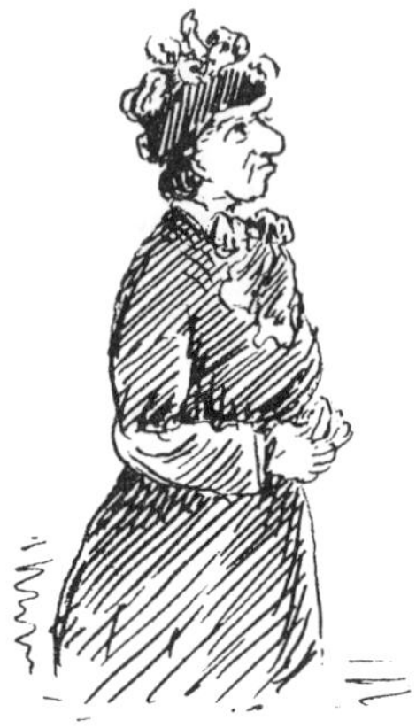

Notes

July 12th 1881 Thought to be Mr Howarth of Harrock.

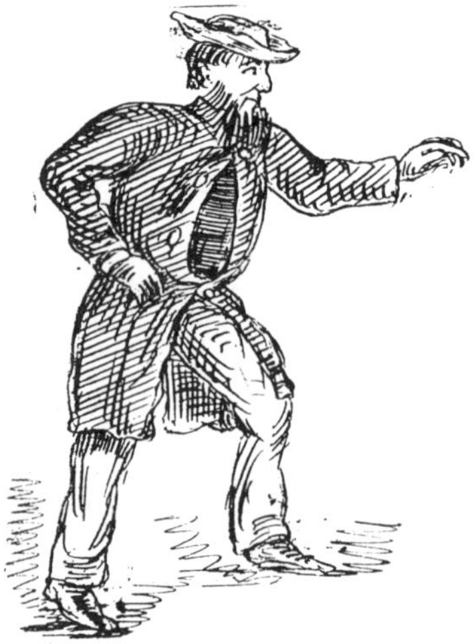

Grange over Sands July 8th 1881... I am paying a hurried visit to Windermere this morning - I am only running over with a view to sailing up the Lake and back again for 'Hum-hah-hay, Hay-hah-hum, The rain comes down today, Teedum, teedum, teedum'. The evening on which we first arrived in Grange (i.e) Monday in last week the air was most clear and the prospect lovely - I rejoiced therein, but alas! that extraordinary clearness of the air was the harbinger and forecast of all the rain, as well as the fierce thunderstorm which we have had since. What poor creatures are we and how uncertain are our pleasures. Hope to see you well tomorrow - shall leave by the same train as last time - Face ache has vanished - Phosferine done it. Yours truly ...

July 11th 1881... The thinning out process has begun. Fanny and Sally have left us this morning - others leave, I think, tomorrow, so that if you come over on Wednesday we can talk over without molestation or interruption matters affecting (our?) hoped for attachment. Believe me Dear - truly ever 'Jemimer Ann' ..

July 12th 1881... I beg to avail myself of the present occasion to address a few words to you respecting current events. We now possess a pig. It (i.e the porky-pine animal or porcine quadruped) came to us last evening. Mr H* on the Hill opposite yesterday with great pains and labour fixed up the lower portion of his flagstaff. Today the riggers will affix the gaff and top piece. 'Mahester Pahecks' of Hillingdon is off to Blackburn this morning and is minded to be in Stafford e'er sunset tomorrow - therefore you will be able to find here the seclusion so dear to you. On Sunday evening a vein which had become varicose just above my right ankle burst - Shall expect you tomorrow evening. Yours ...

July 14th 1881... Look here, Sir, tell me 'What animal is that which walks on two legs in the morning - three in the afternoon and four in the evening?' You don't know - ah well, then I will tell you - It is <u>man</u>. He moves upon his own two legs in the morning of his life - adopts a stick in the afternoon thereof - & totters along in the evening with the aid of two sticks - a perusal of your letter would lead one to infer that you have attained to the two stick or four leg period of Life - I cannot think however that you are yet bordering really on decrepitude - Take warning by Mrs Dombey - make an effort. It cannot be that your declension has yet begun. I regard it merely as a passing whimsicality begotten of circumstances - the weekend be it - come as early as you can on Saturday ...

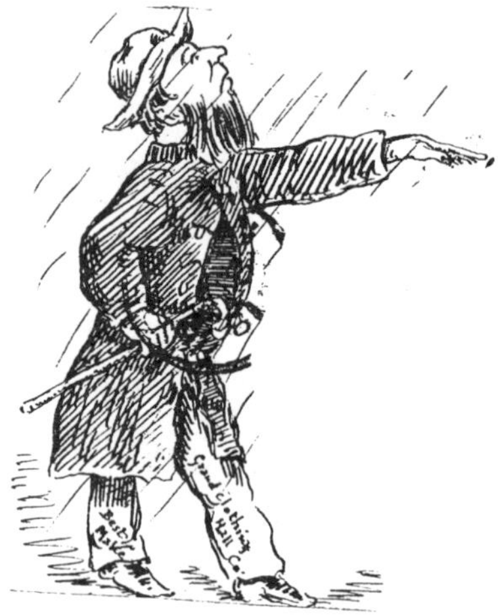
Grand Clothing Hall Co.
Best Make

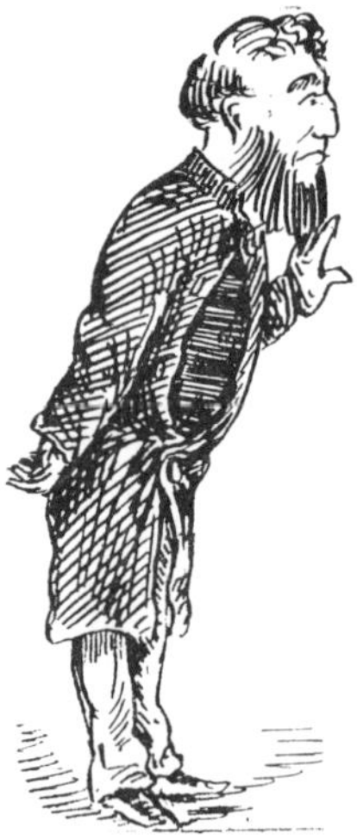

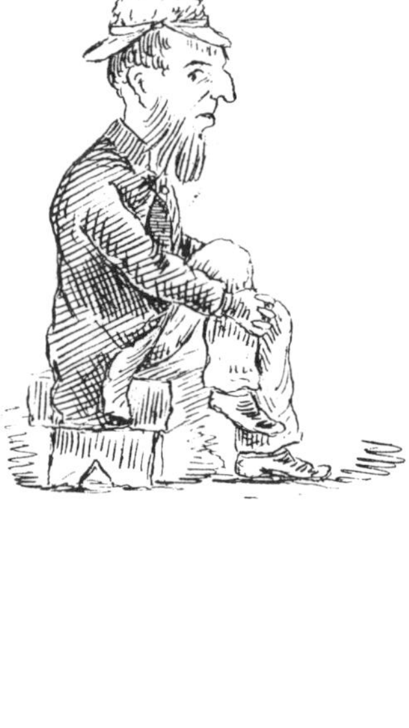

July 15th 1881 (evening)... It is said that the keeper of a place for refreshment once wrote out the Bill of Fare himself & it appeared as follows - Coffey, supe, roste befe, fride hamm, boyled and baked pertators, mutting chops, veal culverts, and hasch. Nearly the whole of this Bill of Fare you have by your resolution to come only at the weekend 'spiled' - outs on your whimsicality - You are rapidly souring by it the milk of human kindness - much responsibility rests on you - Ah me! would ye could see it truly. If we see ye tomorrer we'll have it out with ye. Meanwhile we remain yours most truly ...

July 18th 1881... Honoured & Dear Sir as the saying is - It is a dull and cloudy morning of this 18th day July 1881 and I am not quite sure whether I don't from time to time feel a spot of rain which for aught I know may be the harbinger, pioneer or precursor of a shower. I feel anxious on that account for if it be so, what I ask, or 'Harsk' will become of the Farmer's hay; and ah! (Horror attends the thought) what will or <u>may</u> become of the 'Bags' - by this latter euphonious title I desire, of course, to signify my nether garments - Experience may more accurately than yourself give answer to the second question, meanwhile you never mind. Very truly yours ...

July 21st 1881... No more white hats for me - sunshine or no sunshine, summer heat or winter cold - such as I purchased in your admirable town are not made or at all events not fitted for a world where there is dust smudges, perspiration, rain and 'curiosity-inspired' grate blackers - If you are infatuated enough to invest in one, the day, I feel sure, is not far distant when you will vote them a delusion and a snare - Don't be beguiled but lay out your eighteen pence either in jewellery or a Zulu - A wringing machine now would be a useful investment <u>anything</u> My dear Sir, but a <u>white cap</u>. You must excuse me making it my business to warn you - the importance of this matter is my excuse for interference ...

July 25th 1881... Do you know I have had to nurse my right leg nearly continuously all week. I am still in fact nursing it - when I spoke against the 18 penny white hats I did not intend to disparage at all their comfortableness but to draw attention to their liability to get soiled. They have, I quite admit, their advantages as well as drawbacks - They are light - they are airy - they are cool - Besides, I think they fit nicely and to good figures, <u>like yours</u> and <u>mine</u> they impart quite a military appearance. For my part I feel already as if I had seen considerable service in India and got wounded in my leg - I thought to write more ...

Notes

<u>July 26th 1881</u>

In the auction announcement Pyebrook is described as:- 'A Freehold farm with the dwelling house and other buildings thereon, situate in Town Lane, Heskin, called or known by the name of Pyebrook Hall'.

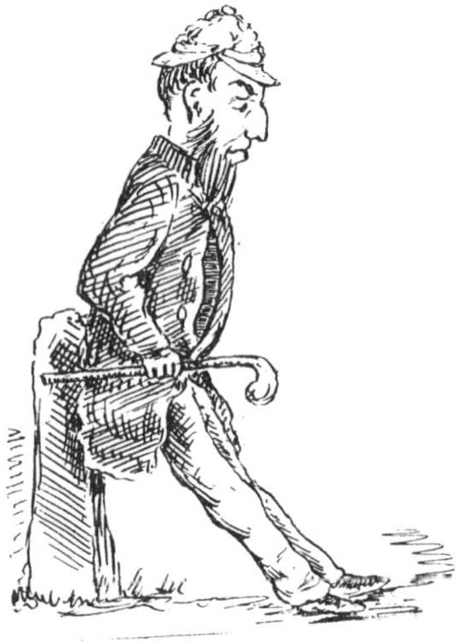

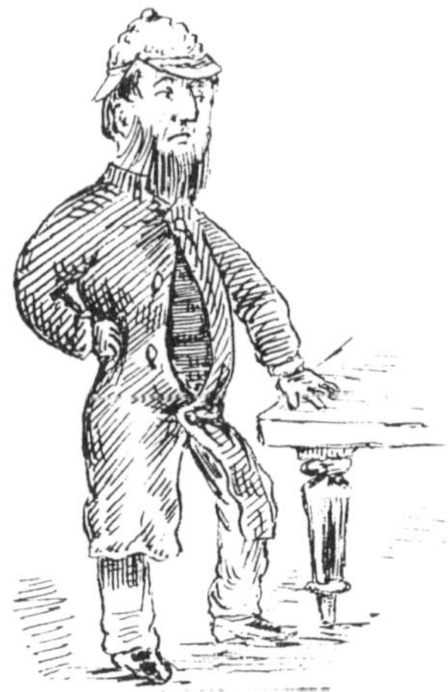

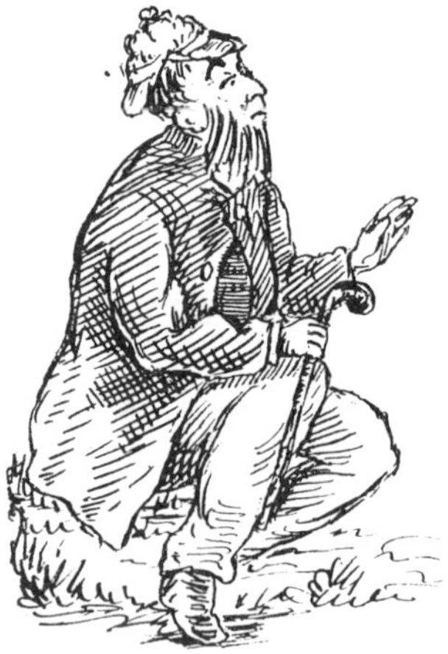

July 26th 1881... this leg still bothers me a good deal and makes it needful for me at times when out walking to stop and rest - You will understand me that my objection to these white summer hats is solely because of their proneness to get soiled - otherwise I am not unaware that they import figures such as yours and mine quite a military looking finish - Pyebrook*, I am told is to be sold at the Oak Hotel, Chorley, on the 17th of August - For further particulars see Preston Papers. I hear it last time 'fetched' only 1200£ and is likely this time to be disposed of for much less. Now is your chance good Sir - your chance is now - Be only at the auction. Remember it is the early bird that picks up the first worm. Mrs S. of Eccleston I regret to hear is very seriously indisposed - The seizure was on Saturday - Of the nature of the illness I can only write from rumour which represents it to be paralysis of the Tongue with great feebleness of the heart. Yours truly ...

July 29th 1881... I have conducted negotiations and effected the purchase of the set of garden tools on your behalf. Receiving promise from the Ironmonger that they would yester even be despatched from Southport per rail to Preston - I shall feel interested in your 'Rake's Progress' and among the tools you will doubtless find out How (or should it be Hoe?, we have not a spelling Bee hereabout) to scrape an acquaintance; and by gardening - Rejoice, Dear Sir, for the cost of the Lot was not so ruinous as you anticipated - 1/9 being the total outlay entailed by their purchase. Have you yet bought a white cap for summer wear? If you have I regard your 1/6 as a lot of money lying idle - for there is no sunshine here away to guard the head against and to wear a sunshade when there is no sunshine will be as incongruous as to carry an open umbrella when it is not raining - We have thunder heat betimes - Thunder rain often but the cold of winter just at present. Yours truly ...

August 1st 1881...Now, my Dear Sir, if any of your friends wish for a white (snow white) summer hat of the current shape they have only to negotiate a commercial transaction in 'head ware' at Messrs Wainman and Cottams, 17, Fishergate Street, Preston where an elegant and affective construction like my own will be supplied to them at something under two shillings. I rejoice that the garden tools have safely arriven - Ply them with diligence and may your toil be prospering. My ankle is improving. This is what we call 'tickle' hay weather - To farmers it is perplexing & occasions them with much anxiety. I am just about to set forth to Eccleston - Sporting myself in a sitting attitude for long standing does not do well for me. Yours most truly ...

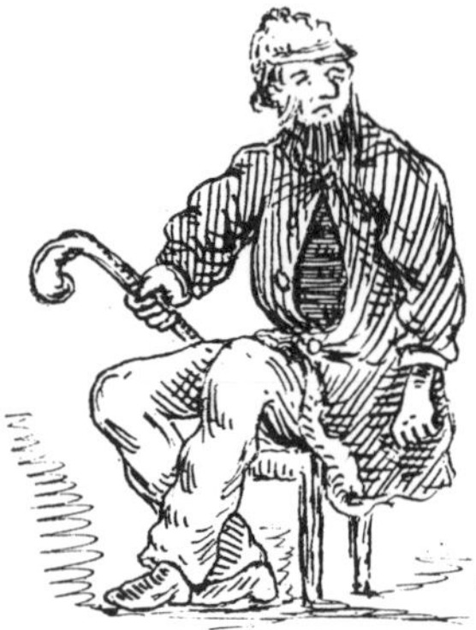

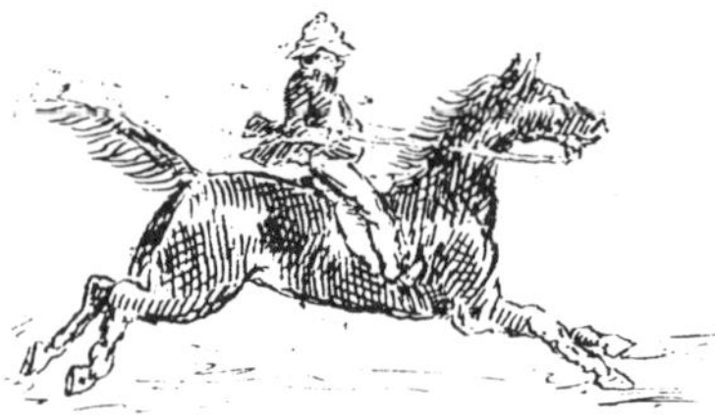

<u>Notes</u>

<u>August 8th 1881</u> The murder of a 16 year-old girl by the man she thought was about to marry her.

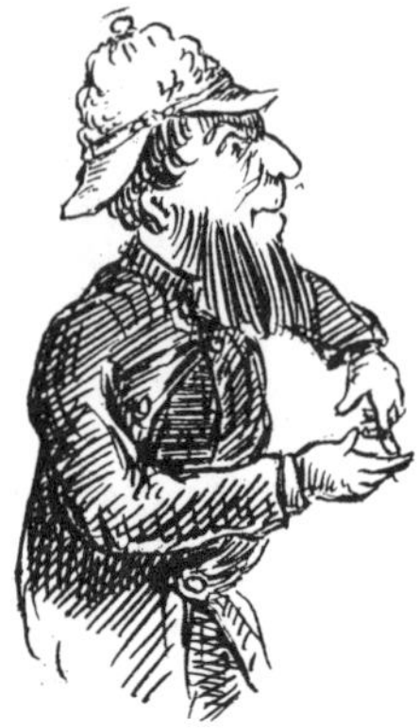

August 3rd 1881... I have today had my house photographed from two points of view and mine own comely figure appears in such picture but do you know I was so stupid I quite forgot to put on my new hat when I went out to pose as an Artist's model. This is an omission which admits of no rectification - The Wigan folks have been here for about eight days - They left this morning with the two children. Our servant 'Pollie' also has been sent off today - Does Miss Worsley know of a good general servant? One that can wash and possesses sufficient sense to be civil preferred - I believe from what I hear that Mr E. of Pemberton is to be married in about three weeks from now - My lame limb is much better and for a day or two has given me no pain but I make a point of resting it as much as possible by sitting when I can.Let me know about the servant - Torpedo well but got rheumatism rather in both hands. Very truly yours ...

Aug 8th 1881... I'm off to Southport and just write a hurried line or so to tell you that you will find these white hats as comfortable for riding as for walking in. Their sole drawback as I have before told you is their liability to get soiled. By the way from what I hear I conclude that in a few weeks from this Brother Evans will be married again - The Bride Elect is I believe a French lady - what an awful tragedy that was on Wednesday last at the Sir Walter Scott Inn* - near St Paul's in your town. I forget whether I told you in my last that I was present at the great Conservative Demonstration in Lathom Park on Monday 1st of this month which as you are aware is known as Lammas Day or a 'Loaf Mass' from the Anglo-Saxon words 'Hlaf' a loaf and 'masse' a feast. Did you on that Feast of first fruits eat your share of a loaf made from this year's flour? How late the seasons are !!!! Yours most truly...

Aug 10th 1881... Now Look You here, Mister. Didn't we come over to see you as we said - then I've a right to expect that 'you' will keep <u>your</u> word and come over hither as <u>you</u> have said - You understand - don't you? Well then let me have no ulterior cause for complaint. Mark that, I beg of you, sir, mark that. What can I say more? I've made it as plain as may be - so look to it and don't plead misapprehension - The white hat is still wearable though a trifle soiled. I'm yours truly ...

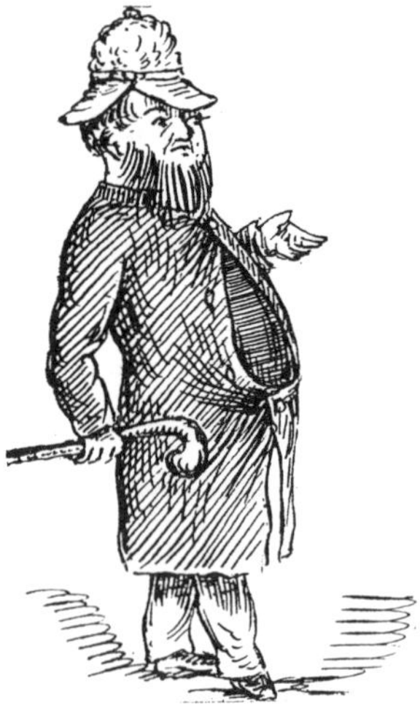

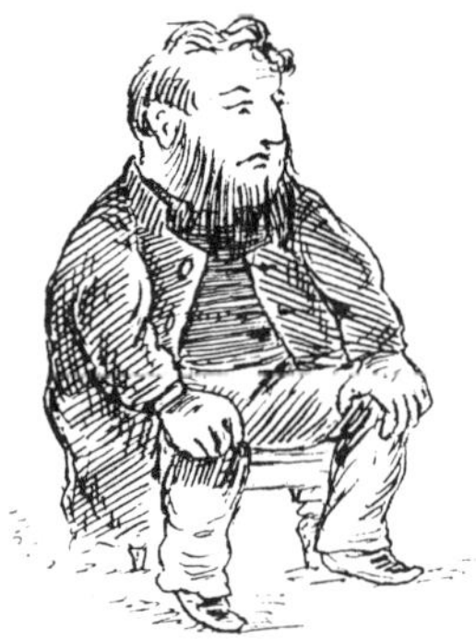

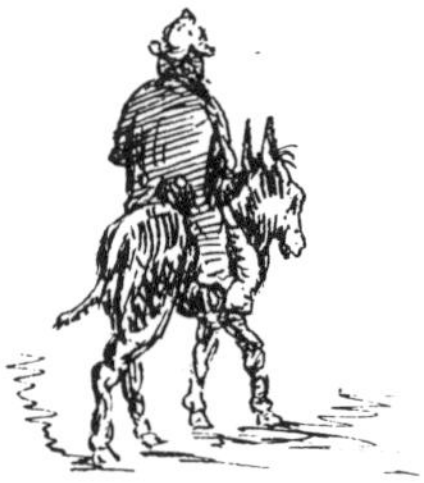

Aug 13th 1881... You know that A becomes An before a vowel or a silent H as 'an acorn' 'an hour' now in the face of this rule the very name itself is ungrammatical. You cannot correctly say 'an riddle' 'an boat' 'an ship' 'an stick' 'an dog' 'an cat' 'an bother' or 'an servant' nor yet 'an policeman' nor 'an web' for none of these begin with either a vowel or a silent H. It would therefore be incorrect to say 'an web' - the proper sign and expression would be grammatically a web. I only mention or allude to this matter that you may regard it from a Sindly Murray point of view. Scholarship, my Dear Sir, Scholarship nowadays is the great thing - We must keep to Scholarship - upon this card cannot write further but am yours truly...

Aug 17th 1881... Ah Mr Worsley, my dear good man - I've been sitting so patient as ever I can weary & worn and expectant and wan awaiting the coming of our 'elp 'Hann'. But How? - you may ask & whence all these cares? Because don't you see I can't go nowheres, since I've got to be Housemaid & watchman & what! Till help has been sought for & help has been got. I'm wanted on all sides yet can't leave my Post for besides being Housekeeper I'm bound to be Host. And now after waiting and feeling distraught the Postman to hand a kind letter has brought, which bids me get on in the best way I can since another has claimed the expected one 'Hann'. Our grateful remembrance and best thanks are due in chief to your sister and also to you. And now, my dear Sir I solicit from thee that thou wilt believe me as ever to be full truly & faithfully ...

Aug 23rd 1881... I'm intending to have a donkey ride either today or tomorrow at Southport - Riding exercise is considered very healthful and after my numerous household duties, as detailed in the previous card, I feel if I am to make progress at all for the next few days with comfort to myself it must be on the back of some trusty sure footed animal - Wrightington was in a state of great excitement on Saturday afternoon - Bunting fluttered profusely in the breeze - to welcome the return home of the squire from his honeymoon. I think Torpedo's Sciatica has vanished but rheumatism in the shoulder has, I regret to say, taken its place - the torture was excruciating on Sunday morning - she however has strength to join with me in kind wishes and I am still yours truly ...

Notes

Aug 30th 1881 From the 'Southport News' 10th Sept 1881..

OPENING OF NEW MARKETS AND PROMENADE EXTENSION BY THE EARL OF DERBY AND THE EARL OF LATHOM.

Southport was almost mad with hilarious excitement on Wednesday when a general holiday was observed with the occasion of the opening of the splendid New Markets and the extension of the North Promenade by the Earls of Derby and Lathom. The Town Council voted £250 towards the expenses of the day's festivities and the Mayor, Alderman Sutton JP entertained the two noble lords and a large number of invited guests to an excellent banquet at the Cambridge Hall. A round of special sports and entertainments of various kinds was got up at the numerous places of public resort; the town was gay with flags and banners, the church bells rang out with merry peals at various intervals during the day; bands of musicians vied with each other in various parts of the town in discoursing sweet sounds; athletic sports took place on the shore, a regatta and boat race from the Pier end, and last though not least in point of attraction and public enjoyment, a grotesque torchlight procession took place at about 9 o'clock in the evening and was witnessed by some thousands of delighted spectators. The Lancs and Yorks Railway Co offered special facilities for visitors to Southport and brought a good many people to witness the grand gala, but not so many as might have been expected. For some time past there had been gloomy forebodings as to what the weather would be like on Wednesday 7th, because so much depends on the state of the elements when a series of al fresco sports and other outdoor proceedings are concerned. Fortunately, however, the Clerk of the Weather Bureau was kind enough to secure a pleasant though somewhat hazy morning, and a genial and brilliant afternoon, followed by a fine evening, for the 'Olde Englyshe Merrie Makinge'.

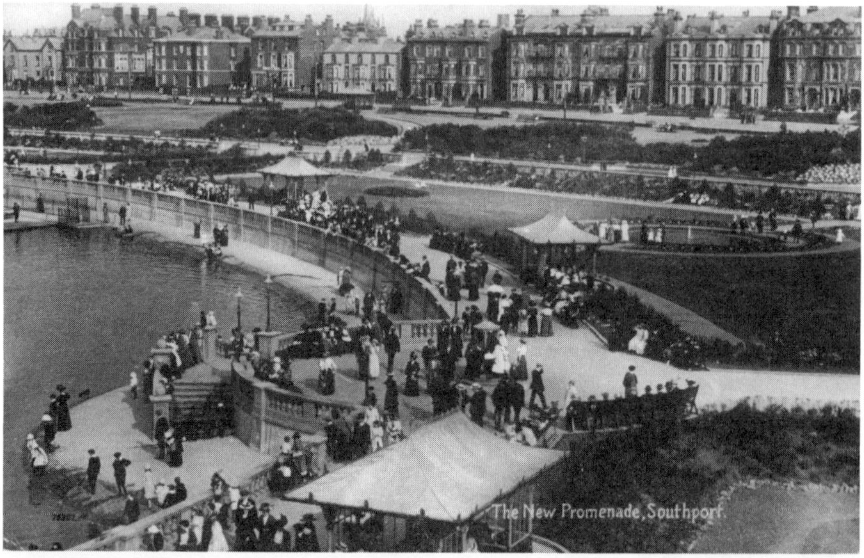

The New Promenade, Southport.

Aug 29th 1881... now I really couldn't write to you last week - I wasn't well and don't look so, do I? It has been so wet that I have got cold - and have to be careful about my ankle - I did not after all get to Southport last week for quadrupedal exercise because the rain was so persistent and heavy - I can't go everywhere, could you if you were as hoarse as a raven and as lame as I am. The Missis wishes to know how your head felt yesterday morning after the stormy, rainy weather and the anxiety as well as excitement of thinking about Jack's birthday. Convey to him for us every seasonable and kindly wish anent this natal day & Believe me ever truly ...

Aug 30th 1881... I did not, as you know, get over to Southport for my Donkey ride, last week but the visit cannot be much longer delayed because health, you know, my dear Sir - health has to be considered so I am minded if weather permit & nothing occurs to thwart my purpose to go to Southport tomorrow - However defective may be the drainage or superabundant the smell of asphalte Southport is Southport all the same - with the sea far off and the new promenade* close to, I am sure I like the place - and a better place than the pier for observing the comet I hardly know - We have a tolerable vantage ground here but the clouds always seem to be in the way - yet on Sunday night I saw the nucleus of the visitant. The clouds hid the tail - but perhaps tonight I may catch sight of the tail while the clouds are concealing the nucleus - your most truly ...

Sep 2nd 1881... observing how perk & spiritful I look as I stand in this position you would not suspect that I am suffering from inflammation in another vein in my right leg - as I was going over the fields to see a sick man yesterday the damp struck through a defective boot sole and the pain became rapidly more acute till last night I was in intolerable suffering - an attempt to walk entails torture - not wishing to pain you unnecessarily I depict myself here to the best advantage. The only remaining aunt of our Glossop friend has departed this life a few days ago. We are hoping to be able to get to Southport on the 7th for the opening of New Market and New Promenade, or perhaps more correctly Promenade extension. I hope we have got back to better weather - certainly the last two days have been an improvement and this morning the sun shines brightly - though it is forsooth at times shadow. Yours most truly & faithfully ...

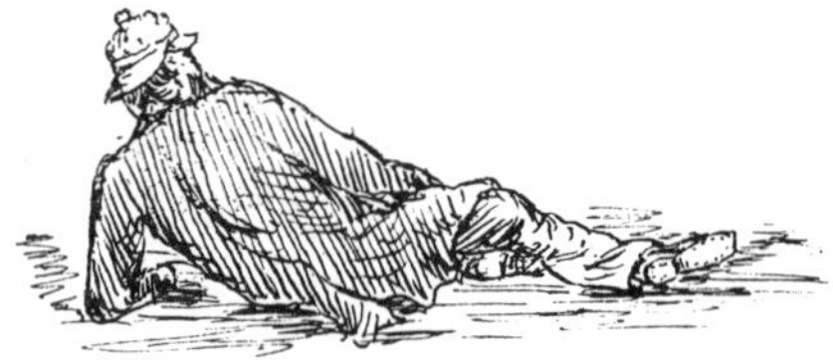

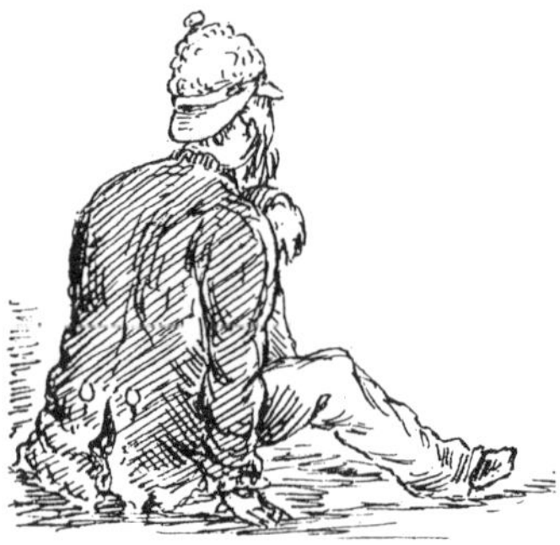

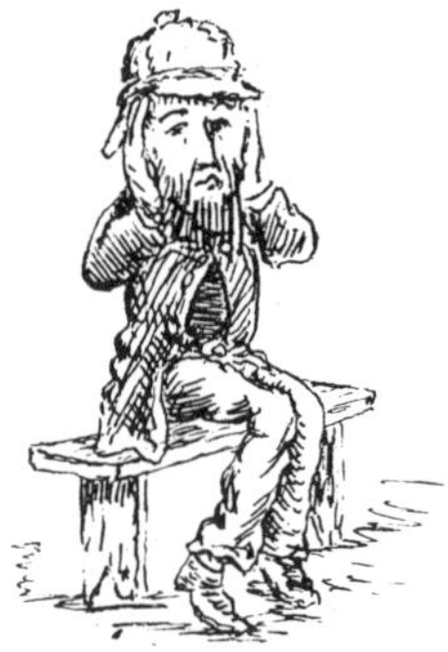

Sep 3rd 1881... I have inflammation in another vein - it set in on Thursday after I had been across some damp fields in defective boots - The attack was preceded by a shivering and all yesterday I was laid up in torture - I applied remedial measures with as much diligence as a sailor would work the pumps of a sinking ship. The pain became a little subdued towards evening - and is milder this morning so that I can bear to move about a little without 'groaning or grunting' as we delight to put it hereabout. Mary Hann has not yet arrived and we have had several offers but being already engaged we could not receive the overtures of any other suitors - There are going to be great doings in Southport for the high jinks there - and buy a pennorth of sweets in the New Market. P.S. Shall you be there helping to extend the promenade to Hesketh Park or to open it when extended -...

Sep 6th 1881... as, my dear Sir, it is as you justly say exceedingly unfortunate that I have again to keep this right limb of mine straight out before me. The pain is much reduced but the ankle I regret & am concerned to say swells now a good deal towards nightfall - You speak of the beauty of yesterday - It is pouring with rain today. You say truly he is 'done for' again - It took place on the 25th of last month - spent the following Sunday in Brussels on the Monday visited the fields of Waterloo - By the way a visit to the battlefield seems scarcely a judicious choice for a pair on Honeymoon except intended to impart timely warning - on Tuesday went to Cologne then to Bonn which they intended leaving on Friday last for Coblentz, and today (Tuesday) or tomorrow are due in Paris again. The Photographs to which you refer will not be executed till after ' return to a settlement in' England. The former i.e 'return to' will be before the 18th Inst - your confidential communication of your idea in re an ppeminent & experienced employer of labour will be respected fully - Hooray! Hooray! My dear Sir, Hooray!!! toss up your cup and shout - Mr Howe has come - His noble figure has just appeared at the window. I should think his shadow has suffered no diminution. Yours ...

Sep 7th 1881... I have not gone to Southport after all for I am not well enough to contend in thronged thoroughfares with pushing Britons - I cannot stand or loiter without great suffering - my poor limb is much more painful this morning - I requested Mr Doig to post in Southport my yesterday's card which I hope you will receive duly - Southport will be a scene of bustle crush clanging bells - braying trumpets beating drums speaking nobles and shouting people - all this I could not do with - the very thought of it makes me hold my ears or rather press them so as to exclude the din - Mr Howe is here - good man he bears me company - seeing my distress and pain he would not leave me. He is puffing the peaceful calumet outside in the mist - which is so dense that a spectator can scarcely tell which is smoke & which is haze - but there is no mistaking the noble & bulky figure of the smoker. I am Dear Sir as ever yours ...

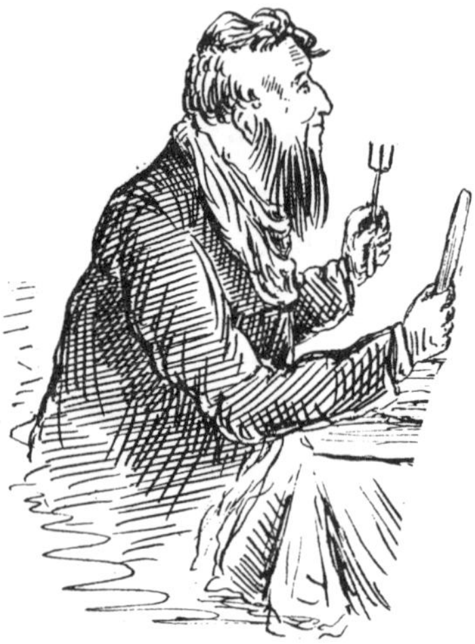

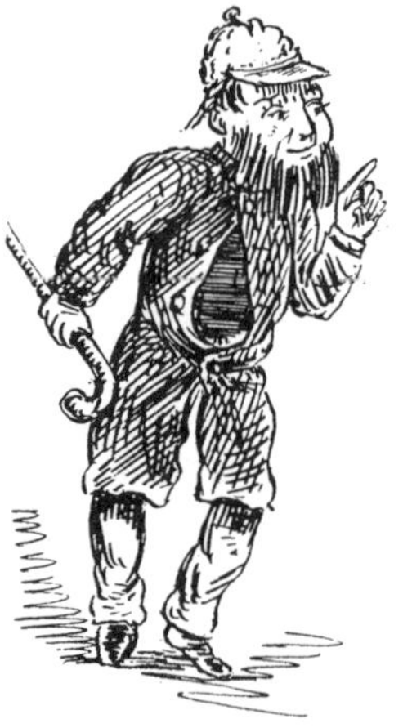

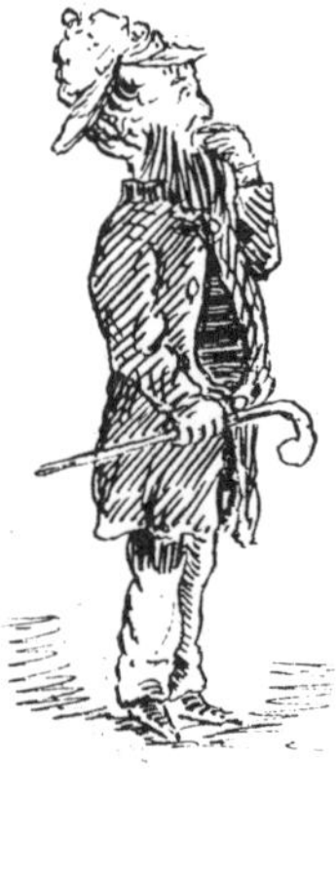

Sep 8th 1881... eh, Mister, how have you enjoyed your grouse and Partridge this season? If well you will feel strong enough to join me in singing - Oh where and oh where has that Mary Hann gone, oh where and oh where can she be, she says she is ill and longs to move on to somewhere that's nearer the sea. Well there, let her go, where the wild breezes blow and drink of the ozone her fill, she had better be there and indeed anywhere than here, defying our will. But this much we say, she has ta'en her own way and therefore she must abide by it. She has thought it the best and as for the rest there's nothing like letting her try it. Meanwhile all about we are both looking out for someone who's worthy and true; and when such we find it is quite in our mind to write straight away unto you. These girls - oh! alas it is hard to get at em and I fancy you saying now, Drat em, Sir, Drat em - Yours most truly...

Sep 10th 1881... Let me see, My dear Sir, wait a bit while I just think it over - Tomorrow, the Torpedo informs me our 'board' will be graced by cold Pork and a Brace of Grouse - so if you be minded to just nip over in your usual quiet fashion we shall be pleased to see you - and you will enjoy an opportunity of perceiving accurately our circumstance - Torpedo is well except for rheumatism in the hands and I am in tolerable general health but my leg in consequence of walking & standing too much upon it yesterday is today very painful - The weather has been for a day or two delightful but today the skies are again darkling & there is little sunshine. To each and all we crave commendation - I am truly yours ...

Sep 12th 1881... Look here now Mister - Never no more of those Hanns for us - No it will be Suss-anne in a week from now - and no more Hanns - neither Jane, Mary nor Jemimer Hann - quite tired of em and besides, you did not turn up yesterday after all. We had no one here but our revered Glossop friend and Mr J.K.M from Southport - Another dark and dismal morning - really how strangely sunless is and has been the present year - Mr Howe speaks of leaving us today, in which case the Southportian will in all probability be making tracks homeward also - Torpedo suffers much from toothache or Tic - I don't know which - Rheumatism likewise torments her greatly - Poor dear soul, she looks anything but well. Grows thinner daily - but is resolved it shall be Sus-anner and not Hann next time i.e. in a week from now if nothing untoward or unforseen meanwhile occurs. All combine in tenderness & remain Dear Sir, ever of thee...

Sep 13th 1881... Here I am in Southport but only for about 3 hours. Mr Howe has left us today & Mr J.K.M. It is to be 'Susanner' is our next help meet and she is due on Monday next at the latest - she is well reported of - able and willing - may she prove so, it is my earnest wish. If she proves herself worthy she will lack no consideration on our part. We are hopeful - Torpedo feels more of comfortable assurance about Susanner than Mary Hann & Hann. Yours most truly ...

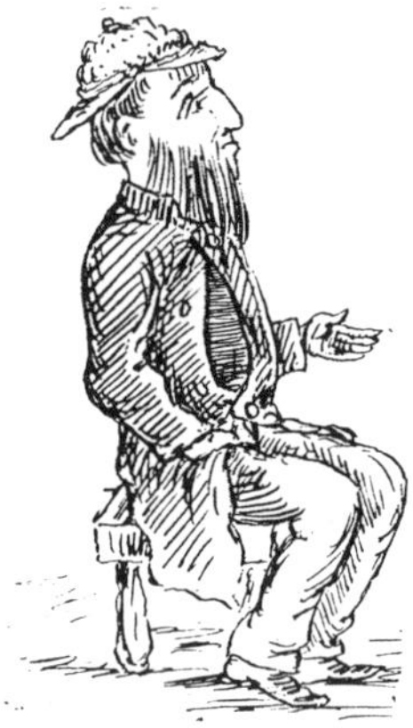

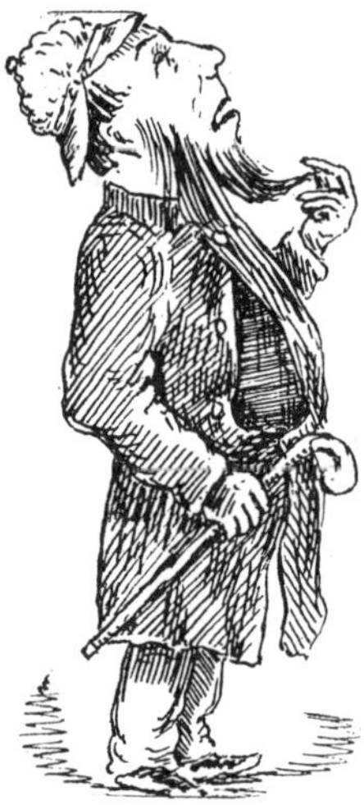

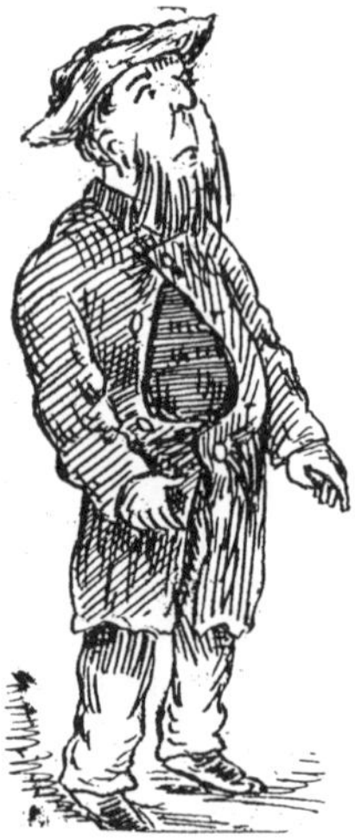

Sep 18th 1881... I waiteth, and waiteth and wonder what next, I don't think in my case I shall be vex'd. If no maidens come such as most people find 'em - let them absent themselves - I'll never mind 'em. I wish I could smoke just a soothing Havanner, I would pass on the time while I wait for Susanner. Torpedo was yesterday suddenly ta'en with a serious & hardly endurable pain. Unfortunately I was away at the time and I don't find it easy to fill up my rhyme. 'Spasms' had nearly driven her wild and nobody with her but Florrie the child. Torpedo she looketh alas! much the worse and wanteth, I thinketh, a suitable nurse. Oh that Susanner would hitherward come, wouldn't we sing, just, the chorus tum tum. I'll write you again when I know it quite plain that Sue by her presence has actually lain the fears that 'Pedo and I entertain, and now dear Sir permit me to be yours indeed and affectionatelee ...

Sep 21st 1881... wait, dear Sir, and let me muse a minute - it really seems as if the very 'juice' were in it. I detect, I fear, a cold discourteous manner in the expected maiden Miss Susanner. She hath not written neither hath she come, Hi diddle diddle, tee-dum, tee-dum, tee-dum. Here I stand awaiting - many excuses making thinking there is some mistaking while all the time I'm quaking. My heart it flutters so - my limbs will scarcely go My tears could freely flow but what to do I scarcely know - I'll peak my beard and twiddle my thumb while you, dear Sir sing tum-tum-tum. I subjoin the music -

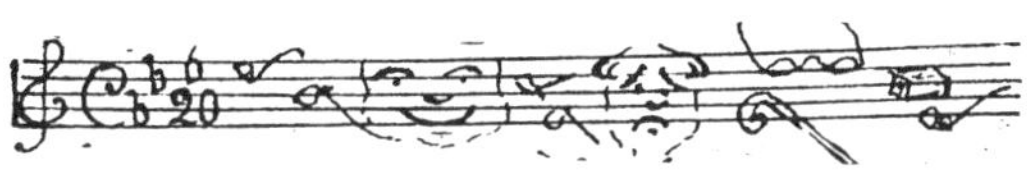

This arrangement will do as well for instrumental as for vocal use - Having sincerity for each and every ..P.S . This face is a rough but exact likeness of the Mary Hann of whom I made mention on a previous card ...

Sep 23rd 1881... Did you ever know such a thing? Susanner's neither come nor written - and we are expecting to have six guests here at the weekend - was ever anybody in such a fix as Torpedo and me? Away with your Hanns - perfidious Mary Hanns and Susanners!!! Miss L of Southport has sent word that she is not well, so she & Miss H have decided to come over on Saturday for a change. We are diligently looking out for Temporary help - failing which the only sensible course seems to be to run away. If you read of a singular and mysterious disappearance in this neighbourhood make your mind easy, we shall return when the weekend is past. Poor Bentham of the Brook House died on Wednesday evening about 9 o'clock ...

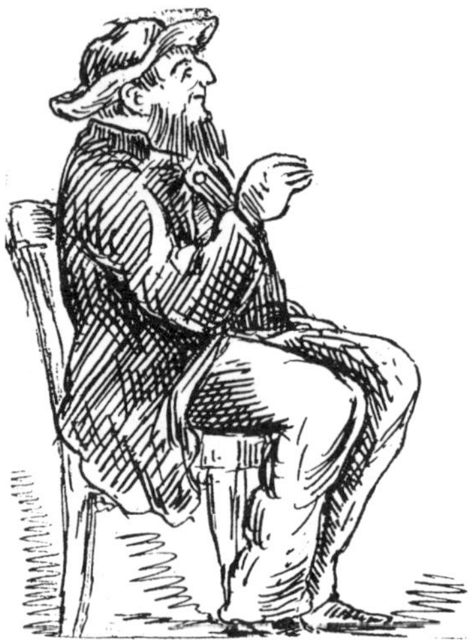

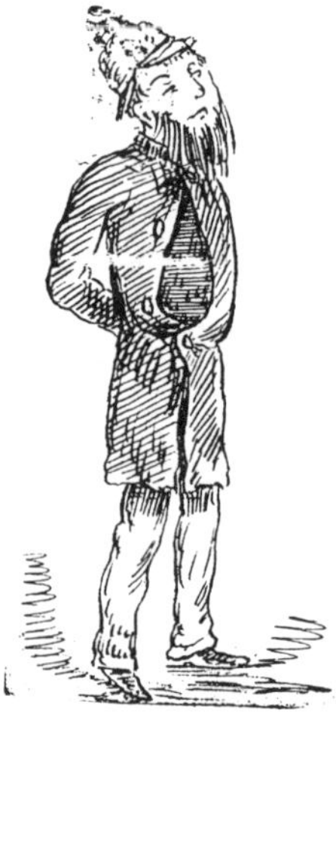

Sep 26th 1881... We didn't run away after all for the rain on Saturday last reduced the number of our visitants to three instead of six or thereabout - moreover help came to hand in a temporary and miscellaneous sort of way - We had an 'Election' and did well - that Susanner's present mistress is trying to keep her - but I mean to have the matter looked into - sit upon 'em - Bring hither the Bell, Book and candlelight - send with 'em a 'praste' and let him anathematise. We pause to weep and now conclude remaining ever your truly...

Sep 28th 1881... We didn't run away last Saturday - It was too wet. I have had occasion to go past your smoke room several times of late & the spot in the sunshine looks lovely now the trees are putting on their autumn tints. We have misty mornings and the country is beautiful. If I was you I would either be content with only one birthday in the year - or if I took myself three or four of them I would fix them upon some day of the week, other than Saturday or Sunday. By the time you've got your birthdays over the autumn will have gone & winter be here - Come whensoever you opine it meet i.e. any weekend most convenient to you ...

Sep 30th 1881... well, Mister, are you coming this weekend? The 'Missis' says she should, or shall, be pleased to see you but she daren't ask you as we have a young lady staying with us and your innate bashfulness would forefend your presence under those circumstances but as the young lady in question is engaged we may perchance even yet enjoy the pleasure of your presence & company unless alas! the birthday, respecting which your letter did not enlighten us much falls on Saturday - Ah! me! I leave it with you - The weather is 'glorious' grand mornings - grand days..P.S. If you come over this weekend please obtain for me from Preston Bank a cheque book 2/6 or there about and bring it with you ...

Oct 4th 1881... Well now, look here, as you have neither written nor come - how will next Saturday suit you - Have you another birthday on for that time? If so if I was you I'd put it off and be born some other day than the eighth of October - I never heard of anybody before being born on the 8th of October - such a thing seems quite out of the question - positively illegal. We had a few bright 'glorious' days but the evenings and mornings are becoming cold and alas! the days are short. Winter, it is all too patent draweth on apace - leaves are falling and russet tints are apparent everywhere - We think of visiting London & Windsor next week. We have not yet had an invitation to stay at the Castle but perhaps may have ...

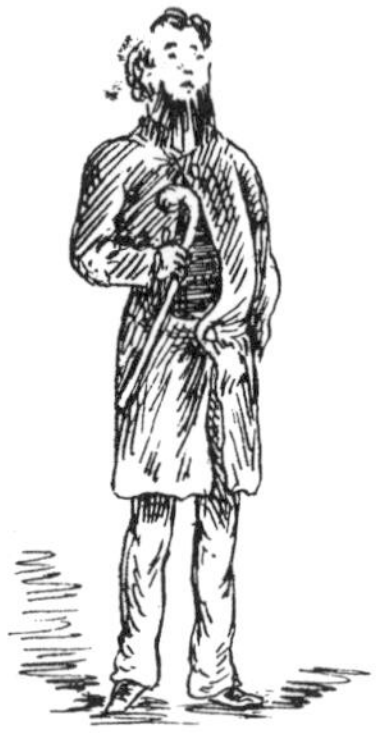

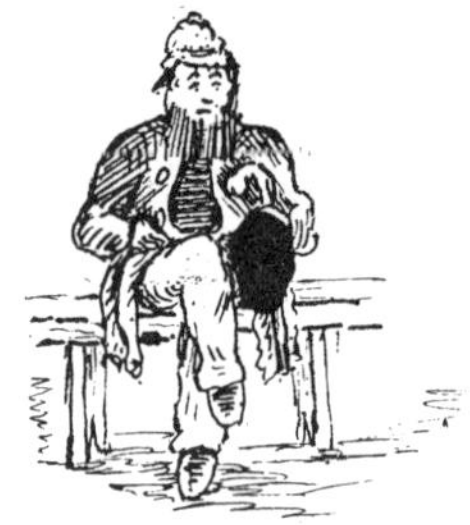

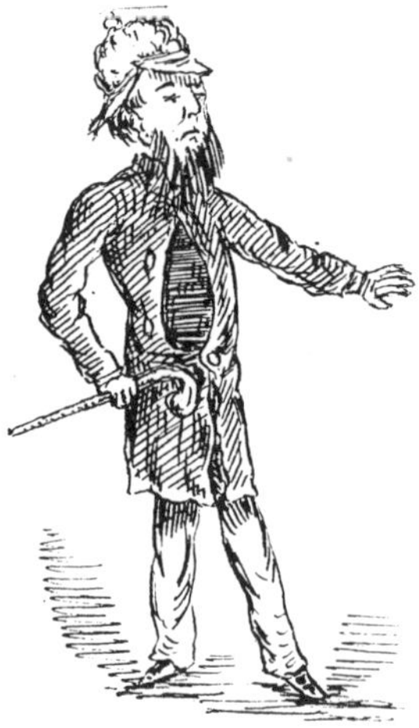

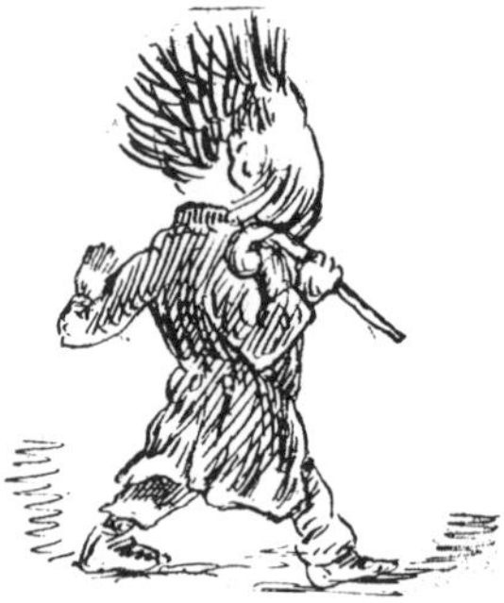

Oct 5th 1881... You see, my dear Mister, I am travelling - I have got to Southport again but on Monday next I am thinking of going further - that will be nice, won't it? The Post had not arrived when I left home this morning and I had only time to just illuminate the left hand corner of this card and put on the address when it was imperative to start forth upon my travels - if I were to catch the train I intended to utilise. You may think what a walker I am, notwithstanding my lame leg, when I can catch a train, especially an express. I must have made the road tremble and the dust fly - Having left before the Postman came to hand I don't know at all whether you have written to me about next Saturday so therefore I cannot say - so no more at present ...

Oct 10th 1881... eh, dear Mister, I cannot go to London this morning after all - I can't go and so it's no use talking. The rain is coming down like anything and my leg seems to have run mad bringing one into a condition bordering on the same state - I am truly in sorry plight. I've got cold and the inflammation has returned upon me with, if anything, greater violence than before. I find we should have had many changings by that train which I had elected to go by. Particularly at the Stations - changing from carriage to carriage - changing of Bank notes into pounds - pounds into shillings, shillings into pence and pence into nothing. It would have cost us a small fortune in necessary refreshments alone - for as Torpedo entertains an insuperable dread of expresses, which she is convinced are always running into something else, I was constrained to select one which would occupy between 7 and 10 hours on the journey - so I rather apprehend we shall have had to spend a night somewhere before getting to Littleton - a Domestick is due today. I wonder if she will come by express or ordinary. If by ordinary we may not see her till tomorrow ...

Oct 13th 1881... come Sir this is inexplicable - not a syllable to say whether you are coming this weekend or not - surely a line would not entail upon you much labour but would afford to me much comfort. We are going to foreign parts next Monday - at least we hope to do. We shall cross several rivers but don't intend to sail. We go first to a place called London and then to a country called Middlesex inhabited by a German people as the name implies - then we return home again and go to rest. If you want to see us before we commence our travels you must come on Saturday - after that we may not be at home for a fortnight ...

Oct 14th 1881... It's very nearly frightened me out of my wits this minute - my dear Sir. I thought the house was blown over and every window driven in - the wind smote them with such fury - and me all alone - my poor Dynamite has gone to Wigan. However will she get there and back - whatever two wheeler can ride out this fearful hurricane. I fear she will get more cold and her tic become unendurable. I wish she was back again. If the storm does not abate a little I shall run away...P.S. Oh dear, worse & worse than ever ...

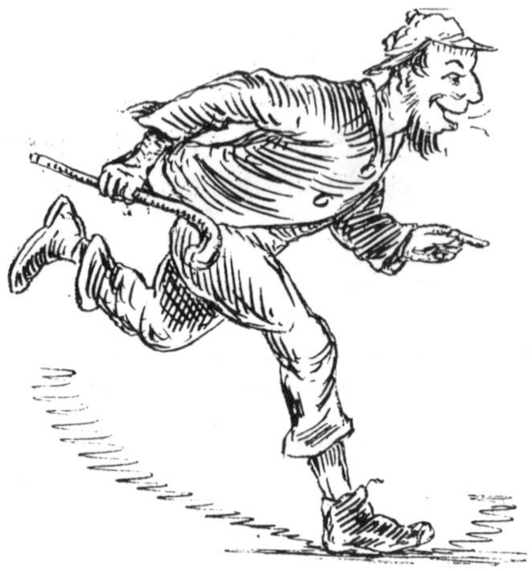

<u>Notes</u>

<u>Oct 20th 1881</u>

Nelson's Column was built in 1840 and Sir Edwin Landseer was commissioned by the government to provide the lions, added in 1867.

Vice-President Chester A. Arthur became President of the U.S.A when President Garfield was assassinated in September 1881.

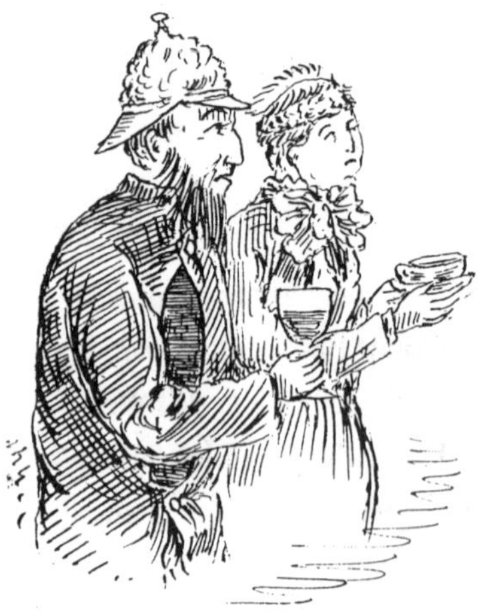

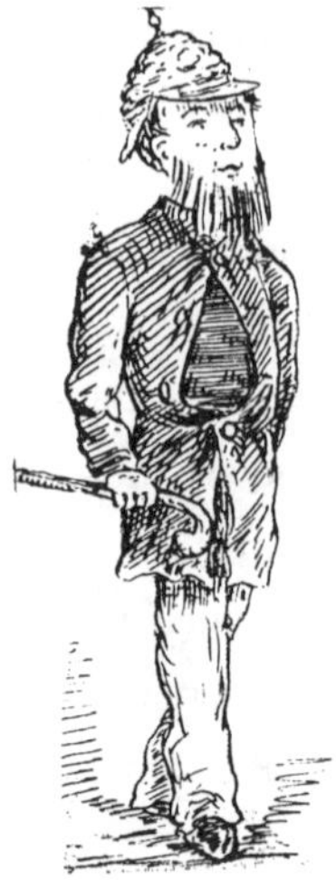

Oct 17th 1881... They're orff - They're orff! Him and Her - both of 'em. They're both off. He's left his fancy hat behind him - so I'm wearing it. If he bethinks hisself and turns back for it I shall have to give it up but meanwhile I'm glad to say they're orff - Him and Her - both of 'em - they're both orff - they're orff my dear Sir - they're orff - they're orff ...

Littleton Oct 18th 1881... We have come abroad and reached these foreign parts in safety - we got out at Stafford to enjoy a glass of coffee with a little warm sugar in it and also a cup of cocoa - greatly refreshed we proceeded but our refreshment craze caused us to be two hours behind the time we intended to get here ...

Littleton Oct 20th 1881... This London is quite a large place. It is larger than Wigan and I almost think it's as big if not bigger than Preston. It is really a big place and has some big people in it - why even the Mayor of the place is a Lord. They have an excellent police system - they put a man on the top of a big pillar in Trafalgar Square* from which standpoint he can look all round London & when he sees a riot or a Burglary or an assault & battery going on or anybody selling short of weight he tells the police who are parading near the foot of the pillar. This hat of mine is becoming more and more military looking - the button on top is getting loose and with its loosening attachment can be drawn out a little and sometimes set erect. We are both well and enjoy our 'out' immensely ...P.S. I suppose the Mayor of this place is also President of the United States*, his name is Arthur ...

Oct 21st 1881... We're off to London yonder this here morning to look at that there tower where it is said they keep the lions. I must know whether they will bite before I go in. After having looked sufficiently at this here and that there we shall return to this place. The rain on Thursday night has taken the wax out of the thread - the loosened thread which holds the button on to the crown of my cap. It is a little peculiar at present but we will see what can be done to rectify it. We have been highly favoured with the weather since we came...

Oct 24th 1881... we have been to the Tower - we went on Saturday last and I feel inclined to admire my cap more and more. By waxing the loose limp thread attachment and drawing out the Button a little it gives precisely the correct shape - You should procure one of them it would set off your figure finely. The effect is considered a great success in my case - our beautiful weather has ceased and we have now heavily pouring rain - ah me! ah us! ah, everybody! It seems the Lions have been taken out of the Tower and have been placed in Trafalgar Square - they are very large and very black ones - they seem to be quite accustomed to the people passing for they never roared - I should think there would be a heavy thick Fog in London yesterday. It got quite apparent here and we are only a matter of a few miles S.W of the great city ... Brother Evans sends muchness ...

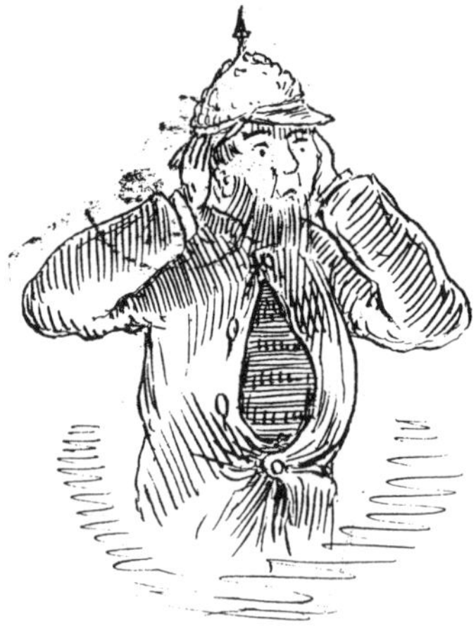

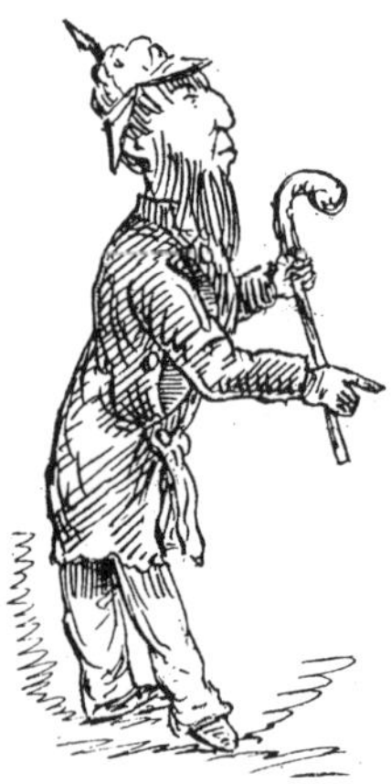

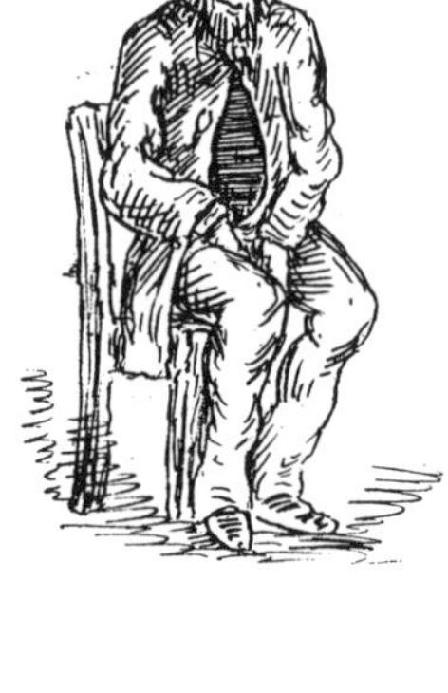

Oct 26th 1881... I have finished my 'sight-seeing' and on Thursday am trudging home again. Please address to me the 'Standards' as formerly. I hear there was a poor fellow run over and nearly killed besides my house the other day. His father was killed about a fortnight ago and his mother died suddenly some time since - I have heard no particulars. We are taking the 'Midland' for our homeward journey - all well here except the dog - He feels sickly rather. Don't you think the waxed thread and elongated button improves the cap - Yours very truly ...

Oct 27th 1881 (Night))... Oh dear, Oh dear, my head is quite bewildered even yet. The roar of trains, the hiss of steam and rattle of cars on the Stoney Street - the Babel of voices and the general hurly burly of travel distract my poor head even to the present time - We returned by the Midland and saw something of the Derbyshire scenery in its Autumn glory - We travelled from 8 or rather a quarter to eight this morning till near the like time this evening. We are tired muchly but have just strength left to thank you for the Cheque Book which awaited us - We have brought Florrie and Joo home with us - I will write more by and bye - meanwhile be assured of our kind remembrance and Believe me Dear Sir very truly ...

Oct 31st 1881... You missed it Sir - You made a great mistake for we had a grand day and two glorious Ducks. You would for sure have enjoyed them greatly - Why did you not come and see us after our great travels. Really how severe the cold has been for some days I can scarcely keep warm and an east wind I think has rendered this frigor more penetrating than it otherwise would have been. We were this evening to have been at a Harvest Tea Party but the cold has retained us at the fireside. We are yours abundantly, Dear Sir ...

Nov 2nd 1881... The cold is dreadfully keen but I have ventured to wrap up and come over to Southport. I am returning this evening and hope the exercise will prove beneficial - For the last two days I have felt quite starved continually - Even a hot fire only seemed to roast me while the unroasted portions continued just as cold as before - Wrapping up I find to be an excellent thing though by some aesthetic people the utilisation of a spotted blue or red kerchief may perhaps be regarded as a slight disfigurement but we never heed them. What we want is comfort, my dear Sir, comfort. Yours very truly ...

Nov 7th 1881... oh dear Mister - it has been cold - during the early part of last week my fingers were almost too numb to write so I had to sit shivering and warming my hands as best I could for we could not get a fire to burn in any of the rooms downstairs. I therefore became a sort of cherub sitting up aloft keeping watch over the Portico for better weather & more genial temperature. I felt anxious and am told looked so. My ankle pained me greatly yesterday - and the pigs broke down their stye door and gave us grievous trouble ...

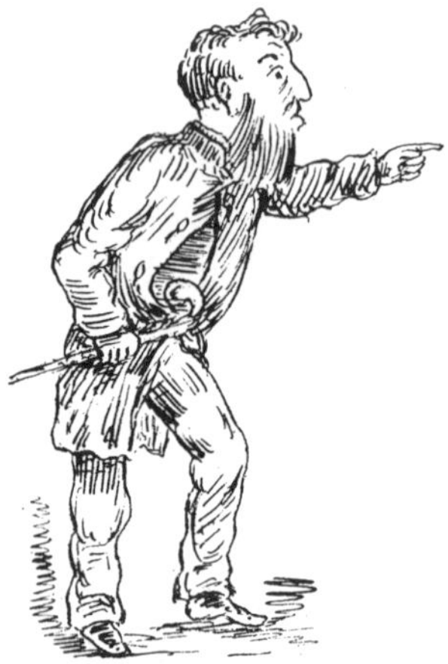

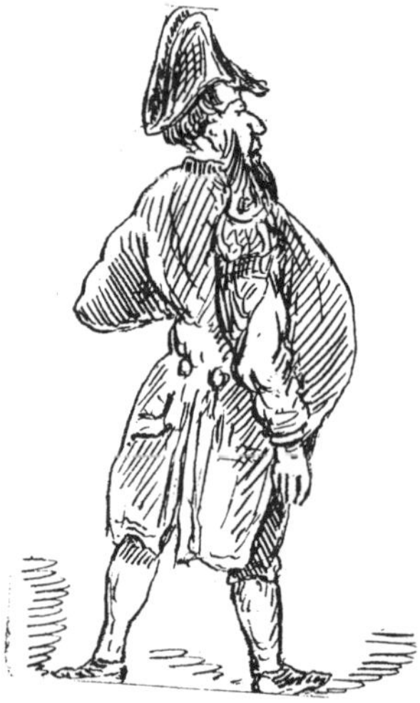

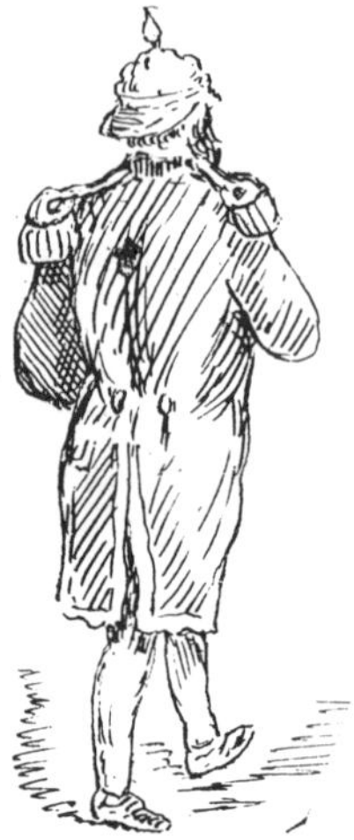

Nov 10th 1881... This fine weather is straightening me up a little so that I can again do the Roman Fall instead of the hunch back bend which e'erwhile my painful limb and distracted head had made a usual accessory to my gait - My leg is still as painful and my head e'en more distracted with figures, but it is the balmy south wind & bright sunshine which does me good & renders me erect. I have so much to do with figures just now that I am almost afraid I may myself be one in due course and if such be the case I should, of all the figures in the Multiplication Table prefer to be number one. It's a busy world - a busy time and I'm a busy man. Every one (i.e.) me and the other me join in muchness ...

Nov 10th 1881... I think in my last I intimated in a brief way the fact that I have not an idle bone in me - so it is & sure so - my thoughts are active - I am diligent in eating and every nerve seems 'on the work'. Every thing, almost, is a 'labour' to me & such being the case surely, my dear Sir, I'm a working man - If you think you know anybody who can do less work in more time than I can, just trot your wonderful specimen out, and let us feast our admiring gaze upon him. We haven't a room in the house just now, except the Kitchen, which does not smoke. Filthy habit - wretched house!...

Nov 14th 1881... If we had deferred for a week or two our visit to the South I might on the 9th have taken part in the Lord Mayor's show - a good stately portly figure adds largely to the effect of a civic pageant - my figure would have been invaluable; and I feel no doubt the Right Honourable the new occupant of the Mansion House would have promptly pressed for my presence in the Guild Hall. However my engagements and arrangements have been adverse to the London show in this matter - Of course I should have walked in a suitable attire - cocked hat &tc - what nice weather we have had so far in this month excepting of course the snow storm on the first - We have had scarcely any fog and the sun has pleasantly shone withal - We have still Florence Eveline with us but at present no one else. My ankle has been very painful this week. We both combine in tender remembrance ...

Nov 17th 1881... Upon a second consideration I don't think - if I had graced the Metropolitan Mayoral show - that I should have consented to have worn one of those unsightly cocked hats - what could have been more suitable than my own trusty and adaptable Preston purchased hat with the button elongated and the attachment threads loosened and stiffened a little with wax. However luck has not been in the Lord Mayor's way this time - How fare ye all amid this hurricane - We hear here the whispers of Eolus with painful distinctness & feel his breath ...

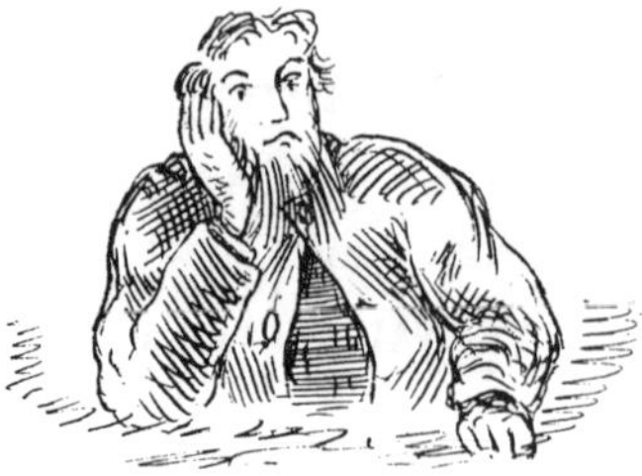

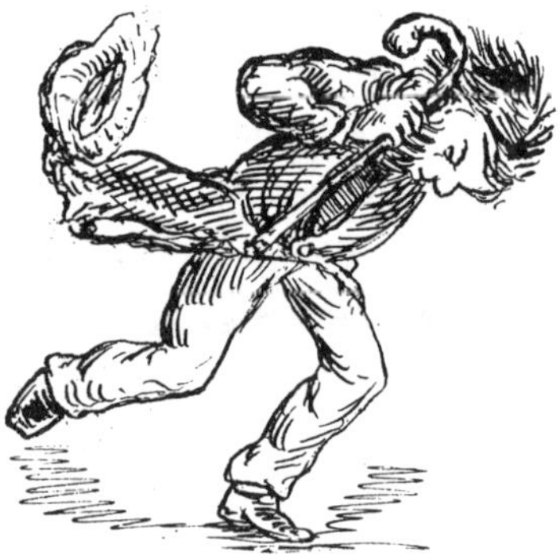

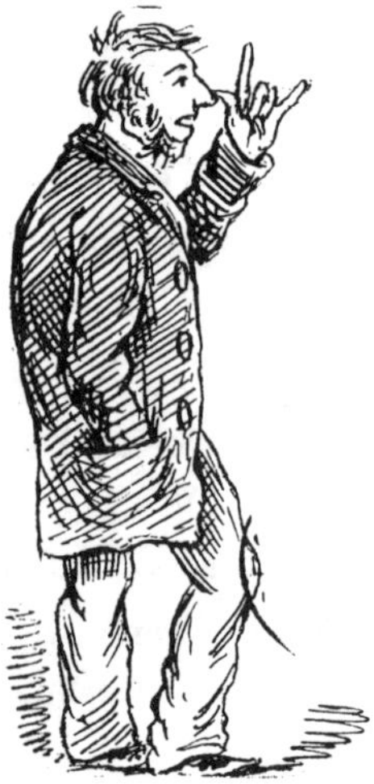

Nov 19th 1881 (Night)... ah my dear Sir I have had an anxious week and feel weary and thoughtful - My poor ankle, foot & leg as far as the calf show signs of 'dropsy' now - one night I found them greatly swollen and though not now quite so much so the presence of water is still perceivable. I have had no opportunity for rest - I have today been at Southport and am tonight considerably pained in consequence - I have a busy day in prospect on Monday next and expect Brother Marsden here in the afternoon - Peradventure another clerical friend will accompany him. The wind howleth. The day has been mild but the wind testifieth of winter's approach. I hope you are all well. Believe me as ever ...

Nov 24th 1881... It is very windy still but I nevertheless hasten to thank you for your letter and Photo - the latter is all right in execution as a work of art but there are points about it that as a likeness don't improve it. You are coming over you say, when the moon sheds her light beams around us sufficiently. Don't give any more of the Photos except to intimate friends until I see you - at all events don't send any of them over hereaway till then & come soon. Yours most truly & in haste ...

Nov 28th 1881... I consider this a rude and vulgar thing for anyone to do - yet this is just what in effect the Land League in Ireland are this minute doing at the Government - a gross return truly but our consciences are clear as neither you nor I have had anything to do with it - The Government and the Land League must settle it among themselves for at my time of life I cannot help them - ah, Ha. Your heart has failed you - the weather occasioned the terror - you durst not come on Saturday - Ha ha you were frightened - you were frightened. We have a young lady from Ormskirk abiding with us & Mr Parkes comes tomorrow I think. He has been in Lancashire a fortnight. Hope you are all well ...

Nov 30th 1881... You must know, my dear Sir, that I was in Manchester on Friday last (25th) the day of the Synod - and such a downpour of rain was there that I am sure you would have pitied such a poor cripple had you seen me plodding despairingly through the wet obedient to a summons from my 'Better'. Manchester does not look enticing on a wet day in this month - Torpedo went with me hoping to get a peep into some shop windows but her hopes were vain. I am expecting Mr Parkes here each minute - I looked for him yesterday but without avail. He is due anytime and so keeps me on the tip toe of expectancy. Yours ever ...

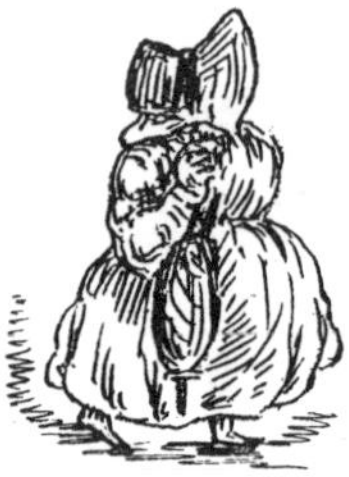

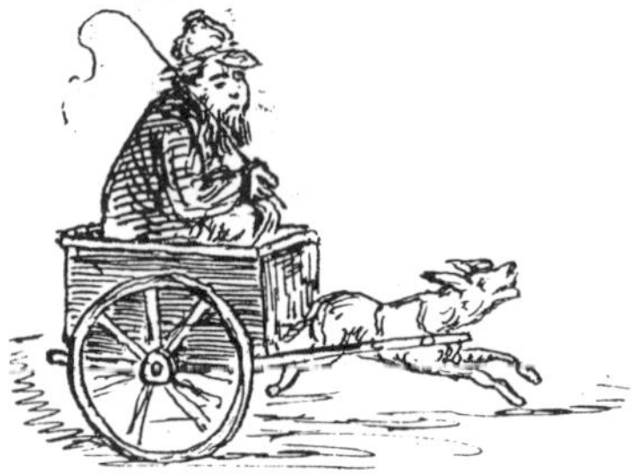

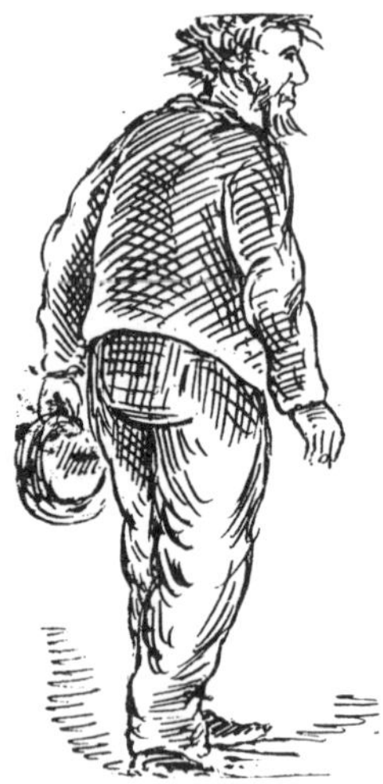

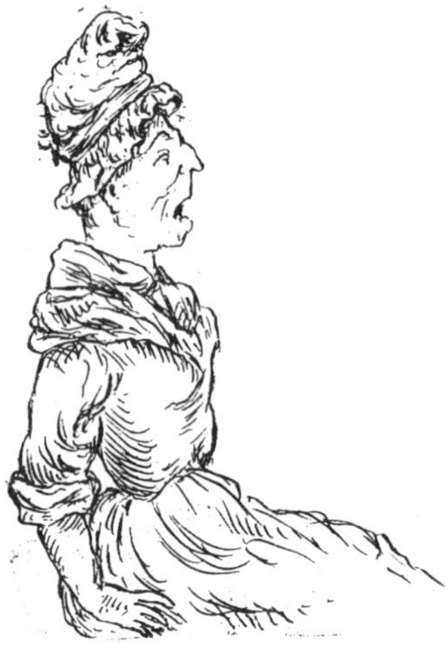

Dec 6th 1881... Well how do you feel my dear after your long ride? The weather at all events has been favourable to you - mild and open. It is really hard to realise that we are galloping through December when usually ice and snow are most prominent factors in the Landscape. Mr Parkes has not yet come to hand nor have we received a line in explanation hitherto. I am today off to Southport for a few hours to enjoy the pleasant showers which enable us to have a bath of that sort without the necessity of paying for it except under the head of Medicine rendered needful by the 'cold thrown in' with the bathing. Dear Mister yours as ever ...

Dec 9th 1881... I really must have a conveyance of some sort - even if it be a dog cart only - for I have a great deal of going about to do on foot with difficulty. November is here at last - I thought it would be - thick fog and plenty of it. We hope you are all well but for Asthma & Bronchitis this will prove very trying. Yours in sincerity ever ...

Dec 13th 1881... get your skates ready, Dear Sir, get your skates ready - put dowels on your shoes and prepare to skim like the 'Swallow' or the 'Swift' over the glass surface of the ponds. Make all haste for the winter and the Frost are here at last - the ground is white and hard and no doubt the surface of the pits frozen. What a fearful fire that in the Ringstrasse at Vienna last week, also that triple collision in the tunnel near London this week. We are fairly well. Hoping you abound, all, in salubrity, I remain Dear Sir ever ...

Dec 14th 1881... eh my Dear Sir you don't surely say you're going off this week and not coming here to see me. I shall be like to see if I can get over to Preston to look at and talk to your dear self for an hour or two next week some time. I don't envy you your journey at this season of Canonbury collidings and London Fogs - not to make mention of a prevailing cold little short of that at the top of the North Pole - why it's almost enough to freeze an unwary traveller to the seat even of a First class Railway carriage. We're expecting company next week but on what day they come I have not information yet - meanwhile for your self and family we hereby transmit our kindest wishes and I remain your ever affectionate Pipsey Popsey ...

Dec 19th 1881... I suppose you'll be home again by this time - and so I will even venture to send you just a line to say that I think some of the gales last evening were more forceful than that which on the 28th day of December 1879 blew the Tay Bridge over. On Friday evening through rain and tempest Mr Howe unexpectedly turned up and is with us now. We are seated by the fireside together - I am thinking and writing while he poor man is tenderly nursing a stomach ache - Christmas is now very near us - a few days more and then the waits and Christmas bells will make the welkin echo. Mr Howe's 'ache' is becoming demonstrative. It has made him jump ...

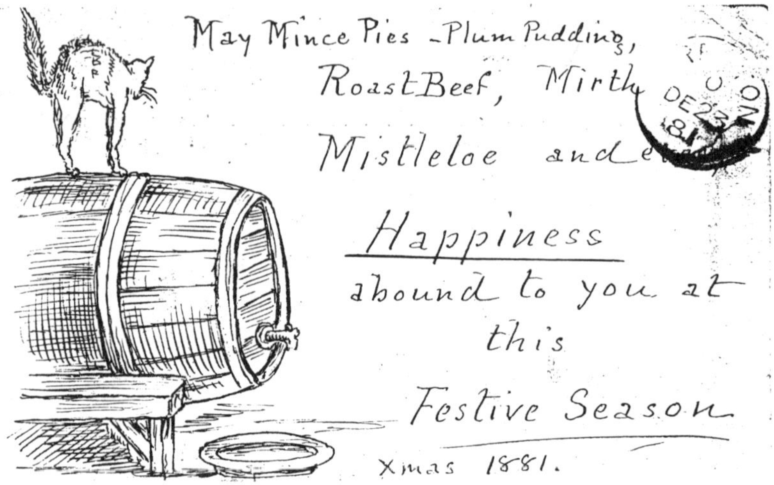

Notes

<u>Xmas 1881</u> Mr & Mrs Evans (Brother Evans) of Pemberton are the couple whose wedding is referred to in August 1881.

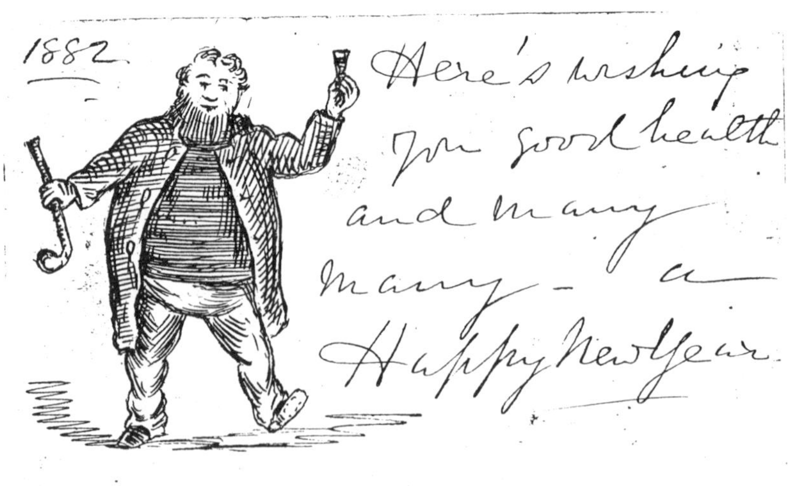

undated... I have really been nearly blown over by the recent forceful blasts. In this exposed altitude - this rural eyerie or eyrie or eerie it has been next to impossible to retain one's foothold. If we had not been fairly possessed of materiality there would probably have been a sort of transmigration of the lot of us. We hope you have sustained no injury from the storm and that ye are all well. Mr Howe joins Torpedo and self in kindly sentiments ...

Xmas 1881... May Mince Pies - Plum Pudding, Roast Beef, Mirth, Mistletoe and every Happiness abound to you at this Festive Season.

Xmas 1881... oh now, My dear - really - aren't we to have mistletoe this Christmas? It's the first time since I was a child that I have not enjoyed the privelege of the mystic bough. We return you a multitude of thanks for the good wishes conveyed per cards - Not much like Christmas is this peculiarly mild wet weather. How are you all? Much happiness be your portion. Mr & Mrs E* are with us. They leave for France shortly, then they propose Italy, Egypt and Holy Land ...

Dec 29th 1881 (Night)... I am running over to Preston as early as possible and shall not fail on that occasion to inflict upon you my presence for a little space - oh, what weather - fog, fog, fog day after day, fog. I should have been in Preston long ere this but the gentleman in Leyland upon whose supervision my visit depends is and has been so busy that he could not return to me certain documents which I must bring with me for signature. We are going to Southport in the morning, health and weather permitting. Mr & Mrs E are in Wigan for a day or two. They are not due here again before Friday or Saturday morning. We started this afternoon for a sale of work at Purbold but the thick mist on the hilltop turned us back again. We greet ye well ...

1882... Here's wishing you good health and many many a Happy New Year ...

Jan 3rd 1882 Night... This is a good vintage of yours and worthy of high commendation. To a weary traveller it is most sustaining. I found my well accustomed chariot awaiting me at Croston station - the ride was a very cold one. I reached my dwelling duly and since, have heard the rain hail & sleet pattering cheerily against the window panes. My heels - o, my!! don't mention them - they form at present a painful subject. I salute you with consideration and am truly ...

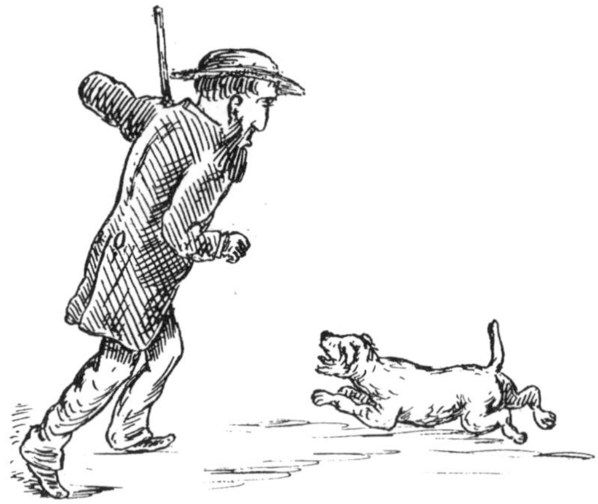

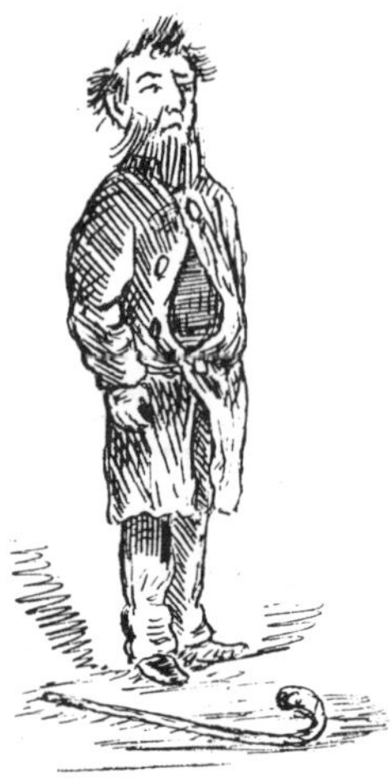

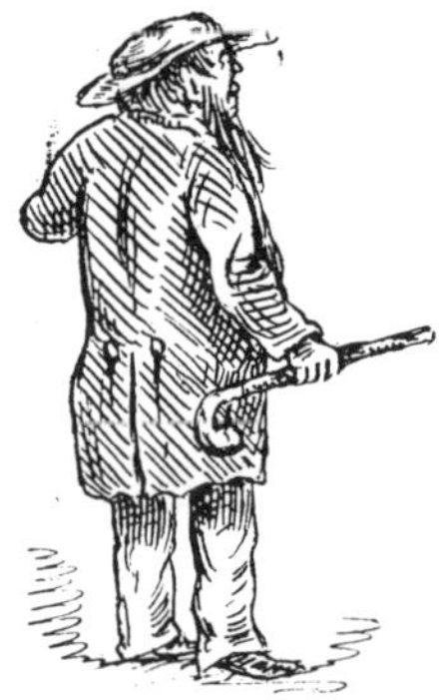

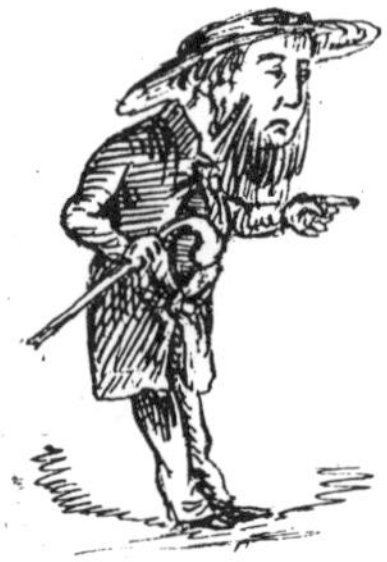

Jan 5th 1882... now my dear Sir How d'you like my new hat? There's no button on the Top of this, you see - my friends here away consider it as quite a Model some say it's 'Pertickler Moddle' and exactly suits my Noddle - The crown is low; the brim is wide A Preston House the Hat supplied. If in its shape you any beauty see To Preston Town must all the honour be. It was not one the Makers had in stock t'was made to order, for my head - the Block - Your letter just to hand - coast clear - Torpedo's pulse seems to beat agreeably - come with a good heart. Your sister of course will accompany you. Hope the weather will prove propitious ...

Jan 9th 1882... If I did not on Dec 31st 1881 lay my stick about that big dog when it was running away after making such havock of my crockery don't I beg you think it was because I feared it - My courage was over balanced by my magnanimity so I exacted no retribution but let it get it gone - right gladly. May <u>you</u> never be upset by a savage quadruped though you deserve it almost for not driving over as arranged on Saturday last. Really what a day yesterday was for rain and tempest!!!! ah me!!!! ...

Jan 14th 1882 (Night)... I rather think this new hat is a little <u>too big</u> for me - My head seems to penetrate a trifle, just a trifle, too far into it. Whether this is due to the head having become smaller or the hat being of too roomy construction I cannot determine - The shape of the Hat is said to suit my figure admirably. Can you get to know for me who are the agents for the Lancaster Banking Co in Wigan and Southport? If you can I shall be grateful for the information. Our guests are still with us - Joo is also here. Our charioteer is very ill - confined to bed. I have had a busy week - and was on Friday in Wigan - Rode hither and thither in open vehicle and got <u>nearly</u> chilled to numbness. All combine in greetings ...

Jan 17th 1882... Torpedo and guests having gone off to Wigan I am this morning <u>'standing at ease'</u> to use a military expression such as I would have done had I been wearing that other hat still - I mean the one with the button on top. Fog still prevalent weather mild and damp but Barometer high. Tomorrow our late Postal messenger Mr Henry Hitch is to be interred. He departed this life on Saturday - The cause of his death I am told was Inflammation of the lungs and stroke. I am renting a field and making it into two by a fence. Affectionate regards multiplied and fervent ...

Jan 20th 1882... My esteemed friend your kind and prompt attention to my enquiry relative to Wigan & Southport agents of L.B. Co places me under an obligation. I thank you very much - and you will be surprised to learn that I have been wildly engaged in multiplying the buildings upon my glebe - structure after structure has been planted thereupon until in a small way my premises begin to resemble to some extent a town. Mr Evans is architect and Clerk of Works and ably he fulfils his functions of his dual office ...

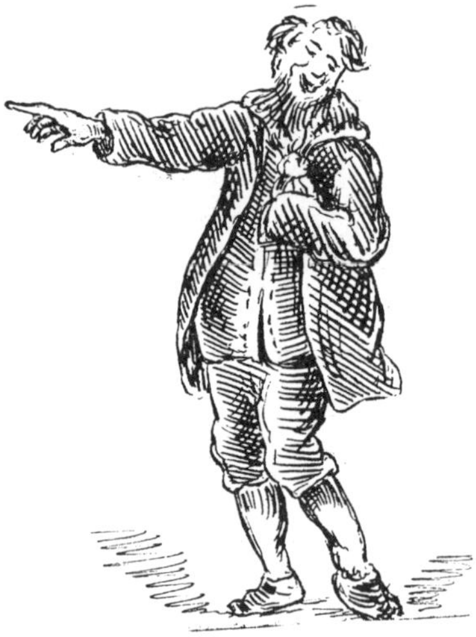

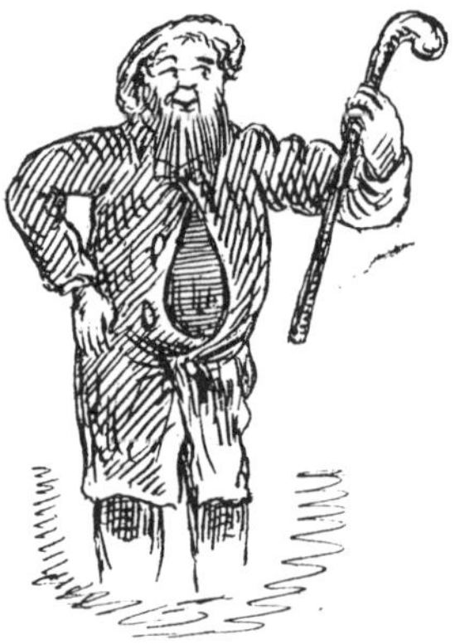

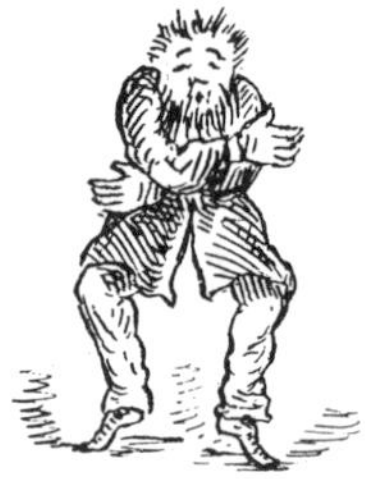

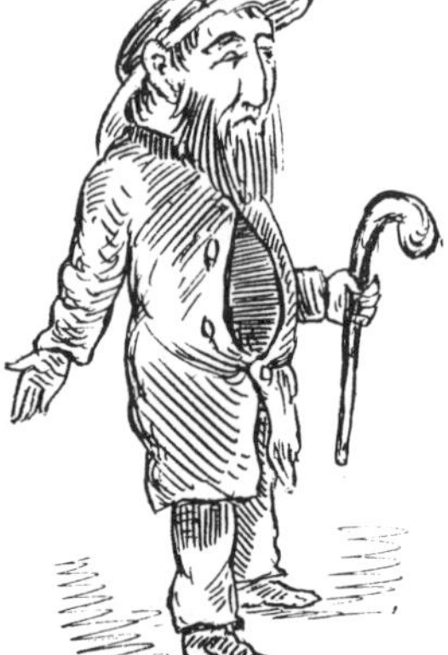

Jan 23rd 1882... Oh, me dear Sir, They're gone, they're gone - They are for sure - I saw 'em this very morning with me own eyes, going up the road in a wehicle. So it's a fact - a real downright positive fact - It's these leave takings and partings as does me up - I can't write - I can't think and I can't do nothink, so no more at present ...

Jan 24th 1882... Hi look you Mister, I am contemplating the giving up of this stick or anyway using it more seldom than I have done. I cannot just this minute tell you why; but you know as I know that we live in an age of changes - Ministries are changed - Land Laws are changed; and my stick is to be changed - It can't be helped you know - but I will advise you further in due course - Coming events cast their shadows before - The prospective event to which I have made reference as inducing me to think of discarding my stick is not Wedding Birth or Pig Killing - When I am in a position to report further I will do so. Mr Howe was to have been here yesterday but has not come - He is a provoking Biped is that Mr Howe. But never mind - let him went - ever faithfully yours ...

Jan 27th 1882... How is it? Please, no Standard, no letter - no nothink by today's post - ah me! ah us! and the North Riding election just settled. By the way talking of Riding just reminds me - Did I tell you in a previous letter, note or Postcard that I have 'bin and took a Farm'? That I have divided the same into two parts - one to put money 'on' - the other to get money 'off'. One for the laying of money 'out' and the other for gathering of money 'in' - Our Hen too has 'layed' twice - we have the second egg in the house now - so you will perceive things seem to be looking up a little - and besides all the foregoing I am expecting shortly to have a trap - a vehicle and a 'Rosinante' or 'Bucephalus' i.e. a mettled steed and here comes in the Riding - North, South, East and West - so no more at present ...

Jan 30th 1882... oh, it's vast cold at least anyway - In fact it is nigh impossible to clap warmth into ones benumbed fingers anyway. Farming is hard and unpoetic work nowadays - It is all very well in spring time and summer when daisies kiss the spade - The sun shines brightly and the modest primrose and clover bows in salutation as you proceed to labour, but with east winds and driving sleet prevailing commend me to an easy chair and comfortable fireside. The wind yesterday was furious in this upland region - You should have been here - it would enable you to form an idea of banishment to Siberia ...

Feb 2nd 1882... Do you know, my dear Sir even this hat does not suit some of them and they even go so far as to say it does not suit me. Now under the circumstances what's to be done my dear, what's to be done? I think I had better have repeated the white one with the button on top. But really one doesn't know what to do for the best - it's a hard case so no more at present ...

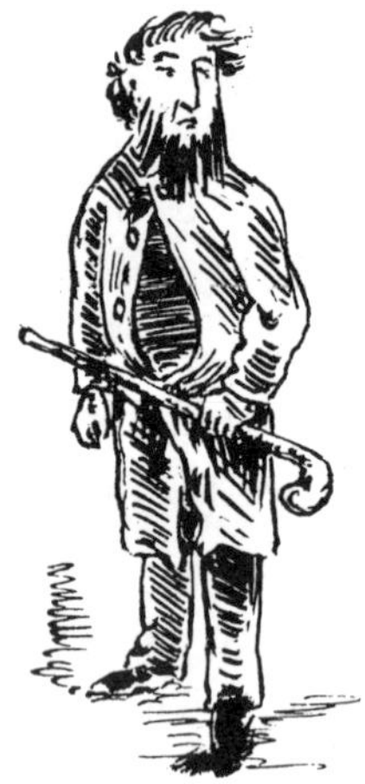

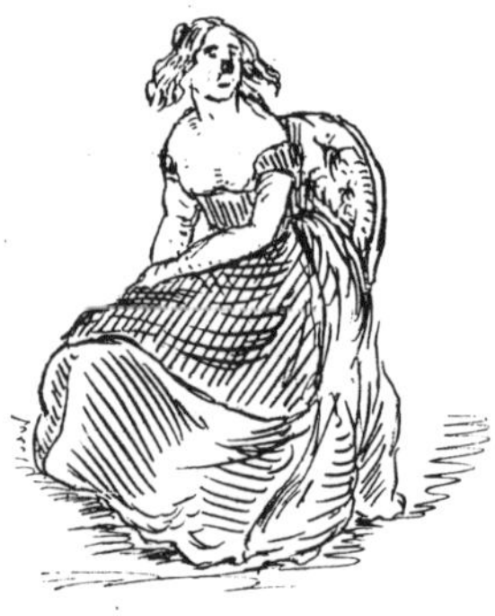

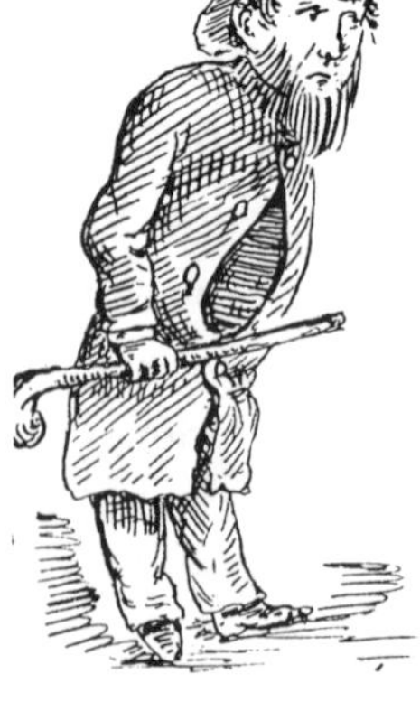

Feb 6th 1882... see, my dear Sir, I look at it this way. There's a Tea Party we'll suppose - room crowded - air hot - some windows open - myself on the Platform. Well - this concatenation of adverse circumstances does not do for me. I was thus situated on Saturday night - It was our Tea Party - I Presided - I was up on the Platform then - I am down in the mouth now for strange to say in the hot room I caught a cold - I am coughing, sneezing and regretting - I think I shall run away and thus try to dodge the cold - colds must be slow moving or else such slow people could not catch them ...

Feb 10th 1882... I'm beginning to be a great traveller. You will doubtless be startled to hear but it is nevertheless a fact that for near half an Octave I have been flying my kite about Liverpool Kirkdale Walton and elsewhere. Today, or tomorrow - I am trotting home again to read the Standards that have accumulated in my absence. My heart is still warm & pulsates in tenderness ...

Feb 11th 1882... We returned from Walton yesterday calling at Ormskirk en route homeward - we feel quite tired this morning and need rest muchly - I am sorry to find a rumour prevailing about Wigan and neighbourhood to the effect that Mr Evans has been drowned through the accidental upsetting of a pleasure boat in which Mrs E. and he were sailing. I trust the rumour is not true - I cannot learn how it originated or where. Hoping you are both well, I remain, Dear Sir ...

Feb 14th 1882... ah my Dear, How much longer am I to be kept waiting? This is too bad!!!! another Valentine's Day and yet no proposal. You'll be sorry for this some time - We looked for you on the 12th as the day was fine, But it seems you're not yet my Valentine ...Hann

Feb 14th 1882... I believe my dear Sir that there is of the 'Tay Party' a report in the Chorley Guardian last week's issue - I am a bachelor today mine gentler and Better Half being from home - she had 'nothing' to go for and I doubt she will very faithfully, cleverly and effectively bring it - The morning is fine - the wind forceful and I think I can descry tokens of change in the not distant future - to rain ...

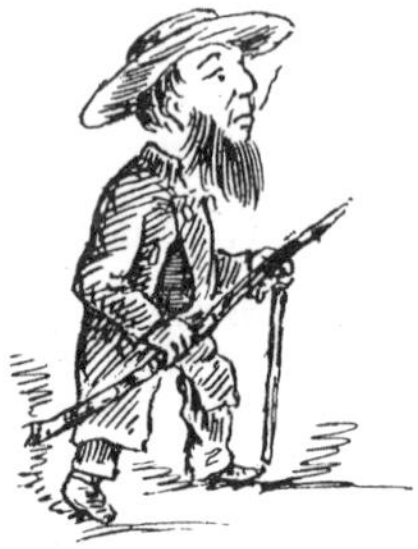

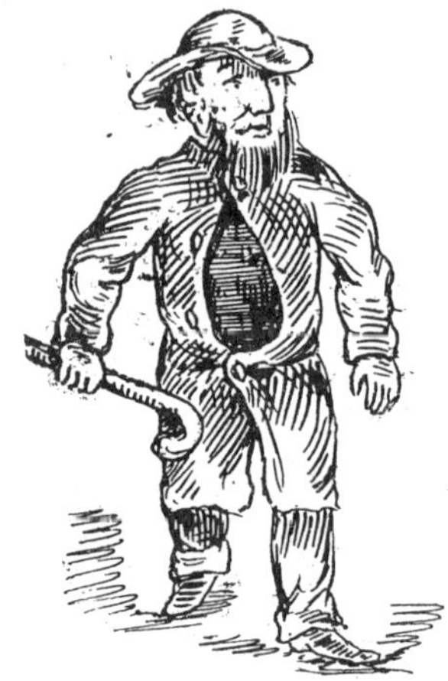

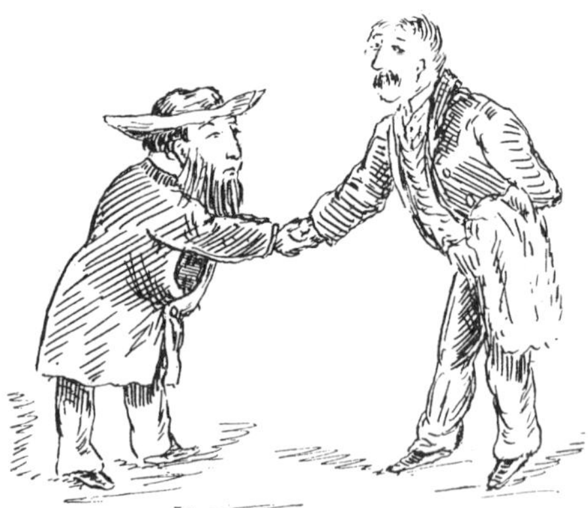

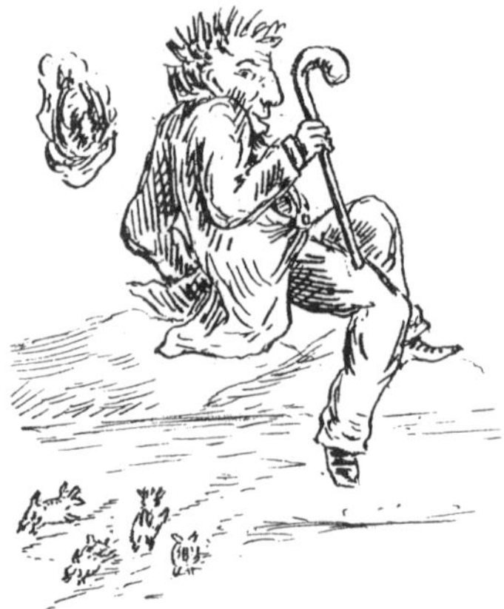

Feb 18th 1882...This is a sugar cane which I brought from Liverpool and will show you sometime when you come. I got it from a man who obtained it from a man, who begged it from another man who was captain of a ship trading to Mauritius who received it from a man who was agent to another man who grew sugar. The thing is genuine - anybody can see that it is neither a cedar nor a pitchpine; and few persons in this country would ever mistake it for an oak and I am sure that you will distinguish between it and my walking stick. I am glad to tell you Mr E. is not drowned - I have heard from him and Mrs E. They are in Paris but about to leave for Spain or Italy - They are undecided which. You must see my sugar cane ...

Tuesday evening Feb 21st 1882... I can wear this New Hat of mine quite easily when the weather is calm and still as it has been today - but in the high winds of Saturday, Sunday and Monday there was no keeping it on so I wore the other and gave no thought to appearance. 'Soos Hanner' or 'Shusan' left us last Thursday so I have now to go errands and look after things a bit. My quadruped and equipage have not arrived yet - Perhaps the disease now prevalent amongst horses may make it desirable not to be hasty in effecting a purchase. My coach house, Hay Store and Stable are made ready so on that point I am easy - I have had too the promise of a lot of Hay &c when my Nag turns up - The Poney Equipage harness and sugar cane will be quite an exhibition for you to look at ...

Feb 23rd 1882... ah my dear and solitary Sir it grieves me see your looks so woebegone. The life of a hermit doesn't suit you - Poor dear man come hither and I will heartily extend the right hand of good fellowship towards you. A night shirt has been aired and awaiting you about three weeks. I am glad to hear you have recommended perambulation in the mornings - Don't pine in solitude, either get married or come hither. I have forgotten almost what you are like. Weather fine snowdrops and Primroses blooming beautifully ...

Feb 25th 1882... Disappointment and hope deferred are enough to weigh any man down - to knock him over and render him generally obfusc. I quite expected this morning a letter to say you would be coming over this weekend to 'jine me' as the saying is - ah me, I sit and loll in sadness - tearful as the clouds this morning. In haste thine ever truly ...

Feb 28th 1882...There was a time once when I could have leaped and bounded after the hounds as lithely as anybody - but such activity I possess no longer. I had a day out yesterday with a neighbour - and did such a power of walking that from stiffness and exhaustion consequent on yesterday's exertions it would be almost more than my remaining strength would admit - would the effort of jumping over a moderate sized mushroom this morning - Yours languidly but truly ...

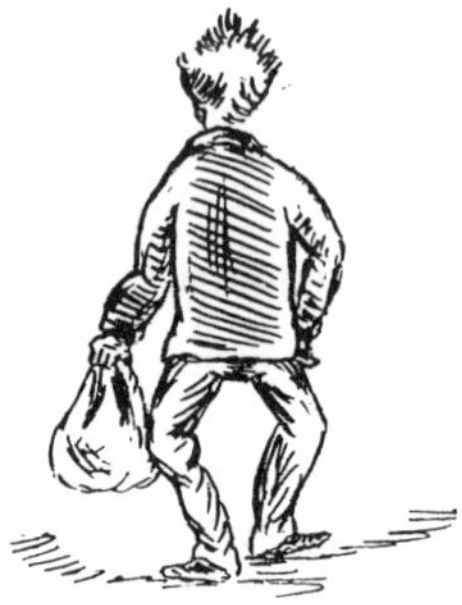

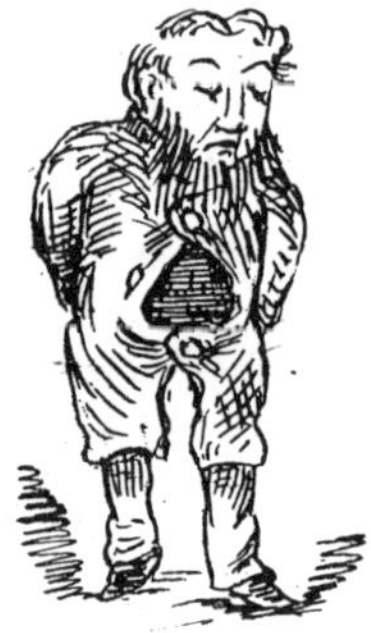

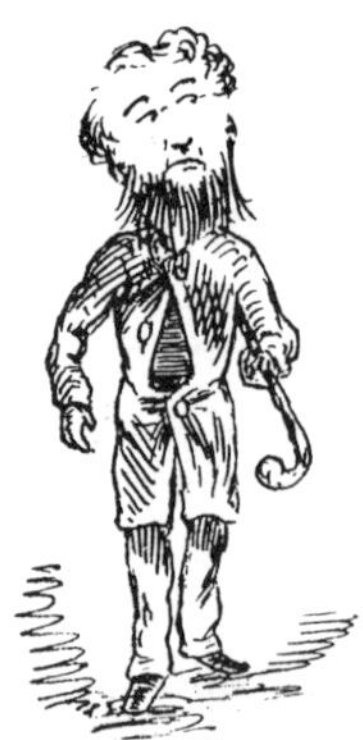

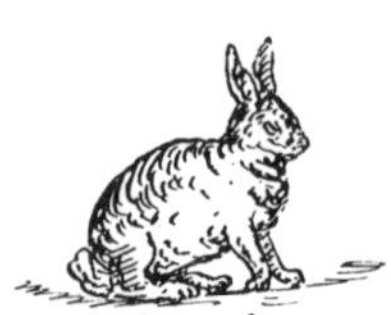

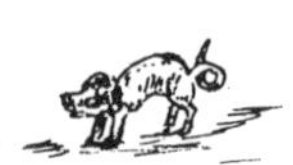

March 2nd 1882... our Guvnr says you have gone and done it - you've been and stopp'd away till it has started raining. He's sent me a-shopping and wants to know whether I shall have to buy anything more than this Handchicuf will hold - All depends on you - whether you are coming this weekend or not. If you are he says I must get two more herrings - a bit of Bacon and another gill of Paraffin. It became so dark at noon yesterday that he couldn't see (for a little while) to read the 'Standard' and a water works co. would charge a good deal for so much water as has come down this morning, I know. The fields are looking green and I hope by Saturday that sunshine will have returned again ...

March 6th 1882... Storrum, My dear Sir, Storrum and Tempist That has been the order of things for some days past - It is perhaps as well you did not come this weekend - I mean the last weekend - you might have been blown away and then what could we have done - a seat would of course be vacant either in Preston or here - and who could we find to fill it? I'm not good at ballooning - I'm now but an indifferent walker and I have as yet no Trap therefore I could not have gone after you. All things considered, I think it well you did not venture in the Tempist and the Storrum. Hoping to have an early look at you I am like Horniman's best tea - Always good alike ...

March 8th 1882... Night.. Your breach of covenant destroys confidence and entails unnecessary inconvenience. You asked me to meet you on Tuesday - I had walked eleven miles but wishing to keep my compact I walked two miles on the road to Croston. I then turned and retraced my steps - The last four miles were unnecessarily added to my day's fatigues. We had to send nearly the whole district over to procure a brace of young fowls - which awaited you in vain. We had not a drop of rain here. The evening was fine & rather cold with wild & grotesque clouds floating in the west. In the night I think rain fell. Yours disappointedly..P.s. old Pyebrook is again empty ...

March 15th 1882... oh, so you are in London are you, my dear Mister? Well, London or no London I don't mind backing in a small way any ordinary Rabbit which we may have about here against that Prize Pocket Mastiff of yours. When you return from the Metropolis I shall be pleased to hear from, or see you farther on the subject - I only stipulate that the canine champion shall wear his new coat on the occasion - with or without a fur collar ...

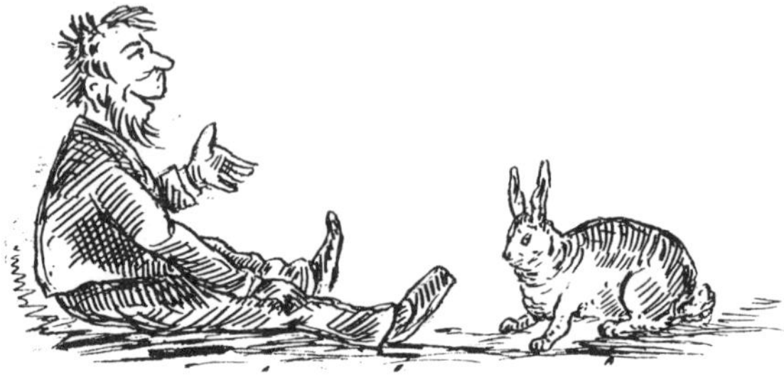

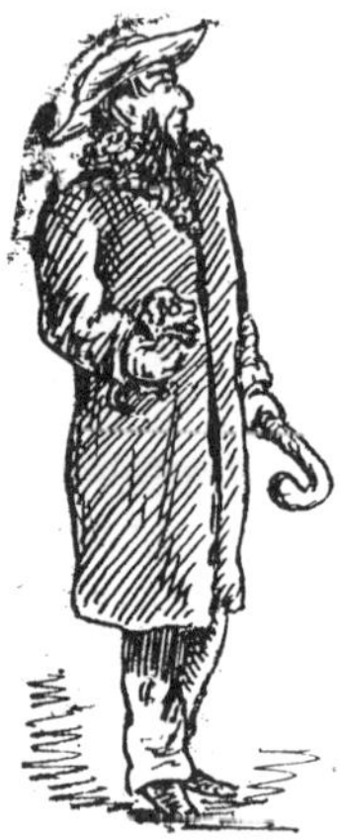

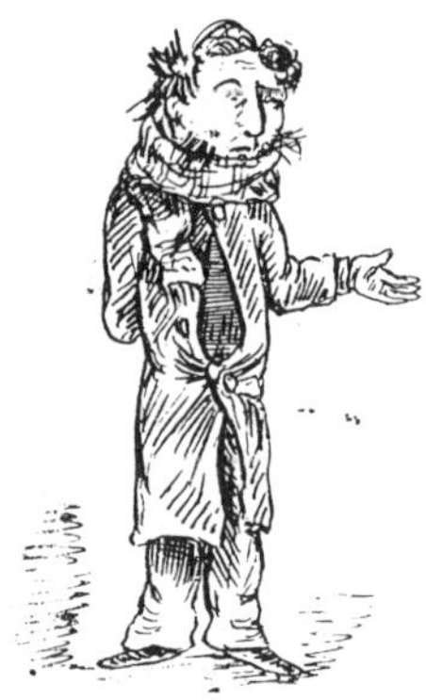

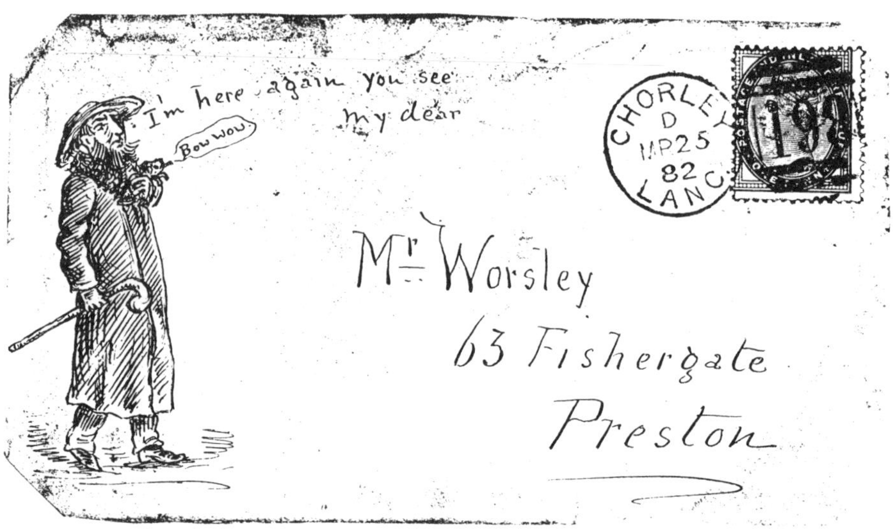
I'm here again you see
my dear
Bow wow
CHORLEY
D
MR 25
82
LANC
Mr Worsley
63 Fishergate
Preston

March 16th 1882... now Mister, what about that there challenge? Yah may tie one leg and one ear of the rappit, or tie both ears and the four legs only leave its tail free - I'll guarantee as it'll soon a druv your fancy house dog clean away. Ah don't mean this rappit in partickler - Yah may tek this or hanny other rappit - wild or tame makes no matter - it'll have your prize pocket mastiff inter a fit in no time - ah horp yah'll not prove wake and let yar dorg show a white fither in it tale - so no more at present from your expectingly ...

March 20th 1882...now Mister I just wish to know how you think I shall look with a wool collar coat on and bearing about with me a little Choctaw spaniel - Isn't the appearance rather the correct thing and withal imposing - Hooray!!! for the Choctaw spaniel - Hooray! for us - 'Heiky, peiky, hooroo - shallaballah shush'!!!! My excellent partner says I have a particularly happy look in your favourite 'get up' - It imports to me quite a noble air - or as Dickens would put it quite ' the air of the Marquis' - You've missed a famous opportunity for coming over for we had a splendid Simnel cake yesterday - grand - superlative - ...

March 21st 1882...now there you are, and it's just iike your wise managements - you've let all the bright and joyful days go by and now - here we are in the midst of storms - bang'd about with icy blasts and battered by the driving hail - No bird songs now and the flowers of late so lovely this morning hold low their stricken heads. But it's just you all over - I've tried and I've tried to get you to see these things as I see them. But where's the use when you won't look - and even if you do see them you'll take your own course - I beg to commend all the teachings of the situation to your thoughtful & patient consideration ...

March 27th 1882...My dear Sir Yes-!!!!

March 31st 1882...This is always your way - are you alone? you ses - Yes says I - I ses - quite alone I ses - Then you wait and you wait on one plea or another until the house gets filled up again - We had five to tea yesterday from all up and down - one guest from Cumberland and one from Skelmersdale, one from Wigan & two local ones - Two had nearly determined to stop all night, but finally all went away - We are again alone but I don't know for how long - In these matters, it's best for you to strike while the Iron's hot - To seize the passing hour & get in between the comings and goings - Mr Parkes is ill & Mr Howe so busy he won't be here for some time - Thanks very many - ses I for your kindness in discharging the little commission for me - and twisting the neck of that risky eleven and threepence ...

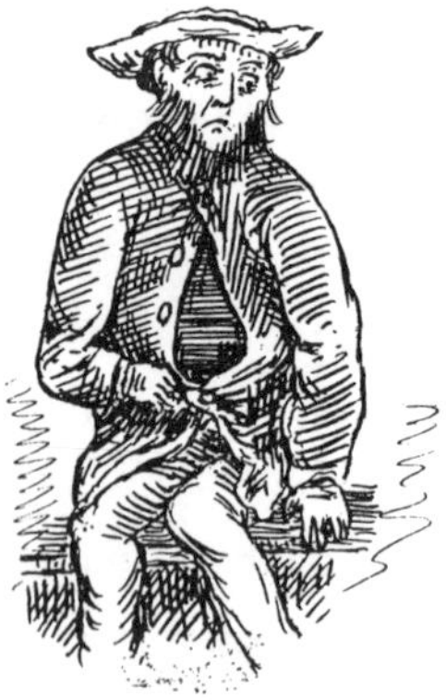

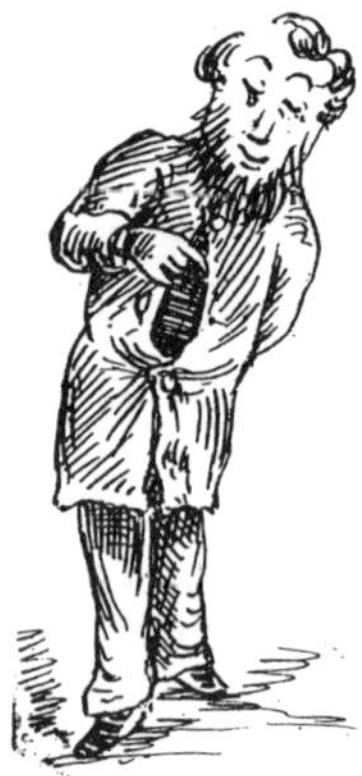

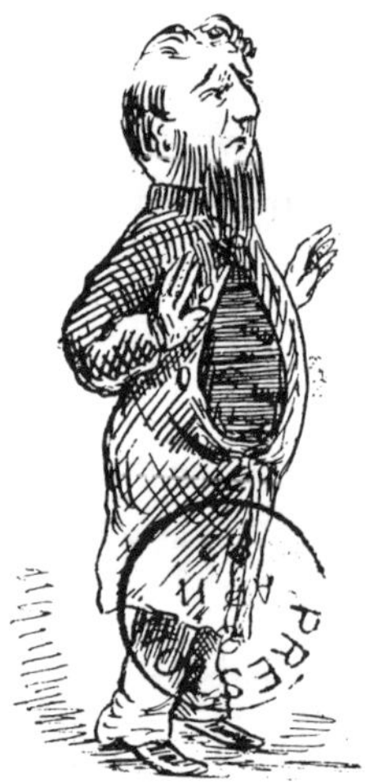

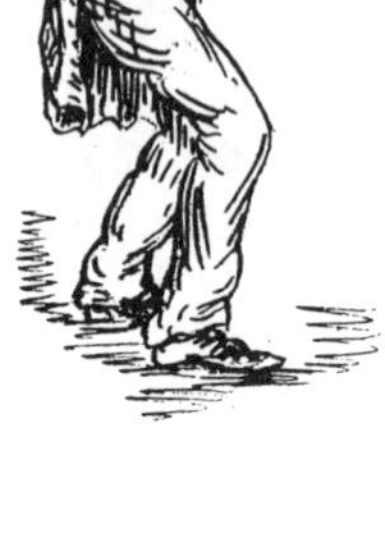

April 4th 1882...I cannot bear this travelling especially in cold weather yet here I am on this 4th day of April 1882 setting off to Southport - what with jolting conveyance and rattling railway cars I am driven nigh wild - when shall we have done with these eastern gales - I hope you are all well - and wishing you a happy Eastertide, I am yours sadly ...

April 7th 1882...Easter is a busy season hereaway - many meetings and many duties keep me fully engaged - The weather is beautiful and the country beginning to look lovely - You would I suppose receive the Southport paper duly - We have my Southport friend here at present - she will remain with us during a portion of the coming week - Miss Julia Jackson is also with us - spending her Easter holidays - we combine in affection ...

April 11th 1882...They're over My dear Sir - they're over - The Easter meetings are over and now I'm easy once again - a placidity overspreads the recently perturbed surface of the stream of my existence. But <u>how</u> and where are you I ask. You seem to be ever either in the wrong box or just one day after the Fair. Here have we been having most delightful weather - the air clear and scenery both extensive and lovely but you forsooth are Easter tiding in Preston or elsewhere and now the glasses have dropped a haze overspreads the earth and the meteorological experts prognosticate a change. It really does not signify - You'll have to do differently yet - make an effort in fact - or you'll always be in the wrong place and time ...

April 14th 1882...The old man who used to garden with such skill that he worked the soil till it was ' as fine as meighl welly' is, you will be sorry to learn, dead - The last adjutant which I have had employed in operating upon the garden has not succeeded in pulverising the soil to a fineness exceeding that of Cocoa Nuts - or very large scaplings. I have therefore to lament the loss of my former horticulturist - his unwearying diligence and unapproachable skill - Rain, Rain a weighty downpour of rain!!!!...

April 17th 1882...This week is mapped out to be a week of travel - I am to be knocking about, so to speak - through the whole of it. Tomorrow - all being well and weather favourable - I am due at Chorley - Next day I trudge off to Wigan and so, day after day, like the Wandering Jew I am to be an examplification of perpetual motion. Send your sympathy and Believe me Dear Sir ...

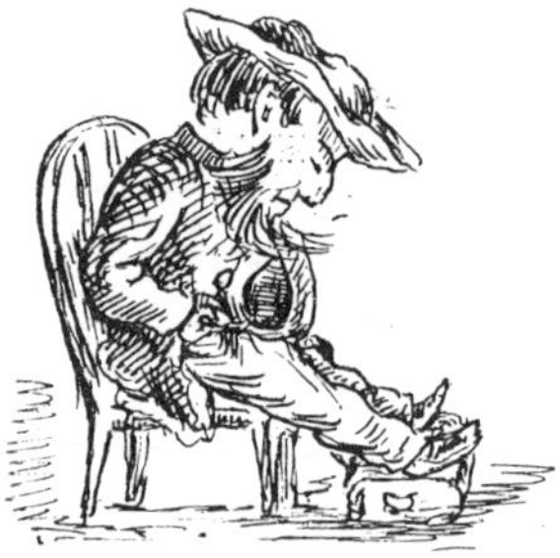

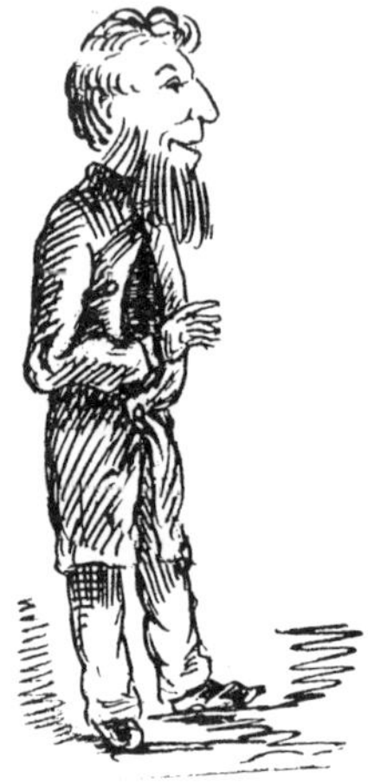

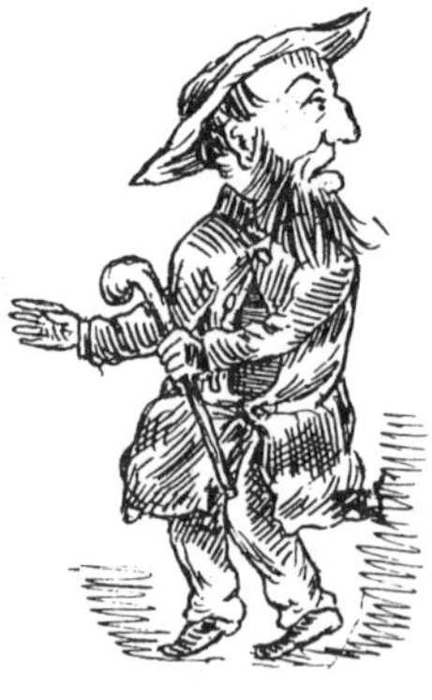

April 20th 1882...Posted at Ormskirk...My Niece is with us Aetat 7 years and is enraptured by the account she has received of your rat-like sleuth hound. Her great desire is to become possessed of it. Her Money Box is not by any means inordinately replete with that detestable dross known commonly as the current coin of the realm but she relies on the potency of an osculatory salutation to wit, in vulgar parlance, 'a kiss' - she ventures to think that two of these if gracefully allowed would suffice to touch your heart and render you pliant to the extent at least of parting with your canine quadruped - at her desire I venture to broach the negotiations. Her grandma is with us almost helpless with sciatica ...

April 24th 1882 Evening...I'm always conscious of a degree of fatigue on Monday. I incline to lay up and rest a little on that day. I am now so resting. Tomorrow the toils of the week begin - all being well at early morn I set forth among my people and my first visit takes me 3 miles nearly from here - To go straight thither and hither again means close upon six miles walking but as I may have divers ins and outs, my walk in the morning may be 10 miles. Sallie is with us - her cousin Fanny (Miss H) is in Southport now - having recently left Eccles. Florrie and her grandmamma are here. Mr Evans is at Milan. Torpedo & self were at Chorley last Tuesday - thence to Wigan and on Friday I went alone to Ormskirk - one day this week I am due in Southport & peradventure may visit Preston shortly ...How's the hound?..

April 28th 1882...I got wet yesterday and have not yet quite got over the fun of the thing. Torpedo got wet also and was apparently much charmed with the experience for she is off to Wigan to get wet again today. She is taking Florrie back but the young lady's Grand Dam tarrieth with us a little longer. Sallie also remaineth - Emblince(?) has resumed her service here - she left her other situation some days ago - from a week to a fortnight since. Had a brief sojourn in Southport where I met with her yesterday - she asked if she might come hither - permission was granted & she came ...

May 2nd 1882...ah my! but it is proving a time of perplexity - I have really more to do and more places to be at than I can manage - one duty calls me this way and then almost contemporaneously another one calls me that way - I may for aught I know to the contrary have to be this week in Accrington Ormskirk Preston Southport Manchester and Stafford - was there ever such a requisite as myself - was there ever such a knock about member of the human race as I? Mr Parkes is in deep affliction - His mother departed this life about 4 o'clock on Sunday morning - excuse more at present ...

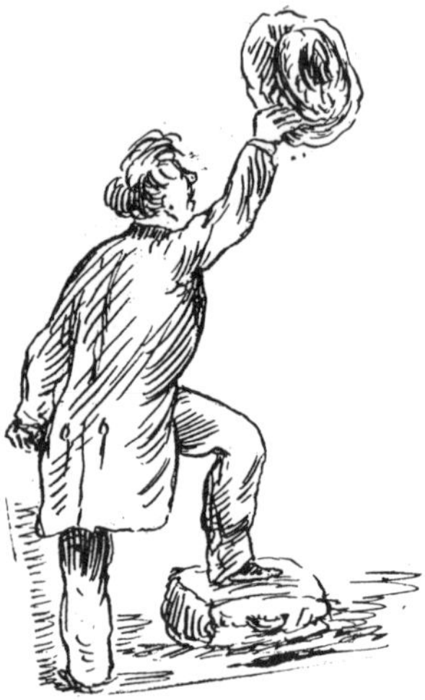

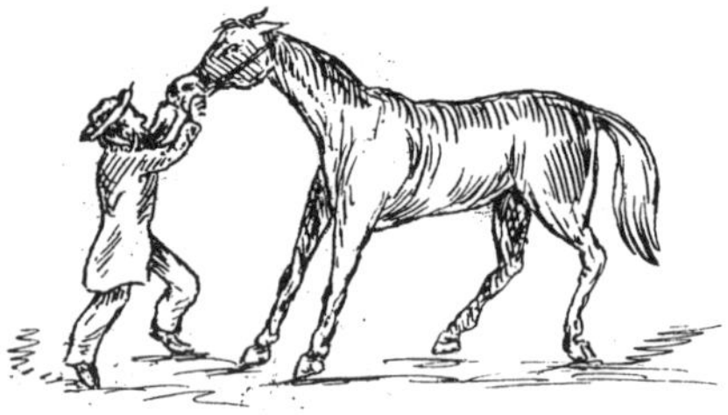

Notes

May 10th 1882 — The assassination of Lord Frederick Cavendish in Phoenix Park, Dublin, on May 6th 1882.

The Southport News, 13th May 1882 -

Lord Frederick William Cavendish, Chief Secretary for Ireland, and Mr J.H. Burke, the Under Secretary, were walking in Phoenix Park, Dublin, after the installation of Lord Cavendish when they were attacked with demoniacal fury by four desperadoes and literally butchered in a few minutes in a much frequented pathway, within the sight of eye witnesses powerless to aid in the arrest of the vile miscreants. The news was first received as a hoax and not believed. A large reward for information was offered by the Government. The assassins were believed to be members of a secret assassination policy, the motive undoubtedly a blow at the new conciliation policy and to cause the Government to revert to coercion which, by keeping Ireland in a disturbed state best suits the designs of those striving for the Parliamentary independence of that country.

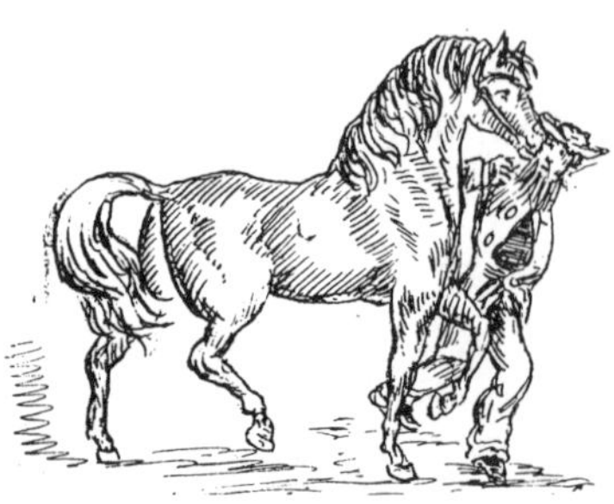

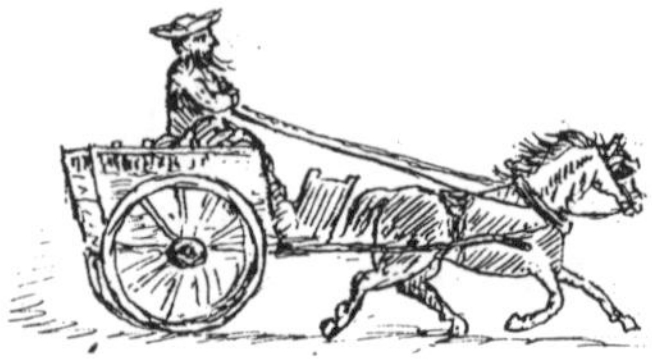

May 3rd 1882...Hooray!Hooray!!! It's coming. It's coming - It's been bought at last and we shall perhaps see you on Friday next - I have a melancholy duty to discharge in the Blackburn neighbourhood on that day and will call on you if I pass through Preston...

May 6th 1882...It has at last arrived. I cannot yet say much about its temper, but it seems decidedly opposed to my committing the imprudence as well as impropriety of 'looking a gift horse in the mouth!' We yester even got home duly and well, albeit the night air felt very cold. I rejoice to add as you will doubtless be pleased to learn, that we found our 'Lodge well tiled' ...

May 10th 1882...We have now had some days experience of the Equine and I am glad to say that it completely answers our expectations. It has a fine spirit as you would remark if you saw me lead it out to grass, and in the vehicle if permitted, will dash along like the wind, yet it is as quiet, modest and unostentatious as we can wish. What a horrible outrage was that in Dublin last Saturday*. What a black disgrace upon our times, our Empire and its Ministers that vile crimes of a like character shall have been permitted so long to take place - why don't the government govern? They were not appointed & put in power with a stipulation attached to their tenure of office that they were to go down upon their knees to thieves, sedition mongers or assassins, but to maintain the Queen's authority - uphold the law & secure peace throughout Her Majesty's Dominions. If I mistake not the stock of the Gladstone administration is fast going down in blood ...

May 13th 1882...Hi! Mister when are you coming? You must know I have not given up walking so I can take a turn round with you as aforetime. The wild Hyacinths are out - apple blossom ditto - Trees nearly in full leaf - country charming indeed and yet I should not wonder if you faddle about - make appointments and break them until the snows of winter are again upon us - the flowers departed, and all the harmonies of nature silent. Poney well, Torpedo well and self well - Hoping ye are well - I am on this bright May morning ...

May 16th 1882...You should just see it out in the field loose merely taking its pleasure as we may say 'My the words!!!' but it would surprise you - you'd nearly think it was the comet that was flitting past and just gently touching the earth to try what it feels like. Weather splendid ...

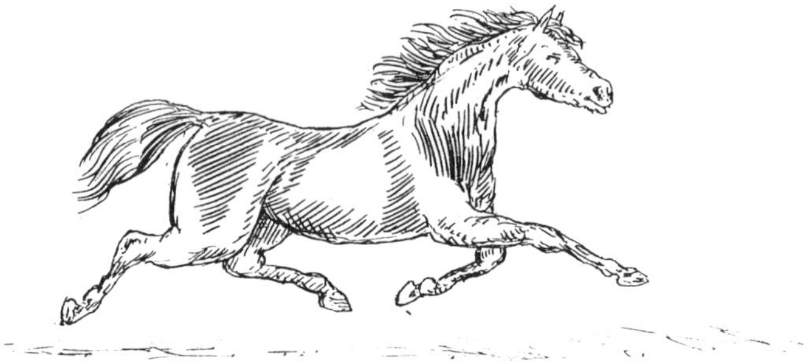

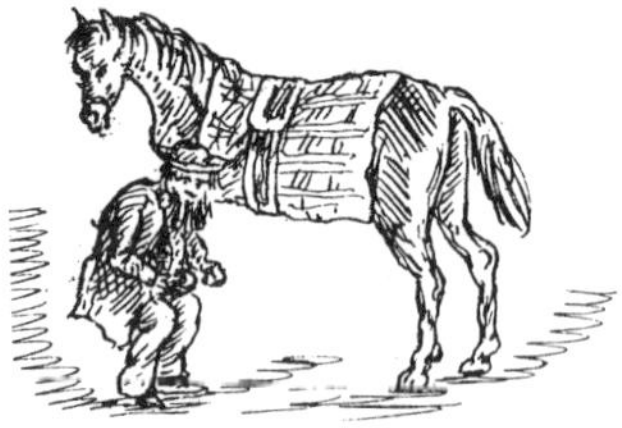

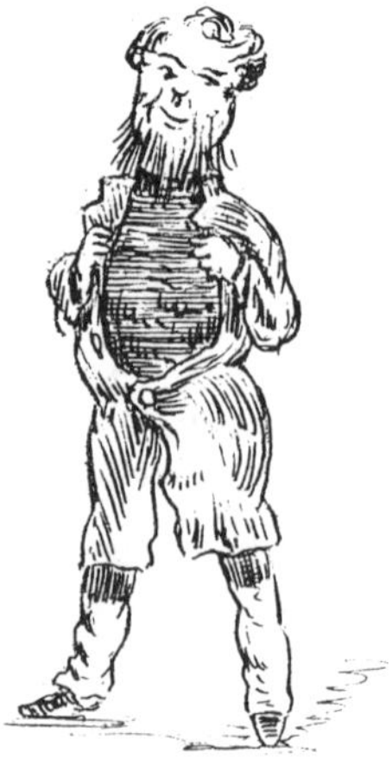

May 16th 1882 (Number 2)...The poney is good and the Dray is good - They run smoothly and well but the harness is done - It goes to smash every time I take it out - It is positively dangerous alike to our life and limb. There is here an opportunity and a great one for any kind good Christian body who feels so disposed (as Mrs Gamp & Mrs Harris might put it) to say 'well now let me have the happiness and privelege of doing something to preserve that valuable life and those gracefully symmetrical limbs of yours - Do let me replace those worthless straps'. Promptitude is urgently requisite - for otherwise I may either have been accidentally flung forth or have hurried to the saddlers myself - in utter despair of any sympathy from a hard cold world - or else try a 'collection' ...

May 17th 1882...I can do really anything about it in the way of 'ossling' - I can give it its food and water - I can brush it down; and at my bidding it will lift a hoof in order to drag the friendly paw. If you'll come over I'll let you touch it. It delights in an osculation so as a particular concession and a mark of especial regard I will let you give it one - after one interview you will be wanting to come over about twice a week to look at it - My Torpedo was yesterday at Southport so I drove twice to Newburgh or Purbold station. In fact I and our Pollie nearly live on the roads this fine weather - The Blue Bells are out beautifully - The smoke room will I expect be just now, a sight to behold. Hadn't you better make haste and get over - say, early on Saturday next so that we could roam the meads and hills at pleasure - Watch the glorious sunset and catch some drops of raining gold flung about us by declining day. Our poetic souls on fire - Fresh air our great desire - We'll breathe it pause & then admire The beauty of the scene..Have just received your letter or rather Miss Worsley ...

Whit Monday morning 1882...Ha Ha I knew you would - It was ever so likely that you'd miss the pure air - the blooming flowers and rural melodies of the country - But then you wouldn't have missed them if you'd stopped among them - A man who never comes into the country; and is as often hurrying out of it cannot help but miss 'em. It is quite in the nature of things that he should do - I don't know whether I make my meaning quite clear - but of course the intention is there all the same, and that is something. This nice warm weather suits me admirably - I can walk about now without my hat and enjoy it only I have a bad sore throat to bear me company which, of course, it's a slight drawback as we can't at all times help - so no more at present only hoping you will have a pleasant week and feel refreshed. Ever yours as heretofore ...

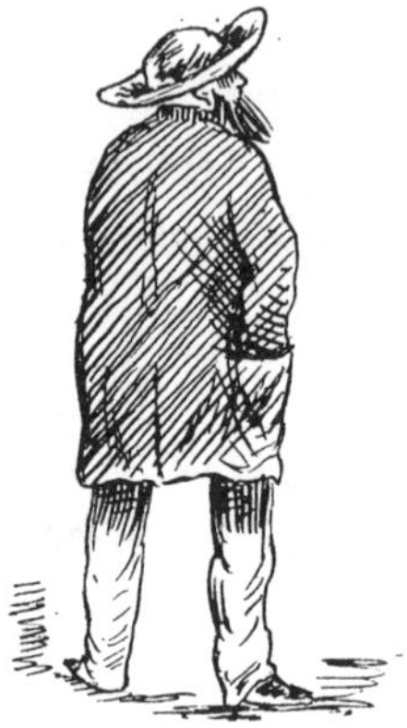

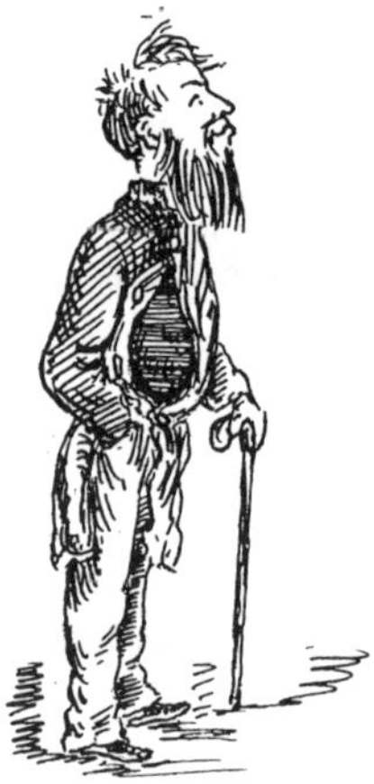

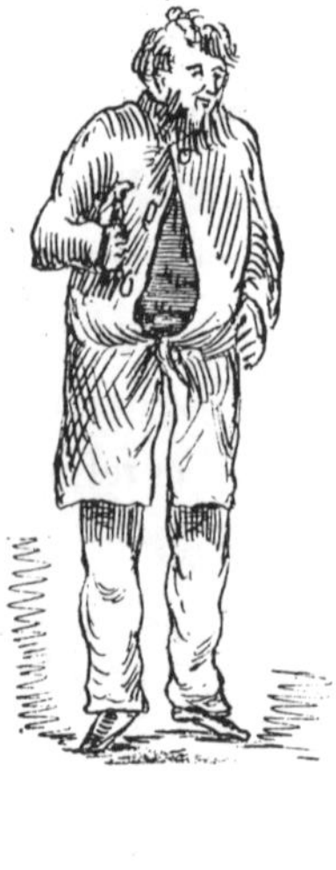

June 3rd 1882...I have been through a sharp but fierce ordeal and am both reduced in strength and bulk - on the very day I posted my last in Croston and not half an hour after I posted it I felt the first symptoms of the approaching onslaught - Four and a half hours later I was in bed - Blankets piled upon me and hot water bottles plentifully supplied yet shivering with cold till my teeth chattered emitting a sound similar to that which emanates from a shaken box of dominoes. I had to evoke medical aid - I am much better but far from well - and my weakness is painfully apparent to myself - I have today begun eating again. You have very nearly had afforded you an opportunity of paying a last tribute of regard by putting up a painted East window to my memory ...

June 6th 1882...Will you kindly tell me whether last Saturday's Standard was posted in Preston <u>last Saturday</u> - and if so at what time - I am writing at half past 9A.M on Tuesday June 6th and Saturday's paper has not yet reached me - Little more than a week ago a similar hitch in the Postal service occurred so I require the facts asked for with a view to institute an enquiry into this recurring irregularity. I should according to arrangement have been now half way to Southport but Nicholas who was to accompany me is at Coppull. If he returns in time I start - I want his trap - it's bigger - but Pollie draws it ...

June 16th 1882...I'm very sorry to hear of your sleepless night and great anguish but yet I feel sure that after being all day on damp grass and in a toothache wind you would have been greatly disappointed if you had not had the privelege of enjoying fully the torture naturally resultant. If you had a night's pain it would not be unaccompanied with satisfaction that you were therein missing none of the attractions of our June Party - our guests are numerically dwindling - only three remain and of these - two leave tomorrow - but the week so far has been to me a busy one. In a few minutes I am off to Wigan in company with Mr G.P who lays to visit Preston shortly accompanied by myself. The coming week may peradventure bring us into your locality <u>but not Monday</u> ...

June 19th 1882...How's your toothache My dear Mister - shall I extract it for you? or is it rheumatic neuralgia that you have got - Perhaps if you wrap a good thick piece of red flannel round the tooth to keep it warm you might experience relief - Every third person or so seems to have picked up an attack of toothache, Face ache or Heart ache at the Tea Party, so there is nothing singular in your painful experience. We all wish you safely speedily and happily through it - I have got a slight cold. I am rather hoarse - I drove Miss L to the station on Saturday through rain - can't fix a day - Dependent on weather partly and partly on engagements - will take pot luck ...

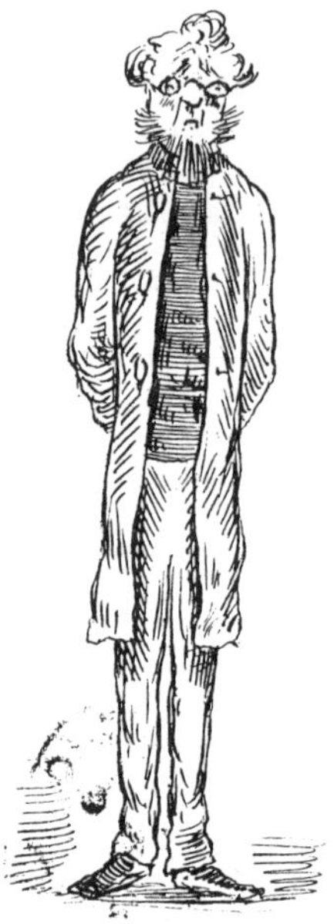

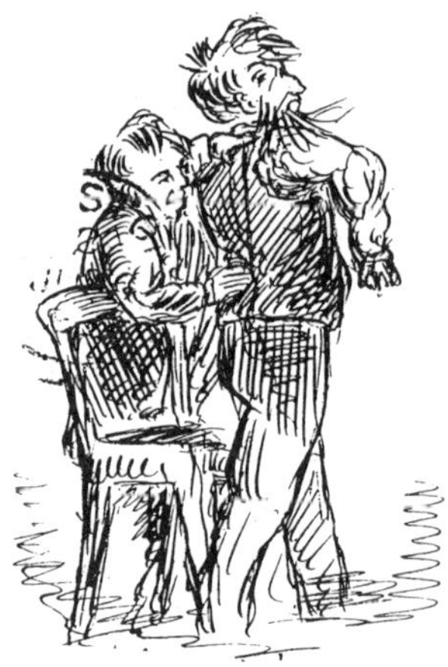

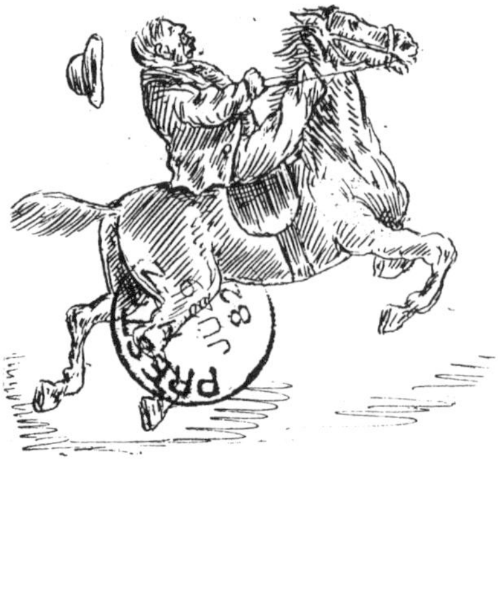

June 21st 1882 (Evening)...I'm home again but these long journeys quite knock me up. They reduce me equally in strength and flesh - Today I've felt quite tired and very thin - I fear travelling in foreign parts would speedily convert me into an impalpable shadow. My companion also grunts about fatigue today and his rotundity of figure is likewise perceptibly reduced ...

June 28th 1882...I am becoming extravagant I fear - I have been measured for a new vest - I have entrusted the important fabrication to a Wigan artist skilled in draping the 'real figure'. He assures me from his measurement that my shadow does not grow less. You have misssed it by not coming over and it serves you very well right. We had a fine day and a plentiful ingathering which would no doubt have been augmented had you been here. I am this morning as hoarse as half a dozen ravens ...

June 28th 1882 evening...Pollie has this morning taken that Mr Parkes to Croston on his way to Whalley and Accrington. If he gets there safely he is intending to return hither on Friday morning - He said before he started that he was already convinced that Pollie could 'go'. He is a pretty fair hand at the reins; but a very uncertain occupant of the saddle - especially when he meets with a spiritful young thing like 'our Pollie'. He went to Preston Market on Saturday last with one of my neighbours to buy a pig - After spending some hours among agriculturists and seeking out those spots where swine vendors most do congregate and finding nought to suit him - He returned with his trusty escort resolved on Friday next to look out elsewhere for a Porcine candidate for Prize (L) at the next Uttoxeter Culture Show. He has enlisted me to aid him in the capture of a First Class Porky pine ...

July 4th 1882...I'm in perplexity for sure for I thought to begin my hay making this morning but instead of bright sunshine as I expected we have a freely descending rain - It is very perplexing to us farmers - <u>My</u> land as you are aware, is not extensive but deary me! I need the hay and am wishful to conserve my fodder - what is to become of Pollie if I cannot get our hay in properly? I commenced mowing yesterday even but by the time I had gotten nine square yards of grass down my scythe point had stuck so often into the ground that the instrument was quite useless further - I shall have to get some man to look to it for me ...

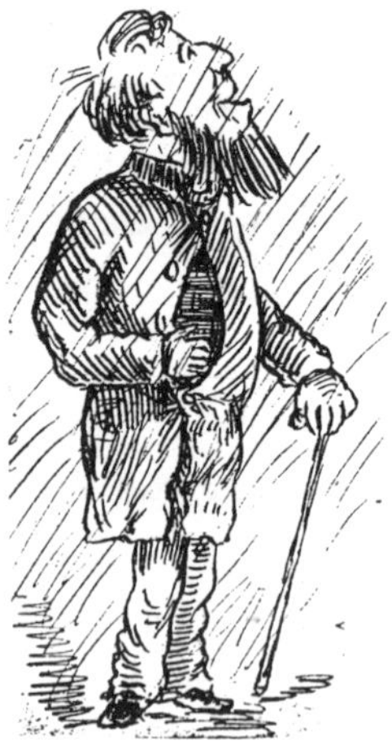

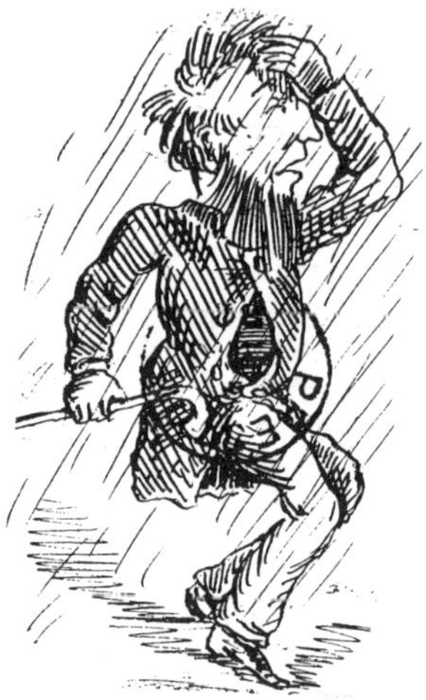

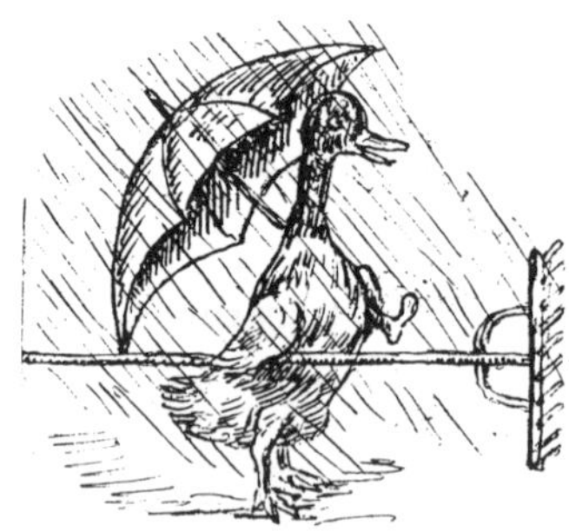

Notes

July 14th 1882 — In 1882 Egypt was under Turkish rule, under khedive Mohammed Tewfik, with a British controller-general, Sir Evelyn Baring. A national movement had been set up by Arabi Pasha, an Egyptian army officer. There was a massacre in Alexandria, and British and French squadrons bombarded the forts there. Arabi surrendered in the September, and British troops occupied Cairo.

July 7th 1882...I can really make nothing of this weather - I don't understand it. Just when I wanted to begin my hay and some portion of the grass is mown - Thunder sets in and the rain fairly pours - The Brooks roar and rush over their banks - I watch and watch the portents of the skies but no gleam to give hope of fair & suitable hay weather appears. It fairly makes my stomach ache while I think about it. The portion of grass which I wish at once to convert into Hay I am told by 'experts' will not keep - It must be mown without delay or Pollie will get no benefit from it. What's to be done my dear Sir? - what's to be done? I begin now to realise fully the anxieties which my neighbours have felt for years. I counsel you to be thankful you are not farming anything but a few rose trees - Your hair would be white in a fortnight if you had a hay field under treatment just now. Yours in perplexity ...

July 8th 1882...My sadness about my hay grass has become at length despair, or very like it. The rain continues all about us and the air is full of thunder - again I ask you what's to be done, my dear Sir? What's to be done? Grass won't make good hay in a flood. In fact I go as far as to believe it won't make hay at all unless we have sunshine & wind. What would you do? Have it mown and then send it into France to be got and returned to England for stacking? Advise me - of your charity I beseech - advise ...

July 10th 1882...I got up with hope of beginning hay today but a bright morning has given place to gloomy clouds and heavy showers - I have therefore brought my rake back again and sought once more the shelter of my dwelling. Notwithstanding the rainfall the Barometers are going upwards - but judging them by the weather which we are experiencing I regard their ascent as descent - their incline as decline - their fair as unfair and their general proceedence as a delusion and a snare. Thank your stars you've no hay out and the horse waiting for it ...

July 14th 1882...ah, Mister, it is raining still - I can feel distinctly the falling drops - what is the cause? My dear Sir - can you tell? Is it due to the near approach of St Swithun's Festival? - or to the cannon of the British Fleet in Egyptian Waters. On Tuesday last (11th inst) Alexandria was bombarded and the storm of Arabi Pasha's* fury may be blowing 'big guns' even yet. Anyway, whatever the cause we've rain; and I cannot get my hay - <u>no</u>body can get his hay this weather so no more at present from yours anxiously.. P.S. Torpedo wants to know when you are sending for us to Blackpool - we have lately enjoyed fresh water in abundance - salt ditto would be a change - now's your Time ...

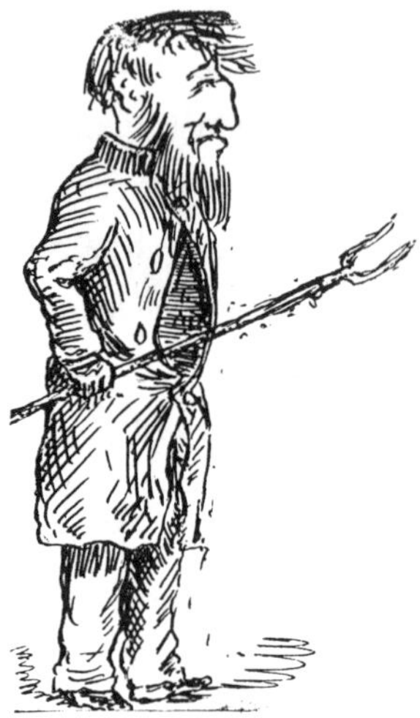

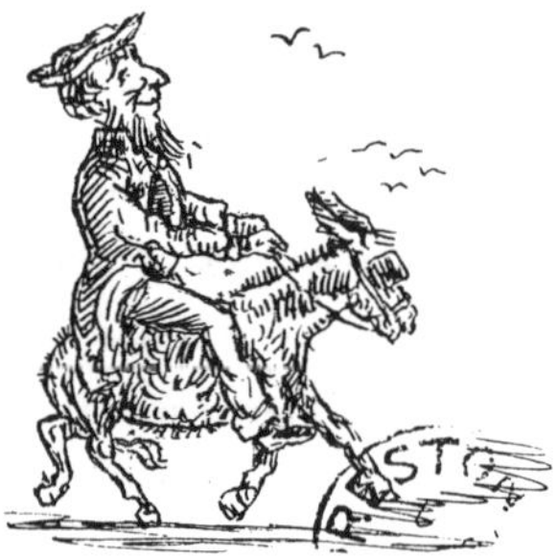

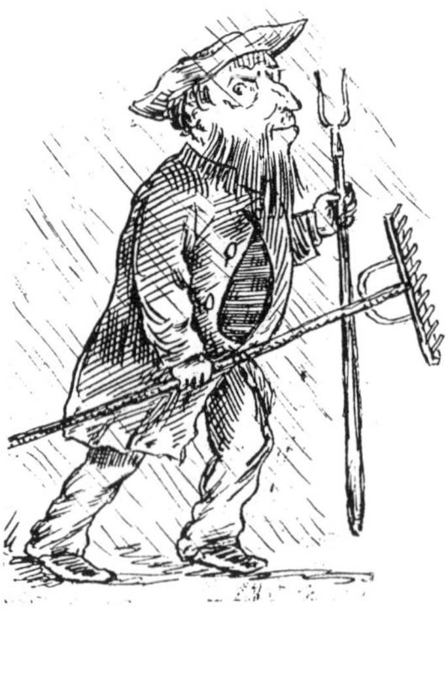

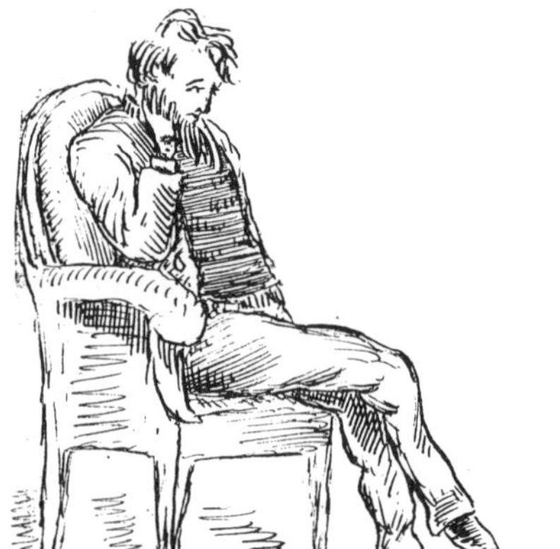

July 18th 1882...I have arrived almost at the borders of my wits - This very day at early morn I went forth to shake with ready pitchfork the sparkling raindrops from the withering grass, but rain, rain, pouring rain drove me quickly back again - all my hay is down and hitherto no weather - Yesterday more might have been done but for two mad bulls which roamed the district & drove all workers from the fields - Today a neighbour has been sorely hurt - having run a pitchfork through his side and broken the prongs in the thickest part - I fear his hurt will have a fatal issue... P.S. The two bulls fought close here. The collision was witnessed by my household - one bull's horns were smashed ...

Valued Mister - This is July 20th 1882 - I have 'got in' my hay this evening and had it stacked; and I think I will now go off somewhere for a pleasure hay time - my workmen estimate that I have hay enough to keep my poney on through the winter and board a Donkey besides - this latter quadruped might come in handy perchance for saddle exercise occasionally. The safe housing of my hay harvest makes me feel very cheerful - My excellent Partner consequently considers this a fitting time to have my portrait taken - my smiles of contentment being truly charming to look upon - why, you don't know the serenity which the consciousness of a well and safely ingotten harvest can produce ...

July 22nd 1882...Having finished my own hay I am going about now in a diligent and benevolent spirit to help other people - I may be said to have a hay making mania upon me just now. My pitchfork and rake, yea even my scythe are at the service of any neighbour in need. It would do you good to get into somebody's hayfield and work hard for a day or two in the wind and rain - for of sunshine we have so little that it would puzzle a philosopher to point out how you could work in it. The most abundant sunshine we've had in our hayfield has been the sunshine of a cheerful disposition each; and our hay I am glad to say is very well gotten, so no more at present ...

July 26th 1882...I feel more and more that if there is one man in this realm who deserves more than another the Right Honourable appellation of a working man that man is 'oneself' - we speak modestly on this matter as is our wont. Weary already I have work that will keep me engrossed the whole day through - I write in haste and with distracted thought for in our lofty mind we are revolving many things. Hoping this will find you robust I am as heretofore ...

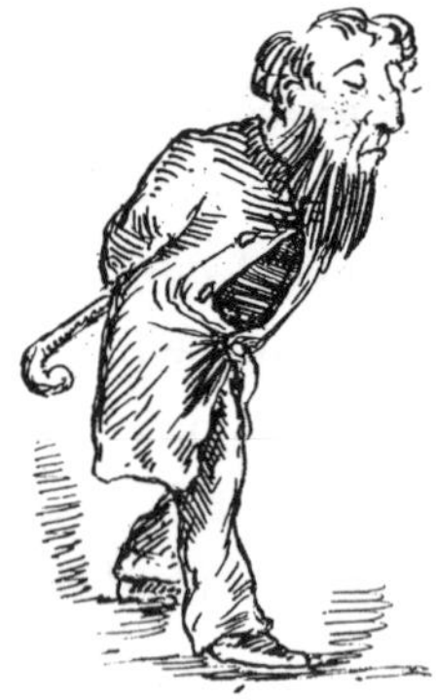

<u>Notes</u>

<u>Aug 1st 1882</u> Preston's 'Guild Week' was held every twenty years.

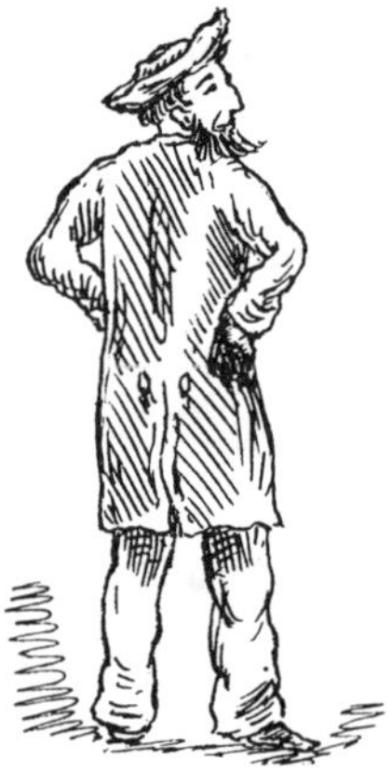

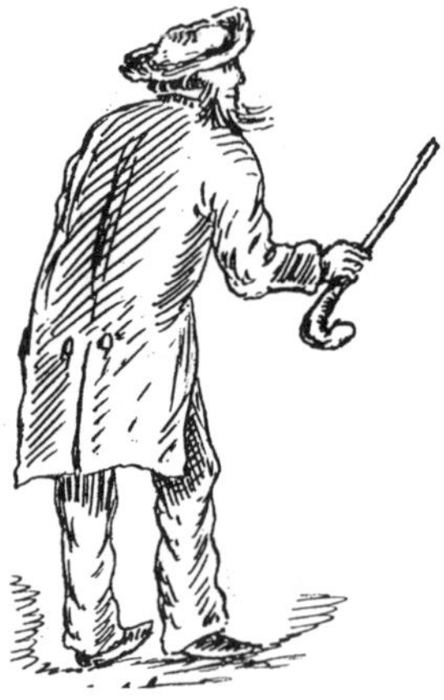

<u>Aug 5th 1882</u> After the defeat of Cetewayo at Ulundi in 1879 he was taken prisoner and sent to Cape Town. He came to England in 1882 in the hope that his rights would be restored to him which they were, the following year. On his return to Zululand he was attacked by one of his old enemies and sought asylum in British territory. He died in 1884.

July 28th 1882...I consider the political situation a very grave one - Being little of a politician I have not hitherto quite fully understood the meaning of a 'Liberal Policy' about the blessings of which I have heard so much. The unloveable fact however is just now made plain to me that it means in Egypt an extraordinary imposition of Ten paras per Feddan or two shillings per acre and in England a threepenny addition to the Income Tax with probable further increase at an early date. I've got my hay in, it is true, but the extra poundage in the matter of Income Tax has yet to be met - My back is nearly broken with the Taxes we have had. I know not how I shall get on with the sundry heavier impositions which loom in the immediate future. How do you feel? ...

August 1st 1882...What we are talking about now very generally is what we call the 'Pressn Guill'* - our grandfathers so termed it and we delight to speak of it after their manner - orthography in a matter of this kind is not accounted of - Tees and Dees may 'gang their ain gate' - for the event which we are anticipating the arrival of is and will be 'Pressn Guill'. Now it would be a very gracious act and one appreciated immensely if - provided you are not running away from town on that occasion - you were to say 'Well, now s'pose you come over some day during the Guill week and see the luminations from the top of our 'ouse' - Don't unless you quite mean it - for if you say these words I do believe you'll make us jump ...

Aug 2nd 1882...I cannot get over this Income Tax augmentation and I feel more and more that we are approaching a time when Income Tax will be Income Tax - You are aware my resources are not great - so where am I to get the threepence from -? It would have looked better of the Government to have made me a grant of the Irish Church Surplus than impose on me this additional monetary burden - In October next I suppose there will be another demand - another threepence and, may I ask, 'for what'? Is it to enact with the Fleet that Dulciquo farce over again and 'Demonstrate' with the Army in Egypt as we have done with it in Ireland - It is strange that the Gladstone who was to abolish the Income Tax should always increase it - The Egyptians have neither rebelled against our Queen as their sovereign nor have they invaded our territory as did the Boers - therefore what I want to know is will there be any 'Blood-guiltiness' in this case and if so upon whom will it rest? ...

Aug 5th 1882...now see, look here, I wish to make just one suggestion about the 'Pressn Guill'. If you see the worshipful the Mayor perhaps you will mention it to him - It would no doubt contribute to make the 'guill' a success and draw much people thereto. My suggestion is that the 'Guill' committee invite Cetewayo* to be present. He arrived in Plymouth Sound by the Union Company's steamer 'Arab' on Thursday last the 3rd day of this month of August 1882 at 5 o'clock in the morning - He might be secured as a 'speaker' at a 'Women's Rights' meeting in the Guild Hall - He would like immensely - I leave the suggestion with you ...

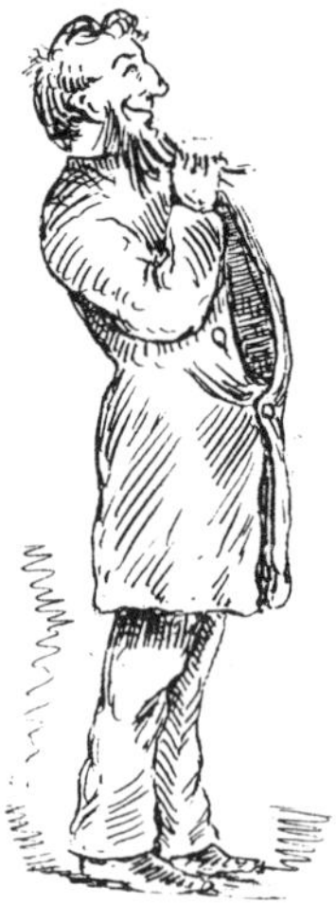

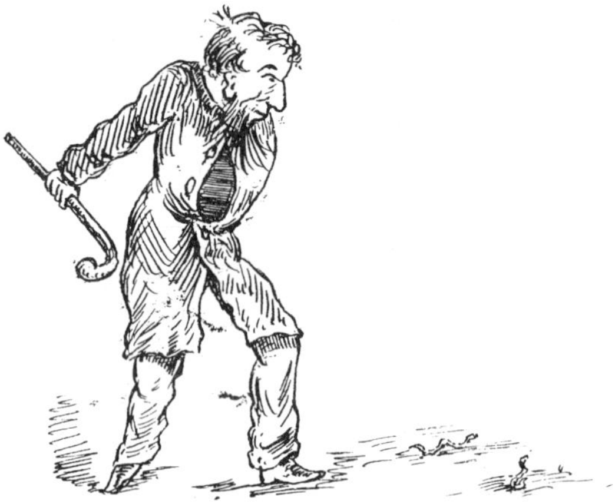

<u>Notes</u>

<u>Aug 14th 1882</u> Garner = granary

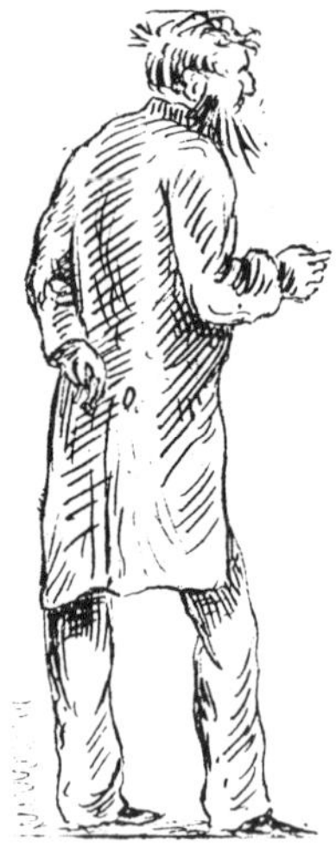

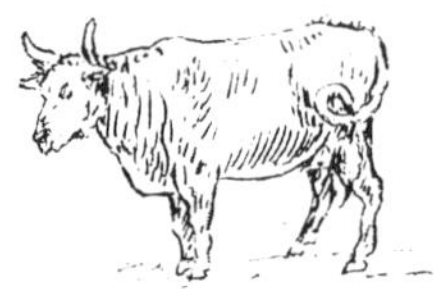

<u>Aug 18th 1882</u> (Oleo)margarine and other butter substitutes had been on sale for about ten years by this time

Aug 9th 1882...We 'mark time' (to use a drill expression) by these 'Pressn Guills' in our locality - Many a 'flighty young thing' who went to the last 'Guill' is a flighty thing no longer - Raven locks that excited admiration or envy at the last Municipal celebration have lost their ebon line and suggest a hard rub against the North Pole. Many who like ourself were then supple of limb and swift of foot, are now like us glad to rest and be thankful - so greatly in fact do I prize repose and quietude that were I a resident in Pressn I should, like you, feel a burning desire to flee from the hubbub during the 'Guill' week - I have taken the opportunity of speaking very generally about your purpose, to wit that you are letting your house for the week and hieing ye to Baden Baden or elsewhere with the view of obtaining a meet replenishment of your health - We have a wet mist prevailing here this morning - The weather perplexes us - It looks as if the sunshine were putting off its 'outing' till the Guill. We are all well and hoping you are ditto. We remain each and every of us ...

Aug 14th 1882...I was in Coppull yesterday and only just got home before the rain came down yester even. In fact the shower began as I was coming up the front. I see the 'Guill' begins with a Masonic display, don't be beguiled hereby to abide in Town - Haste and get ye forth, Lodge or no Lodge, or don't feel surprise if we Brethren, attached and unattached, visit the 'Guill' in force and avail ourselves (or in the expectation that we may avail ourselves) of the conveniences and hospitalities of the 'Temple' opened at 63, Fishergate - that first day will be a time of special peril to your garner* & your store as also to your Domestic quietude & privacy - Next unto it - the day of the opening of the County Buildings ...

Aug 15th 1882...You know how great is my antipathy towards all the snake family since I was bitten by a viper. You may therefore imagine with some degree of ease how startled I have been when twice during the past week while walking along the road I have nearly trodden upon an 'anguis fragilis' - they are not large or dangerous but big enough to awaken memories of the past; and cause me to pause and contemplate their movements - You should have been here you could have afforded to your naturalist proclivities a plenary gratification, for the roads have presented a degree of resemblance to a serpent house ...

Aug 18th 1882...We are off to 'Wiggin' this morning and were in Chorley only last Wednesday - really how we do travel about. But then there is this to be said we always do it sensibly - we don't attempt the 'desert' nor yet the ocean - and I have heard, what inclines me to think we shall stay more at home shortly (for we cannot very well go away then -) viz. that my Domestic Regulator has decided to add to our livestock a cow. The advantages shadowed forth as likely to secure therefrom are that we shall have plenty of work, plenty of milk and some little Butter - a little spoiled perhaps in the making but yet - Butter - not oleomargarine* - Butterine - or any other mysterious device of ingenious men. Hoping you are well ...

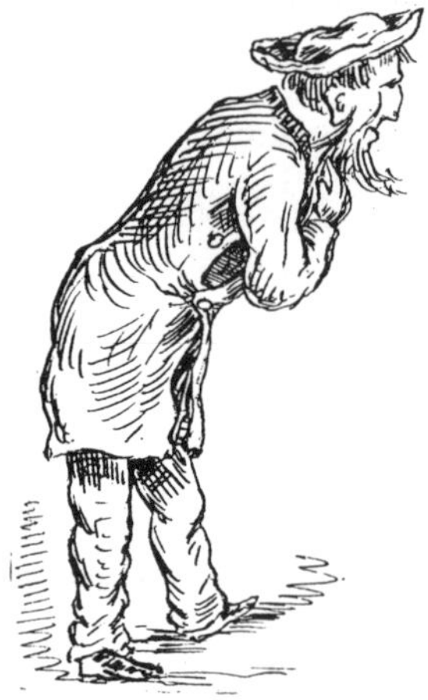

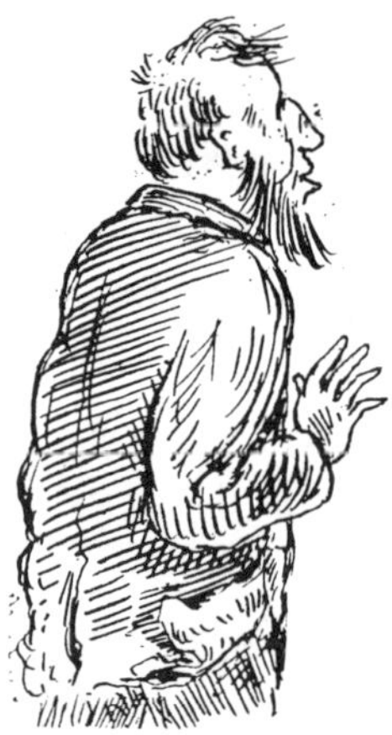

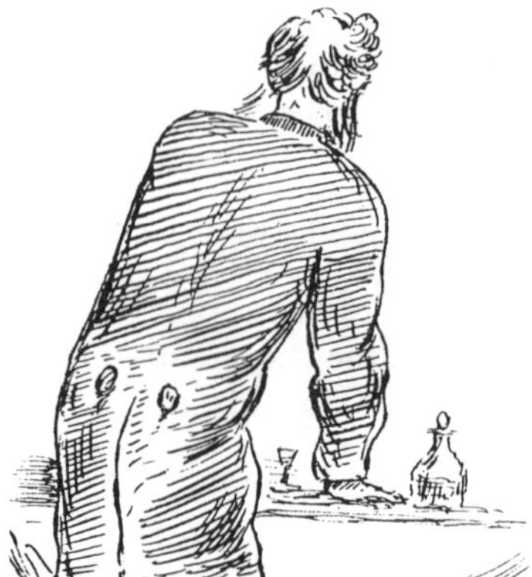

Aug 19th 1882 evening...I rise to order as we say in Parliament when we've got nothing particular to speak about. I am told that there is holden at Treacle Row in the Parish of 'Church' near Accrington, a Fair called 'The Treacle Fair'. It is merely a 'pleasure fair' to which people go for the 'pleasure' of consuming Treacle - I don't know what time of the year it is usually held but if it be the first week in September I feel it will greatly injure the 'Pressn Guill'. If you see the Mayor it would be a very proper thing to tell him so that he might ascertain the date and if need be postpone the Guild until the Treacle Fair is over. The air this evening has just a flavour of winter in it - a frosty feel I mean ...

Aug 24th 1882...I feel very sure that they need a good head or two in the Preston Council to wisely devise means for making the oncoming celebration a complete success - If therefore the Mayor - President or Committee, or any other high functionary having meet authority in the matter would signify their desire to that end I would bring them mine - and at the same time lend them my pastoral staff to be carried in the procession by the corporation mace-bearer - It would be a bauble much less cumbrous than the mace; and I flatter myself not inferior in dignity or comeliness. The arrangement would be a very nice one for all parties, and a free Ticket for all the Banquets, Balls and Revelrouts during the Guild week would be accepted as a sufficient and satisfactory 'quid pro quo' - Though a little top heavy perchance and bulky as to our paunch we still retain aptitude for the gracefully active saltations of the Ballroom - weather cold and steeping - rain, rain, cold rain ...

Aug 29th 1882...If you go to Blackpool during the 'Pressn Guill' week, my dear Sir, whatever else you do, keep away from the 'watterside' - we don't want you perished through the incoming tide nor overpowered and crushed by the forceful pressure of an Arm of the sea - should you unhappily become the victim of some ravenous shark we could do nothing but be whale you. Do be careful, my dear Mister, do be careful..P.S. Have not yet decided about next week - so will write to Miss Worsley tomorrow ...

Aug 31st 1882...Mr Worsley, Mr Mayor and gentlemen - I rise on the present occasion to crave your indulgence while I point out the wisdom of my former counsel - Had ye compliance with my suggestion secured His Majesty of Zululand as one of the Patrons of your 'Guild' ye might have tided over the present crisis without much difficulty by still presenting the attractions of Royalty to a Throne-loving people - and furthermore methinks that had ye but fully explained to the Ebon sovereign of the Zulus how important a position your Guild holds among the celebrations of the Whitemen he might have been induced to set aside his longing to be back in his own country, and so defer his departure from ours for the space of one week in order to impart by his presence and support that eclat to your famous Guild which is so desirable - with these few words I beg leave to sit down ...

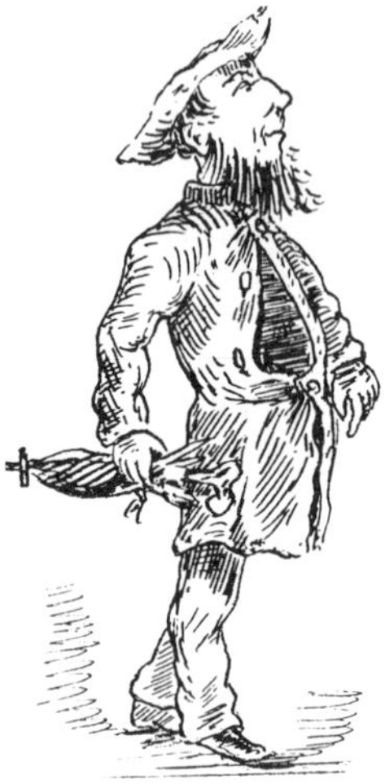

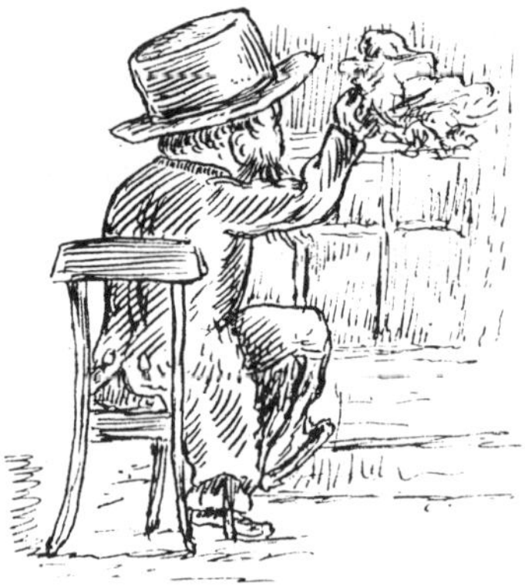

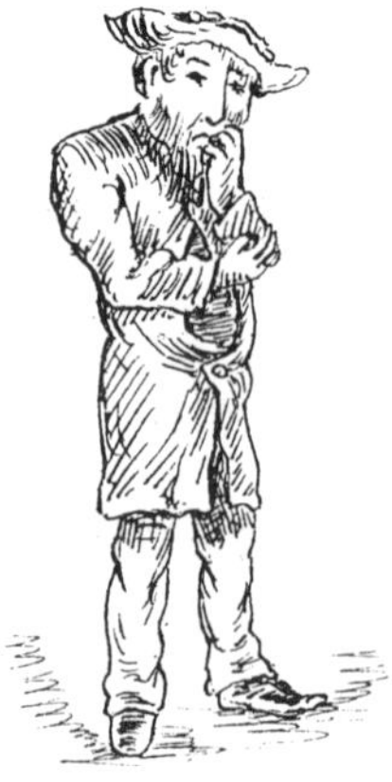

Sep 2nd 1882...If I was you - as soon as the Guild commences I should go out for a walk afar from the bustle and throng and take my umbrella with me. Among the 1,000,000 persons who will diurnally crowd into the town of Preston during the Guild Week I should be nobody, and probably unnoticed but as a Bona Fide traveller at a country Hostel let me but order a substantial dinner of Eggs and Bacon; or a first class Meat Tea consisting of pickled herrings and a pair of eggs - a sliced cucumber and a lump of cheese I should be somebody and noticed - I should feel myself a power in the land - surely this would be much preferable to mingling heroically in the crush of the Guild Week and coming thereout with fractured ribs and the regretful remembrance of a watch that once was mine. No, my good Sir, take my advice - bid the Guild avaunt and hie ye thence ...

Preston Guild 3rd Day Sep 6th 1882...Hooray for the Dook!!!! Hooray for His Grace the Dook!!!! Who to open the Guill did undertook: And that we might get at him a good look Did come to Preston - the Marshal Dook. Wave then the Kerchief - the Kerchief white - Out through the window and full in sight of the Bands that are playing with all their might And troops all with colour and sheen bedight As well as the folks who with liquor are tight - Let it wave for the while the day is bright Wave it likewise at approach of the night When the streets are ablaze with Electric Light. Hark to the bugle, the Clarion and drum List to the thousands who from everywhere come, Bang with each broomstick & rattle each can - Since the Guild is now open'd by a great Noble man. So hooray for the Dook - the great Marshal Dook Who's so nobly accomplished what he undertook ...

Sep 9th 1882...The Preston Guild of 1882 concludes today - By the time this reaches you the bands of musicians will have ceased to play - Much too of the gewgaw and glitter of Demonstration will be laid aside until the biquentennial Festival comes round again - Perhaps some are already wishing that the guild had never been - aching heads - rifled pockets and absent watches will in some instances render the Guild memories not pleasant ones. When I passed through Standish yesterday I was informed that a man lay dead there who drank so excessively during the guild excitement that in a state of helpless inebriety he by some means fell upon the fire and was roasted to death - The event so lately spoken of as the next Pressn Guild will now be mentioned as the last Pressn Guild - so it ever is - Today will be yesterday 'tomorrow' ...

Notes

Sep 12th 1882 — Sir Garnet Wolseley was commander in chief of the Expeditionary Force sent to Egypt. A distinguished soldier, he was created a Baron in 1882, and a Viscount in 1885.

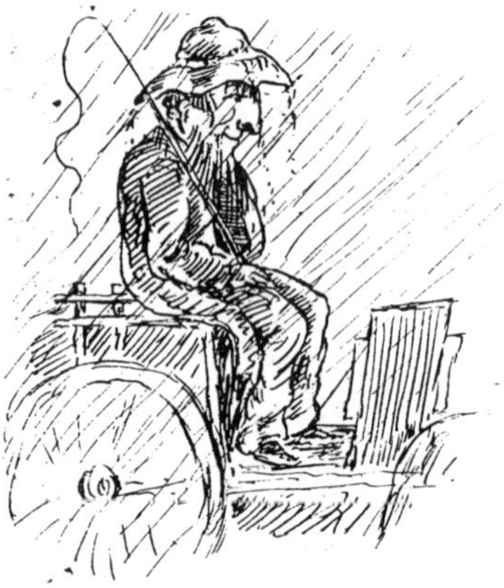

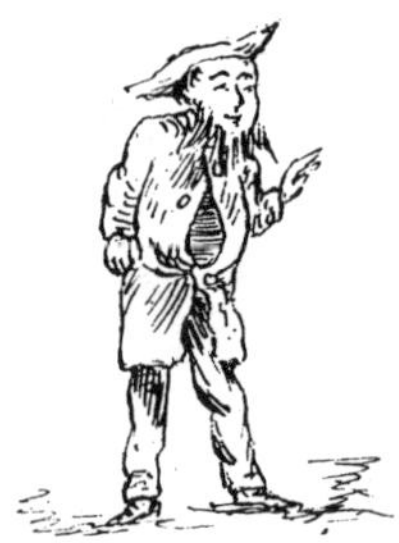

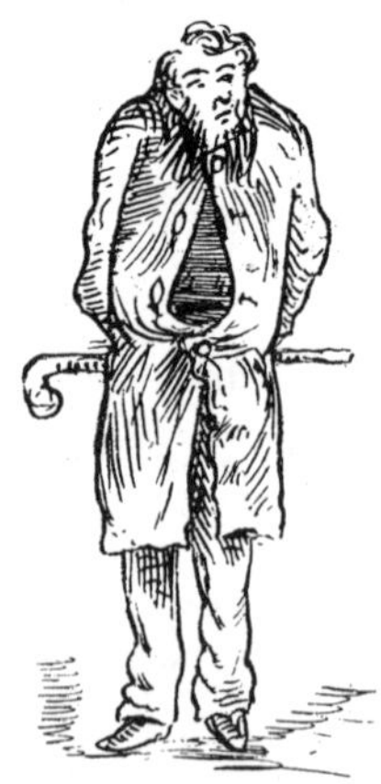

Sep 12th 1882...It is my proud boast, Dear Sir, that I went nowhere near the recent Guild and I can add further that I am now treating with the same indifference the 'Wakes' of Eccleston. I am told that festival is on this week but I am not going to it - Mr Howe is with me as is also Mr Parkes so what need have I to festivate - some of us visited Southport yesterday to bask awhile and enjoy a brief promenade by the rivage of the briny main - I could not stand it - methought I should be sea sick if I tarried by the seaside longer - The saline mixture, as before, proved to my Wimstow friend a benefit indeed - Engagements are the order as to the present time - I have one at Heskin school tomorrow - Sir Garnet* had one in Kassissin in Egypt on Saturday ...

Sep 14th 1882...Thunder and weighty rain this morning renders it unreasonable to think of going out for a drive - I have been wet to the skin several times during the recent drenching weather - over Harrock the sky looks very dark and the air thick - Thankful I am that it is not urgently needful to go forth anywhere this morning - The egression would be attended with much discomfort. I hope your sea trip has been beneficial - Mr Parkes still here also Mr Howe who is busy writing - all join in good wishes - Tel el Kebjr taken yesterday - Hooray ...

Sep 18th 1882...You little know the excitement we are in - The Pressn Guild was nothing to it as an instrument for disturbing people's equanimity. We are to have a railway at last - a railway from somewhere to here; and from here to everywhere - Engineers have been a week surveying - taking measurements and levels so we begin to feel that we may have a railway any day - We who are near to nowhere are now going to be neighbours to every body - can you imagine the iron horse disturbing the quiet of our fields and awaking us diurnally from our slumbers. The Derbyshire giant is with us still - He has just been out to enjoy his Matin pipe ...

Sep 19th 1882...ah me! My Stafford guest has left me - at ten o'clock this morning he passed down my front walk and went for the vehicle wherein he bridged the distance hence to Capull station - I went with him - He took the noon train from Wigan which all being well would land him in the Stafford station (not Police I hope) about 40 minutes past one. Tis evening - wintry wind prevailing - hear rain threatening - and on the whole surroundings might be more cheerful ...

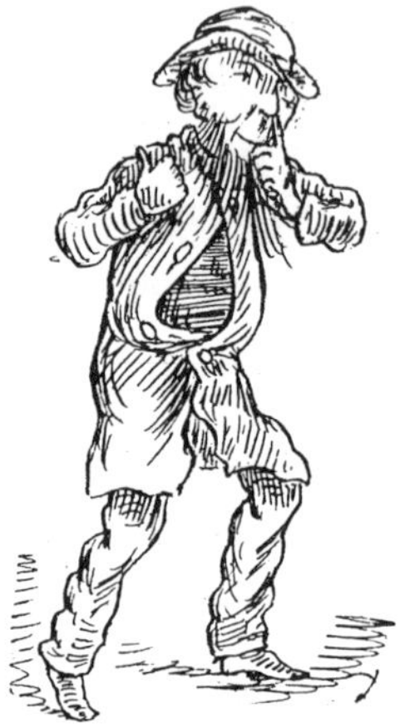

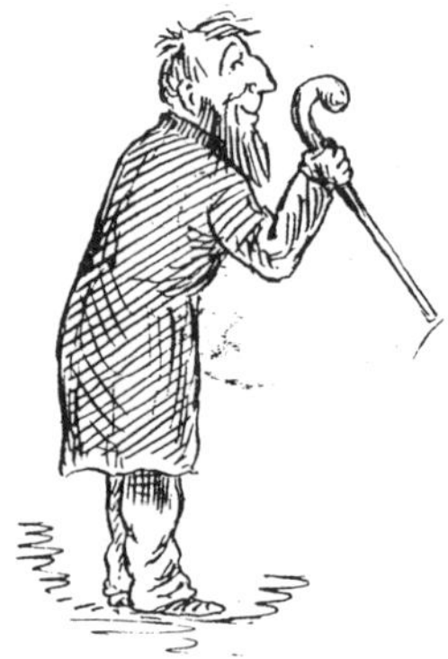

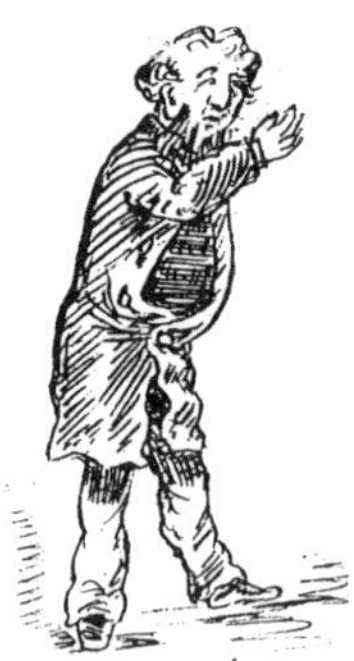

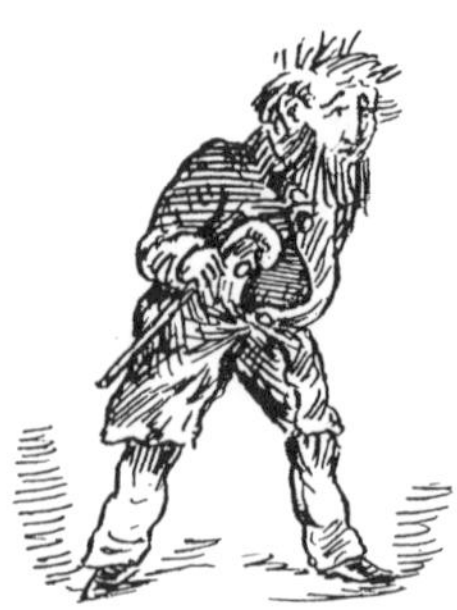

Sep 21st 1882 (evening)...He's off is the Derbyshire giant. He went away over yonder towards Standish with his 'portmantel' in his hand about one o'clock. He will be tired just now - I know - you see he's very heavy of foot and slow withal in movement - In fact he's truly a great man - steady going - often sitting and weighty both in council and out of it - We hope you are well - I don't feel in extra 'fettle' myself today but am expecting to go into Derbyshire for a few days soon ...

Sep 23rd 1882...Hi! Look here Mister - Did I tell you in my last that that there gentleman what gave me my 'gee-up' and veekle - my <u>Poney and trap</u> as yah may call it has become a 'family man' - It was on Tchuesday morning last (Sep 19th) that his little son was born - I've been so excited by the news that I don't recklect whether I mentioned it on any previous card this week - I cannot yet say for certain whether, or when, I shall get to go into Derbyshire this beautifully fine Mickklemas summer. I mean to look up Buxton, Chatsworth &c when there, but if I don't go I <u>shan't</u> look 'em up so no more at present ...

Sep 27th 1882...It is a moment of anxiety - I await the arrival of the Post with indescribable impatience, for my Derbyshire visit trembles in the Balance - which way the beam will incline I shall not know until the Post comes. The matter stands thus - (A) writes to (B) (that's me) and asks him to come over into Derbyshire and do something - (B) thereupon goes to (C) and asks him to write to his friend (D) and get him to come over and do something for him (B) while he (B) is over doing something for (A); after a week's delay (D) responds regretting that having to do something for somebody else he cannot come over and do something for (B) so that (B) may go over and do something for (A) as aforesaid - consequently (B) (that's me) goes off at once to see (E) and ask if he or his coadjutor (F) can come and perform the function at first set apart for (D) - (E) will have great pleasure but must first consult with (F) and (F) not being comeatable at the time (E) requests (B) to let the matter stand over till he can see (F) when (F) and (E) will discuss the possibility of helping (B) that he may be free to help (A) and have his fortnight in Derbyshire ...

Sep 30th 1882...What do you say? a what? a <u>wedding</u>!!! <u>you've</u> gone to a wedding over in London!!! Well I never!! They are dangerous occasions for Bachelors and Widowers to be present at. I feel much alarmed about you - Your position is critical. It is like riding on an ammunition wagon at Cairo when there's a lot of warm sunshine & spontaneous combustion about. Do let me hear from you when it is all over, that I may know whether you are safe - <u>You</u> going to a wedding! I never knew such a thing - My dear Sir wherever is your discretion - wherever is your sense of self-preservation? Do have a care - whatever you do - do have a care ...

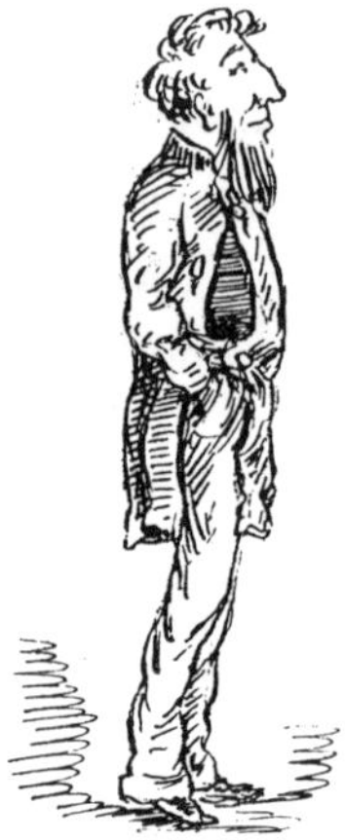

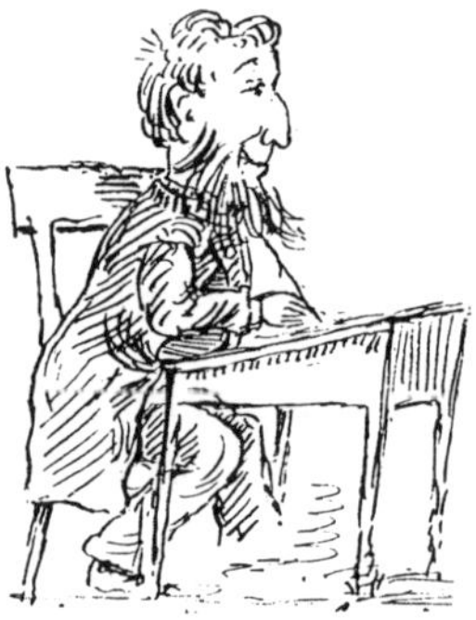

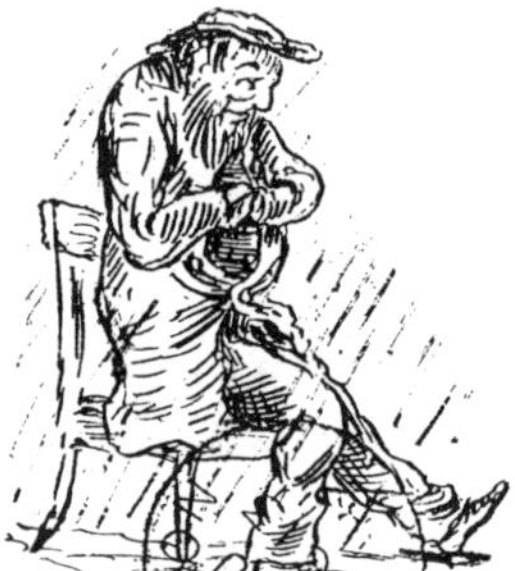

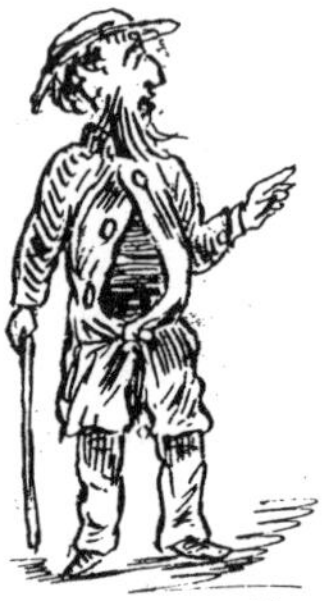

Oct 3rd 1882...well - How have you enjoyed it all? I assume that you will be back at home again by the time this card of enquiry passes through the portals of 63, Fishergate. How do you feel after the wedding jinks - the breakfast - the rice throwing (I might have said wasting) and the ball? I hope you have caught no coolth and do, my dear Sir - do say, have you come back quite free? I have trembled on your account for I considered your risk a great one - I'm off to Derbyshire in a day or two - Have engaged to be there on Sunday ...

Oct 9th 1882... I am not in Lancashire at all just now, so you don't need to look for me there - I am in fact at present with my Domestic Regulator enjoying the fresh breezes which sweep over the Peak of Derbyshire - I write this at the Breakfast table for as soon as our fast has been broken and our wearied frames have received resuscitation we trip forth into the bright sunshine to do feats of pedestrianation such as a Weston might envy - Don't know what day we shall return but hope to send you a line again by and by reporting the progress of the Tour ...

Tuesday Oct 10th 1882...I write these few lines hoping they will find you quite well as it leaves me at present so no more at present except that dear to me as to the humming bee the nectar stored in the cup of the woodbine are the fresh sweet breezes which sweep gently o'er these heathery heights - mists unfortunately have begun to obstruct our range of vision - but kindness unremitting lights up our countenance with gladsome smiles and we are both happy ...

Oct 13th 1882...oh Mister! I've been all through the Peak on a 'Tower' as we say; and the clock had struck six a good deal when I awoke this morning - I got a 'shower' bath at Matlock yesterday - from which circumstance I suppose the valley receives its name. The rain came down its hardest - The roads became a bed of mud - We are but human - and humanity is ever frail - cannot sustain much toil at my time of life - not very ..Off home this morning ...

Oct 16th 1882...ah, me - My dear good Sir - I'm back again and mean to be so for some time - Torpedo has brought home a sciatica and I am enjoying a first class headache - We left rain in Derbyshire and have found it here - will it be the same rain, do you think? It looks like it - we have considered the matter from a political -liberally political - point of view and determine that the Comet and the rain are alike due to Lord Beaconsfield's policy - My headache wages me to a conclusion, so without further apology ...

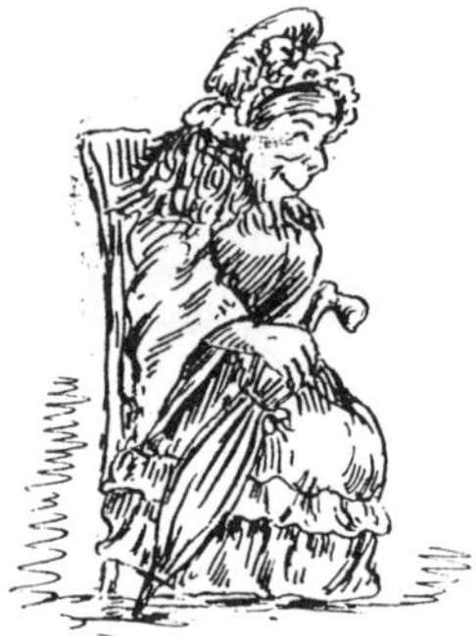

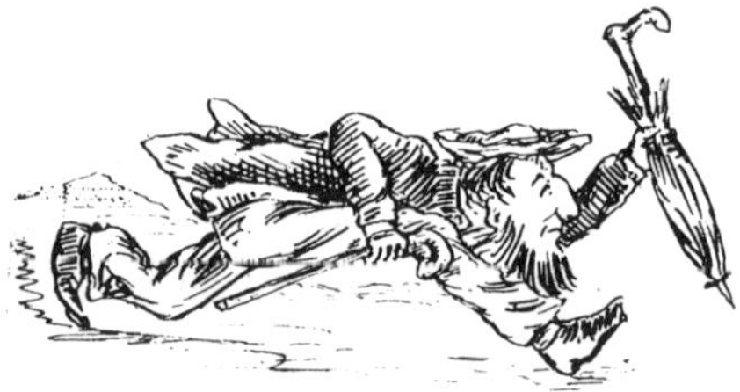

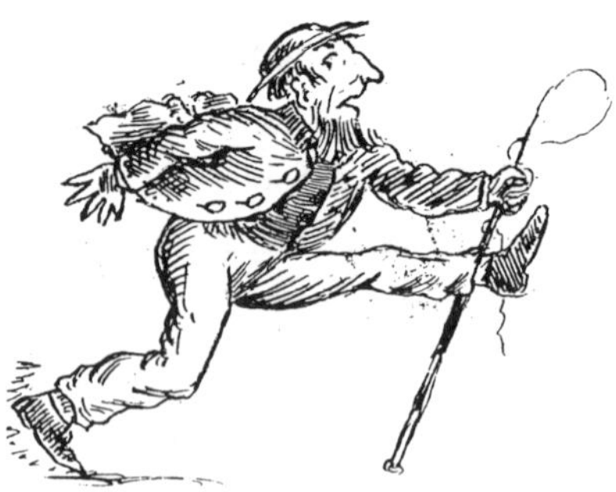

Oct 21st 1882...Mister - my 'usband - Dear good man - he bin at Southport a tuthrey days and only come back yester which it were dark when he got here, and me with 'im as is not used to travvil - my poor limbs was near broke with walking and me umbrella quite wet through and me no goloshers on, nor strong boots, nor nothink - but we're leaving 'ome aggen in a few days - Sorrer 'aunts us as we cannot ask you over just yet and make all comfuthubble - but we know you wouldn't come if you knew - and so will arsk you wait and we will explain more fully - Meanwhile cherish Dear Sir - a spirit of patience and contentment - assured that all may yet be well - We old folk you know has to do it betimes and so 'oping you are all quite well as we remain so - only a little unsettled, like which it's no matter mostly but now believe us - Mister - with distinguished regards.. P.S. we've just got Two Partridge which it makes us cheerful like rather ...

Oct 23rd 1882 (Monday)...Wet or Fair I am meaning to be off tomorrow - at early morn I start and take Torpedo with me - we shall be away from home some <u>time</u> - in fact we shan't be back till evening - It is not London, nor Llandaff - nor Worcester nor Malvern nor Scarboro to which we are going - as we had our first snow or sleet in this 'fall' yesterday and the air is still cold we shall not venture far afield but only <u>run away</u> as far as Ormskirk accompanied merely by my umbrella and stick - while hasting on travel we will think of ye ...

Oct 25th 1882...I beg your pardon for intruding again so soon - my excuse is I am a little bit ruffled - my hair nearly stands on end, and so would yours, if I told you all about it - I've had a haxident as might have 'killed off' both myself and partner - one or both or either. You'd have been ruffled also if you'd been there which I rejoice you weren't - for it was enough to give one Bronchitis in one's back hair - we went to Ormskirk yesterday and today I can scarcely move. It's my left knee - it is, as done it - so no more ...

Oct 27th 1882...I think I told you of my accident - now - if you wus driving - say - in a high back'd car if you will and chanced inadvertently to druv over a wheelbarrow so that a regard - an earnest and thoughtful regard - for your personal safety made it indispensable for you to take a sudden and hasty stride that would have done honour to a Colossus - in fact a stride from the vaulting vehicle into the hedge four yards away - would <u>you</u> like it? I should think <u>not</u> and no more do I - I can say no more ...

<u>Notes</u>

<u>Nov 1st 1882</u> This was the innovation of the bustle.

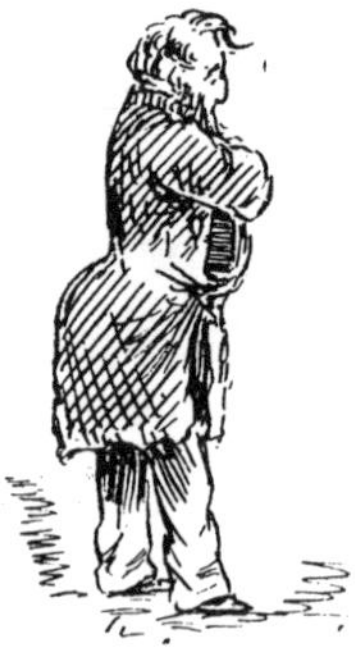

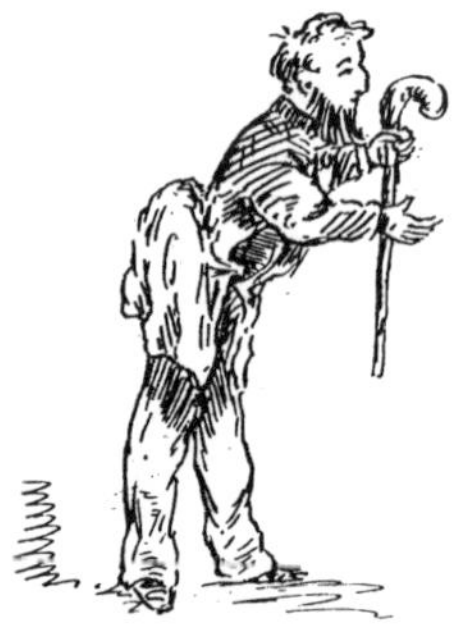

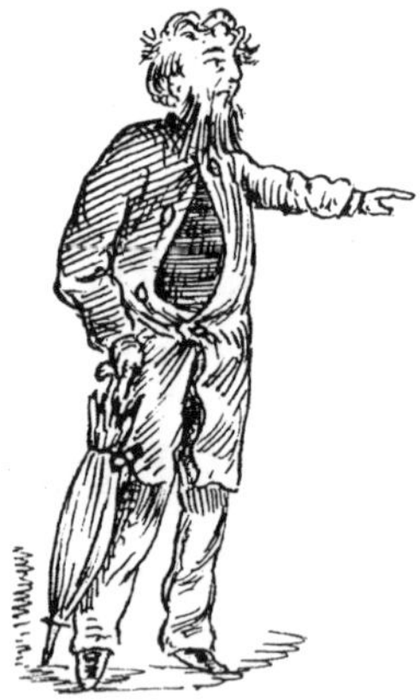

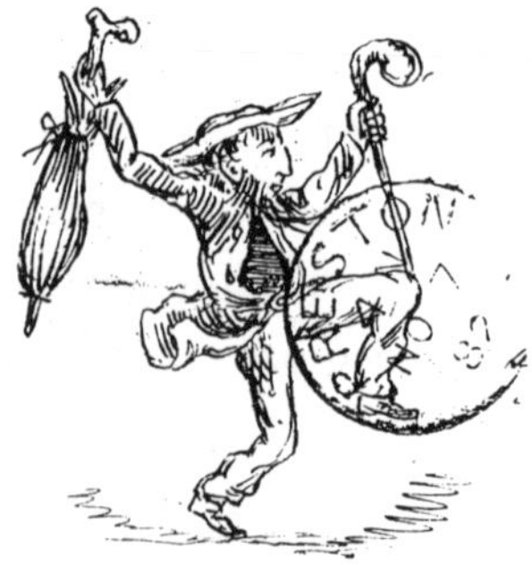

Nov 1st 1882...What a deal people see and know who live a long time - For instance if I had died 30 years ago I should have missed seeing many things that human ingenuity has since devised - I was shewn the other day in a shop window a wonderful arrangement which most impressed me - They call it I believe a dress improver* because it is thought to import such an airy unanimal appearance to the human figure - As you are aware that I have - though a slender - not by any means a wasp waist - How do you think a dress improver would answer in my case? As represented in the portraiture hereon - the effect seems noble and impressive - since our humiliation in the Transvaal our people appear to have run after Dutch proportions ...

Nov 2nd 1882...I am convinced that these 'Improvers' as they call them won't do in my case unless I make previous special arrangements with the gentleman who deftly drapes my figure - to wit the Tailor to whom I am indebted for my much admired garments - The effect of the Improver as here shewn falls slightly short of elegance - If weather permit I am going to Southport for an hour or so today - Hoping you are all well ...

Nov 2nd 1882...I got quite to Southport today - and very nearly got drowned - such rain!!! I couldn't make you believe - I really couldn't, and so I shan't try - But, I remain ...

Nov 6th 1882...I send this to inform you that I am just going off to get my hair cut - There's a little tuft at the crown which I fear the last tonsorial operator clipped too short - It consequently persists in sticking up on its own account and resolutely bids defiance to hair oil, pomade and brush alike - It is of course just possible I may hang about for a day or so in order to pick up a little corporeal vigour before my busy time comes on. I have been nearly blown out of the house this last weekend and the rain showers have been quite appalling ...

Nov 7th 1882...I quite anticipated enjoying today the refreshing coolness of a well clipped pate - and to have been parading the promenade at Southport - the admired of all who can appreciate what is noble in figure and character, who by the way would be rich in speculation as to the identity of that foreign looking gentleman - but alas! It may not be - a dense fog has set in which renders travelling dangerous - Torpedo dare not venture either herself or me. I can only see from my windows to the shrubs opposite - Nobody therefore would be able to see my fresh cut hair in Southport if I went - so my purpose for the present abandoned ...

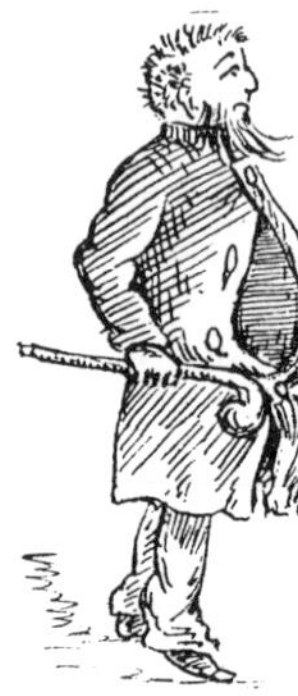
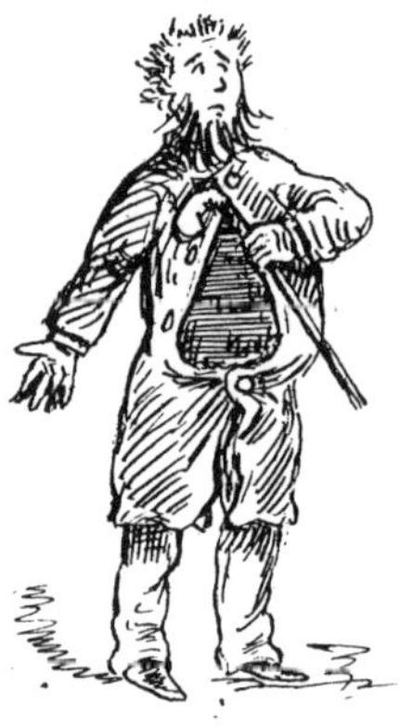
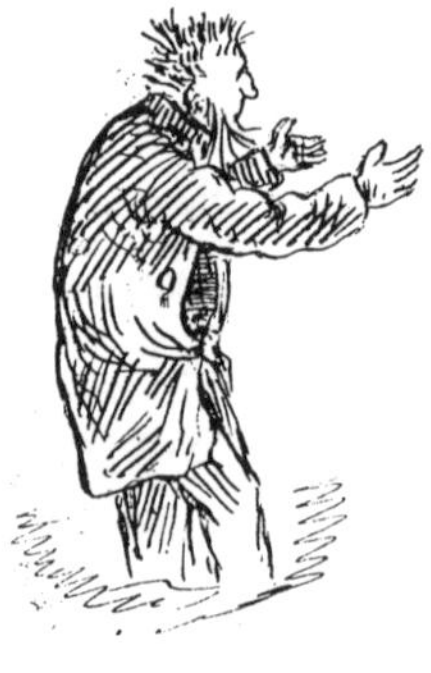

Nov 7th 1882P.M....I told you I was coming and I have done so - Torpedo's following me - horray horray!!!! She's coming via Wiggin - whereas I have come via nowhere but straight on. The Fog cleared away after I sent off my other card so that our prospects brightened and there is now some prospect of the hair-cutting being done. I shall then look fine and modernised, you may depend on it. I have brought with me little sundries needful for my comfort - a little protection from probable rain; and a little support when pedestrianating - in other words an umbrella and a walking stick - I have not time for more at present - so no more ...

Nov 11th 1882...Thanks for your letter which I found awaiting me on my return home this afternoon - I don't feel quite what you may call first class. It rained all the way nearly. The roads consequently were bad to travel on - I am very tired and yet more very rheumaticked - I was a spectator of the first public Tea Feast in connection with St Luke's Church Southport on Tuesday evening last (Nov 7th) - a great occasion - a wonderful success - I cannot say this last about my hair cutting - the Tuft at the crown still pokes up too much after the manner of a celery brush - but after it has been operated upon by a frost or two it may become more tender and display less the qualities of an upstart. Twenty six letters awaited me upon my return. In haste ...

Nov 16th 1882...How very much one's personal appearance depends upon the tact and ability of one's hairdresser - any one can see that he's made a change in me. I am truly busy, too, just now - Florrie's Mamma had an apoplectic fit a few days ago - life for a time despaired of - paralysed - but signs of improvement last evening - nearly been an end to both Torpedo and self too. Driving home in the dark we got into collision with some heavy jingling carts - we unfortunately had no lamps - as we expected moonlight - Instead we encountered Fog and carts ...

Nov 17th 1882...If there is at this time a 'Working Man' upon this fair earth who distinctively merits the title - be his hair recently operated on or not - I modestly claim to be that man. I'm over ears and head in a flood of work - even the 'celery brush' looking tuft which proudly garnishes my apex can scarcely appear above it. We have also had another accident - on Wednesday night (15th inst) in the fog and darkness when returning from a visit to Florrie's Mamma we collided with some coal carts and damaged a wheel - It is quite time we old folks stayed in at nights ...

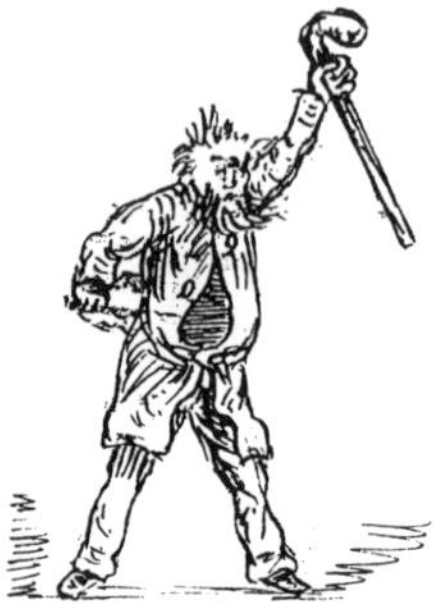
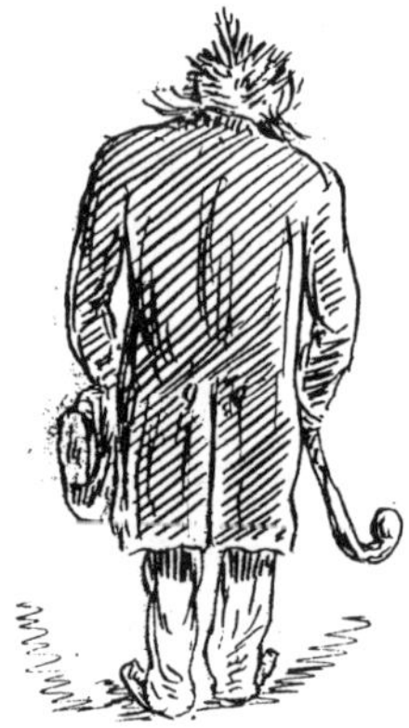
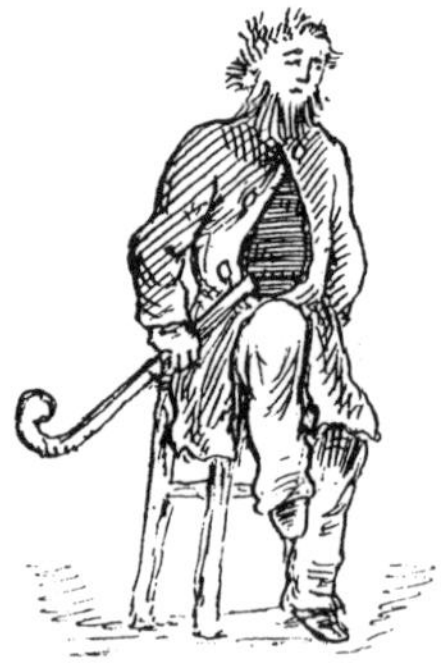
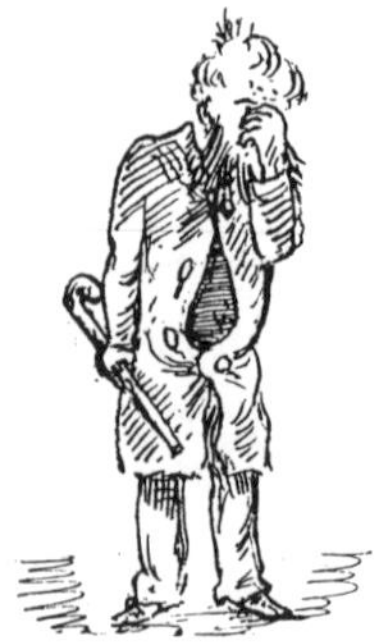

Nov 20th 1882...see here, My Dear Sir, see here - Whatever you may say - 20th of November though it be I stick to it - aye my dear Sir - I stick to it that if there be a working man - a distinctively working man - living - him's me, or, I'm him - Why therefore am I not a Member of Parliament? Why don't you propose me for Preston in the labour interest - especially 'Interest'? I leave it to you however - and as heretofore I remain ...

Nov 21st 1882...Just a word with you before I commence the active duties of today - It is this - when you propose me for the Preston vacancy make it clear that I am a representative of 'Labour' - in fact myself a working man - It must be understood too that if honoured with the suffrages of the Electors of your ancient and distinguished Borough - I must go as a paid candidate - one thousand a year and a cosey house rent free up in the Metropolis will enable me to represent them with some degree of comfort to myself - all may freely vote for me as I will, to suit my constituents, support both the present administration and the Conservative opposition - I shall support the former by saying nothing therefore practically accepting the Cloture and not impeding or obstructing by any exuberance of my own verbosity the progress of important legislation - on the other hand my vote will on all occasions be Conservative - I leave the rest with you ...

Nov 25th 1882...I see by an Article in the Standard that there are two candidates for the Representation of your Guilded Borough - Am I one? Did you in proposing me specify clearly to the Electors the indispensability of an annual allowance and snug house within easy walking distance from the Palace in Westminster - the annual 'thousand' I should like to have paid to me in advance and guaranteed for five years at least so that a change of Ministry or appeal to the country may not take immediate effect on me. I was in Ormskirk on Friday and got drenched with sleet and nearly as numb as a Russian Cabman on a winter night ...

Nov 27th 1882...oh dear, oh dear, you have done it to let this opportunity pass - and after I had given you such particular injunctions and instructions, too. I have been so busy that I did not open the Saturday's paper till this morning and there I saw the Election at Preston is over and you never even proposed me. It makes the tuft which the Barber left on the apex of my head stand up worse than ever - and I now have to mourn the loss of the yearly 'thousand' for which I stipulated as well as the Parliamentary honour - oh dear, oh dear, you shouldn't do so...

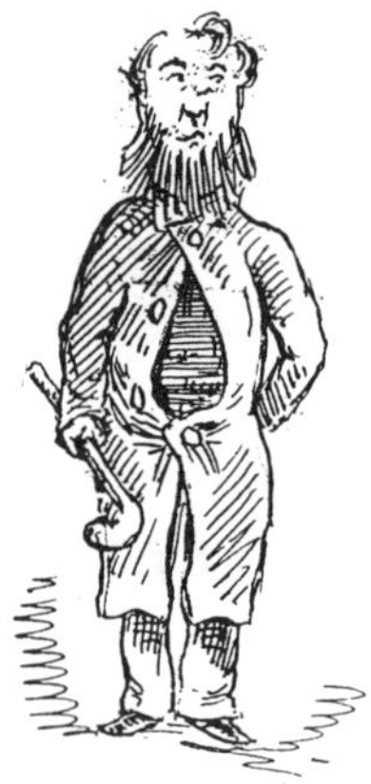
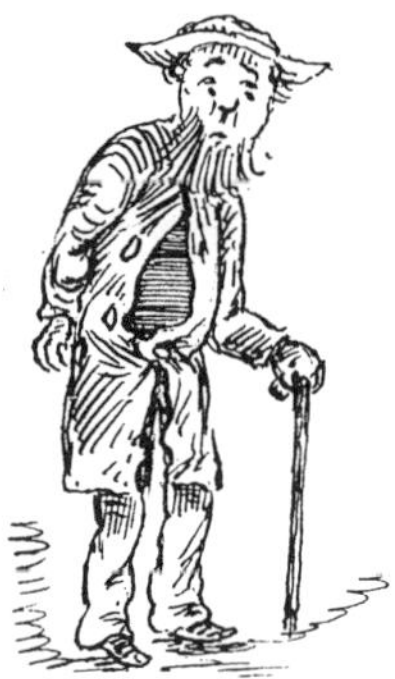
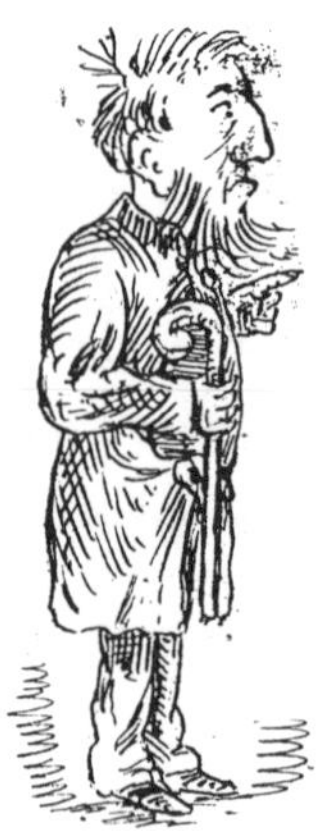

Dec 2nd 1882...We've had a gloomy and perplexing week so that I have not felt myself at all - nor have had the mood for Post Cards - I have been up to my chin in accounts - a curvilinear 8 would persist in changing places with an angular 4, while sickle like 5 & vertebrate ones, billhook looking twos and warming pan nines sneaked in here and there mingling with the crowd and soon lost to sight, while I despairing and undone, dashed madly in pursuit. My duties have in fact been sometimes as perplexing as those of an Irish man who was to drive a drove of pigs through a Fair - or those of Mr Gladstone in making Ireland orderly. The weather has been cold - this morning it is bitter raw and bleaching - Mrs Jackson departed this life on Tuesday evening last and is to be interred here today. Her mother is with us and has been several days. Hoping ye all are well ...

Dec 2nd 1882. Night...I can't walk out much this weather - can you? Keen Southeast winds - sleet, and rheumatic knees don't encourage pedestrianism - of course I want to go out, and would go, but when it's not fit, what's the use? I like to preserve a grave and tranquil demeanour when I go out anywhere but nobody could do that in this wind which is sweeping with hurricane violence outside. I shall have to get down to Eccleston by some means on Monday, but whether on horse back or by road or rail I have not at present decided - much must depend on the weather and state of the roads - but if it is like it is now, what's to be done? for that I don't know - Do you? ...

Dec 4th 1882. Night...Bless us! Your note has knocked me all of a heap, almost, my dear Sir - What can I do? I can't help it - if you'll just unbethink you - you will recollect I mentioned a month or two ago that there existed at that time a cause which restrained our movements - and restricted greatly our freedom in the household - I promised to explain when I could get to see you - that obstacle has gone, but what's the use? others have arisen - In fact now our household is augmented by the addition of three members permanently and a fourth occasionally - I hope e'er long to be in Preston & then can open out to you the arcana of my heavy bosom - explaining in what manner and degree I have been of late 'fowten' ...P.S. Thanks for the Mite's portrait. It is lovely ...

Dec 8th 1882...It has just occurred to me that mayhap you'll be able to unbethink you again that we have had one or two accidents - that once we left the vehicle rather abruptly and on another occasion collided with some empty carts in fog and darkness. The roads too are infested with Traction engines about which our poney is very timorous and so in this wise or from divers causes we are not enthusiastic about riding out - Don't therefore, I pray you, find in the possession of a poney and trap an argument for our getting about at all times - for Torpedo as you know doesn't soon forget, or get over, a fright once received. I was in Leyland a few days agone & so may shortly look you up ...

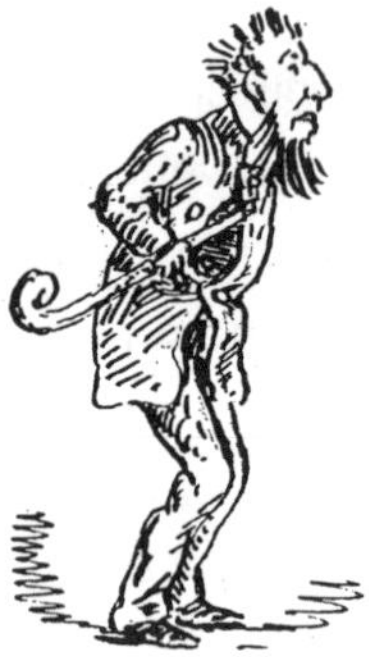

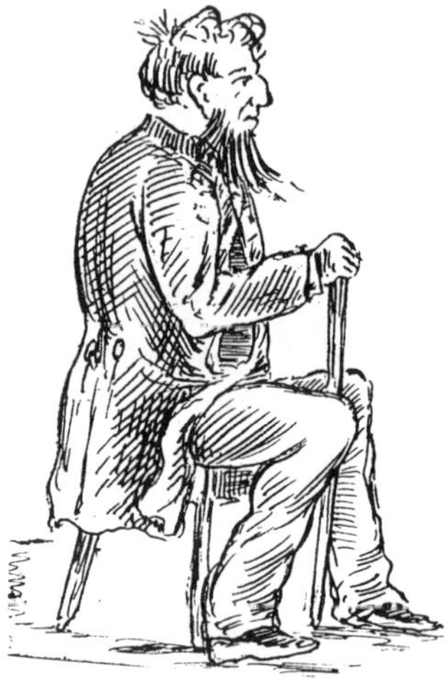

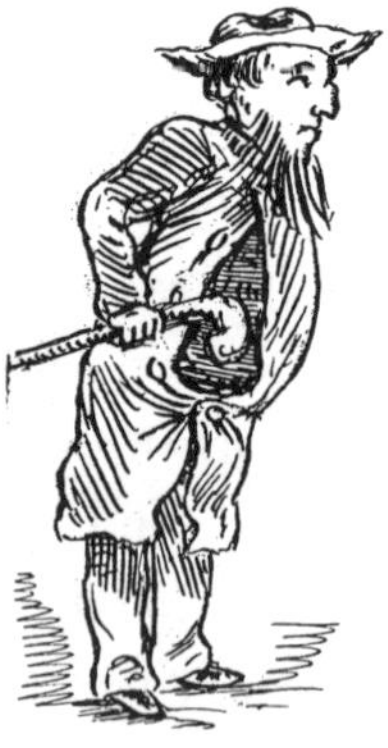

Notes

Dec 18th 1882

The pantomime was even then a feature of the Victorian Christmas, although the style known today was not introduced (from Drury Lane), until 1893. They were, even so, great spectacles, sometimes employing casts of hundreds, with as many as a dozen changes of scenery.Perhaps the most famous 'dame' was Dan Leno, who began his pantomime career in 1886, reaching the Theatre Royal two years later.

Dec 12th 1882 Night...We're Ice bound and in snow enveloped - That is just how we are at present - and nobody needs to blame us, for we can't help it - of course we can't. There's the ice and the snow and we have to do the best we can with both - We got two loads of coal brought on the day before the snow set in and we feel proportionately happy in consequence - But then the coal won't last for ever so if this weather does our present felicity will terminate - I have got a severe cold - Hoarse as a Nutmeg grater or for that matter - as a lesser Nutmeg. Nicholas, our quondam charioteer made on Wednesday 6th Inst a journey to Hoole - his last in this earthly life - Paralysis seized him on the road - perhaps induced by the severe cold. He died in Hoole on Friday 8th and was interred on Monday the eleventh - We cannot get out anywhere and our poor poney is nearly distracted at her imprisonment - but the roads are so slippery she couldn't stand upon them ...

Dec 16th 1882...The simple truth is this my dear Sir - That I've been on these very premises unable to go out and get off them since last Monday - I had then a cold and it has taken me all my time to keep it as a cold and prevent it becoming Bronchitis - My throat is less sore and the pricking scrapey sensation on or about the Larynx or upper portion of the Trachea is all but gone, yet there lingers a dry, hard shaking sort of Tussis - (nice word 'Tussis' -it's the short for a cough). A Thaw is proceeding so that this morning the 'green fields' begin to be pretty plainly visible - Our poney is thoroughly sick of this weather and craves the freedom of her pasture if only for one hour in the day - Mrs Marsden is with us but so broken down with Age and her great trial that you would hardly know her - Florrie too is here and Joo returns to us for the holidays. I have heard nothing from Leyland yet - but by each Post I expect to do ...

Dec 18th 1882...My dear 'Postcard receiving' Friend - Did you ever? This is intended rather as an ejaculatory enquiry than as a positive interrogation - I am being bang'd about rather with Bronchitis - an East wind on Saturday changed my cold into that old foe of mine - my cough is hard, dry, shaking, head splitting, chest rending, and 'biler busting'. I hope it will get no worse and that I may be directed to something that will speedily bring about or compass its subjugation - Our Tea Party is on Saturday next - Will you nip over and join us at a dish of the exhilarating beverage on that occasion? We have a wondrous programme for length and quality - varied as well as stimulating - "you won't need to visit no Pankymine* at after" ...

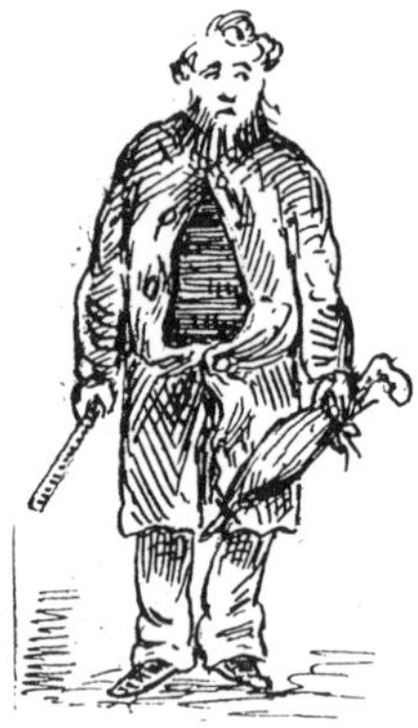

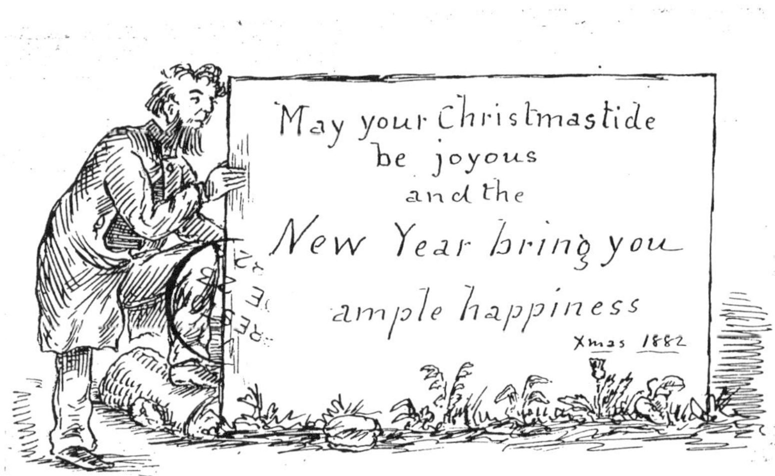
May your Christmastide
be joyous
and the
New Year bring you
ample happiness
Xmas 1882

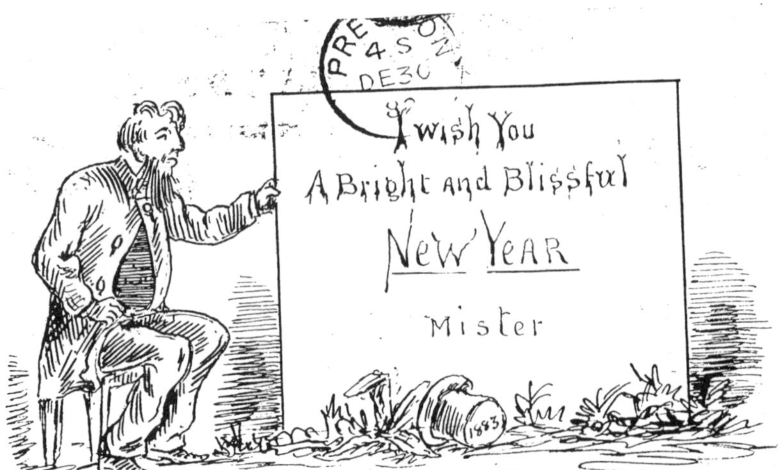
PRE
4 S
DE30
I wish You
A Bright and Blissful
New Year
Mister
1883

Dec 21st 1882 Night ...I've been ready each day for some time past to pick up my umbrella and stick with a view to setting forth to Preston, but alas! from Leyland yet no sign or sight or sound - We've look'd each post, and look'd in vain - Your letter also has taken the stiffening out of one a little - T'would have been a pleasure to see you at our Feast but such, it seemeth may not be - The advertisement which you were good enough to enclose had not been previously seen by me. I had heard rumour that it was to be, but nothing more - Torpedo not very well - out of fettle slightly as we may say - As for self - though I have been exposed to the cold a good deal today I think my Bronchitis is rather better - It has been hanging about for some days as a sort of bosom 'associate' (I can't write 'friend'), I speak of the thing as I find it, and what can I do more - would you? We've had a drain stopped and nearly all the premises taken up to rectify it - Holes here and there as if there had been an Alexandrian Bombardment and many shells bursting ...

Xmas 1882...May your Christmastide be joyous and the New Year bring you ample happiness ...

Dec 27th 1882 Night ...Well, I declare we're here!!!! By here I mean this dwelling, I mean home. The roads were heavy by reason of the recent rains - and to the like cause may be ascribed the darkness & cloudiness of the heavens - we walked splendidly however and got home alright - to find a lot of duty waiting me - Torpedo like myself is tired - and who would not be who had walked all the distance we have done - come early ...

1883...I wish you a Bright and Blissful NEW YEAR Mister ...

Jan 3rd 1883...I hasten to inform you that this week is likely to be to me a continual running about - at Purbold & Highmoor and Heskin Green today - Eccleston last Monday - Ormskirk yesterday - Southport tomorrow - a meeting at Eccleston on Friday - Round about Standish on Saturday but next week I hope to enjoy more of home quiet - what a mixture of rain and sunshine - tempest and calm - hot and cold this week has been so far - I never venture out far with my umbrella now as well as stick ...

Jan 8th 1883...I was away a good deal last week and I expect to be at home a good deal this - so now's your sorts and now too is your time - I am awaiting patiently but really what changeful weather - sunshine and rain - warm and cold - India and Greenland both in one day - oh, what complaints everywhere - Biliousness, sore throats, coughs - et cetera, and sundry. Eh my! Don't ask me to write any more this fitting - so be satisfied and please excuse ...

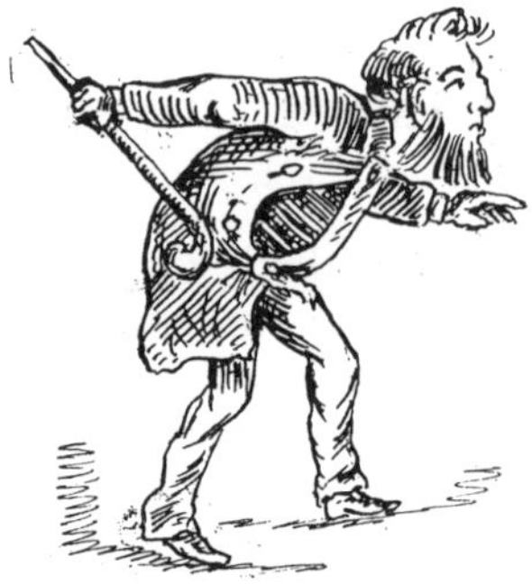

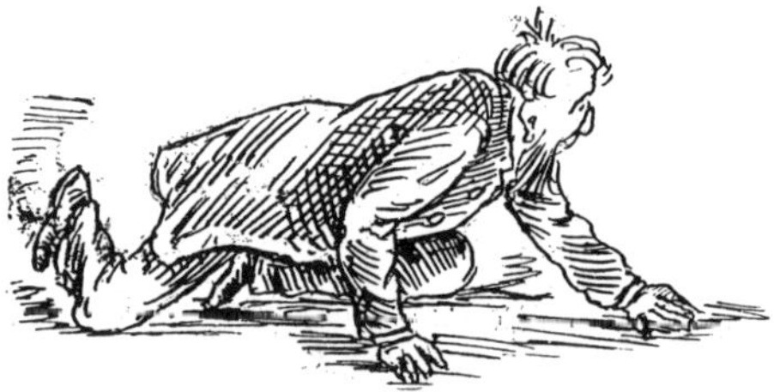

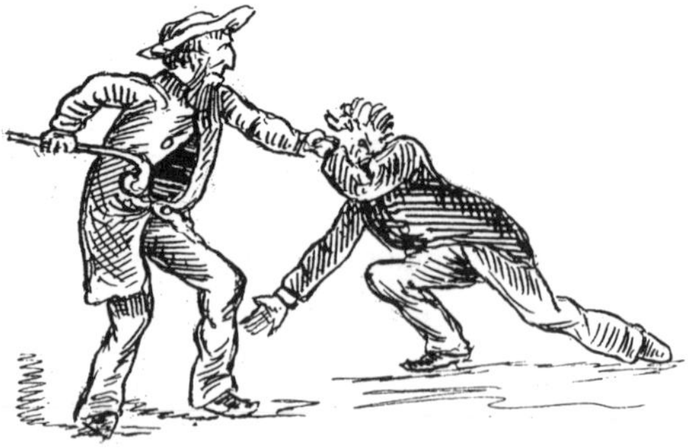

Jan 13th 1883...yah Mister! see you, look hither, and don't you go for to blame me this time - Day after day we have looked and longed but I suppose circumstances over which nor you, nor I have in anywise control have forfended - Mist, rain, and east winds have sturdily interposed between Fishergate and this dwelling. Roads slippy, fields spongey, and chimneys smokey have of necessity rendered the country unattractive. Measles are abounding and most people complaining about something - where health was unimpeachable the weather has formed the ready subject of complaint - Hoping the coming week may have more sunshine in store for us ...

Jan 15th 1883...It's really enough to floor anybody in this weather but I'm crawling on through it as best I can - a cutting east wind doesn't enliven me - far from it - but then - more's the pity - I have it to face and wind or rain are no deterrents. I have to go forth at Duty's call and do my do with most alacrity. Through cold or tempest, wind or rain I may diurnally be seen moving; and even into the shadows of night my vehicle and self, or self alone may be beholden. A neighbour is ill, and brotherly obligations rest upon me. I'm off to the adjoining country again today - I have lady visiters expected on Thursday in addition to the two we already have ...

Jan 16th 1883...oh, come now, my dear Sir, it will never do for you to get so 'down' as that - Let me try to raise you up a bit - have patience for a little time - It is true we cannot control this weather but we can wait, you know, till sunshine comes again and roads are passable. Don't give way for that I assure you will never do - You may be knocked over a bit, but don't go quite to the ground - cheer up, my dear Sir, cheer up and all may yet be well - The springtime lays before us - think of that and be thereby comforted ...

Jan 22nd 1883...If you feel anything like I do, you feel tired - Plainly speaking let me ask you, were you ever at a Concert? I have been. In fact you did not drive over on Saturday fine as it was - I went off to a concert to comfort myself - It cost me sixpence! Now as a friend you ought not to drive me to such desperation - the concert was downright exhilarating, and I feel better though, as I have already said, tired - You should try a concert - I consider it an excellent thing when you feel weamish - It did me good but still I feel weary -...P.S. I think I over exerted myself in listening ...

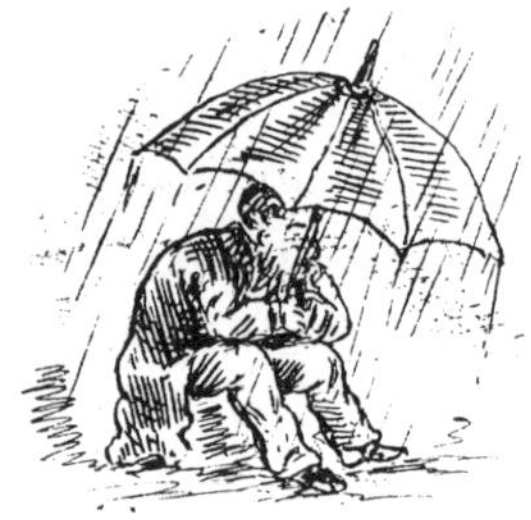
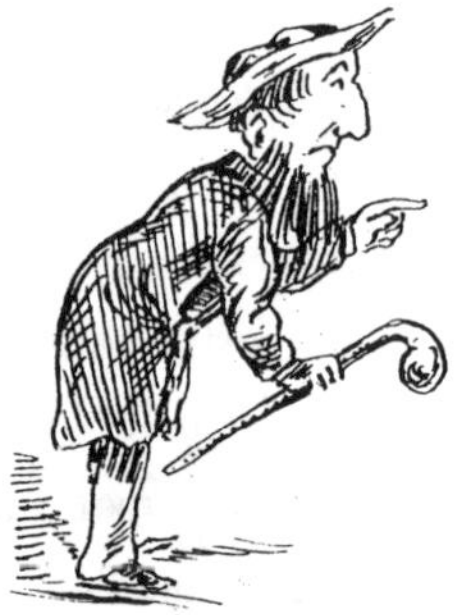
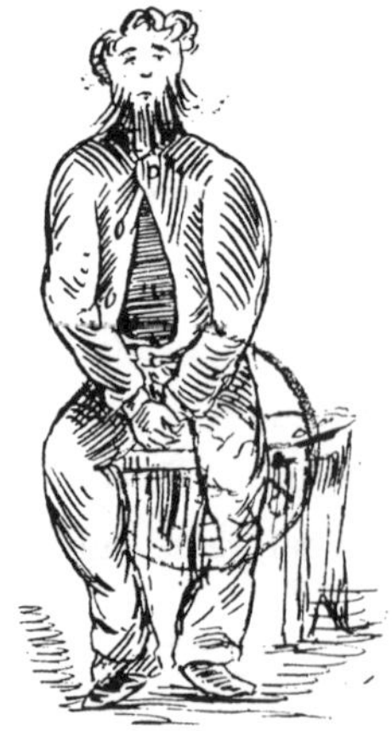
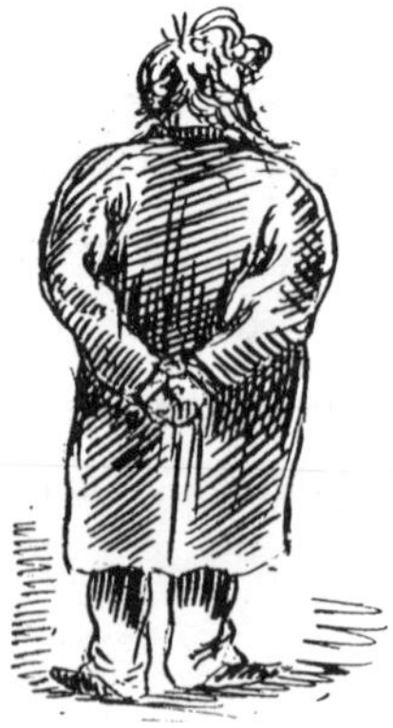

Jan 24th 1883...To be sure what a day it is - I have this very day an important function at a marriage service and here is the rain coming down like a wolf on the Fold - and the wind is both forceful and cutting and cold. I yesterday drove to Rufford and back again and never before felt so nearly cut in two by the wind - Neither Sirocco nor Harmattan could exceed it in penetrativeness. My stiffened fingers scarce could grasp the reins - Poor weather this for country visits and outdoor recreation. The elements after the manner of Mr Wartok have blocked hitherto very successfully the Bill of our aspirations ...

Jan 29th 1883...excuse me, my dear Sir being in a hurry this morning - like a famous Prime Minister I'm off - not to Cannes but to the second city of the Empire. Verily my purpose is to be in Liverpool before nightfall, but how long Torpedo and us will there abide I cannot say as tidings have reached me but an hour agone of the sudden death of an old man. An inquest is pending and I know not what day my presence may be looked for again. If these gales don't satisfy you no 'blow out' will ...

Jan 30th 1883...I'm in the Second City of the Empire at last - Like the 1st City in ditto, it has got a thick fog in it - The houses opposite are scarcely visible. We have made such good use or diligent use of our time that we already begin to need rest - Old folk cannot bear what young ones can. Earnestly wishing you happiness and very much so ...

Feb 3rd 1883...Even in this 'second City of the Empire' we cannot remain for ever - It began to rain and snow - eh my!!!! such as ye never seen afore - I am slightly within the mark - if anything, when I say it druv us on - We stampeded past Ormskirk to Southport and thence hither - We're tired, Sir, tired - and need in no small degree, rest. We got home last night Feb 2nd and on the evening went to Philharmonic Hall, L'pool to see Irving Bishop's experiments in 'Thought Reading'. They are enough to drive one nervous - If you go to see and hear him tie your hair down first for his pin seeking makes the hair fairly jump up and unless tied it might jump off ...

Feb 5th 1883...I've got back it is true but I cannot do with knocking about now like I once could. I was knocked about in a pleasant like way in the Second City of the Empire and now reaction has set in so that I may be a little time before I am, so to speak, all right - I walk about languidly but still my form is upright and I trust a few days' rest will set me all right - I look towards you, wishing you good health and much happiness - I remain your ever truly what's gotten home again ...

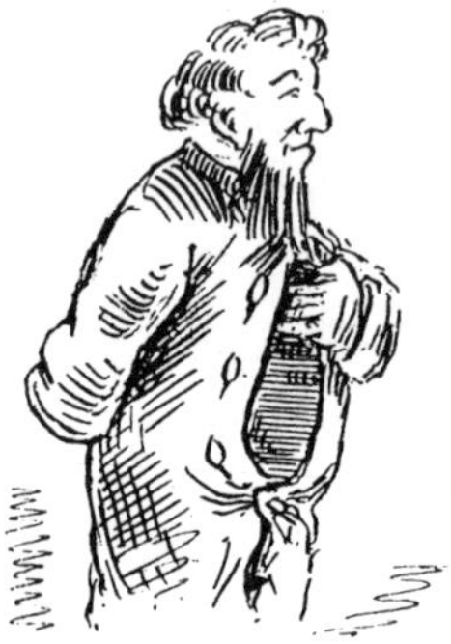

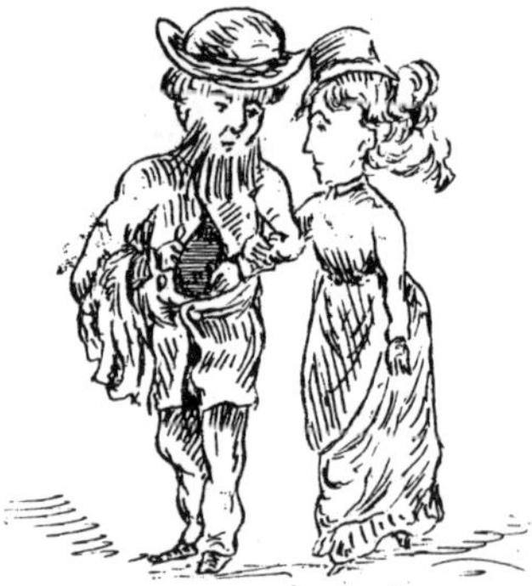

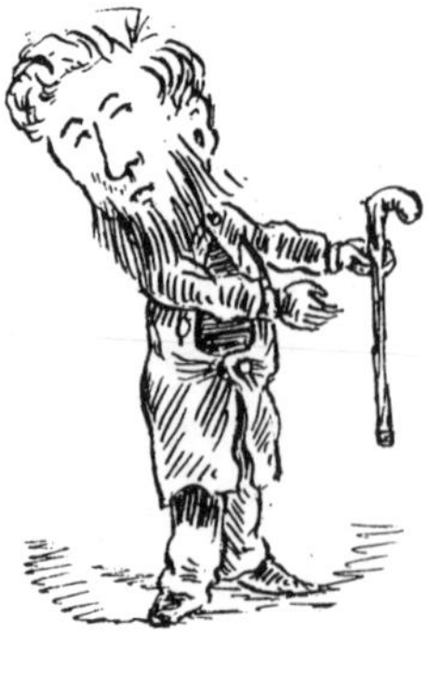

Feb 7th 1883...I'll tell you one thing my dear venerable Sir - and that's not two - these persistent gales from Orient are very trying to the chest - If you ask what chest? I reply my chest - your chest or anybody's chest - I know because I'm out in them all day through, and day after day, but then it matters not - we can't help it - There they are and here we are - so since grumbling's neither here nor there why indulge in it - It won't save either your shoe leather or mine but it may make us bilious - My advice is Don't grumble but wear a chest protector ...

Feb 10th 1883...oh, I'm ill this morning - my dear Sir - downright ill - completely out of fettle in fact - The combination and culmination of a number of Bile evoking factors - I feel fit for nothing at all - oh dear, oh dear - weep with me and pour out thus your sympathy abundantly - I am sure you would if you only knew fully what I feel, for ye were alway the possessor of a tender and loving heart - looking fervently and lachrymosely towards you ...

Feb 16th 1883...We went off to enjoy a brief repetition of the Honeymoon at Ormskirk yesterday and there got all Pollie's shoes renewed ...

Feb 17th 1883...oh dear, oh dear, these gales do frighten me - and these whistling draughts I can't endure - I have no need to practice civilities in my house by raising my hat when my wife enters the room for when she opens the door the in-rushing currents are brisk enough to set my hair apeak and lift my hat. I have been pursued from room to room by them till I have finally had to take refuge in a den which I seldom haunt - the library - should this prove untenable I must step outside and brave awhile, if not the battle - yet - the Breeze. We have got through Spring cleaning so we feel like getting on to summer nicely were it not for these gusts, these awful gusts ...

Feb 20th 1883...I cannot hold out to myself or any one else any hope that this poor old stick of mine will have any rest - Rain or fair - wind or calm - sunshine or shadow - warm or cold, it has to go plodding along with me by the side of it - Tis true I occasionally take out Pollie but only betimes & even then my stick goes in the vehicle. We have been several hours in Mawdesley today - the pair of us - our staff and self. Does the weather mend at all in Preston? It is here very diversome to say the mildest of it - My eyes are so irritated I can scarcely see to read or write - so I sigh for bed - my dear Mister - I sigh for bed - and remain at 10p.m. ...

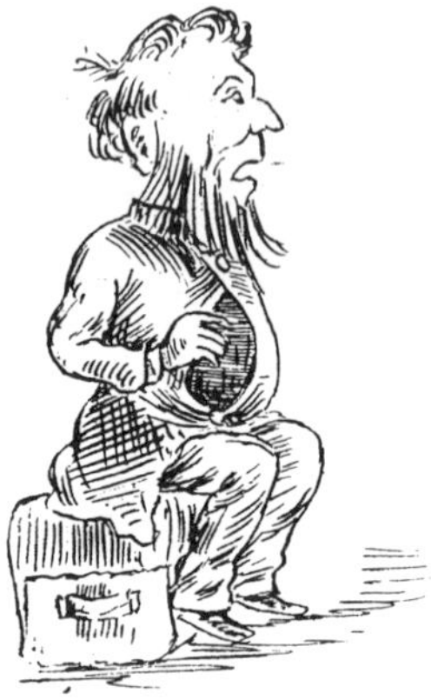

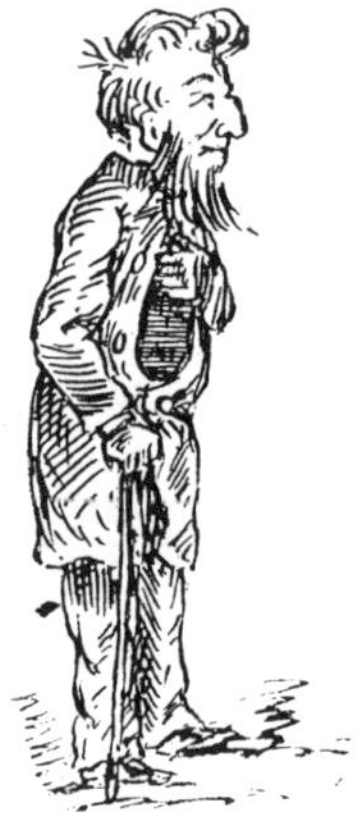

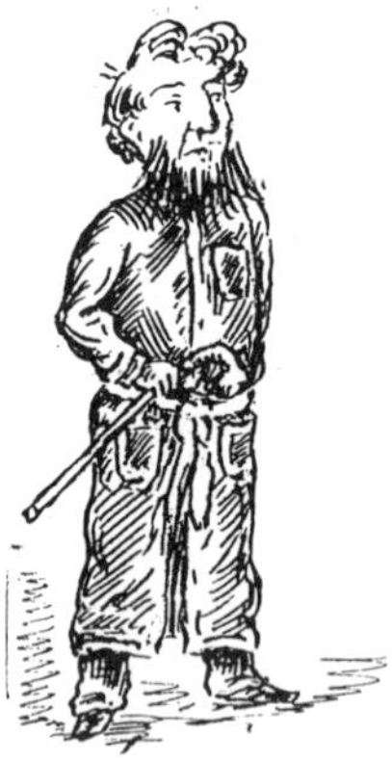

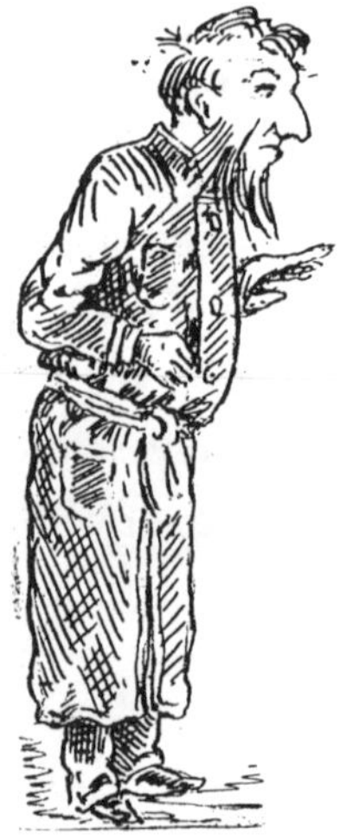

Feb 24th 1883...Whatever are they doing up in that there Parliament my dear Sir? It quite startles a nervous person like me, to read of their uproars - I suppose that cries of 'Name, Name' in that august assembly is equivalent to 'Turn him out - Turn him out' in our less dignified rural meetings - I hope it will all 'turn out' well, but still it fills me with apprehension. I wish you were here to reassure me because you understand such things. Perturbation forbids more ...

It is the 27th day of February 1883. I have been busily engaged in agriculture and really toiling hard - Though really, no worse for my exertions but better, I feel very tired and have a great appetite for slumber this eventide - My chest feels slightly cold as if some of the effects of this fierce cold wind yet hang around it - but on the whole I incline to think that bed is all I need to set me right again. I regret to inform you that Miss Marsden who lived a little below your smoke room died this morning about 6 o'clock after a week of most distressing illness. When are you coming to see me? I am going off for a day or two this week and will write you when I get away. We have a bidding to Ormskirk for a couple of days next week but cannot go, so if the weather's fine, here we are ...

Feb 28th 1883...Did I not notify you, my dear Sir, to the effect that I was coming? To be sure I did, my words were 'I'm going off for a day or two this week' and here you see I'm come - having brought my new coat with me too - It is no outcome of the Clothing Hall - It is a garment of ample dimensions & possessing a noble gracefulness. Torpedo has come with me - We are here not on pleasure merely but on diverse business - I consider it probable that tomorrow we shall be off home again - for I cannot be spared long from my sphere of diligence and this is saying a great deal. The health-inspiring breezes from the ocean only stimulate my affection - so that I subscribe myself only too too yours ...

March 2nd 1883 Night ...oh! so you're coming at last are you? It's this new coat of mine that's done it. I just thought at the time that it would fetch you if anything would. I quite expect you've not been able to get a wink of sleep since its splendours were first flashed upon your gaze through the intermediary of a Post Card - You'll feel easier when you've seen it and will doubtless rest better. You have acted wisely in resolving to come at once - far better this than pining away in wondering; and ungratified speculation. I shall drive to meet you, but as my poney has been resting for a full fortnight if it runs away I may meet the train at Burscough instead of Rufford as I shall have to go where the animal elects to take myself and vehicle ...

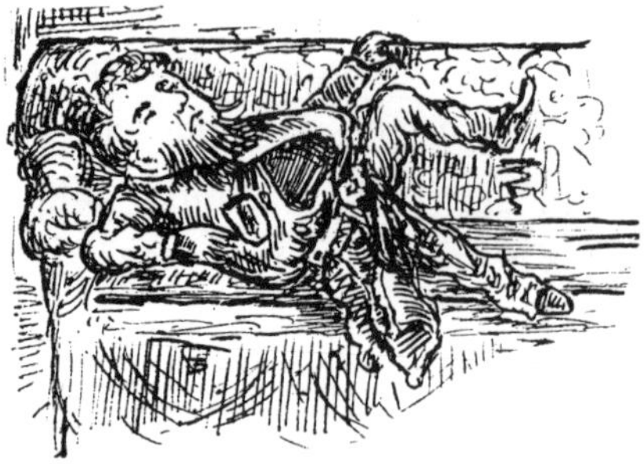

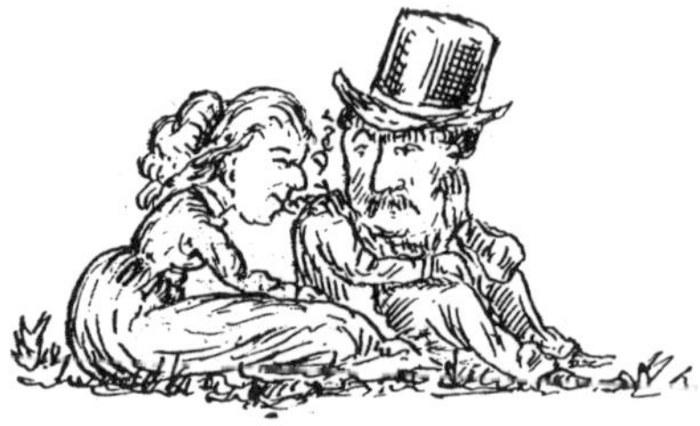

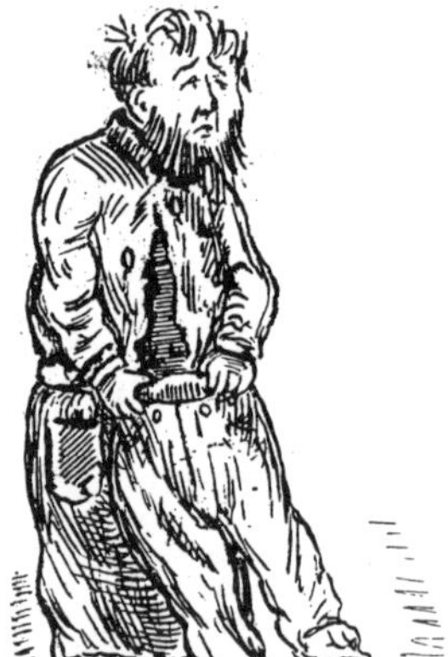

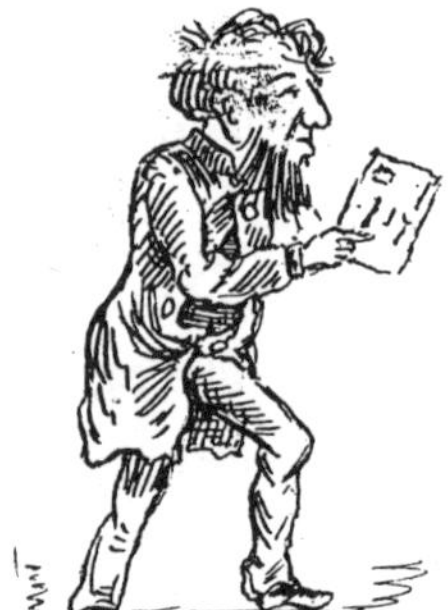

March 8th 1883...ah! my dear Sir - I hope you got home well, comfortably and without prejudice yesterday. I got home all right myself before ten o'clock, having made a call or paid a visit en route, but dear me! after such a starving I put on my new and 'Preston Guild-like' coat to recline therein on the sofa till warmth and resuscitation came back to me; and have hither come today (Southport) ...

March 12th 1883...Mr Worsley, Let us for honeymoon go to Southport - There are occasionally such nice quiet Tides - such was the case on Saturday last - The sea came creeping in with no tossing billows but a continuous succession of gentle undulations. Besides when we consider the cleanness and beautiful arrangement everywhere you must confess that it is a truly Tidey place - Bring a member of the Psychological Society with you when next you come to see me as I have got a Ghost ready for your investigation - It is quite a new one and according to information received (as we say in the 'Force') persistently vivacious and objectionable. This may import additional interest to your visit ...

March 15th 1883...ah, ha! so you were Installing at Wigan last night, were you? Well! don't you think now my dear Mister, that you'd all have felt more comfortable by your own several firesides than travelling through the nasty piercing East wind - I'm personally quite convinced that it was far too cold for any good work to be done with mallet chisel and stone. It is my purpose to visit Wigan today and should dearly like to see any bit of walling which you Masons did last night ...

March 17th 1883...Have you a cast off pair of nether garments - I mean those outward and visible casings or envelopes for the lower limbs of which society is wont to speak tenderly - to give me? Now I ask the question in all seriousness. I want a pair for a poor old lone man who is lame and poor - He is almost without garments. This weather is very cold & his state is cheerless - He knows just sufficient to enable him to alter a pair to his own convenience - The last pair of my own I gave some two or three weeks ago - or this man should have had them ...

March 21st 1883... Thank you, thank you, my dear Sir, for your early response and kind promises - You see I've just this minute received your letter - we are, I rejoice to say, all in good health but bothered by the East wind...Business - My Insurance premium is due - will you kindly pay for me to Mr Easterly, agent of the 'Alliance' company at Mr Alison's office 11/3 on Policy No. 428.065 ...

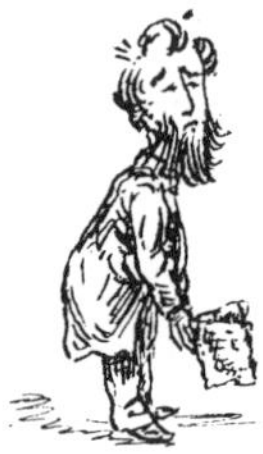

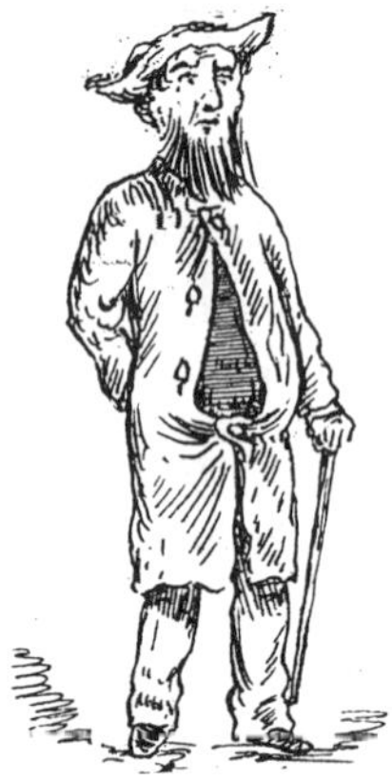

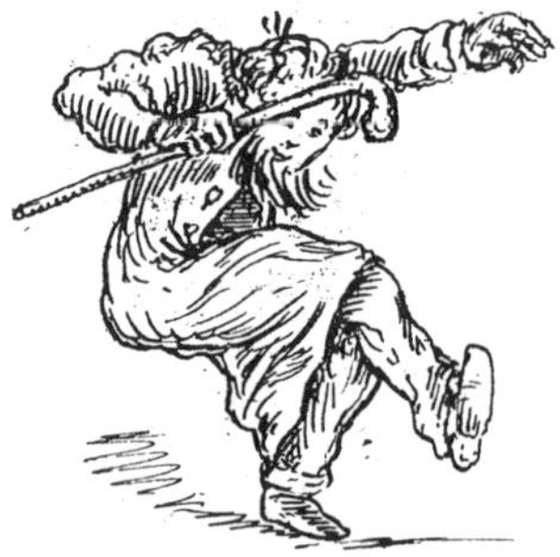

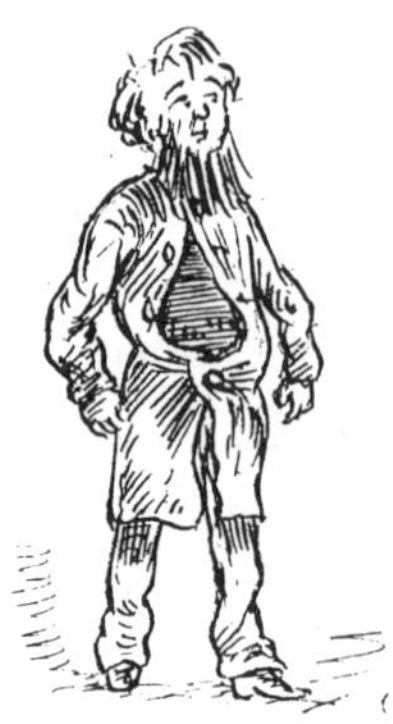

March 23rd 1883...o thank you! Thank you! My dear Sir - This is really very prompt and kind of you - I will repay the Bullion when I see you next which will probably be when you seek a retreat here or temporary refuge from the Temptations, provocations and discomforts of Spring cleaning - It is an ill wind that blows nobody good - and even this wind with its accompanying frost postpones the spring & so holds off for a time that Domestic torture the cleaning incident to that otherwise blissful season - With overflowing gratitude ...P.S. New Rector (Rev. Humphrey W. Bretherton) was inducted at Eccleston on Tuesday 20th instant ...

March 28th 1883...I am in perplexity - I don't know what to do - I have to go to Southport and I have to spend a day in Ormskirk. I am bidden likewise to a feast. I have besides a multiplicity of home and parochial duties - I have the Misses M. of Ormskirk temporarily abiding with me as also some friends from Newburgh coming to spend one day this week with me here. My perplexity is - what day must I fix upon to go to Ormskirk & which to Southport since I know not when my Newburgh friends are coming. Thought they would be here on Monday, then expected them on Tuesday. Drove in despair to Rufford & Mawdesley. Will they arrive today or shall I make tracks to Southport - shouldn't like to be off however if they do come - Morning beautiful - sunshine very bright, yet air cold ...

March 31st 1883 (My Birthday)...I'm done up - I've had to trust to my legs again. When starting yesterday for Ormskirk I discovered my conveyance was broken - The fraction was in a portion of the iron work but with a view to prevent its extension to a bone or bones in my own body, I had the horse unharnessed again and proceeded on my journey otherwise - I feel so stiff this morning that I walk with difficulty - When does your Spring cleaning begin? This morning is beautiful but wind still cold ...

April 6th 1883...I saw a great fire last night or about one o'clock this morning over anenst Eccleston - where and what was it? You will see some account of it doubtless in the papers - Two clerical friends from Southport - both Brother Masons - have been with me - one of them witnessed the leaping flames together with - we gazed & we gazed and we think and think but had after all to seek repose without having determined the exact place whereat the fire raged. Poney ready we're off to Wigan - morning lovely ...

April 7th 1883 (Saturday)...I saw a great fire over yonder in Eccleston on Thursday night or rather Friday morning - Though far away it greatly upset me so that I 'thunk' and 'thunk' as well as looked and looked - Today we had an accident in Pollie's meadow whereby a poor horse got a shaft of cart driven into its thigh - Night's lengthening shadows were closing in when this sore mishap occurred ...

Notes

April 16th 1883

Lawn tennis became popular with the advent of the lawn-mower, and the first Wimbledon championships were held in 1877, and regarded as something of a novelty.

Moody & Sankey were American evangelists who visited Britain at this time - Moody preaching and Sankey singing and playing the organ. They published a hymn book 'Sacred Songs and Solos' in 1873 and their gospel hymns were largely taken up and popularised by the Salvation Army.

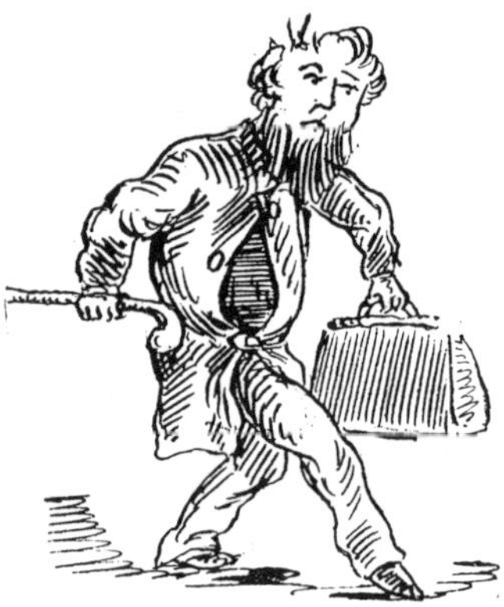

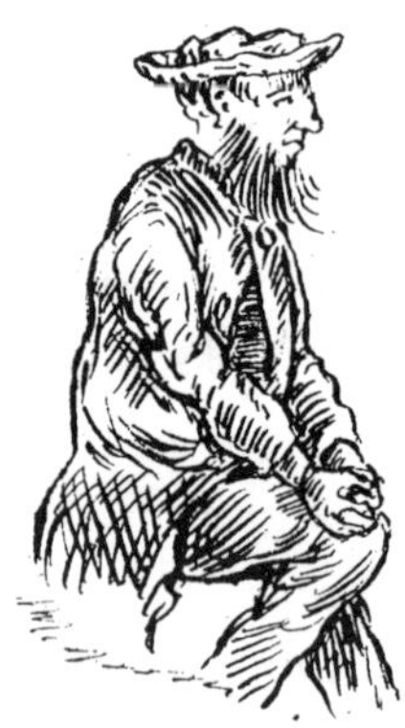

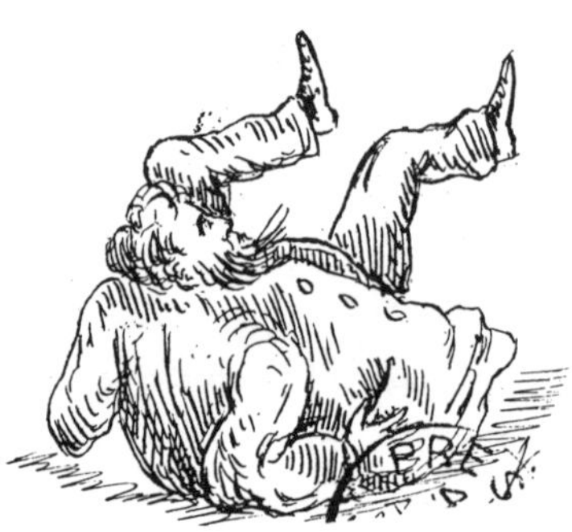

April 16th 1883...I played my first game of Lawn Tennis* on Friday last (April 13th) and don't like the pastime. There is in it more promiscuous LOVE than is proper for a married man; and too much of the 'deuce' about it to be agreeable to a clergyman - If my Torpedo had overheard the talk of Love there would have been on that lawn a Racquet such as is not commonly used in the game. She would have ba(w)lled and batted up finely, I know, and besides the Inner and Outer Court, the Police Court would have been utilised and probably also the Divorce ditto. I went to hear Moody & Sankey* on Tuesday last - only heard Sankey, and that at an overflow meeting. Our Southport friend is poorly - Miss H. is with him ...

April 16th 1883...I'm nigh beside myself - I feel I need a change and so methinks to pack my scanty surplus raiment in a comely bag of nigrous leather and nip away to some secluded spot where joys abound and sorrows rarely come - Tell me, Mister, where such glad retreat awaits - or else I'll fling my coat aside, select an axe and hew a cherry tree instead. Oh for a snow storm - a cutting wind and Delective witness of my desperate energy ...

April 18th 1883...I thought I should - I had nowhere convenient but here so I've come - but my engagements won't let me stay so I'm off again - well, well, such is life - That fire was in Parr Lane or Beadley Lane - I think Parr Lane, Eccleston - a Barn full of Hay. The Barn, known locally as Hope's Barn formerly in the occupation of Mr Ralph Miller - all destroyed but no loss of human or cattle life. I am writing in a dark and shadowy corner so no more at present ...

April 20th 1883...I'm off - I'm off to Wiggin this morning - we were at Standish yesterday - there was a confirmation there. Miss H. was there having left Southport for a few days to see the confirmation and get a temporary change of air and scene. I am as you will perceive in a hurry and cannot write more. Time forbids - Hoping you are quite well as also whole household ...

April 23rd 1883...As you see I'm upside down again - in other words upon my back once more - It's hard work nothing but hard work that has done it - I feel more and more that I am in the highest sense of the word a working man. The past week has been to me an exhausting one but now I hale with some satisfaction the prospect of rest - a temporary rest. East winds prevail and somewhat neutralise the springtide sunshine - Receive my benison ...

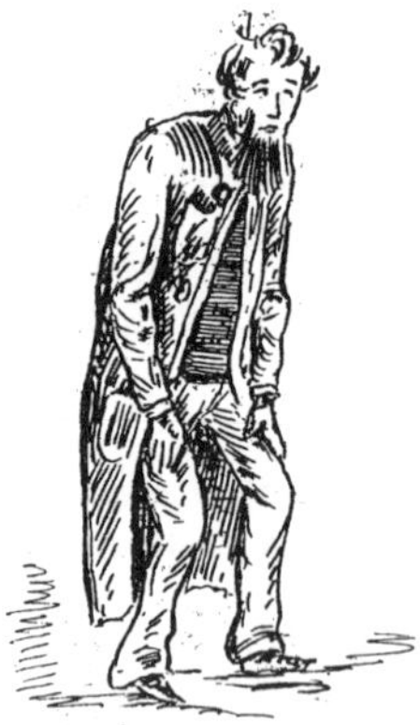

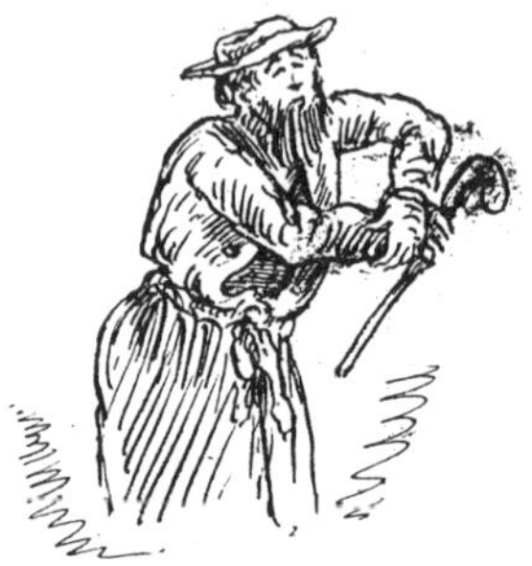

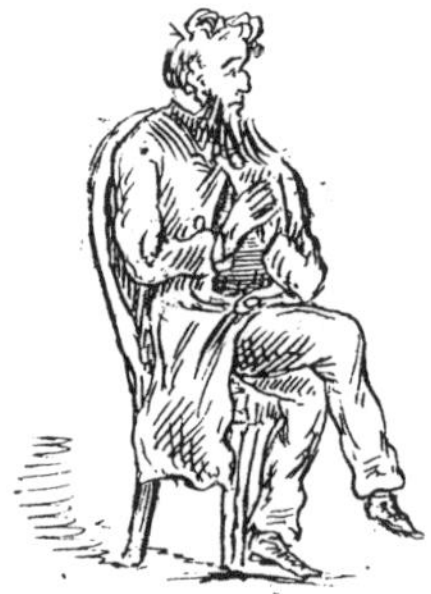

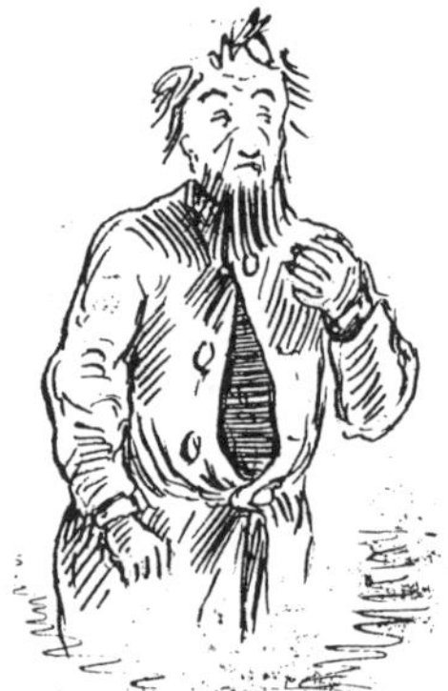

April 28th 1883...I've heard it this very morning, at eight o'clock, for the 1st time this year - The cuckoo and the rain have come together - oh this rain is grand, golden, grateful, - Hedgerows green - Tree buds opening - 'May' flowers preparing - birds singing, all Nature joyous - In just one hour from this I have a wedding to attend and by the way this very day is the anniversary of my own - The associations of this 28th Day of April are manifold and gladsome. With very fervent desires for your health and happiness - I am ...

May 3rd 1883...With the exception of rheumatism in my right arm - Ditto in both knees, the same in my right hip - a strain in my back - a slight gout in my right big toe joint and a 'art ache - I am quite well & so going this morning with my 'Nitro Glycerine' 'Domestic Torpedo' or what not, to Ormskirk - also Mrs Sephton accompanies me. Mrs Grundy has summoned a man for threatening her life. Pollie is well - I saw her about five minutes since looking over the stable door and apparently speculating on the duties of the day ...

May 7th 1883...I feel a wreck - I need rest - I have got an inflamed big toe joint and yet have to be continually hobbling about - sad accidents here and a wave of sickness keeps me continually on the move - on the 21st Inst two friends from the Peak in Derbyshire are due to abide with us till the weekend - a lady friend from Ormskirk is at present with us. We have had a hatch of nine chickens and I suspect this increase in the egg-laying power of the country has brought down the markets for our lady friend informs us that eggs are now 12 for one shilling instead of 8 as was the case a short time ago - Enterprise thoughtfully directed may achieve much ...

Whit Monday 1883...It's in the chest, partly on the left side extending to me head and all over. My difficulty indeed is to fix upon a place where it isn't. I've been unable to get forth all the week - I have been truly ill - unfit for yesterday's duties. I am much reduced in strength but fervently hope this week may restore me the health which last week took ...

May 16th 1883...unhappy me - I've trouble in my right leg again. It is very painful and much caution is needed at all times. It has come very rapidly - I am nursing it as much as possible - We shall be open to receive you after Friday 25th -all other guests will have come and gone by that time except our young friend Sallie who is athirst to come as soon as the school breaks up. Mr Howe turned up unexpectedly just a week since today - weather glorious ...

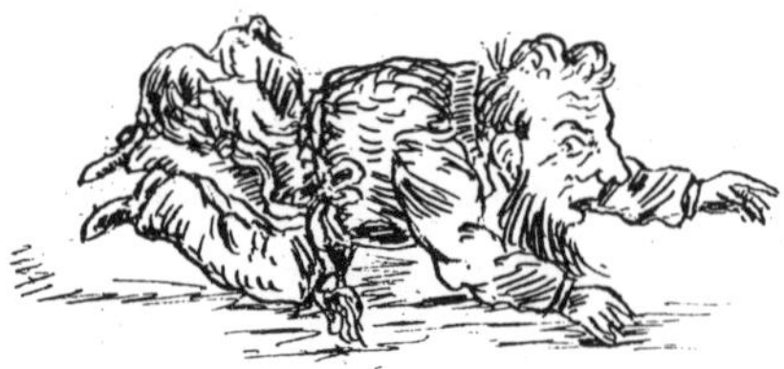

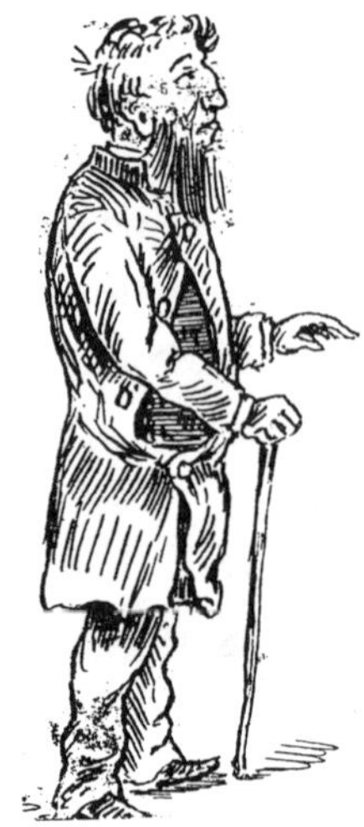

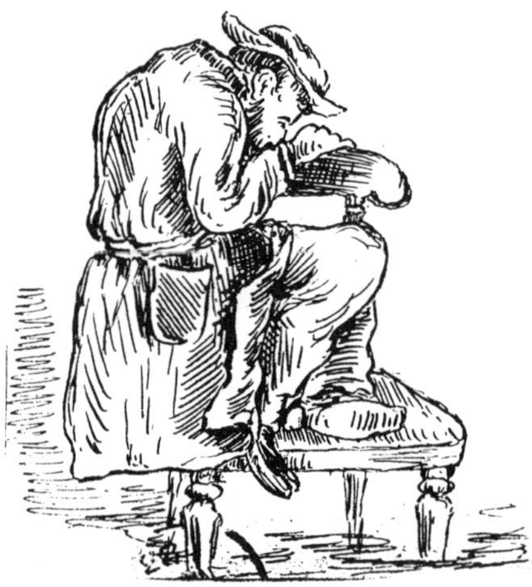

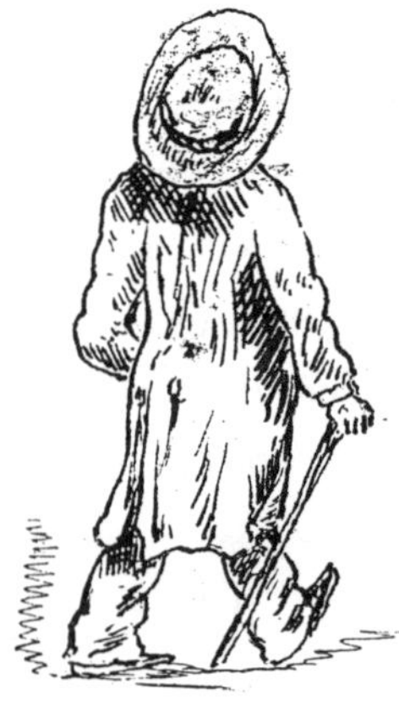

May 19th 1883...In agony.. I have been walking about rather too much of late - I've been here, I've been in Southport, then Liverpool, then Southport, then here again and I have such a pain in my back and right leg that I cannot without suffering sit up, I am therefore writing this while reclining on the sofa - what's to be done, my dear Sir? What's to be done? for Monday is a busy day with me ..P.S. Delay'd in transmission - I am under Doctor's care ...

May 26th 1883...I've burst - I'm a little easier now but very prostrate yet now as heretofore ...

May 28th 1883...I suppose you got home and didn't hurt yourself. My bottle of physic reached me a little after 9 o'clock. It's good but it isn't nice - It makes me strength, and a wry face at one and the same time - Improvement continues in me - whereat like myself ye will ardently rejoice ...

May 31st 1883...I think I may say that I continue to improve but still I am not completely restored - There are times when I'm compelled to twist about upon my chair and wriggle myself into all manner of attitudes - yet can scarce discover one easy posture - weather glorious - air still pure and bracing. Torpedo, alas! has got Lumbago and toothache ...

June 4th 1883...I am out and about upon my legs again but my dear Torpedo is quite knocked up. She complains of aching limbs and general weariness and sighs for a brief period of complete rest before our summer cleaning begins - The Whitewash brush has begun to whisk briskly in such parts as its services are permitted in. After a few days' rest the whole house is to be turned inside out, or upside down - My Reverend Southport friend and I have held two sessions this last week; and been very busy - a Brother Mason of yours from Rufford walked over hither on Tuesday last - Hoping you got home safely and with comfort ...

June 9th 1883...I'm glad to get out and walk about as best I can just now for our home is turned inside out as nearly as can be with plasterers, white-limers &c - I can find nothing, and do nothing, so I seek the retirement of the fields - everything is in its place there for white limers and their art do not there intrude. I find my snow white summer wideawake a light and grateful protection for my head against the solar heat when fleeing from Domestic upset. Sick at heart ...

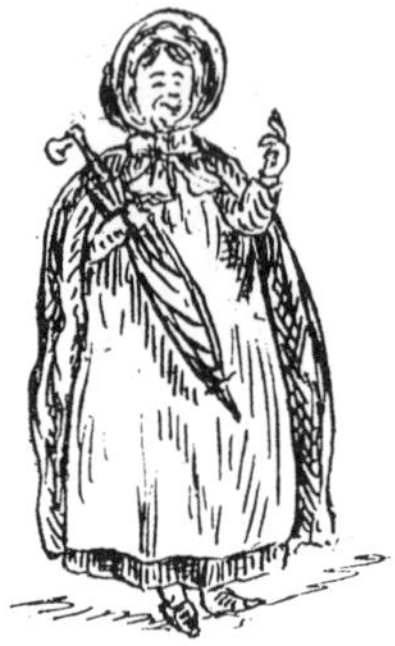

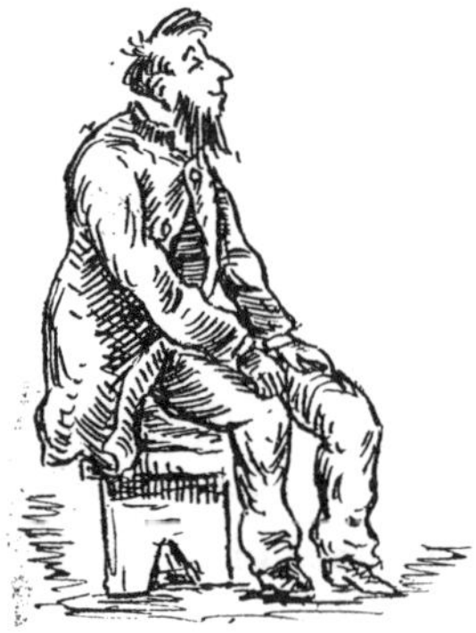

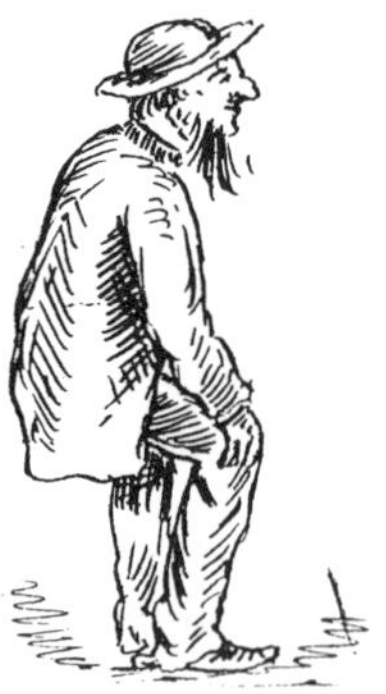

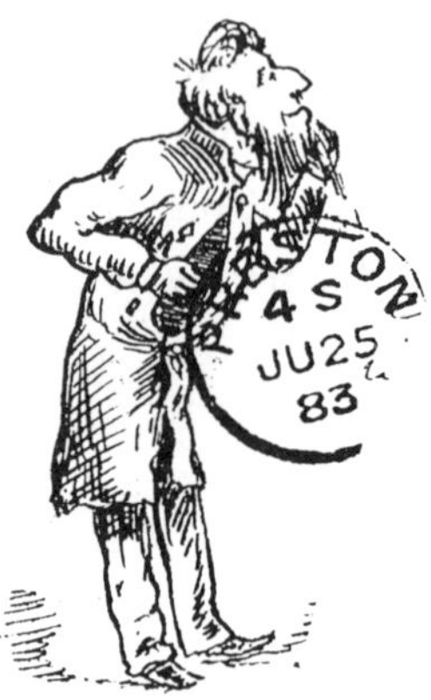
4 S
JU25
83

June 12th 1883...eh my Dear, My thoughts are often with you - when shall we decide upon the happy day - I'm going off to the Peak of Derbyshire on Saturday so that you will be prepared for other postmarks - I will apprize you from time to time how I am getting on. I thought to have been in Preston today to buy a new hat as my present head arrangement is a little out of date and obfusc withal i.e. It has gone a brownish green or snuffy red instead of the Black as heretofore and as you well know I like to appear 'respeckable' where I go - a hat with a Feather in it, and some blue 'ribbing' will about set me up. Fare well my dear Sir till I see you or write again ...

June 16th 1883...oh Mister, I don't know what to do - I've promised to go to the Peak and I'm not fit, I really don't know what to do when I get there if I don't feel better - I couldn't make you believe - I really couldn't - you will see by my portrait that I look a weary mortal and that's just how I feel - Somebody tells me that I require change of air and that it will do me good and that I ought to take plenty of it - I can't take much for I have very little appetite for anything - Oxygen likewise was pronounced by scientists to be very intoxicating a little time ago - now that would never do - It must be taken in moderation - plainly in moderation ...

June 18th 1883, The Peak, Derbyshire...I'm <u>here</u> my dear Sir and <u>have been</u> very much so since I came - I was very tired on arriving - Travelling doesn't agree with a debile being like me. I have rested a little and trust, when I have had Breakfast I may feel equal to a walk. Ye have cuth of my activity when in health.. I will write again...

June 20th 1883...Yah - I'm in Buxton Mister - Ha,ha,ha - git off now ...

June 20th 1883...ever truly, I've borrowed a hat for the occasion, and am getting about the Peak pretty considerably on foot - I'm looking about me a good deal and hope to return with an enlarged knowledge of the Geography of England. High up or low down - on Mountain or in vain I am yours as heretofore ...

June 21st 1883...I have seen a good deal of the Peak; and being slightly wearied with walking am returning proudly to my domicile tomorrow (Friday) - Buxton may be all very well for people with the rheumatic but it's nothing for me - you see - I can't get up and down the hills like those favoured ones - so no more of Buxton for the present ...

June 25th 1883...Let me see, my dear Sir, our Tea Party and popular Festival is fixed for Monday next July <u>2nd</u> - come one, come all!!!! Your presence will fill to overflowing the measure of our felicity - You will perceive that we are back again from the Peak and remain, as before we went thither ...

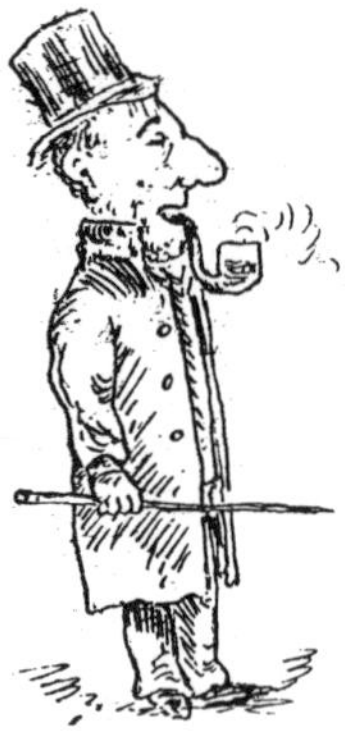

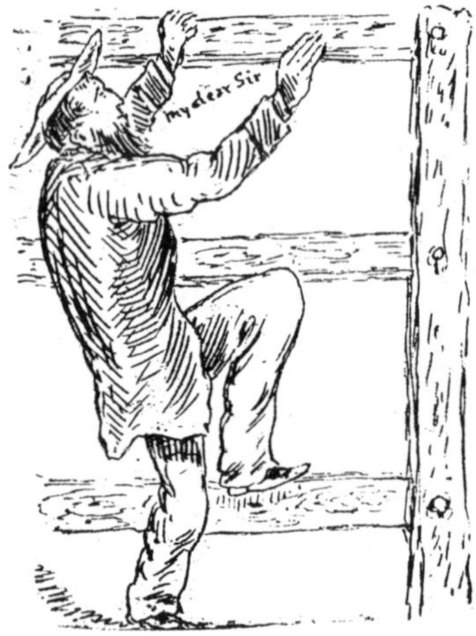
my dear Sir

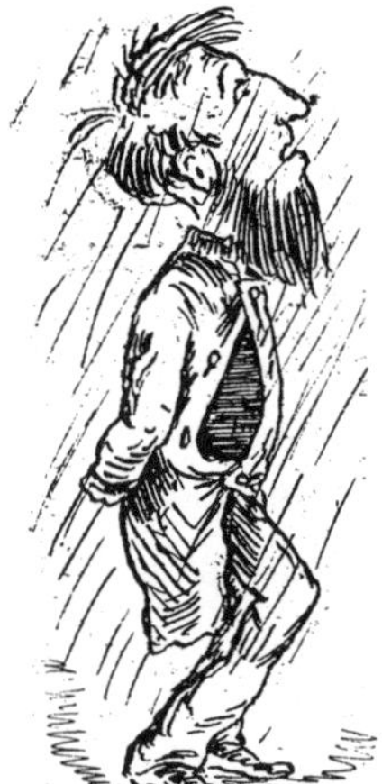

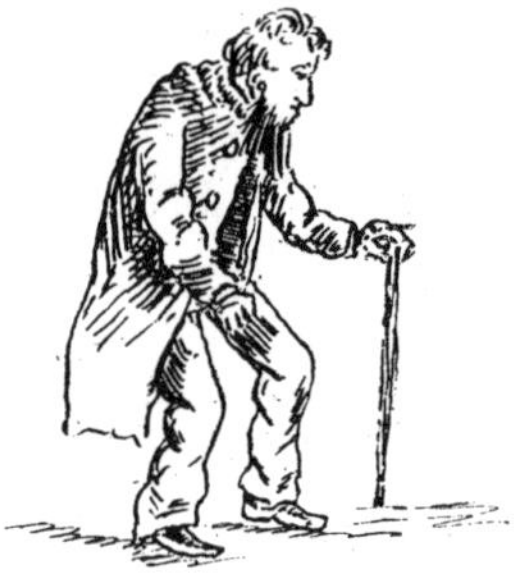

June 27th 1883 Night...You did - and I freely admit the fact - You did (as you assert) send me a letter last week, which I received on my return - I am not sure whether the Peak of Derbyshire does not include the whole mountaineering portion of that county - My Headquarters being at Mellor I consequently hailed from the 'Peak' - as the name implies it is situate on one of the Mels, Meols, Mulls or Fells of that county. I trust this explanation will prove satisfactory - Did you get Buxton Herald...P.S. Alas! that ye cannot come ...

July 4th 1883...It's over and done with except in so far as meeting the incidental liabilities is concerned. These parties entail a large pecuniary outlay but this is counterbalanced to some extent by the income of our Glossopian or East Glossopian friend -whose shadow grows in a very trifling degree less as circling years glide past and each to each succeeds - His appetite too is vigorous for he comes off a very eating stock - His ancestors by all accounts having done a great deal of mastication in their time - Though it is midsummer and occasionally very hot just now he as a precautionary measure often wears his coat collar turned up to near his ears. He's a dear delightful man and very properly exercises caution at all times ...

July 7th 1883...I'm beginning at last to pull myself up a little and once more to feel as well as the heat will let me - But oh! how great is the diurnal sultriness - 'Bleak House' is thinning fast again - only seven of us now but as there are two young ladies in the number the clatter of tongues which continually is awaking the Domestic echoes is about equal to what would emanate from a whole cohort of the other sex - Our Glossop friend has gone so no more at present ...

July 9th 1883...I believe I reported favourably of myself when I last wrote to you but this Monday morning July 9th finds me, my dear Sir, feeble, weary and feeling as if weighted with the burden of age - after my own duties were over I drove last night to Shevington, to wit, 'Crooks' near Wigan, and returned thence in pouring rain, to which latter circumstance perhaps may be attributed my slightly antique condition this morning - Miss L. abideth yet with us. We hope you are both well ...

July 12th 1883...alas! alas! how it doth pour! The rain comes down here more and more, Commingling with the tempest's roar - The raindrops on the window patter Keeping up a ceaseless clatter Till we nigh wonder what's the matter. No bird about essays to sing Nor busy bee on humming wing Attempts to fly from well-stored hive - By industry resolved to thrive. In Southport we should be this day But vainly wait to get away ..P.S. Post here ...

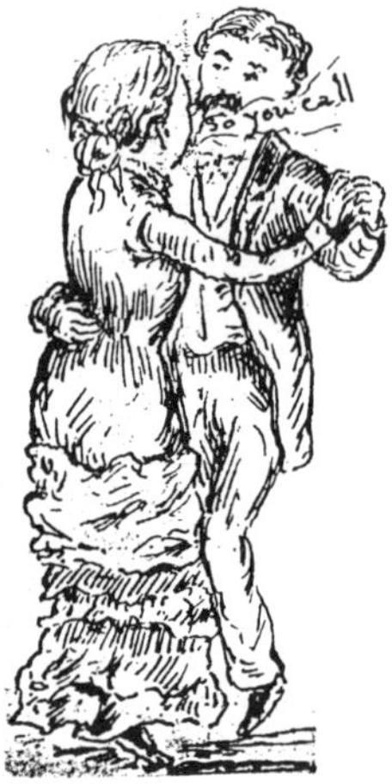
so you call

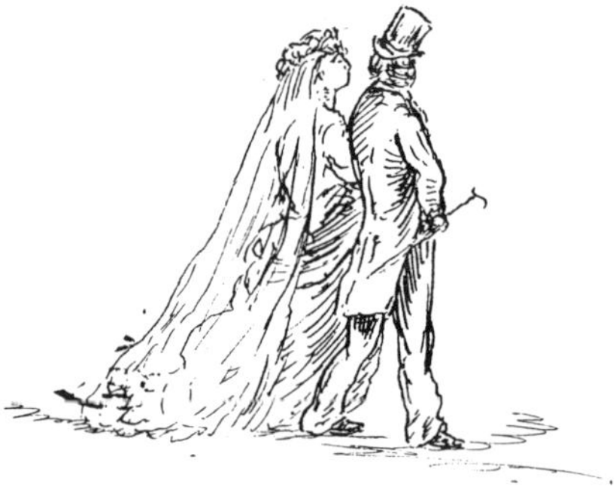

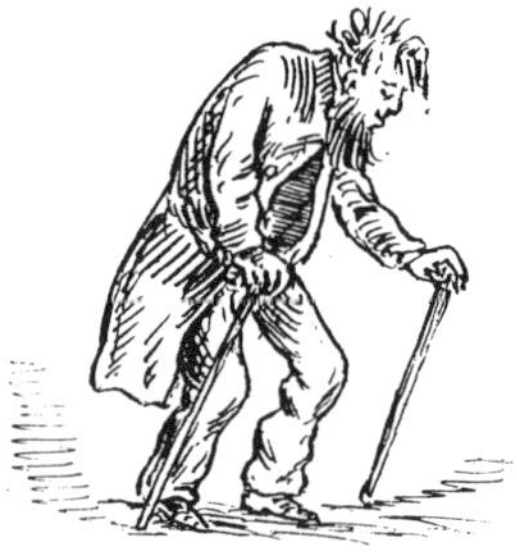

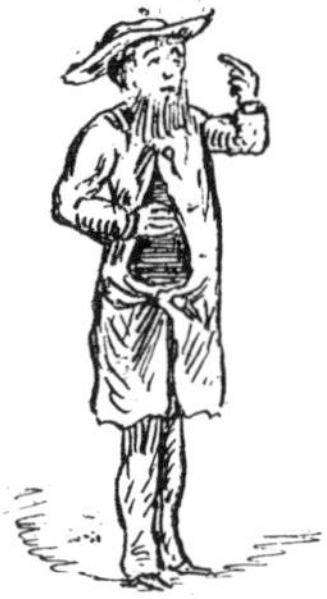

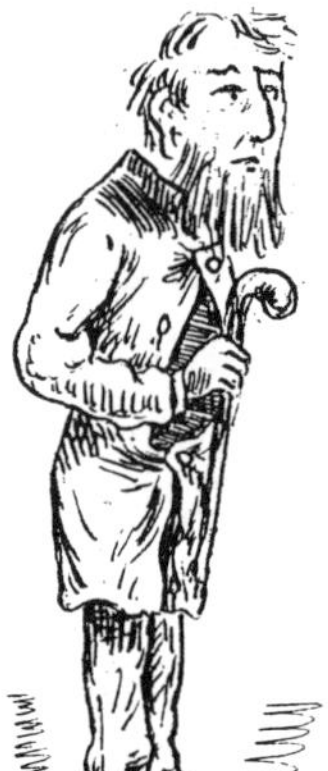

July 17th 1883...so you call this sort of thing 'Quiet' do you My dear? If you do - then let us have plenty of quiet for I am rather partial to it - until we saw in the Paper yesterday that the Happy event had come off on Tuesday we were blunderingly thinking it was fixed for the 10th prox; and rather spreading that impression by our converse. Our confusion respecting the matter is probably due to the bustle and upset - You perchance would say the 'Quiet' - of the past three weeks. We are replete with best wishes and I am ever ..P.S. Never mind - it will be our turn next ...

July 21st 1883...When are you thinking of doing this sort of thing some more ...

July 21st 1883 Night...ah! my dear Sir, excuse me trespassing on your notice so soon again. I do so with a view to inform you that on yesterday July 20th I scried my third accident and our vehicle presents in consequence much the appearance of a vessel that has been in collision on the High Seas - a temulent man in a state of almost helpless inebriety returning from market galloped his cart into us when we had pulled up at the roadside to let him pass - It nearly makes my hair stand up to tell it ...

July 25th 1883...I am sorely afflicted with an acute Lumbago attack again - I am at home today and have not gone out anywhere because when I rise from a seat I can scarcely toddle about - Rheumatism too makes manifest its presence in my knee joints so you may conjecture how I am by thinking how you would be in similar circumstances - I do my endeavour to preserve a cheerful exterior notwithstanding but it requires an effort - I can assure you it does - Torpedo has toothache badly so she has not much time to condole with me ...

Saturday July 28th 1883...we're quite gay in the country today - Don't you know it's the Mawdesley Tea Party and a Festivitating doment also of the Eccleston Methodists - While some scholars from Rochdale also are drinking deeply from the cup of pleasure in our midst - We haven't had such a bit of Fun thrown our way since we had the measles. The day is splendid - bright sunshine and refreshing wind - Miss Heaton arrived last night - Missis is ill. We ourself have mown in the Hayfield till we have got a bad back - can hardly straighten ourself after sitting ...

Aug 1st 1883...Let me see - This is what day of the month - oh! August 1st 1883 and me with my hay grass uncut still - Losing quality and not increasing quantity. What's to be done, my dear Sir, what's to be done? Others are finishing their ingathering but here I am with winter before me and no hay in prospect - I feel perplexed indeed but I am going out to Tea today; and this peradventure may prove of some advantage to me - I hope this may find you all quite well & with warmest regards ...

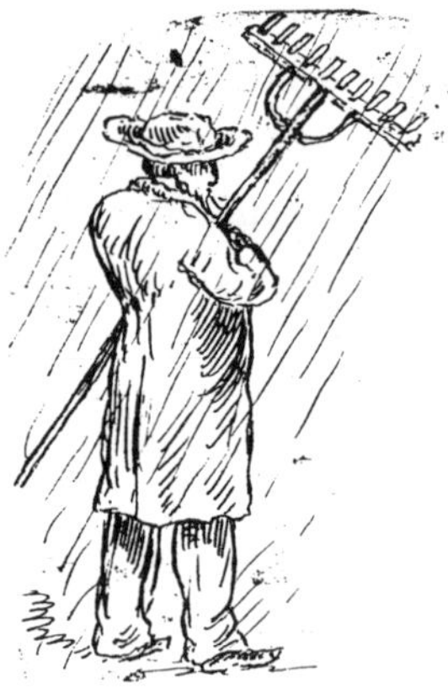

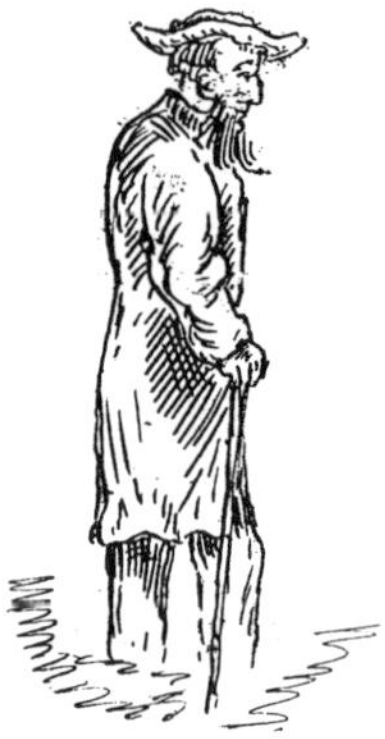

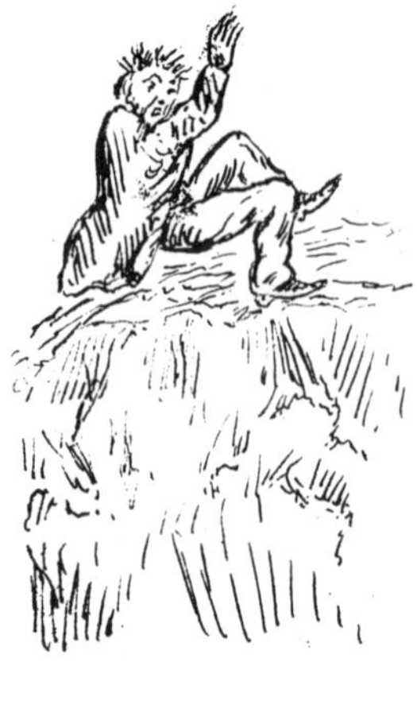

Aug 3rd 1883...Don't you see my dear Sir It was in this wise you got the paper yesterday. I put on my white Summer hat and went off to Southport. I had business there in course 'twas that and the train (assisted part of the way by Pollie) took me - Programmes for St Luke's Autumn Bazaar are out - They are very elaborate and too costly in first instance for many to be gratuitously distributed. They comprise each 31 pages, many and beautiful engravings - I understand they are purchasable at Mr Witham's - I don't know the price - Quite new and original ...

Aug 9th 1883...ah my venerated friend these are indeed perplexing times - Besides the Political aspects of the age I have to consider the prospects of my hay harvest - I have my whole crop down - and such a crop!!!! I think I never saw one so light - as it lays spread out upon the ground it gets to the thickness of a wafer in some parts, and in others there is none at all - so if the weather spoils the entire crop it won't spoil much. Herein I find solace as I am ...

Aug 11th 1883...My Hay is out still because of the unsettled weather - enough to make one melancholy - However it can't be helped so I mean to run off somewhere next week - If I can get my crop in before I go so much the better but anyway I am quite purposed - nothing intervening to forfend - that off somewhither I go. How feel you amongst it? shall we elope to Zamatave whence we may unobserved watch how the world gets on without us - Believe me ...P.S. Drove to Chorley yesterday ...

Aug 13th 1883 Afternoon...Well I declare my dear Sir - If this doesn't beat everything. It is positively enough to make the heart of a stone sad - This very minute I ought to have been in Southport - yet this very minute my hay is all uncarried and this very minute, too, there is every show for a speedy rainfall - misty clouds - soft south wind, and dropping weather glasses - My chickweed barometer cheered me this morning but this afternoon its testimony is like that of other authorities, prepare for rain - Till my hay is got in I can't go out - it would be folly to go to the <u>sea</u>side and leave my hay crop <u>out</u>side. I passed your smokeroom - looked in and heaved a sigh this very morning - when I see or meet a happy smiling face nowadays I conclude that that belongs to a party whose Hay is housed - would you were here to solace ...

Aug 16th 1883...oh my dear and venerated Friend these recent prevailing winds have been quite a peril to me - I have been standing for a fortnight on the very edge or brink of a precipice of Bronchitis and they (the winds and drafts) have nearly blown me over it - I have come to Southport to recruit myself. 'Twas noon yesterday when I reached this beautiful town and peradventure tomorrow I may hie me hence - Has Mr Maynard yet returned to Preston? ...

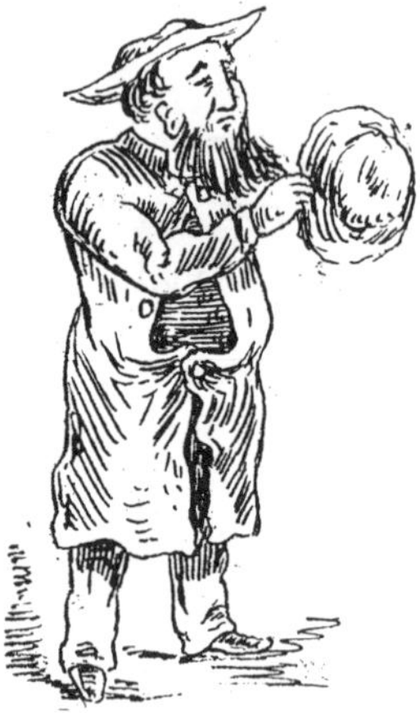

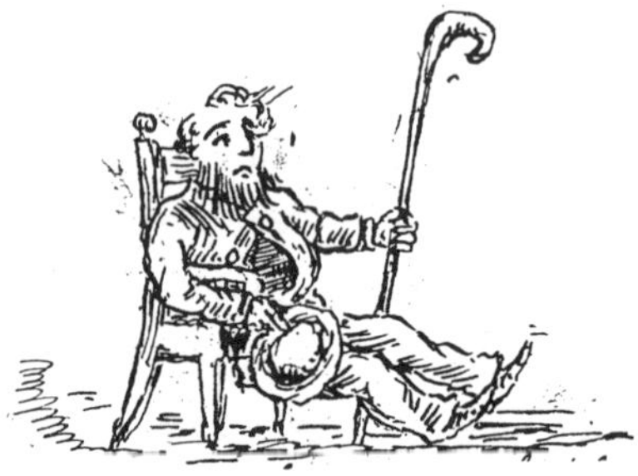

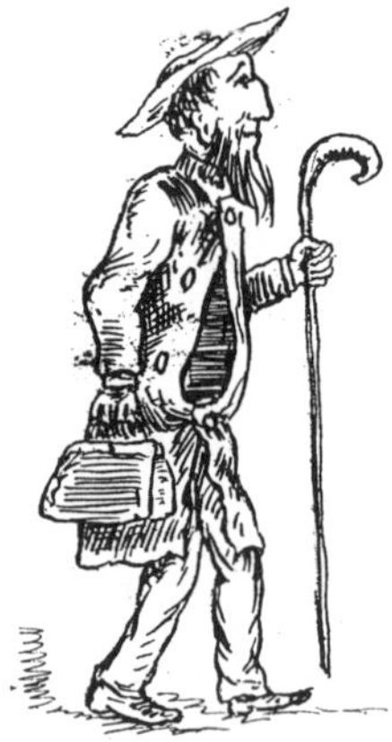

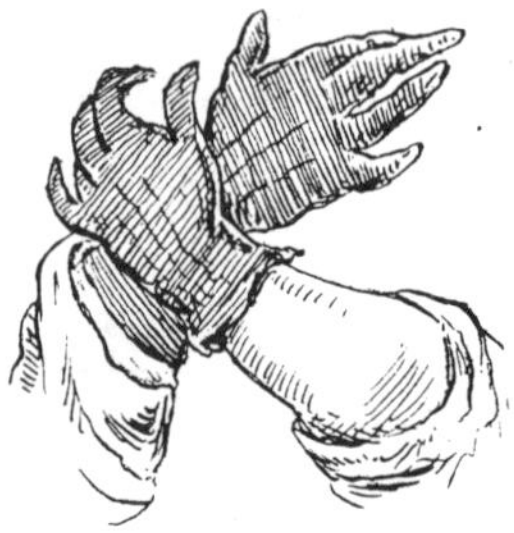

Southport Aug 17th 1883...I've been and bought a new hat - I got it yesterday (Aug 16th) at Hobbs' the Hatters in this Town - when I put it to Adelaide St it was pronounced 'Lovely!' I feel so charmed with it that I could keep looking at it all day - I think I may say that it is universally admired - I am coming to Preston to get my Portrait painted one of these days and will bring the hat with me that you may behold and admire likewise ..P.S. am back again today ...

Aug 20th 1883 Night...Really my dear Sir What changes one lives to see - This year of grace 1883 will be ever memorable for two events viz:- There has been purchased by me a new hat: and there has been given to me a new stick - which may be used as a walking stick, an alpenstock - a shepherd's crook, a jumping pole, a Pastoral staff, a fishing rod, or a gate rail - Its longitude is near five feet - it supports me and I carry it - Truly you must see the article to appreciate it. I am rapt in admiration - I only got it on Saturday last ...

Aug 22nd 1883...I had fully purposed to be in Preston today to get my Photo taken 'Life size' in colours - I put my Staff last night where I could promptly find it this morning - Moreover I was up early, but lo, and behold you, I was detected to have a swollen lip. This discovery was fatal to my Preston visit - Torpedo does not want a Photo of my under lip in its present abnormal condition - The visit therefore has been postponed till my lip looks rather less as if a Bee had been gambolling about it than it does just now ...

Aug 27th 1883...I have reason to believe that the world sighs for the possession of a during and reliable portrait of me on a liberally large scale - I am therefore coming to Preston to have it taken and I shall probably bring with me my new walking stick - Our hand maiden is off for her holidays so I know not if my visit will take place this week. We are pretty well. The missis has not had toothache for three days until last night - We are expecting a large Party for Luncheon today. I have too, 'much work and long walking' - Mr Parkes is at present at Grange while I remain here...

Aug 29th 1883...Your note of caution, Explanation and information is to hand this morning - Thanks many and fervent - We will keep off the days you name - a member of my household who is famed for her prowess at Bezique says oh, if he is going up to London remind him about my gloves and tell him my sizes are 7 and a quarter - Hoping you may have good weather for your trips we combine ...

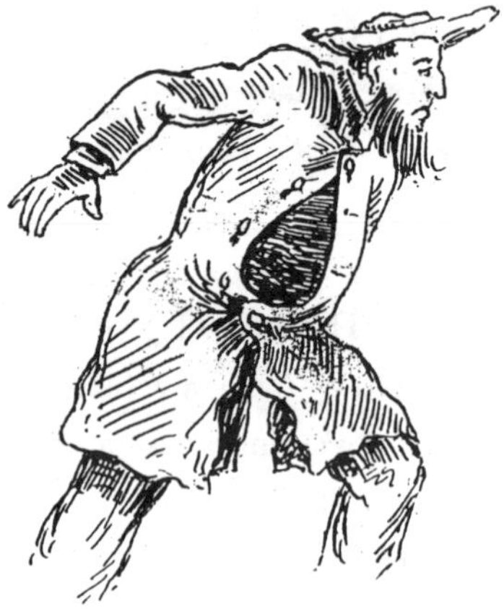

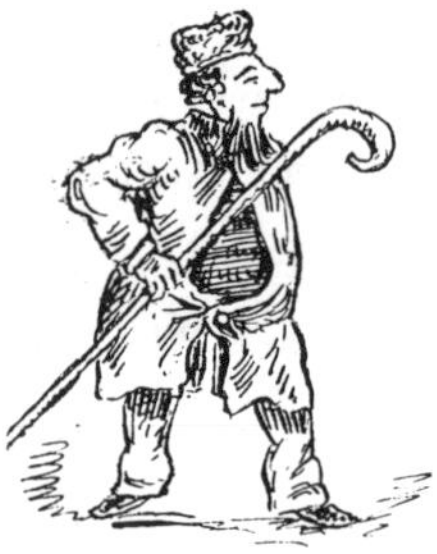

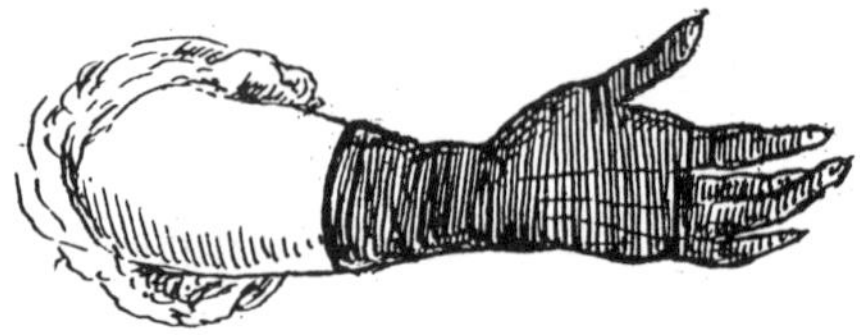

Notes

<u>Sep 18th 1883</u> The British Association for the Advancement of Science's annual meeting was held in Southport in 1883, and reporting the occasion the 'Southport News' remarks:-

"It is true we have little in the town or district of a scientific nature to offer for the inspection of the members of the British Association if we except the ice-making process at the Glaciarum, but there will be some minor geological excursions to Scarth Hill, Ormskirk, where the Keuper may be seen resting on the upper bunter formation; to the mouth of the Alt at Formby, and to Leasowe, on the Cheshire coast, where are examples of submarine forests; to Shoreton, where sections of the Keuper formation and footprints of the Cheirotherinan Storetonense are to be seen; and to Bispham, where the Permian formation crops up with a thin bed of limestone. The botanists for their part are manifesting much interest in the sandhills with which region they seem to be remarkably familiar."

There follows an account of the excursions some four days later including: "<u>Rufford</u>. On Saturday a party consisting of about 60 ladies and gentlemen left Southport about 2 o'clock in the afternoon and paid a visit to the charming little village of Rufford. On alighting at Rufford the party was met by the Rev. J.T.Wilson, Vicar of Wrightington, who courteously acted as guide."

Sep 3rd 1883...I hope sometime during the present week to enjoy the pleasure of offering you the hospitality of my Box. On Monday I have duties elsewhere so can't come on that day. I have got an eruption on my lip consequent on cold which I fear will hardly be completely eradicated even by Tuesday. But one cannot tell - If my hair be sufficiently grown and my lip better we may come over any day for the portrait. The world should possess a presentiment of us. Everybody admits that so we are going to have one taken ...

Sep 5th 1883...It is, It is. It are the new gloves - Truly beautiful. But wherefore did he not send over here and bring them since the Fates alas! forbid our visit this week to Preston. Mr Parkes expected here on Friday. Thanks - thanks, many thanks ...

Sep 10th 1883...I shay likkeer Mishter 'ts Eccleston Wakes this week (hic) sho can't write nymore at preshn't but when Wakesh over'll write then (hic) sho m'dear flo shept besht thanksh and give ush besht shupport thish Wakesh...

Sept 15th 1883...Sad are the tidings which I convey - I went to 'Wiggin' yesterday and I got alas! my toe crushed or to be very accurate a toe crushed - for I have yet happily more toes than one - Mr Parkes hath been with us, abiding certain days so yesterday I took him 'on' to Wigan and thence he took himself 'off' to Stafford. Hoping you are well ...

Sep 17th 1883...Permit me to inform you that the world-famed association found themselves short of one without whom the machinery for the Advancement of Science would not work - so theyv'e sent for me. I leave for Southport on Tuesday ...

Sep18th 1883...ah-ha I'm here, you see - looking after the 'Sociation* and fully equipped in every way for the duties of the occasion. I will report further as our labours progress - won't you join us? Surely you ought to do something for science. It's a great work! - Indeed it is ...

Southport Sep 19th 1883...come on, my dear Sir - come on - Somebody must do something for the advancement of Science. I am and why not you. I've concluded an engagement today and am leading an advance on Rufford next Saturday - I was never so scientific in my life before as now. Come on my dear Sir, come on - and bring everybody ...

Sep 20th 1883...I've obtained a charge 'The Charge of a Light Brigade' (limited to 50) which I am leading to an advance on Rufford next Saturday. Our operations will be chiefly confined to reconnoitering the locality - The Detachment under my command will return to this town (into cantonments) the same evening - The Commission with which I have the honour to be entrusted has been duly Gazetted in the publications of the Association ...

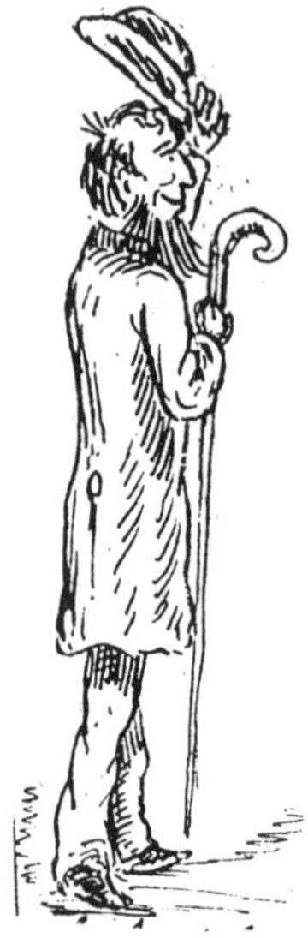

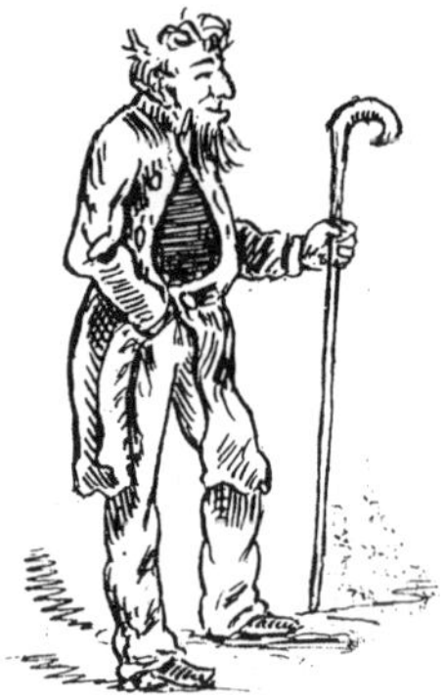

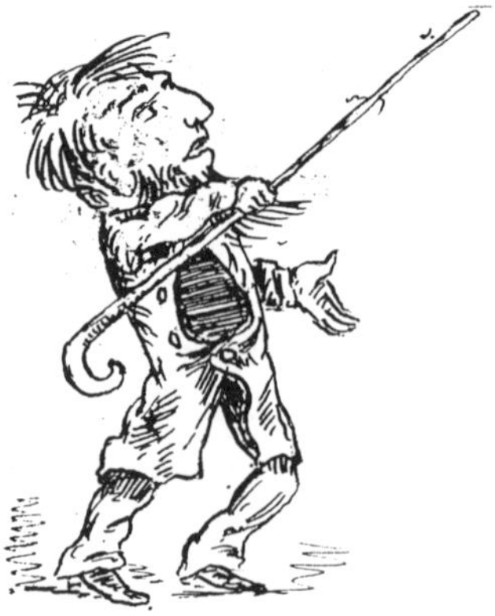

Sep 24th 1883 (evening)...'Ladies and gentlemen Good Day - How are you tomorrow? I shall have great pleasure in seeing your Party at my house yesterday if weather and circumstances permit. I hope you are always quite well generally some times - In this wise I thought to salute 'em when I met 'em at Rufford on Saturday last, the 22nd Inst, but they looked so severely learned a party that I deemed it prudent to refrain and so stepped promptly into the pathway of archaeology and general science. Herein our hearts pulsated sympathetically. We were happy together ...

Sep 27th 1883...It came in handy this 'crook' did - and I don't know what we should have done without it. It is very dear to me this stick is, very dear. Today I believe the British Association have their final excursions and tomorrow disperse. So my dear venerated Friend have the goodness to bear in mind that the 1883 meeting of this learned Brotherhood was holden at Southport - that the 'Assembly' took place on Tuesday Sep 18th and the concluding excursions on Thursday Sep 27th. The President's 'Inaugural Address' on Wednesday Sep 19th and the Rufford as well as other <u>intermediate</u> excursions on Saturday September 22nd ...

Sep 29th 1883 (Night)...They have dispersed until next year when they hope all being well, to meet in Montreal. It will be very nice for them no doubt - but they will <u>miss</u> <u>me</u>. I shan't go <u>there</u> - no. It is not for me to cross the wide Atlantic now at my time of Life. Why - it takes me weeks and weeks to get to Preston - It would take me years and years to get to Canada. By the time I got to Montreal the British Association would have visited New Zealand, Australia, Spitzbergen, Borneo and South Africa and have fixed for their meeting in India. Therefore I shan't attempt it. I should have been in Staffordshire all this week and at this very minute - but adverse circumstances forefended ...

Oct 5th 1883...I'm going, my dear Sir - next week over to Southport to the great Bazaar. I'm taking with me my pole as perhaps may be of service in pointing out things. I shall meet you there on Tuesday Oct 9th (the Opening day) or any other? 'Twill be a stirring scene you may depend and the enterprise is a vast one. I am an Interpreter at the world 'Gathering' Treasure search so I can protect you partly and make it smooth all round like - You'll be very 'appy there if you can only spare an hour or two - Hoping for the pleasure ...

Oct 8th 1883...I am ready now for the Bazaar and was on the point of starting this minute but the fog has set in so thickly that I know not what to do; - besides the 'Missis' has begun to cough and talk of Bronchitis but if she said she feared the railway travelling in fog more than Bronchitis it would be more in accordance with fact - yet fear of Bronchitis is made the scape goat for entailing in me disappointment ...

Notes

Oct 9th 1883 The 'Southport News' reported on 13th October 1883:-

St Luke's Bazaar This bazaar has been crowded every evening with a very fashionable assembly, and a large amount of business has been done, although the receipts have not reached the very high, and we must say, rather too high expectations of the promoters. A most energetic effort has been made by a small army of lady assistants and a devoted band of masculine attendants. Entertainments of various kinds are continually going on and Mr Bernasconi, with his various accomplishments in the art of creating fun, may be said to have been the heart and soul of the bazaar, and has made himself a universal favourite. The receipts up to last night were £1835.

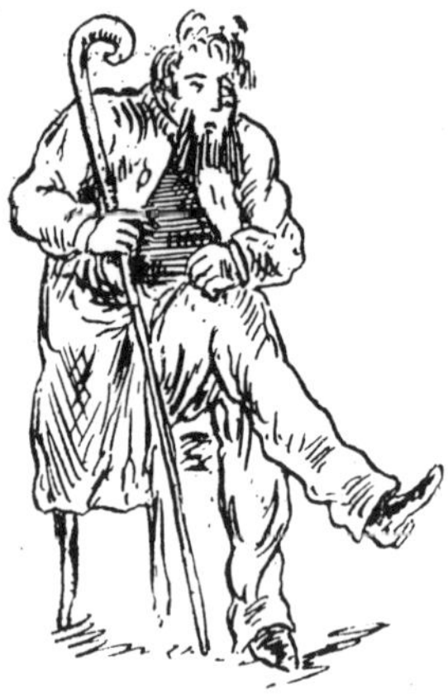

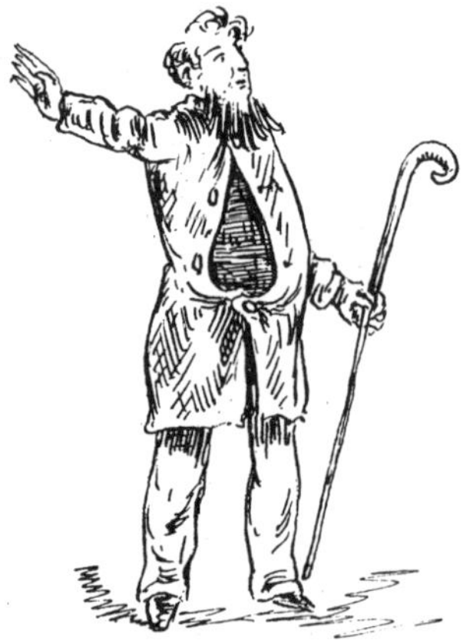

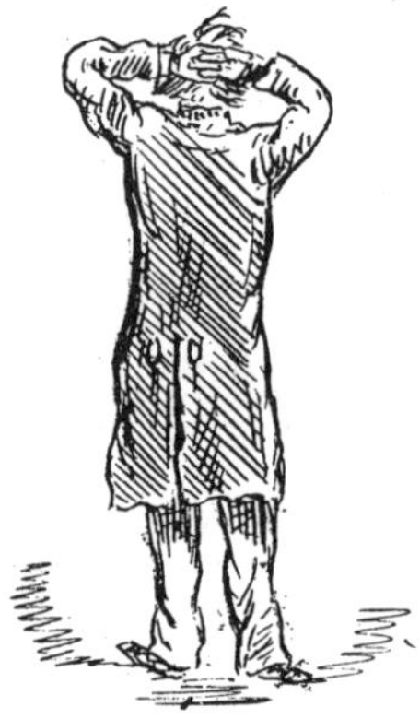

Oct 9th 1883...I've scarcely slept a wink all night and so have risen very early this morning to titivate myself up and arrange my back hair decently for the Bazaar* - Everybody will be there to look at it, and if you would just run over every body else would then be present - I shall have not got any fancy costume hired for the occasion and so shall go disguised as a clergyman merely - I shall probably write again before this day is over - so no more at present ...

Oct 9th 1883 - evening...I'll tell you what - This Bazaar opening's a vast tiring business and I don't care who hears me say so - It is as hard work as the Manchester Arts Exhibition - and if the public thinks I'm going to stop here all week the Public's greatly mistaken ...

Oct 12th 1883...Dear and Dejected Sir - We've just pass'd over another weekend without seeing you. The fact is a strange one that you are always occupied now at weekends. When the roads are impassable by reason of the snows of <u>winter</u> you will be just beginning to have leisure to get out into the country which may then be impenetrable - I'm ready, as you may be well assured to do anything in reason to promote your health & happiness even to the lending of my 'crook' - but then you don't give me a chance - so how can I? ...

Oct 19th 1883...I'm sure you'll be sorry to learn that I have had a bad cold ever since I was in Southport - and this is partly due to two causes viz:- 1st - If anything (as you know) I err on the side of politeness - consequently 2ndly Having got to know and be recognised by so many people I seldom, during my stay, had my hat on - I soon catch cold and (I may add) <u>have</u> caught cold. <u>So it is</u> - and I can not help it ...

Oct 23rd 1883 Night...ah me! I'm done up - I'm quite tired of these storms - stopping in the house day after day, looking through the window at rain clouds and fugitive leaves. Ambition should be made of sterner stuff - Caesar <u>crossed</u> the Rubicon with decision and I am <u>decidedly</u> getting 'cross' likewise - The existing reign made him and the prevailing rain makes me - In Towns you hardly comprehend these things but we in running our rural race are indeed and truth familiar with them - I send these plaints to Preston 'press'd on' by the weather's influence ...

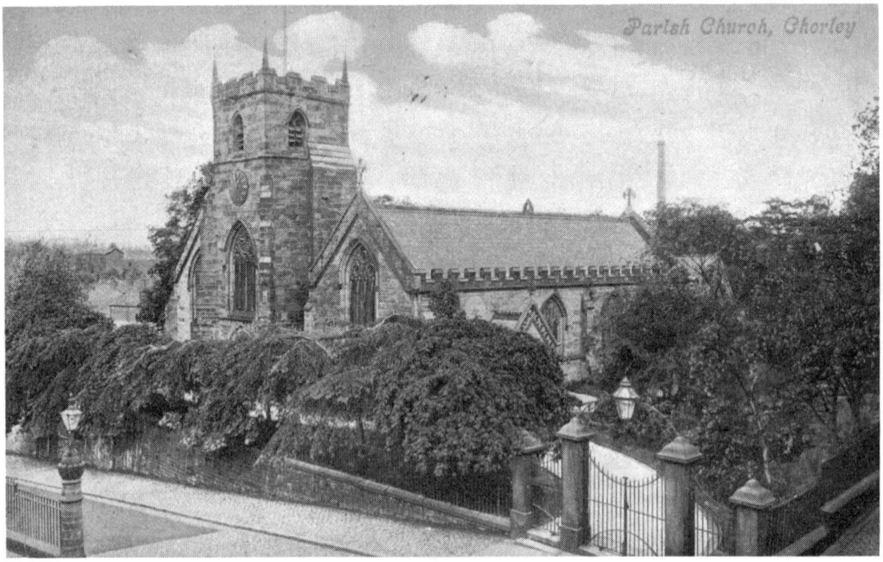
Parish Church, Chorley

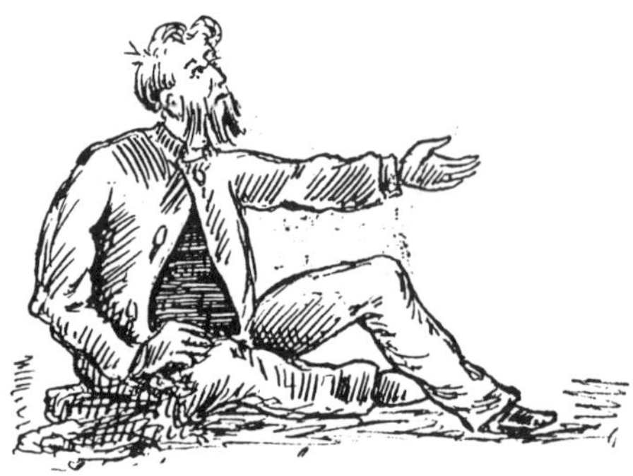

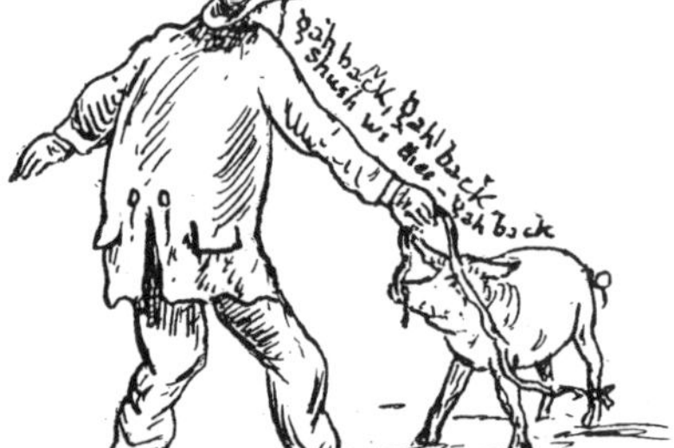
Gah back, Gah back
shush wi thee - gah back

Oct 27th 1883 (Night)...If you'd been living out here in the country this last fortnight you would have acknowledged the utility of both my pastoral crook and an umbrella. They have both been anything but superfluities - Now wherefore are you so reticent? When are you going to name a day for a visit hither and keep it? We shall soon have winter down upon us - If we have a few days fine and fair weather now e'er the frosts come on we could enjoy a drive out into the surrounding country - I exhort ye to snatch an early opening for at this rate we shall have Christmas here before we have the pleasure of gazing on ye by our own fire side ...

Nov 2nd 1883 (2nd day of Mahometan 14th century from Mahomet's Flight)...now isn't this hard - My dear Sir - They really will not let me rest a minute - I'm tired out - have rheumatism in my back, knees & foot - yet must walk hours per day & now this morning they want me to go to Chorley. I have this morning received a note informing me that Miss L. of Southport has resolved to come over in a cab to spend a few days out here in the country before the winter sets in severely - When are you going to favour us with a 'look in' & a stroll out ...

Nov 5th 1883...Come I say - I thought you would really have either written or come over, or both but then 'upon me word' you've done neither; so may I now be permitted the privilege of asking '<u>How's which</u>'? I don't understand it - Of this I'm convinced that you might with an effort get hither. Of course we must now take our luck of the weather. Who could have told it would prove so stormy yesterday? Pluck up courage my dear Sir and call resolution to your aid - It's no great distance - Take some day an early Train when the weather is favourable and likely to be so for a 24 hours or more. We shall be at home all this week and perhaps the next one also - Certainly this week and for ought I know the next as well. Receive my warmest protestations of cordial regard ...

...No news except the leaden fingered November is upon us spreading fogs and cold & damp all round. Not a line have you favoured us with nor promise to look us up as ye were wont to do aforetime. Mr Booth has made Mr Parkes a present of a pig of rare and strange breed on condition that he takes it about the country to show it. I fear the condition will be unfulfilled as Mr P will find it a perplexing thing to travel with - a pig is diversome in its ways ...P.S. Letter just to hand - shall expect you e'er long ...

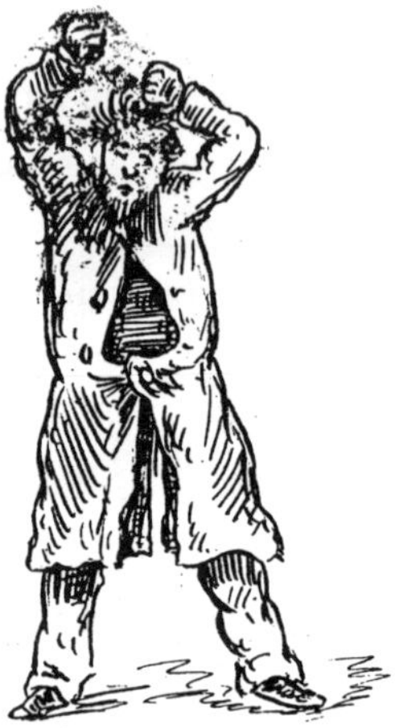

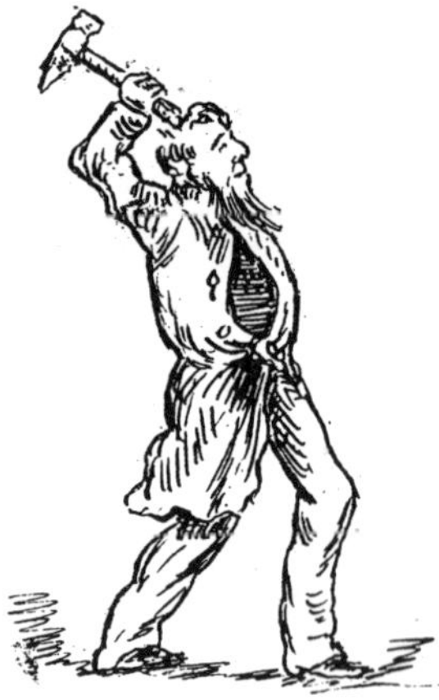

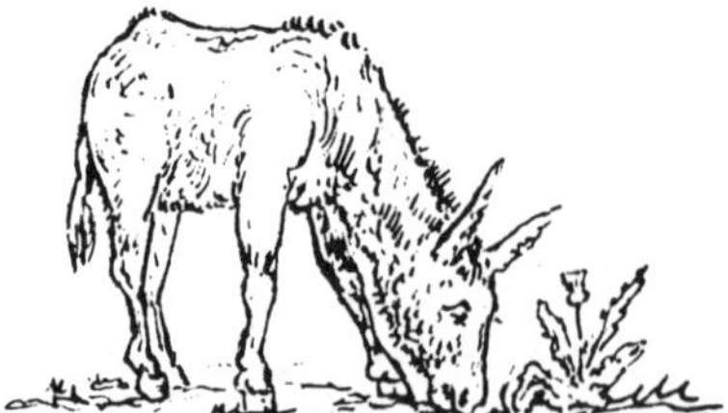

Nov 13th 1883...a beautiful bright frosty morning the New York storm warning notwithstanding but there is no rest for me - over fields thick with rime - over hills and vales - stiles and rough roads I have to plod e'er nightfall. I am inclined to think this regular and undue exercise is beginning to make me quite thin. I am sorry to report that Typhus Fever has broken out among us - We have at present one case only and I earnestly hope that the disease may not spread. We were grieved to learn that Mrs Maynard was so unwell. How is she now? Do drop us a line which we trust may convey more favourable tidings than your last note brought us - Excuse brevity and haste as the daylight nowadays is so short-lived and the duties to be performed in it so many ...

Nov 21st (Night)...Dash my Buttons - My dear Sir - Dash anything - but if you knew all I've got to do just now and how I'm suffering from rheumatism your dear sympathising heart would nearly bleed for me. I'm nearly driven out of my wits, and walked off my feet - We rejoiced to receive your letter and were grateful to have conveyed to us the happy tidings of which it was the vehicle - Why did you not come last weekend - I'm sure you would have enjoyed it ...

Nov 24th 1883 Night...strike, My dear Sir, Strike!!! always strike while the Iron's hot - Now I quite expected you over here last weekend to the concert - This weekend has not been fit but how about the next one - you'll be having the young folks home soon, and lots of Xmas engagements - No time like the present so Strike, my dear Sir, while the Iron's hot ...

Nov 29th 1883...Your letter to hand - alas! it seems next to impossible to get you over here nowadays - of course the Programme was sent to indicate a time when we should have some pleasing excitement to offer you - come any day when you find yourself at liberty - we can always find you a bed and shall not be away at night for weeks. If you are not fairly speedy I shall fetch Pollie out of her pasture - yoke her up and drive over to see about it - She has got her winter coat on now and presents an appearance at once charming & rural - sorry to hear of Miss R's indisposition - We trust it may prove to be only temporary & not serious. Hie hither, come ...

Nov 29th 1883. Night...You said, my dear Sir, that there were only seven more cards wanting to complete another album - I sent one this morning and you see I have come with another. At this rate the number wanting will soon be supplied ...

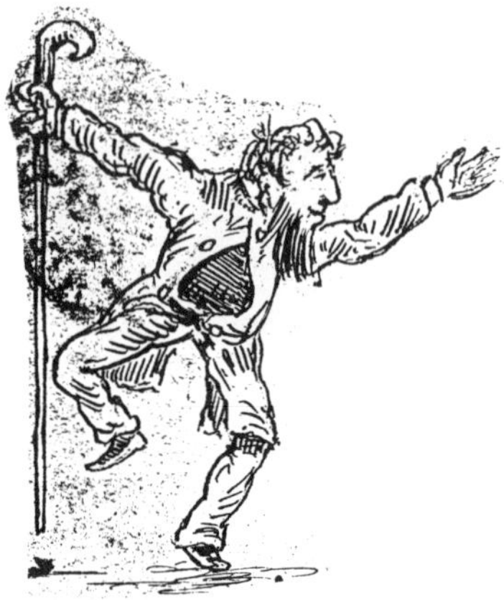

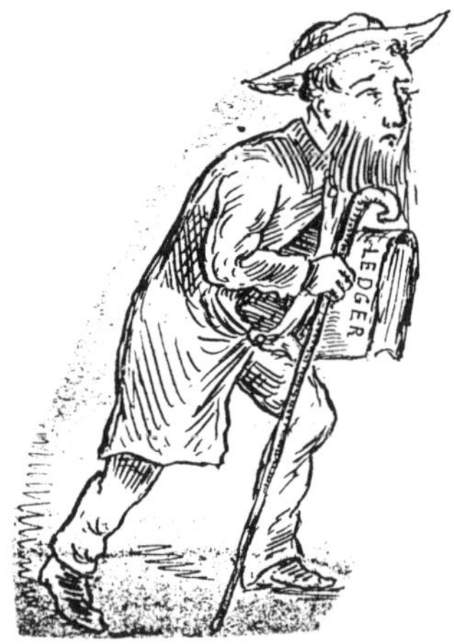
LEDGER

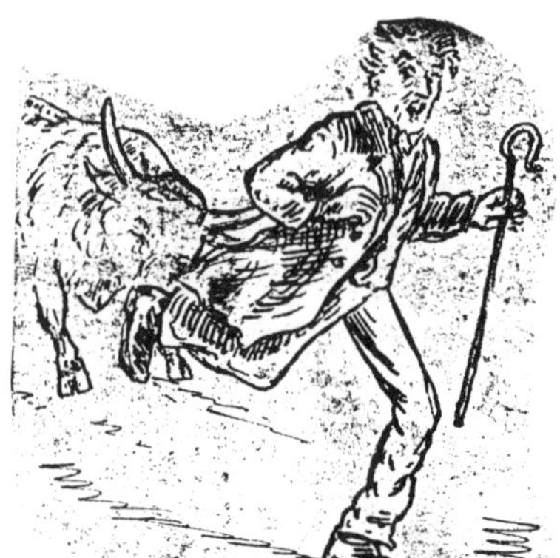

Dec 1st 1883...I'm off to Leyland my dear Sir, I'm off to Leyland - I've knock'd all the figures into fits - floored the papers and got ready for Leyland - Hooray! Hooray! Excuse haste. In a hurry now - more time presently - good day, Good day! ...

Dec 5th 1883...I was too sanguine - Far too sanguine. I could not get to Leyland after all - and so I did not go. No, I have that trudge before me still, and a storm predicted - I generally have bad weather and so I suppose it is going to be again - I am waiting for an important paper from London which is behind its time ...

Dec 7th 1883...Why don't you come over into the country to enjoy yourself a little - Today for instance is just the sort of weather for getting a good run over the fields - and the pleasure of a run is always so much more thorough - I think - when you have a definite object in view ...

(The final two cards of the collection were obliterated...)

From 'The Wigan Examiner' December 3rd 1910 -

The Late Vicar of Wrightington

Last week we announced with regret the death of the Rev. J.T. Wilson, B.A. ex-vicar of Wrightington, at the age of 73. The rev. gentleman had been in failing health for some time and passed away on 23rd ult, four months after the death of his wife. He was the son of Rev. Mr Wilson of Windermere, a contemporary and friend of the poet Wordsworth.

He was of deep learning and marvellous memory, and though unable to take an active part in public life he had a keen interest in all the questions of the day. Mr Wilson was the Vicar of St James', Wrightington, for 43 years, but owing to ill-health resigned in August last, but through the courtesy of the newly-appointed vicar he had remained in residence at the Vicarage, where he passed quietly away.

The interment took place on Saturday, many friends and parishioners attending as a mark of the esteem in which he was held. Among them were Rev. Father Melling, Rev. T.A. Walton, Rev. A. Aldridge, Mr W.S. Waddington, Mr Marsh, Mr Hubbard, Mr Morris and Mr Holding. Mr H. Haworth, Harrock Hall, intended to be present as a mark of respect, but was kept indoors with a chill.

The mourners were Mr Baxter, Dr J. Aspinall Marsden, Miss Waddington, Dr Wilson, and members of the household.

The officiating clergyman was the Rev. T.W.J. Baker. The march in 'Saul' was played as the body was borne from the church by ten of the church officers, followed by the choir who sang one of Mr Wilson's favourite hymns 'Lead Kindly Light' at the graveside.

Messrs. Middleton and Wood (Wigan) were the undertakers.

On Sunday the Vicar, in the course of his sermon, referred to the great loss the parish had sustained by the death of the late Vicar, whose long and faithful ministry had endeared him to the officials of the church and the parishioners generally. He was a man of many parts. Their only consolation was that their loss was the late Vicar's gain.